Remembering Wolsey

Remembering Wolsey

A History of Commemorations
and Representations

J. Patrick Hornbeck II

FORDHAM UNIVERSITY PRESS

New York 2019

Fordham University Press has no responsibility for the
persistence or accuracy of URLs for external or third-party
Internet websites referred to in this publication and does not
guarantee that any content on such websites is, or will
remain, accurate or appropriate.

Fordham University Press also publishes its books in a
variety of electronic formats. Some content that appears in
print may not be available in electronic books.

Visit us online at www.fordhampress.com.

Library of Congress Cataloging-in-Publication Data
available online at https://catalog.loc.gov.

Printed in the United States of America

21 20 19   5 4 3 2 1

First edition

CONTENTS

Color plates follow page 148

A&M   John Foxe, *The . . . Ecclesiasticall History Contaynyng
               the Actes and Monuments* (London: J. Day, 1570); other
               editions of *Actes and Monuments* will be denoted by
               the year of publication
Cavendish   George Cavendish, *The Life and Death of Cardinal
               Wolsey*, ed. R. S. Sylvester, EETS o.s. 243 (Oxford:
               Oxford University Press, 1959)
CCA   Christ Church Archives, Oxford
EETS   Early English Text Society
Hall   Edward Hall, *Union of the two noble and illustre fami-
               lies of Lancaster and York* (London: Grafton, 1550)
Holinshed   Raphael Holinshed et al., *The Chronicles of England,
               Scotland and Ireland* (London: J. Hunne, 1577); other
               editions of *Holinshed's Chronicles* will be denoted by
               the year of publication
L&P   *Letters and Papers, Foreign and Domestic, of the Reign of
               Henry VIII*, 21 vols. (London: Longman, Green,
               Longman, & Roberts, 1862–1932)
Schwartz-Leeper, Gavin Schwartz-Leeper, *From Princes to Pages: The
Princes to Pages Literary Lives of Cardinal Wolsey, Tudor England's
               "Other King"* (Leiden: Brill, 2016)

ACKNOWLEDGMENTS

It is impossible to write any book—particularly one that seeks to engage with multiple disciplines and styles of scholarly inquiry—without incurring a great many debts. My early interest in Wolsey was stimulated by the remarkable opportunity that the Governing Body of Christ Church, Oxford, offered me to serve as Senior Scholar at a college that, as this book seeks to demonstrate, very much still considers itself the cardinal's. Since my leaving Oxford, my relationship with Christ Church has been sustained through countless dialogues with Mishtooni Bose and, more recently, through the generous friendship of Martyn Percy, who will no doubt be remembered as one of the House's most socially engaged and courageous deans. I could not have written the sections on Wolsey's relationship with Oxford without the gracious assistance of college archivist Judith Curthoys and her colleagues Cristina Neagu and Alina Nachescu.

My current academic home, Fordham University, and its outstanding Theology Department have been exceptionally generous as this book has taken shape. I am grateful to the University for granting a Faculty Fellowship and providing financial support that permitted me to conduct archival research and write the first draft of this volume, and to the Theology Department for releasing me from a semester's service as chair. (To Karina Martin Hogan, who served admirably in my absence, and to Joyce O'Leary and Anne-Marie Sweeney I owe great debts indeed.) Joseph M. McShane, S.J., has been a tireless cheerleader and mentor, even if he still thinks this book should have been about that other English cardinal, John Fisher. Anne Fernald and Terrence Tilley, two of the most insightful people I know, generously read and commented on draft chapters; these pages are far better for their assistance, and that of the three anonymous readers for the Press, although I take full responsibility for all the shortcomings that remain. Successive graduate assistants Elizabeth Keohane-Burbridge, Alexandra Wright, and Adam Beyt provided invaluable help, particularly in gathering sources and preparing the manuscript for the Press.

x *acknowledgments*

I grieve that one of those who most inspired me in my academic vocation and who provided constant encouragement and support will not see the publication of this volume. The late Stephen Freedman, over the course of his eleven years as Fordham's provost, epitomized the openness, dynamism, compassion, and commitment to justice that I have learned to associate with Jesuit higher education. I am only one among many whose lives and careers he helped shape and who will miss him dearly.

My research in the United Kingdom would have been impossible, not to mention far less delightful, without the gracious hospitality of Gwen, Andrew, Andrew junior, and Alex Griffith-Dickson, along with the indomitable Joan Griffith. For assistance with bibliographic inquiries and advice on the trajectory of my research, I am grateful to the staff of the Ipswich Museum (especially Eleanor Root), the York Minister Library and Archives, the Bodleian Library, the British Library, and Historic Royal Palaces (especially Brett Dolman). John Cooper, Felicity Heal, David Rundle, Robert Swanson, and William Sheils all engaged in candid and thoughtful dialogue about Wolsey and Reformation historiography, raising questions and challenging me to produce the best possible book.

It is impossible to say enough good things about the editorial staff and board of Fordham University Press. I am grateful to Fredric Nachbaur and his team for the care with which they shepherded this project from proposal through to publication, and to my multi-disciplinary colleagues who, as board members, have been willing to support creative and groundbreaking scholarship in the humanities.

Remembering Wolsey could not have come to fruition without the thoughtfulness and encouragement of many friends, including those mentioned above. I wish especially to thank Eva Badowska, Jonathan Crystal, Robert Glenn Davis, Benjamin Dunning, Christine Firer Hinze, Susan LeVangia, Debra McPhee, and Peter Stace. This is the second book I have finished as a guest of the Brothers of the Society of St. John the Evangelist, and their abundant hospitality has always provided nourishment for the body, mind, and soul.

Finally, my husband, Patrick Bergquist, has tolerated the presence of Thomas Wolsey in our lives for more than two years, and he has done so with constant grace, patience, reassurance, and love. I am more grateful to him than ever I can say. *Mihi adiutor* indeed.

J. Patrick Hornbeck II
August 24, 2018

Let me tell you what I wish I'd known
When I was young and dreamed of glory
You have no control
Who lives
Who dies
Who tells your story?
　　　　　　　　　—Lin-Manuel Miranda

Memory and Representation

I began writing this book shortly after the premiere of the hit Broadway musical *Hamilton*, a hip-hop reimagining of the life of the early US revolutionary and politician Alexander Hamilton. The brainchild of the acclaimed composer Lin-Manuel Miranda, *Hamilton* transposes, and transgresses, the usual boundaries of discourse about its subject. The actors are predominantly African American and Latino/a; the plot renders Hamilton as hero and Thomas Jefferson as villain; the language is anything but eighteenth century. Miranda's book and lyrics offer an alternative, well-researched, and compelling representation of the first treasury secretary, and his musical comments directly on the processes of history and memory making. In *Hamilton*, the questions of what counts as history and who deserves to be remembered are never far from center stage. As the character of George Washington sings twice, once in each act: "Let me tell you what I wish I'd known / When I was young and dreamed of glory / You have no control / Who lives, who dies, who tells your story."[1] And indeed, the historical Alexander Hamilton could likely never have imagined—and might well not have given his blessing to— Miranda's interpretation of his life.

The absence of control over the ways we are represented and commemorated during and after our lives is of course not unique to Hamilton's case. Details about the lives of many well-known individuals are contested both within and beyond academic circles. Debates about the facts and significance of a life often flourish for centuries after the person in question has died. Such debates pose many of the same questions *Hamilton* asks—questions that this book, likewise, seeks to ask about a historical actor from a very different time and place, and one whose character has more often than not been taken to hew closer to that of Hamilton's nemesis Aaron Burr. Why and how are representations of historical figures generated, why and how are they passed down and changed over the years, and what structures of discourse and power shape and resolve disputes about the representation of controversial lives? These are matters about which historical scholarship has something to say. Yet they, in turn, prompt questions about meaning, ethics, and values that transcend empirical investigation but are critically important for the ways we think about and represent the past. Who has the right to narrate someone else's life? For what ends? And what does it say for our beliefs in our agency and autonomy that those very capacities often fail us when we seek to dictate how we will be remembered?

This book seeks to contribute to our understanding of historical memory and memorialization by examining in detail the commemoration and representation of one particular life, that of Thomas Wolsey, the sixteenth-century cardinal, papal legate, and lord chancellor of England.[2] Wolsey was born in the early 1470s in the East Anglian market town of Ipswich; he was sent to Oxford at an early age and distinguished himself academically; and after a somewhat halting start, he began rapidly to ascend the ecclesiastical hierarchy in the early 1500s. Thanks to the patronage of King Henry VIII, who acceded to the throne in 1509, by 1515 Wolsey had become one of the most powerful men in England, styled *alter rex* (the other king) or even *ipse rex* (the king himself) by foreign ambassadors such as Venice's Sebastiano Giustiniani.[3] He held at one time or another the offices of lord chancellor, legate *a latere*, cardinal priest, archbishop of York, bishop of Lincoln, bishop of Winchester, bishop of Durham, abbot of St. Albans, royal almoner, and many more besides. With a portfolio that covered virtually all of Tudor government and that Giustiniani recognized as equivalent to "all the magistracies, offices, and councils of Venice," Wolsey's sphere of influence encompassed foreign policy, legal affairs, university education, church reform, the contest with Luther and Lutheranism, and, fatefully, King Henry's proposed annulment of his marriage with his first wife, Katherine of Aragon.[4] Following the failure of a legatine court presided over by Wolsey and the Italian cardinal Lorenzo Campeggio to deliver the verdict that the king and his intended, Anne Boleyn, had hoped for, Wolsey was dismissed as lord chancellor, exiled from court, and ultimately sent north to York. After more than a year in legal and political limbo, he was arrested for high treason in November 1530. Traveling south to stand trial in London, Wolsey fell ill, died at Leicester Abbey, and was buried there, unmourned by many. The circumstances of his death— whether it came as a result of grief and stress, poison, or suicide—have been for years the most hotly contested features of his biography.

Over the course of the nearly five centuries since his death, Wolsey's name and image have been invoked in a bewildering variety of contexts. Unsurprisingly, he has been most prominent in retellings of the early English Reformation, whether in the works of chroniclers, historians, theologians, dramatists, or more recently film and television producers. But Wolsey has also figured in narratives about the development of British democracy, early modern English foreign policy, and Tudor architecture and humanist education. He has been represented as a favorite and a dutiful son of his hometown, Ipswich, where three streets, two theaters, an art gallery, and a shopping center are all named in his honor. Representations of his galero, or cardinal's hat, adorn walls, furniture, silverware, notepaper, and countless other objects at Christ Church, the Oxford foundation that succeeded his Cardinal College, and the institution proudly displays what it claims to be Wolsey's original hat.[5] Somewhat more frivolously, in the nineteenth and twentieth centuries his name and image have been used to sell a range of commercial products, even furniture and underwear (see Plate 1).[6] Of course, many of these representations of Wolsey have had their own afterlives. William Shakespeare and John Fletcher's play *King Henry VIII (All Is True)*, for instance, has provided fodder for countless artistic works and pieces of political propaganda, including a peroration in favor of the US Constitution that concludes one of the early numbers of the *Federalist Papers.*[7]

Why has Wolsey been remembered and represented? Overwhelmingly, he has been invoked by those wishing to advance their arguments about the events that led up to the break between the Roman Catholic Church and what was to become the Church of England. In this regard, posterity has rarely been kind to our cardinal. For some, Wolsey epitomized all that was wrong with the traditional religion of the later Middle Ages, and for them, his fall was a harbinger of the reformation to come. For others, his failings were personal rather than systemic, and it was his arrogance, vengefulness, and greed that led him to steer King Henry into schism. Works of both these kinds have regularly appropriated Wolsey as a dramatic foil or, to borrow a phrase that the Reformation historian Peter Marshall coined in another context, an "ideological football," depicting him in ways that buttressed their authors' preconceived theories about the origins, merits, and theological significance of the Henrician reformation.[8] As Felicity Heal has pithily reminded us, "History has frequently functioned as legitimation for the present."[9] Other works have focused more directly on Wolsey as an individual, and these have often explicitly avowed the desire to rescue the cardinal from the purported calumnies of his critics.[10] Both of these impulses—to employ Wolsey as a means for telling the story of the early English Reformation or to free an "authentic" Wolsey from defamation—have led authors to treat the cardinal as a moral exemplar as much as a historical figure. There are also works about Wolsey that have sought to link him with specific localities, especially Ipswich, Hampton Court Palace, Oxford, and Leicester—the scenes of his birth, power, largesse, and death. And, especially in the twentieth and twenty-first centuries, some works featuring Wolsey have had entertainment as their primary objective. None of these purposes necessarily excludes any other, and most of the works that we will encounter here aim simultaneously at more than one end.

Remembering Wolsey seeks to survey the history of the anglophone commemoration and representation of Wolsey from his death on November 29, 1530, through the early twenty-first century. Its goals are broadly historical but occasionally theological as well. I aim to show how representations of Wolsey have been one of the vehicles through which historians and theologians, in particular, have contested the events known collectively as the English Reformation(s).[11] Over the course of nearly five centuries, Wolsey has been at the center of the debate about King Henry's reformation and the virtues and vices of late medieval Catholicism: This book therefore seeks to chronicle how representations of the cardinal have performed important work in narratives about English religious history. An important caveat is in order, however: Wolsey's historiographical role has not been limited to the sphere of religion, and as I have already hinted, he has been invoked in contexts ranging from the development of England's judiciary to the promotion of humanism in its universities. The book will consider some of these contexts as well, but only briefly and in passing, insofar as they illuminate the history of Wolsey's representation as a churchman and ecclesiastical statesman.

A second overall purpose of the book is to make a small intervention in ongoing scholarly discussions about commemoration, representation, and cultural or collective memory. As this Introduction will argue, recent theo-retical insights about memory and its cultural mechanisms can help us trace and explain shifts in the representation of Wolsey across changing historical, intellectual, and theological contexts. However, insofar as many theoretical formulations about memory have emerged out of the disci-plines of oral history and Freudian psychoanalysis, they need to be adapted to the concerns, textual productions, and cultural circumstances of (writing about) early modern England.

Of necessity, *Remembering Wolsey* examines commemorations and repre-sentations of the cardinal in a variety of media as well as across multiple genres within any one medium. Throughout the past five hundred years, Wolsey has been depicted in nearly all of the textual and artistic forms known to European and US anglophone cultures. Almost certainly, one of the first representations of Wolsey following his death was a farce staged by Anne Boleyn's father, the Earl of Wiltshire, in which the cardinal's soul was shown descending to hell.[12] Since then, Wolsey has been represented by chroniclers and historians; by propagandists and pamphleteers; by poets, playwrights, and pageant masters; by novelists and short-story writers; and most recently by screenwriters and documentary filmmakers. Other repre-sentations go wholly beyond the textual: There are portraits of the cardinal, paintings of scenes from his life, busts, waxworks, and statues. Sometimes these and other objects have been brought together in museum exhibits, and in other instances, people have created memorials to Wolsey in places of significance for him. Only some of these forms of representation employ academic discourse, and so, to write a full history of the representation and commemoration of Wolsey, it will be essential not to privilege academic writing, implicitly or explicitly, as necessarily more accurate or more impor-tant than any other form of representation. Indeed, as I will argue, often-times the depictions of Wolsey that have emerged out of or been directed at popular cultures have been the most broadly or persistently influential.[13] Therefore, this book often juxtaposes representations of the cardinal that were produced for different audiences, noting the rhetorical advantages of each different form of discourse in which Wolsey has appeared.

Of equal or greater necessity, this book is selective, in some instances highly so. Wolsey has been depicted literally hundreds of times since his death. If we leave aside a flourishing manuscript tradition and consider only printed works in English, the approximately twenty texts featuring Wolsey that were published in each of the sixteenth, seventeenth, and eighteenth centuries pale in comparison to the nearly eighty such texts from the nineteenth century, the more than three hundred from the twentieth, and the more than a hundred already produced since 2000. As my analysis advances through the years, therefore, I will be able to consider an increasingly limited slice of the extant sites of representation. The texts and other materials I have chosen for particularly close analysis are those that have had the most substantial or longest lasting influence, those that have advanced the most innovative or distinctive portrayals of Wolsey, and those that have thus far escaped notice by scholars who have been interested in the cardinal and his posthumous reputation. Since this book seeks to offer a history of Wolsey's *anglophone* representation, I focus almost exclusively on works composed in English, with the notable exception of a few Latin texts written by sixteenth-century English exiles on the European mainland.

Reception, Commemoration, and Representation

For centuries, scholars have written about the reception of canonical texts, not least among them the scriptures of Judaism, Christianity, and Islam. Researchers have become accustomed, for instance, to tracing the ways in which particular psalms or gospel pericopes have been read in different cultural contexts and new moments of history. Similar if perhaps less influential work has been done on the reading of literary texts and the hearing of musical compositions. By analogy, it might be tempting to say that this book constitutes a reception history of Wolsey, an effort along comparable lines to excavate his changing fortunes in the hands of new writers and readers.

However, there are important differences between the reception of a text and that of a historical personage, even when, like Wolsey, he is long dead and no longer able to speak for himself. First, with an individual like Wolsey there is wide scope for interpretive conflict. No written text is entirely stable, and late medieval and early modern texts in particular often underwent change as they were copied and disseminated, but it has frequently been possible for reception historians to establish with reasonable certainty what text was or is being received. Not so with a life, or at least not with Wolsey's life. As we will see throughout this volume, the cardinal's interpreters have operated on the basis of widely divergent claims about basic elements of his biography, stretching from the circumstances of his birth through those of his exile and death. With Wolsey, unlike most canonical texts, we cannot help but find conflicts over fact as well as interpretation. At the same time, whereas most reception studies have depended primarily on written texts, sometimes to the exclusion of other kinds of sources, we have already seen that Wolsey has been remembered across a wide variety of media and genres. This is not to mention oral traditions about him, some of which took years, if not decades, to be committed to writing, and others that have left little or no trace at all.

Something more than a standard reception history is therefore needed if we are to grapple with the complexly evolving portrayals of Wolsey across the centuries. Over the course of recent decades, scholars have increasingly turned to the categories of memory and commemoration to understand how individuals and societies conceive of and interact with the past. Theories of social or collective memory began to emerge in the early twentieth century, in the work of the French sociologist Maurice Halbwachs and of the German art historian Aby Warburg. But it was not until the 1980s that what has been called an "explosion of interest" in the "scholarly boom" of memory studies began to be felt.[14] Since that time, historical studies that take memory as a primary category have proliferated, with some of the most productive work being done with regard to the collective remembrance of traumas such as the Holocaust (or Shoah) and the Argentinean "dirty war" of the 1970s.[15] The category of memory has been applied outside the frame of trauma as well, and early modern historians such as Judith Pollmann, David Cressy, and Andy Wood have considered how sixteenth- and seventeenth-century European cultures sought to remember and commemorate their past.[16] As of this writing, a new, interdisciplinary "Remembering the Reformation" project, a collaboration of two British universities, has been formed "to investigate how the Reformations were remembered, forgotten, contested, and re-invented."[17]

Among theorists of collective or cultural memory, Jan Assmann, a German scholar of Egyptology, has been particularly influential. In his 1997 monograph *Moses the Egyptian*, Assmann coined the term "mnemohistory," the prefix *mnemo-* coming from the Greek word for memory. For Assmann, mnemohistory "is concerned not with the past as such, but only with the past as it is remembered. It surveys the story-lines of tradition, the webs of intertextuality, the diachronic continuities and discontinuities of reading the past."[18] Assmann's mnemohistory differs from traditional historical writing in a number of significant ways. First, it does not seek to make claims about the facticity of any given memory, since memories can be faulty, repressed, or manipulated. Instead, it seeks to explore what has been remembered, what has been forgotten, and why. Therefore, in Assmann's words, "mnemohistory analyzes the importance which a present ascribes to the past."[19] Second, mnemohistory is for Assmann primarily a history of discourse, of the ways in which it has been (and is) permissible to talk about the past.[20] Finally, mnemohistory seeks to chronicle the development of what Assmann calls cultural memories, narratives about the past that provide coherent and often intentionally curated accounts of cultures' histories and identities.[21]

Assmann's mnemohistorical method, like other constructive interventions in the ongoing debates about history and memory, has its advocates as well as its detractors.[22] On the one hand, scholars have explicitly employed Assmann's ideas in studies of subjects as diverse as the Salvadoran peasant massacre of 1932, the biblical exodus and its recollection in modern Judaism, and the representation of Queen Elizabeth I in Stuart writings.[23] On the other hand, critics have charged Assmann with insufficiently theorizing his approach, in particular with regard to the epistemological problems that arise when memories are contradicted by documents or other kinds of historical sources.[24] Some scholars have accused Assmann of moving facilely and therefore misleadingly between history and mnemohistory, sidestepping pieces of evidence unfavorable to his conclusions and instead privileging unsubstantiated impressions of what belongs to the realm of collective memory.[25] Others have observed that Assmann's theory relies too heavily on Freudian ideas about traumatic memory and the return of the repressed. For instance, Wulf Kansteiner has observed that although an individual might not be able to repress a trauma without memories of it returning in some other form, it is not clear that the same dynamic operates for cultures.[26] What is more, critics have alleged that Assmann's theory assumes "a basic commonality of social memories" that cannot always be found in modern, pluralistic societies, and they have asked whether Assmann sufficiently takes into account the role that authoritative social actors play in influencing the content of collective memories.[27]

These and other critiques deserve careful attention, but they do not require us to throw out the mnemohistorical baby with its Freudian bathwater. Assmann's argument about the collective return of the repressed that he identified in the relationship of ancient Egypt and ancient Israel may not be universally accepted, but Assmann's work advances an insight of enduring value, namely that a history of what he calls collective memory, or of what I will call commemorations and representations of the past, is available to be told alongside a more typical history of events and their consequences. Some mnemohistorical concepts, however, do require additional nuance. As Assmann's critics have shown, collective memories are not uniform in content or universally embraced in practice. In any given moment, such as England during the early modern period, multiple and conflicting versions of the past may be treasured and transmitted by different groups: Susan Royal has demonstrated, for instance, that various sixteenth- and seventeenth-century English religious historians portrayed the medieval heretics known as lollards or Wycliffites quite differently, often as a consequence of those historians' confessional or denominational allegiances.[28] In addition, mnemohistorical work has not infrequently elided the difference between memories and commemorations, thereby perpetuating the questionable assumption that if the past is invoked, it is invoked in large part in order that it be remembered. Likewise, even when something has been *held up to be* remembered, it is not always the case that it has in fact *been* remembered as intended. As Kansteiner concluded, histories of memory must therefore take into account not only "the intellectual and cultural traditions that frame all our representations of the past [and] the memory makers who selectively adopt and manipulate these traditions" but also "the memory consumers who use, ignore, or transform such artifacts according to their own interests."[29]

To address these concerns, which are substantive as well as terminological, in this book I will distinguish as carefully as possible between memories, commemorations, and representations. When I write about memories, I am primarily interested in individual people's recollections of the past. Admittedly, in only a limited number of cases is it possible even to suggest that a particular individual remembered an event or person in a particular way (at a particular point in time). Memoirs, or texts that commit memories to writing, are often our best (or only) sources in this regard, at least prior to the availability of data from oral histories.[30] However, as James Fentress and Chris Wickham have cautioned, memoirs and memories are not identical: "Writing . . . transforms memory, by fixing it."[31] Because memoirs are limited and, at least for the early modern period, rare, it is necessary to acknowledge straightforwardly that almost all memories of Thomas Wolsey are lost to us. What we have instead—with a few, almost always elite exceptions, such as the life of Wolsey written by one of his gentleman-ushers, George Cavendish—is evidence of the ways in which Wolsey has been commemorated and/or represented in a variety of media, from scholarly works to paintings and historical fictions.

A further distinction is also necessary. When I write about commemorations, which can include written texts, museum exhibits, public memorials, speeches, and other forms of communication, I am speaking about intentional attempts to call something to the memory of others.[32] The forms that these attempts have taken have varied dramatically over time: As Pollmann and others have shown, techniques for remembering and memorializing differ substantially between the early modern period and

subsequent centuries.[33] Commemorations are often, but not always, laudatory in their overtones, and they are often highly local or specific. As an
example, we might note that in 2011 the town of Ipswich sought to commemorate Wolsey by proudly unveiling a statue of him that still sits on
St. Peter's Street, yards from the presumed location of his boyhood home.[34]
Whereas commemorations have the express purpose of creating, shaping,
and transmitting memories, when I write about representations, portrayals, or depictions—I alternate among the terms to avoid repetition, but I
mean roughly the same by each of them—I am interested more generally
in all kinds of likenesses, images, and assessments, whether or not they have
a commemorative intent. As with commemorations, we will see that forms
of representation have undergone significant change over the centuries.[35]
Some texts, objects, and performances are at one and the same time commemorative as well as representative. To take an example well removed
from the subject of this book, consider several hypothetical representations
of the Vietnam War. A diary kept by a soldier during the conflict would
be a memoir, a freeze-framed version of the soldier's memories at the moment that he recorded them; it would also be, in an important sense, a
representation of the wartime experience, although it may not have been
written with commemorative purposes in mind. The Vietnam Veterans
Memorial in Washington, DC, by contrast, is clearly commemorative,
but it is only in symbolic terms a representation of the war. A scholarly
monograph on American policy during the conflict written by a tenured
historian would be the opposite; it represents certain aspects of the war
without intending to call them to mind as the memorial does. A television
documentary that seeks to convey to its viewers a sense of what the war
was like for those who fought in and survived it, drawing upon memoirs
like soldiers' diaries, would be simultaneously commemorative and
representative.

Distinguishing carefully between memories, commemorations, and
representations will help us carry out the work of this study, which is to
recount something of the history of the commemoration and representation of Wolsey over the *longue durée*, from the time of his death through
nearly the present day. *Remembering Wolsey* is a mnemohistorical book in
the sense that it is emphatically *not* a new biography of the cardinal, and
accordingly, it does not set out to resolve any of the contested questions
about the details of his life.[36] Not to be found here, for instance, is an answer to the long-debated conundrum why King Henry spared Wolsey from
execution when he dismissed him as chancellor in 1529 yet ordered his
arrest for high treason just over a year later.[37] In turning aside from

questions of fact to focus on those of commemoration and representation, I am following the lead of a number of scholars who have recently performed similar excavations of the representation of other figures and events. By way of three examples, consider Susan Bordo's work on the afterlives of Anne Boleyn, Michael Evans's study of the depiction of Eleanor of Aquitaine, and, of greatest significance for our purposes, Gavin Schwartz-Leeper's book on the portrayal of Wolsey in a series of particularly significant Tudor and early Stuart texts.[38] Apart from Schwartz-Leeper's work, however, Wolsey's representation has been the subject of relatively little scholarship. Sybil Jack's 2004 entry on the cardinal in the *Oxford Dictionary of National Biography* includes a brief overview of writings about him, to which the last section of Stella Fletcher's 2009 semipopular biography, a chapter entitled "At the Sign of the Red Hat, 1530–2009," adds a range of popular sources, including works of art, drama, film, and television; there are also unpublished theses and dissertations.[39] This dearth of attention to Wolsey's representation reflects a broader level of disinterest in the cardinal, who has not received the same level of sustained treatment as other leading figures of the Henrician court. Only ten book-length biographies of Wolsey have appeared in English since 1900, as opposed to more than a hundred of Henry VIII and more than thirty of Anne Boleyn.

The Enduring Power of Representation: The Obese Wolsey

This book seeks to demonstrate what we can learn from chronicling the representation and commemoration of Wolsey over the centuries. For now, let us test briefly how such an analysis might play out, taking as a case study one of the few claims that many people believe they know to be true about the cardinal: that he was obese. As Schwartz-Leeper has demonstrated, many hostile Tudor and early Stuart accounts of Wolsey deployed metaphors concerning his size. Schwartz-Leeper has traced a majority of these images back to the works of the poet, satirist, and onetime royal tutor John Skelton, who produced a series of poems critical of Wolsey between approximately 1515 and 1522, prior to making a volte-face and accepting the cardinal's literary patronage for the remainder of his career.[40] As Schwartz-Leeper has shown, Skelton's poems are replete with images connecting obesity to corruption. In *Magnyfycence* (c. 1516), he described an evil counselor with a "gowne so wyde / That he may hyde / His dame and syre / Within his slyve."[41] *Speke, Parrot* (c. 1521) obliquely identifies Wolsey as "that fat hog of Basan," and *Collyn Clout* (1522) criticizes the girth of bishops more generally: "'Bysshoppes, yf they may / Small households woll kepe,/But slombre forth and slepe,/And assay to crepe/Within the noble walles/Of the kynges halles,/To fatte theyr bodyes full.'"[42] Subsequent writers embraced Skelton's imagery with enthusiasm. Abraham Fleming and the team of compilers who prepared the second edition of *Holinshed's Chronicles* in 1587 employed corporeal language to describe the adverse public reaction to Wolsey's creation as cardinal:[43]

> And now that he was thus a perfect cardinall, he looked aboue all estates, which purchased him great hatred and disdaine on all sides. For his ambition was no lesse discernable to the eies of the people, than the sunne in the firmament in a cleere and cloudlesse summer daie . . . for that his base lineage was both noted and knowne, in so much that his *insatiable* aspiring to supereminent degrees of dignitie kindled manifest contempt and detestation among such as pretended a countenance of good will and honorable dutie unto him, though in verie deed the same parties . . . would have tituled him a proud popeling; as led with the like spirit of *swelling* ambicion, wherewith the rable of popes had beene *bladder like puffed and blowne up*.[44]

Following Holinshed's lead, John Speed's *History of Great Britain*, published in 1611, described Wolsey as having been "swolne so bigge by the blasts of promotion, as the bladder not able to conteine more greatnesse, suddenly burst, and vented foorth the winde of all former fauours."[45] Nearly contemporaneously, Shakespeare and Fletcher, in the first act of *King Henry VIII*, also characterized Wolsey as obese, with their Duke of Buckingham expressing "wonder/That such a keech can with his very bulk/Take up the rays o'th' beneficial sun/And keep it from the earth."[46]

This unflattering palette of images was not limited to the written and spoken word. As Fletcher has shown, the earliest extant paintings of Wolsey include an anonymous portrait, dated 1589–1595 and now in the UK National Portrait Gallery (see Plate 2), and a set of two other portraits executed in 1610 by Sampson Strong. All of them portray the cardinal "as a man of more than ample proportions," and, as Fletcher continues, they "came to influence many subsequent paintings, prints and performances on stage and screen."[47] In particular, their successors include a number of direct adaptations, along with a series of paintings executed by Sir John Gilbert from the 1860s through the 1880s. Finally, a painting of Thomas More confronting a stout Wolsey in the House of Commons was commissioned by Parliament in the 1920s as part of a series of depictions of key moments in the history of British democracy (see Plate 3).[48] As with the portraits, a substantial majority of the actors who have played the role of

Wolsey have been of notable girth.[49] Perhaps most memorably, Orson Welles's cardinal in the Academy Award–winning film *A Man for All Seasons* (1966) was a Wolsey of exaggerated size and self-confidence. Even the medical guild has assumed that Wolsey was a man of bulk: In a 1901 editorial, the *British Medical Journal* opined that lean political leaders were more likely to be ambitious, while fat ones were inclined to be complacent. The journal's editors cited Wolsey as one of those, like Louis XVI and Napoleon, whose greater size in his later years made him susceptible to misjudgment and overthrow.[50]

However, despite all this attention to Wolsey's size, Fletcher, Schwartz-Leeper, and others have made clear that no extant text or artwork from the cardinal's lifetime indicates definitively that he was unusually large. To the contrary, several pieces of evidence suggest that Wolsey's figure may not have been obese at all. The Venetian ambassador to the English court, Giustiniani, represented the cardinal in a 1519 dispatch as "very handsome, learned, extremely eloquent, of vast ability, and indefatigable."[51] Likewise, an extant copy of a lost drawing of Wolsey from the 1510s captures a man who, if not especially thin, is also not overly large (see Plate 4).[52] Many early critics, such as Wolsey's former associate Polydore Vergil, did not lampoon his size, despite, in Vergil's case, labeling the cardinal "so proud that he considered himself the peer of kings" and condemning him for "arrogance and ambition" and "odiousness," all in a single paragraph.[53] It might be expected that Cavendish, Wolsey's onetime gentleman-usher, discreetly omitted comment on his master's physical appearance, but Oxford, Bodleian Library MS Douce 363, which contains a copy of Cavendish's *Life* dating from the last quarter of the sixteenth century, includes a series of drawings of the cardinal that depict a thin, elderly, bearded man wearing a black robe, not the scarlet-clad, clean-shaven bulk of the dominant tradition (see Plate 5).[54]

It is strands of representation like these that *Remembering Wolsey* seeks to identify and to trace over time. In this case, we can conclude that Wolsey has been remembered as a fat, even a morbidly obese, man, for reasons that usually have had little to do with the limited and ambiguous evidence available. Instead, it has been polemically useful for the cardinal's opponents to caricature him physically in ways that mirror and reinforce the claims they have made about him morally. As Greg Walker was the first to demonstrate, Skelton's satires, from which many subsequent representations of Wolsey's purported obesity took their cue, were not intended to convey what we might call a historically accurate portrayal of their target. Instead, as Walker argued, "Much of what appears to be purely political or biographical commentary in the texts proves on closer examination to be a subtle utilization of conventional models, arguments or assumptions for deliberate effect."[55] For Skelton, Wolsey's alleged bulk symbolized his gluttony, rapaciousness, outsized authority within the political and ecclesiastical realms, and many other faults besides. The images that Skelton made available provided fodder for verbal portraits of the cardinal by chroniclers such as Holinshed and Speed, who in turn bequeathed their images of Wolsey to playwrights like Shakespeare, whose carefully cultivated metaphors reified the representation of Wolsey as a fat man whose size betokened his moral failings. Yet while this has been the most influential and popular representation of Wolsey's appearance, it has not enjoyed a total monopoly: The thinner Wolsey of the imagery of Douce 363 and of more recent portrayals by the actors John Gielgud, Sam Neill, and Jonathan Pryce constitutes another strand, even a counterstrand, of representation, which has performed a different set of functions in narratives about the cardinal, King Henry, and the early English Reformation. This representation of Wolsey has been more sympathetic, highlighting instead of faults and ill motives Wolsey's relative lack of agency in the matter of the royal annulment, his poor treatment by King Henry, and his frustrated attempts to reform the ecclesiastical system of which he was such a visible and indeed infamous part.

Plan of This Book

What the preceding section aimed to accomplish with regard to Wolsey's obesity, this book attempts to achieve with regard to the overall representation of the cardinal. Paying particular attention to the ways in which Wolsey has been portrayed in connection with Henry's "great matter" (that is, his projected annulment) and the subsequent beginning of the Henrician Reformation, *Remembering Wolsey* traces the sometimes competing strands of commemoration and representation that have been woven, passed down, refashioned, and sometimes cut off over the course of the approximately five centuries during which the cardinal has been remembered. While we will discover that no two representations of Wolsey have been exactly alike, one of the overarching arguments of this book is that since his death in 1530, most portrayals of Wolsey have borrowed, consciously or otherwise, from what I will be calling three prototypical representations of him, versions of each of which had become available as early as the mid–sixteenth century. I will say more in Chapter 1 about what it means to describe these representations as *prototypical*; for now, let me briefly describe each of them. One is that of Wolsey the papist. According especially to evangelical writers like Edward Hall and John Foxe, Wolsey symbolized all that was wrong with Roman Catholicism; he was a literally bloated prelate who was more loyal to Rome than England and whose arrogance knew no bounds. A second representation depicts Wolsey as the author of the English schism. Here, Catholic controversialists such as Vergil and Nicholas Sander deplored the cardinal for the role that they believed he had played in encouraging King Henry to pursue an annulment, resulting eventually in England's break from Rome. According to this archetype, Wolsey was morally flawed, often fatally so, but his flaws were personal failings rather than reflections of the structural or institutional corruption of the Roman church. Finally, there is the representation of Wolsey as repentant sinner. Epitomized in Cavendish's memoir, this prototype is not blind to the cardinal's faults but instead portrays him as a hard-working, sometimes morally ambiguous, often put-upon administrator who sought to do the bidding of his royal master even as King Henry made increasingly impossible demands on him. Throughout the book, I will seek to demonstrate that almost every serious retelling of Wolsey's life, and in particular almost every account of his role in the saga of Henry's annulment and the ensuing schism, incorporates elements from these prototypes. Successive writers have balanced competing memories in no small part according to their own political and theological concerns and those of their day.

The book is organized primarily in terms of chronology, with each chapter covering approximately a century in the history of the commemoration and representation of Wolsey; in a few instances, I have left the boundaries between chapters somewhat fuzzy in order to treat together pieces of evidence that are closely related but that cross chronological divides. Chapter 1 begins by tracing more fully the three prototypical representations I have just sketched, elaborating how a series of sixteenth-century writers adapted and interwove memories and texts in order to construct their accounts of the cardinal. The final source in the chapter is Thomas Storer's 1599 verse elegy *Life and Death of Thomas Wolsey Cardinall*, the first of many representations of Wolsey to be produced by a member of Christ Church.

Chapter 2 steps briefly back into the sixteenth century, exploring the literary fate of Cavendish's *Life* from the time of its composition at the end of Queen Mary's reign through its first appearance in print, in a highly expurgated, theologically and politically partisan edition of 1641. The chapter's main concern, however, is the representation of Wolsey under the first two Stuart monarchs. The years leading up to the outbreak of the English civil wars saw the publication of numerous texts featuring the cardinal, including several pamphlets critical of the churchmanship of Archbishop of Canterbury William Laud. The chapter considers these popular publications alongside a series of early Stuart dramas and more learned texts such as the church histories of Francis Godwin (1630) and Edward, Lord Herbert (written 1639, published 1649).

In Chapter 3, which encompasses the greatest chronological sweep, 1641 to c. 1860, I survey the representation of Wolsey in influential histories of the English Reformation, such as those of Thomas Fuller, Gilbert Burnet, and John Lingard. The chapter observes how a number of these texts were written with contemporary ends in view: Lingard, for instance, worked amid the controversy over Catholic emancipation and calibrated his portrayal of Wolsey to the disputes of his day. The period covered by this chapter also witnessed the publication of the first book-length biographies of the cardinal, most of which sought to defend Wolsey from what authors like Richard Fiddes (1724) and Joseph Grove (1742) considered to be the slanders of his critics. The chapter concludes with an important moment in popular engagement with Wolsey's legacy, namely Queen Victoria's decision to open Hampton Court Palace to the public in 1838. The history of restoration work and commemorative display at Hampton Court is itself a fascinating one, intersecting with the heritage industry's changing canons of preservation and authenticity.

Chapters 4 and 5 bring the story of Wolsey's representation up to the present day. Even though they cover shorter spans of time, they draw upon the most extensive archives of materials. Chapter 4, which covers the period from c. 1850 to c. 1960, begins with a new genre of representation that came into its own only in the nineteenth century: historical fiction. The chapter addresses some of the interpretive challenges that historical fictions present and offers new readings of two early stories about Wolsey, both set in his native Suffolk. The emergence of historical fiction occurred nearly contemporaneously with rapid and far-reaching developments in academic historiography. With the publication of copious original documents from the Henrician period, especially in the collection of calendars entitled *Letters and Papers, Foreign and Domestic, of the Reign of Henry VIII* (1862–1932), came new resources for the study of Wolsey. The chapter explores the work of such historians as James Anthony Froude and J. S. Brewer, alongside the Wolsey biographies of Mandell Creighton (1891), Ethelred Taunton (1902), A. F. Pollard (1929), and Hilaire Belloc (1930).

It observes how Victorian historians were often zealous about policing the boundaries of their discipline—a different way of contesting the proper forms of representation, and one that in subsequent years has never quite vanished entirely. Finally, since it is from this period that we have the earliest evidence for the public commemoration of Wolsey, the chapter explores the ways in which the cardinal was remembered in early-twentieth-century civic pageants in Oxford and Ipswich and on the anniversaries of his Oxford foundation.

Chapter 5, which takes as its chronological starting point the premiere of Robert Bolt's historical play about the life of Thomas More, *A Man for All Seasons*, considers Wolsey's representation in academic writings and influential historical fictions in the second half of the twentieth century and the first decade of the twenty-first. The chapter explores the five biographies of the cardinal that appeared during this period, discussing at the same time how Wolsey has been represented in the broader historiography of the early reign of Henry VIII. While revisionists of the 1980s and 1990s demonstrated little interest in Wolsey, their discoveries about the early English Reformation have shaped the most recent academic representations of the cardinal. At the same time, however, some of the most *influential* representations of Wolsey in the past half-century have been fictional, and therefore, the chapter also analyzes Bolt's play, the controversial television drama *The Tudors*, and Hilary Mantel's *Wolf Hall* novels. A brief Conclusion examines the latest public commemoration of Wolsey, the statue that was unveiled in Ipswich in 2011. It argues that this most recent portrayal, like its predecessors, strategically both highlights and elides certain features of Wolsey's life in order to achieve a desired effect. Rounding out the book are some observations on what all this means for the study of the cardinal, for mnemohistory, and for the enterprise of commemoration at large.

If the myriad representations of Wolsey have anything in common, it is that almost all of them reflect their creators' attempts to make meaning out of earlier memories, commemorations, and representations yet also to do so in light of the circumstances of their own day. Each chapter of this book contains numerous examples of the ways in which contemporary realities—the furor over Archbishop Laud's churchmanship in the 1630s, for instance, or the emergence of new forms of historical revisionism in the 1980s—have shaped the representation of Wolsey. Indeed, more often than not, writers and other cultural producers have used Wolsey as a foil, appropriating his biography and achievements selectively, and sometimes cavalierly, in order to tell their preferred stories about late medieval Catholicism and the origins of English Protestantism. In the most recent years, commemorations and representations that are more sympathetic than disparaging have predominated, but it is uncertain how long that trend will continue. The history of Wolsey's representation has been a history of almost constant change.

CHAPTER I

The Basic Ingredients (1530–c. 1600)

The contest to shape Wolsey's posthumous representation began within weeks of his death. When George Cavendish came to court with news about Wolsey's final hours, both King Henry and Sir William Kingston, the constable of the Tower of London, urged Cavendish to be circumspect in sharing his memories. The king commanded him to "let me alone kepe thys gere secrett bytwen yor self and me, And lett no man by privye therof," referring specifically to the whereabouts of some £1,500 that Wolsey had given away before he died.[1] Kingston, for his part, admonished Cavendish not to share too many details about what had transpired in Wolsey's sickroom: "ye shall be examyned of suche certyn wordes as my lord yor late m^r hade at hys departure. And if you tell theme the treuthe, q^d he, what he sayd, you shold vndo yor self for in any wyse they wold not here of hyt."[2] Cavendish complied, telling the Privy Council that he had been concentrating so intently on ministering to Wolsey's physical needs that he had

---

I adapt the title of this chapter from that of Chapter 7 of Bordo's *Creation of Anne Boleyn*.

not attended to his words. In any case, they had been only "idell words as men in suche extremes" tend to say.[3]

Cavendish was rewarded for his silence with more than thirty pounds, along with six horses and a baggage cart, and retired from court to his family's Suffolk estates. It was not until the reign of Mary Tudor, more than two decades later, that he ventured to commit to writing his memories of Wolsey.[4] In contrast, the late cardinal's opponents lost no time in advancing critical assessments of his life and legacy. Anne Boleyn's father, Thomas, recently ennobled as Earl of Wiltshire, took it upon himself to stage a play mocking Wolsey's memory. On January 23, 1531, the imperial ambassador Eustace Chapuys reported to Charles V that "the earl of Vulchier [Wiltshire] invited to supper Monsieur de la Guiche, for whose amusement he caused to be acted a farce of the Cardinal going down to Hell; for which La Guiche much blamed the Earl, and still more the Duke [of Norfolk, Wiltshire's brother-in-law] *for his ordering the said farce to be printed.*"[5] Chapuys wrote the words I have italicized in cipher, perhaps because Norfolk's edition of the play was unauthorized; almost certainly the print run was small, and no copy remains extant today.

Wiltshire's play was a particularly tasteless salvo in an ongoing campaign to discredit Wolsey, one that had begun during the cardinal's lifetime and had intensified as hopes for the annulment of the king's marriage had met with greater and greater frustration. Yet whereas much of the anti-Wolsey propaganda of the 1520s had sought directly to affect English policy, later representations of the cardinal aimed at different ends. These depictions emerged from all points on the spectrum of Tudor religious and political opinion, from evangelical authors like Edward Hall and John Foxe just as much as from Catholic writers such as Polydore Vergil, Nicholas Sander, and of course Wolsey's loyal servant Cavendish. This chapter explores various representations of the cardinal in influential Tudor writings, including chronicles, histories, martyrologies, memoirs, and poems. It covers some of the same ground as Gavin Schwartz-Leeper's recent monograph *From Princes to Pages*, which analyzes in detail the appearance of Wolsey in texts by John Skelton, Cavendish, Foxe, Raphael Holinshed and his successors, and William Shakespeare and John Fletcher. However, here I treat a number of texts Schwartz-Leeper omits, and I identify a series of literary resonances he overlooks. The focus of this chapter is also substantially different than that of Schwartz-Leeper's book: Rather than being interested primarily in the *portrayal* of the cardinal in literary terms, my analysis concentrates chiefly on writers' *assessments*—theological, political, as well as literary—of Wolsey's role in the events leading up to the break between England and Rome.

My argument, broadly speaking, is that texts written about Wolsey from 1530 through the end of the sixteenth century collectively established what, in retrospect, we may call three prototypical representations of him. Before describing what precisely I mean when I use the label *prototypes*, I hasten to add that I see them as analytic tools that can help us bring together, for observation and discussion, sets of discursive elements that analytically cohere with one another and advance a particular characterization of Wolsey. I regard the three prototypes that I will be identifying along the lines of Weberian ideal types, each consisting of attributes, features, narratives, tropes, and so forth that collectively constitute a distinctive way of representing something. But I intentionally identify these three representations as prototypes, rather than archetypes or ideal types, for two reasons. First, because especially in the first half of the sixteenth century they appeared in a somewhat embryonic state: Their manifestation in the earliest representations of Wolsey is far from complete, and later writers added to and embellished the accounts of their predecessors. And second, because the earliest representations of Wolsey were consciously employed by later writers as models or blueprints, just as engineers might use a prototype of a mechanical device to construct their own, more efficient version.

It is not necessarily the case—and indeed it will not *usually* be the case—that any particular representation of Wolsey will be identical with one of my three analytical prototypes; instead, the prototypes serve as idealized models that bring together, for clarity of discussion, similar claims and narrative elements.[6] As we will see, the writers whose works we will be exploring draw upon one another, as well as upon earlier cultural productions, in expanding, intensifying, nuancing, and even refuting one another's representations of Wolsey. Indeed, as time went on, writers began to employ elements or incorporate materials from earlier sources that belong analytically to more than one prototype; the resulting complexity of these later representations makes them all the more interesting. Of course, each text also bears traces of its own, highly specific historical, cultural, and political milieu. In this chapter, therefore, I will seek to identify not only the interrelationships among texts but also the contextual factors that shaped their production and reception.

The three prototypical representations I will be tracing are specters that have haunted almost all subsequent accounts of the cardinal's life and legacy. One prototype, that of Wolsey the author of the schism, was primarily the product of English Catholics writing at home as well as on the continent. This Wolsey is a man of personal vice and disastrous statecraft, whose jealousy and desire for vengeance, as opposed to any structural defects in traditional religion, cost Rome the obedience of England. Wolsey's fall, according to this representation, is a due reward for his ill policies. But his disgrace is not sufficient to halt the progress of schism: The cardinal had enabled King Henry, politically and psychologically, too much for that. A second prototype, that of Wolsey the papist, has until recently dominated anglophone accounts of the early English Reformation. In this version, Wolsey epitomizes the decay of late medieval Catholicism, constituting a leading symbol of its corruption and pointing toward the speedy overthrow of papism by men of the gospel. According to this prototype, Wolsey's ignominious fall and death set the stage for the submission of the clergy, for King Henry's divorce, and ultimately for a definitive break with Rome. While the first two prototypes adopt an overwhelmingly negative attitude toward Wolsey, the third prototype is substantially more complex: Wolsey as repentant sinner. This account admits Wolsey's not insignificant shortcomings, but it attributes the English schism to the caprice and passion of Henry and the ambition of Anne Boleyn and her family. Far from encouraging the king, in this telling Wolsey sought to restrain him. Most notably, in the final year of his life the cardinal experienced a conversion, coming to perceive Henry's character as tyrannical and cruel.

These three prototypical representations of Wolsey offer a set of analytic tools to examine the sixteenth-century texts that laid the groundwork for later accounts of Wolsey's life and significance. Subsequent chapters will highlight the ways in which later writers appropriated elements of these prototypes and adapted them to the needs of their day. For now, in this chapter we will explore the emergence and early articulation of these three ways of thinking about Wolsey by treating a period of some seven decades, from Wolsey's death through the end of the sixteenth century. We will do so by analyzing in detail an influential text that captures the key features of each prototype, then situating that text in the midst of others like it.

Wolsey the Author of the Schism

It is worth pausing, before proceeding further, to observe that few written accounts of Wolsey appeared publicly between the time of his death and the end of Henry's reign. On the one hand, it is likely that Henry retained ambivalent feelings toward his former chief minister, who had died accused, but not convicted, of treason. While Cavendish is not entirely a reliable source (as we will see later), his report that the king wished after Wolsey's death "that leuer than xx M^{lli} he had lyved [that rather than £20,000 he had lived]" seems both too specific and too much in line with comments that others attributed to Henry during the period of the cardinal's exile to be fabricated out of whole cloth.[7] On the other hand, the unpredictable contours of Henry's reformation, which alternated between decrees and initiatives that moved England in an evangelical direction and those that sought to retain and enforce elements of traditional religion, revealed that Henry, an instinctive conservative, was uneasy about going too far. The political and theological uncertainties of the second half of his reign made it dangerous for writers of all stripes to engage with a legacy as complicated as Wolsey's. In some ways, it must have been easier for them to allow the cardinal to slip temporarily out of memory, vanishing from sight just as Henry's workmen plastered over Wolsey's coat of arms above what came to be known as Anne Boleyn's Gateway at Hampton Court Palace.[8]

Following the onset of schism, which received legislative sanction in the parliamentary acts of the early 1530s, writers whose religious allegiance remained with Rome found themselves in a tenuous rhetorical position. They regarded what they took to be Wolsey's numerous moral failings as one of the leading causes of the schism, but at the same time they were wary of inadvertently lending credence to the evangelical argument that it was the teachings and practices of the Roman church that had given rise to, and condoned on an ongoing basis, the cardinal's excesses.[9] There was also another, even more politically tricky question: How should Catholic writers represent *Henry's* involvement in the schism? As Peter Lake has recently demonstrated with regard to texts written by Catholic critics of Queen Elizabeth I, such writers could choose from a spectrum of discourses. The safest option was to argue that the monarch had fallen prey to the invidious designs of so-called evil counselors. This time-honored approach excused the sovereign from personal responsibility, even if it ran the risk of portraying the king or queen as a figure with less than full control. However, as Lake has argued, the line between this more politic argument "and one directed straight at the person of the monarch could be paper-thin. . . . Various authors or factions, and in some cases even particular texts, might slip and slide, with relative ease, between accounts of tyranny centred on evil counsel, and alternatives centred on the very personal rule and malign will of the ruler/tyrant in question."[10] While Lake's research focused on Elizabeth rather than her father, his insight is equally true of Catholic authors who were writing about Henry and his onetime cardinal-minister. As the century continued and circumstances changed, such authors presented increasingly lurid accounts of Wolsey's motives and, at the same time, became increasingly prone to attacking Henry's character outright.

One of the most influential treatments of Wolsey by a Catholic writer appeared in the third edition of Polydore Vergil's *Anglica historia,* which was first printed at Basle in 1555, the year of Vergil's death. He was an Italian scholar, diplomat, and inveterate political intriguer who had lived in England from 1502 through 1515 and again from 1517 through 1533. Vergil was well known to Wolsey, who had made use of him in the 1514 negotiations that won his cardinal's hat. However, relations between the two men soured the following year, when Wolsey imprisoned Vergil in the Tower of London after authorities discovered that he had indiscreetly written letters against the cardinal to correspondents on the continent.[11] Following his release, Vergil remained embittered: He no longer engaged in politics on Wolsey's behalf and instead sought revenge on his former patron through the craft of historiography.[12] The *Anglica historia*'s most recent editor, Denys Hay, has written that Vergil's primary purpose was "to put a favourable interpretation on the rise of the house of Tudor" and especially to chronicle the achievements of King Henry VII. However, Hay added, Vergil did not miss any opportunity to slight Wolsey. His animus not only colored his judgments but also prompted him to represent incorrectly some facts of which he was, as a contemporary, likely to have been aware. "His attitude of uncritical abuse makes suspect every passage in which Wolsey is mentioned."[13] While Hay later revised his judgment, concluding in his 1952 biography of Vergil that the Italian "may have been spiteful but he appears to have been right," the scholarly consensus remains with his earlier view.[14]

The first two editions of the *Anglica historia* cover the earliest days of England up through the accession of Henry VIII in 1509; the third edition, in which Wolsey is portrayed at length, extends the narrative through 1537. Hay has argued persuasively that even though the third edition was not published until 1555, Vergil had written much of his account of Henry VIII's reign contemporaneously with the events he was narrating. In making this claim, Hay upended the theories of earlier scholars who believed that Vergil had depended for his material on the chronicle of the London evangelical Edward Hall.[15] Instead, Hay demonstrated, it is more likely that Hall, along with later Tudor and Stuart historiographers, depended instead upon Vergil. The recurrence of tropes from Vergil—"from the wicked uncle to the grasping prelate"—in later works marks Vergil as a writer of considerable influence and the *Anglica historia* as a text of broad circulation. In the language of memory theorists such as Assmann and Kansteiner, Vergil was an influential producer of cultural memories.[16] Indeed, the *Anglica historia*, as the first substantial work of English history to employ Italian humanist norms of scholarship, shaped the narratives of many other writers we will encounter in this chapter, including Hall, Holinshed, and Shakespeare.[17]

Wolsey appears midway through the lengthy final book of Vergil's history. The words that introduce him characterize him as a figure to beware. Vergil recounts that with King Henry during his French campaign of 1513 was, among other retainers, "Thomas Wolsey the almoner, a clever man and endowed with a . . . spirit, who had suddenly become so dear to the king that he could scarcely have been dearer."[18] Vergil here conjures the image of a royal favorite, just barely leaving it to his readers to associate Wolsey with the other evil counselors they had encountered earlier in his book.[19] As he rises in Henry's service, Wolsey appears to bring England peace and economic well-being through his careful administration, but he "gloried exceedingly," Vergil writes, "as though he alone were responsible for the great good fortune in that his authority was now supreme with the king. But he was also more hated, not only on account of his arrogance and his low reputation for integrity, but also on account of his recent origin."[20] Here we can identify, in the space of a few pages, three of the charges that were frequently leveled against Wolsey: that he sought and guarded an inappropriate level of influence with the king, that his moral judgment was questionable, and that he had unreasonably transcended his low origins.

Indeed, many of Vergil's criticisms of Wolsey emerge from the ways in which he represents the cardinal upending the proper order of things. Wolsey sits as a judge despite being ignorant of the common law; he forces the great lords of the realm to serve him at mass; he collects a multitude of bribes; and he exiles from Henry's presence anyone, even great lords, who might threaten the privileged place he holds as the king's indispensable counselor. In the sphere of religion, the cardinal is as vicious as he is innovative: When he attempts to sway the people in his favor by dispensing them from the Lenten fast, "far from this Wolseian benefit being taken to be beneficial, it was regarded as an act of malice, for it drove very few (and precisely none who were good) to abrogate the former law for living life."[21] Even worse for Vergil is Wolsey's decision to dissolve a number of monasteries to pay for his colleges in Oxford and Ipswich (the latter, "an unimportant place"). "This singular wickedness resulted in the pope being gratuitously disliked in England, but Wolsey much worse."[22]

Vergil's criticisms of Wolsey mount as his narrative develops. At one point, he describes how the cardinal, "acquiring so many offices at the same time, became so proud that he considered himself the peer of kings."[23] Unlike some of the other writers we will be encountering, Vergil does not imply that Wolsey had persuaded Henry to demand Archbishop of Canterbury William Warham's resignation as lord chancellor, but he does depict Warham, along with Richard Fox, the bishop of Winchester, withdrawing in sadness from royal service as the scope of Wolsey's influence over the king became clear. Some years later, Vergil returns to the contentious relationship between Wolsey and Warham—a topic we will explore throughout this book—to illustrate the cardinal's jealousy about his prerogatives. When Warham familiarly addresses Wolsey as "brother" in a letter he sends after the cardinal had been made legate *a latere*, Wolsey takes great offense, exclaiming "that he would soon arrange for [Canterbury] to learn that he was not even his equal let alone his 'brother.'"[24] Vergil tells this story immediately after describing Wolsey's practice of having two crosses carried before him, in comparison to the one that preceded Warham. Some later writers conflated these two anecdotes, representing Warham feeling slighted that Wolsey had any crosses at all carried before him in the presence of the more senior archbishop.[25]

For Vergil, however, Wolsey's greatest crime was his attempt to procure the annulment of Henry's marriage with Katherine of Aragon. In the *Anglica historia*, this is entirely Wolsey's conception, but in contrast to the seriousness of the matter, Vergil represents him imagining a royal divorce somewhat casually: "It came into his head to change his queen and to find a new one, whom he wished to be like him in conduct and character."[26] Henry at first resists attempts by Wolsey and John Longland, the royal confessor, to persuade him to divorce Katherine, and it is only later, after negotiations about the annulment have been going on for some time and after Cardinal Campeggio has come to England to sit as a judge in the case, that Henry develops a romantic interest in Anne Boleyn. Wolsey's opposition to the king's projected match with Anne, which Vergil represents as the first major decision of Henry's over which Wolsey had no influence, prompts the cardinal to reverse himself. Wolsey writes secretly to the pope to urge him not to grant the king's petition.[27] Hence Wolsey reveals himself to be not only an evil counselor but a counselor acting directly in contravention of his monarch's wishes. For that reason, Henry almost immediately decides "to reduce to the lowest ranks this man who was so forgetful of his favors."[28] Only a paragraph in the modern edition of the *Anglica historia* covers Wolsey's dismissal as chancellor and his banishment to York, arrest, and death. Henry's decision to charge Wolsey with high treason comes on the heels of the cardinal's plans to be installed as archbishop "in triumphal fashion," with the king intending to "stop him becoming haughtier and acting like a madman."[29] Vergil has little to say about the manner of Wolsey's arrest and death and attributes his downfall primarily to his presumptuousness in seeking to procure the divorce: "Wolsey flourished in importance and wealth: when he set in motion the marriage project, which he considered would be a fine thing for him, it brought him ruin."[30]

Vergil's *Anglica historia* served as a prototype for subsequent Catholic representations of Wolsey, but Vergil's successors embellished features of his narrative. Writers who had not known Wolsey or been received in a friendly manner at the court of Henry VIII, as Vergil had, concocted increasingly sensationalistic claims about Wolsey's motives and, at the same time, began to assign the king greater responsibility for the schism. Nicholas Harpsfield, the former Oxford legal scholar who served as archdeacon of Canterbury under Reginald Pole, claimed in his *Treatise on the Pretended Divorce* (1557 or 1558) that Wolsey sought the royal annulment as a way to take revenge upon Queen Katherine's nephew, Emperor Charles V.[31] Harpsfield's argument rests on the assumption, common to many criticisms of Wolsey, that the cardinal desired above all else to become pope. Charles had promised Wolsey assistance in the conclave but failed to deliver, so (according to Harpsfield) Wolsey "maligned and hated" Charles "because he would not serve and content his immoderate ambition."[32] However, events rendered Wolsey's vengeance impotent: Wolsey did not envision that King Henry's favor would fall upon Anne Boleyn, thus catching the cardinal on the horns of a dilemma of his own conjuring. Wolsey may have been successful in persuading the king that his marriage was invalid and that only Wolsey's elevation to the papacy could guarantee an annulment, but Wolsey "could in no wise fancy" the prospect of a marriage between Henry and Anne.[33]

We find an extended version of this narrative in a more influential, if less often studied, Catholic work of the late sixteenth century, Nicholas Sander's *De origine ac progressu schismatis anglicani*, which first appeared in 1585 and went through at least fifteen printed editions by the end of the century (see Plate 6).[34] Like Harpsfield, Sander was a legal scholar. They overlapped briefly as fellows of New College, Oxford, but by the beginning of Elizabeth's reign Sander had left England; he subsequently lived in two of the continent's Catholic intellectual centers, Rome and Louvain. Christopher Highley has recently dubbed Sander's work the intellectual and literary rival of Foxe's *Actes and Monuments,* "arguably the major Protestant history with which the *Schismatis Anglicani* was in dialogue."[35] The tone of Sander's writing earned him, among the barbs of many other critics, the epithet "Dr. Slanders" from the Stuart church historian Peter Heylyn. Bishop Gilbert Burnet dismissed Sander with the claim that he "did so impudently deliver falsehoods, that from his own Book many of them may be disproved."[36]

Sander represents Wolsey as "daring and ambitious beyond his fellows."[37] Like Harpsfield, Sander writes that Wolsey, who had Henry "utterly in his power," seized on the divorce as an opportunity to revenge himself upon Charles V.[38] But also like Harpsfield (and Vergil before him), Sander observes that Wolsey had not expected that Henry would insist upon making Anne Boleyn Katherine's successor. For Sander, like his predecessors, the schism therefore emerged from "the interplay of impulses both inside and outside the king."[39]

Wolsey was not, however, the only character in the drama of the Henrician period that Harpsfield and Sander represented differently than Vergil did. As Eamon Duffy has argued, Reginald Pole's return to England as cardinal legate marked a turning point for Catholic representations of King Henry. Whereas traditionalists like Bishop Stephen Gardiner and his protégé Thomas Martin, the civil lawyer who was the chief prosecutor at Thomas Cromwell's trial, had previously demurred about the events of Henry's reign, "after Pole's arrival, the gloves were off, and the Marian episcopate now routinely described the heresies and disorders of Edward's reign as the inevitable outcome of Henry's schism and spoke of Henry himself as a tyrant."[40] It should not be surprising that Harpsfield's *Pretended Divorce* borrows from Ezekiel 8 the language of "abominations" and "idols," which Harpsfield argues "the King did secretly worship."[41] Harpsfield also quotes from royal letters to foreground Henry's willingness to foment a schism should it have been necessary to secure his annulment. According to Harpsfield, when Pope Clement VII fell seriously ill in 1529, Henry planned that if the ensuing conclave did not elect Wolsey, then the English and French cardinals should leave Rome, proceed to another city, and elect their own pope, while Henry would "offer a presidie [garrison] of two or three thousand men to be in the city for the time of the said election."[42] Henry's willingness to plunge the church into the kind of schism that had done such damage in the fourteenth and fifteenth centuries demonstrates that he had subjugated the church's good to the fulfillment of his lustful desires.

For Harpsfield, writing in the final years of Mary's reign, Henry may have been recklessly corrupt. Sander and his later editors, however, pressed the case against the king in far more disparaging terms, working from the safety of the continent at a time when Elizabeth I, Anne Boleyn's daughter, had been excommunicated. Sander opens his *Schismatis Anglicani* with a comparison of Henry's and Katherine's conduct: She lived a life "of soberness and modesty, the king one of levity and wantonness. No more repugnant pair of opposites can easily be found."[43] (He adds in an aside that Wolsey's "works were more like the king's than the queen's.")[44] In the late sixteenth century this was conventional enough, but Sander adds a lurid and almost unspeakable claim, one that prima facie constituted treason. He argues that when Henry pursued Anne Boleyn, he was seeking to marry his own illegitimate daughter, the product of an affair with Anne's mother. Sander adds that Thomas Boleyn was aware of his daughter's paternity but had reconciled himself to the situation at the request of the king and senior nobles.[45] The *Schismatis Anglicani* presents an unflattering physical description of Anne, with Sander linking her physical attractions and courtly behavior, on the one hand, and her sexual immorality, on the other. After becoming involved with at least two of her father's servants, Anne was sent to the French court, "where she was commonly called by the French *Hacnea*, or the English mare, because of her shameless behavior; and then she began to be called the royal mule, when she became acquainted with the king of France."[46] That Anne's religious opinions were Lutheran was, for Sander, only in keeping with her way of life. (While the queen-to-be may indeed have been inclined to religious reform, I must hasten to add that there is little evidence for Sander's incredible statements about her.)[47]

To appropriate Peter Lake's terminology, we could say that as the sixteenth century wore on, English Catholic writers by and large shifted away from ascribing the ills of the Henrician reformation to evil counselors like Wolsey. Instead, they began to launch direct rhetorical attacks on the king. Vergil had represented Wolsey as having persuaded an initially unwilling Henry to pursue an annulment, a course of action that eventually led to Wolsey's downfall. Harpsfield criticized Henry, but Wolsey's ambition for the papacy remained at the forefront of his narrative. In contrast, by the time Sander put pen to paper, he was prepared to cast the king as chief villain.[48] Shifting responsibility for the schism from Wolsey to Henry provided Sander with the opportunity, if not to exonerate Wolsey, then at least partially to rehabilitate him. Sander argues that even though Wolsey had been the first to raise the possibility of an annulment, he "was sorry for the counsel he had given" once it became clear that Henry wished to marry his illegitimate daughter rather than another, more suitable woman and that Anne Boleyn's "monstrously productive body" would become, as Highley has put it, "a locus of schism."[49] When Henry banished Wolsey from court after the failure of his annulment proceedings, this, for Sander, served only to confirm that the king was tyrannical and capricious: "The very sin for which he punishes Wolsey so severely is the very sin in which the king obstinately persists. Therefore, O king, art thou inexcusable!"[50] And with regard to Wolsey's arrest and death, Sander's narrative again reflects a surprising degree of moderation. In the *Schismatis Anglicani*, Henry orders Wolsey's arrest because the cardinal "was living in great state in York, giving feasts, using solemn pomp, and demanding from the king the restoration of his miter fashioned with precious stones."[51] About the circumstances of Wolsey's death, Sander presents conflicting evidence:

> Reports were spread abroad that he had taken poison. This, however, is certain, that on being arrested for high treason he said, "Oh, that I had been as guiltless of treason against His Divine Majesty! Now, indeed, while intent only on serving the king, I have sinned against God, and have not pleased the king."[52]

The ascription to Wolsey of a parting aphorism about the respective merits of serving God and the king distinguishes Sander's account from those of Vergil and Harpsfield and points to the possible influence of George Cavendish's memoir, *The Life and Death of Cardinal Wolsey*, which (as we will see later in this chapter and in Chapter 2) started circulating among English Catholics soon after its composition in the late 1550s.

It is clear that the bounds of acceptable Catholic discourse about Wolsey, Henry, and Anne expanded over the course of the sixteenth century. Catholic writers began to attack not only evil counselors like Wolsey, William Cecil, and Robert Dudley but also the sovereigns they served. The most vicious criticisms of King Henry and Queen Elizabeth appeared in Latin works such as Sander's *Schismatis Anglicani*, which (as Lake has argued) "was designed more for continental than for domestic English consumption" and which, once translated into the vernaculars of Catholic countries such as Spain, "operated as a work of both propaganda and counsel, advocating and legitimating active military intervention in England."[53] While it is true that, intentionally or otherwise, these writers created space for slightly more sympathetic portrayals of characters like Wolsey by shifting responsibility for the schism away from counselors and onto the monarch, no Catholic text sought to absolve Wolsey entirely from blame. What works such as Vergil's, Harpsfield's, and Sander's have in common are what we might designate as three distinctive features of the prototypical representation of Wolsey as author of the schism. First, they depict him as a man of personal vice, including in particular his ambition for the papacy. Second, they claim that the schism emerged at least in part out of Wolsey's desire for vengeance against those whom he held responsible for his failure to attain that office. And finally, they represent Henry as either a duped or a willing participant in Wolsey's scheme, with the level of the king's personal malfeasance generally increasing in proportion to a writer's geographic distance from England and chronological distance from the events in question.

Wolsey the Papist

Yet Catholics were by no means the only Tudor writers who produced works critical of Wolsey. Evangelical writers were even more censorious, freed as they were from the necessity of defending the religious system of which Wolsey was a prominent part. Forming the dominant strand of anglophone historiography long after the close of the sixteenth century, evangelical writers remembered Wolsey as a papist villain. Their works reflect a second prototypical representation of the cardinal, a representation that dwells on his allegiance to the papacy, identifies him as an emblem of the thoroughgoing corruption of the Roman church, and vilifies him as a dangerous source of foreign influence over the affairs of England.

To a greater extent than the Catholic writers we have just been considering, evangelical authors borrowed ideas and images from satires and polemics written while Wolsey was still alive, such as the poems of John Skelton and tracts by William Roy, Jerome Barlow, and William Tyndale.[54] These texts do not fall chronologically within the remit of this book, and Schwartz-Leeper has recently carried out the important work of demonstrating how their tropes—Skelton's invocation of animals like the jackdaw, wolf, and spider as metaphors for Wolsey, for instance—shaped subsequent writers' treatments of the cardinal. While these pre-1530 works will therefore not figure directly in the following discussion, it is important to observe, along with Schwartz-Leeper and earlier scholars, that authors like Skelton and Tyndale drew many of the terms of abuse that they directed at Wolsey from the literary conventions of the late Middle Ages or from unsubstantiated assumptions, rather than from direct observation of the cardinal and his way of life. For the purposes of the present study, these conventional claims take on two interrelated forms of significance. First, as Greg Walker has argued with regard to John Skelton: "Skelton's satires are not . . . a fair picture of Wolsey. Neither are they evidence of a personal hatred for the Cardinal on the part of the poet. They are a collection of writings aimed at the vilification of Wolsey, written to further the poet's own fortunes."[55] At one and the same time, however, "Skelton's legacy is persistent. His fictionalized Wolsey still influences subconscious judgments about the historical original."[56]

For the same reasons we discussed above, few evangelical commentaries on Wolsey's life appeared between 1530 and the late 1540s. In 1548, the first edition of Edward Hall's *Union of the Two Noble and Illustre Families of Lancaster and York*, more commonly known as *Hall's Chronicle*, was published, with a revised edition following in 1550. Both came from the press of Richard Grafton, a staunch evangelical who from the beginning of Edward VI's reign held the title of King's Printer.[57] Before his death in 1547, Hall had conveyed to Grafton a draft of the *Chronicle* covering the years 1399 to 1532, along with notes on the remainder of Henry's reign; Grafton added to this draft his own account of the ensuing years.[58] Hall had been a lawyer who sat in the Commons during the Reformation Parliament, which met from 1529 to 1536 and, among other significant pieces of business, adopted the Act of Supremacy that declared the monarch to be supreme head on earth of the Church of England.[59] In its first year, Parliament also considered, but at Cromwell's urging ultimately rejected, a bill of attainder against Wolsey. Hall brought to the work of compiling his chronicle both his evangelical faith and his loyalty to the city of London, which he served as a judge and undersheriff.[60] It is not surprising, therefore, that his *Chronicle* attends closely to the fortunes of Londoners and, in particular, those of the merchant class.

Wolsey is a more or less constant presence in *Hall's Chronicle*, from his earliest appearance in Henry's fifth regnal year (1514/15) through his death. Until 1528, Hall represents Wolsey as the king's alter ego. For example, when in 1518 a delegation from the city of London comes to Henry to beg pardon for a recent riot, the king refuses to deal with them and sends them to Wolsey instead: "at this tyme we wyll graunt to you neither our favor nor good will, nor to thoffenders mercy, but resort to the Cardinall our lord Chau[n]celour."[61] Wolsey sits at the king's right hand in Parliament, he prepares the way for the king's travels abroad, he entertains foreign ambassadors on Henry's behalf, and he reorganizes the royal household. In the church, he dissolves the convocation of clergy in Canterbury province when he believes that it poses a threat to his authority as legate.[62] Moreover, Wolsey's dominance is not confined to England: The French king, Francis I, sends him a "patent of power" that was "taken for great loue that the Frenche kyng had geuen so greate power to the kynge of Englandes subiect."[63]

Hall is not shy about identifying Wolsey's vices: pride, arrogance, and the inability to tolerate rivals. Indeed, Hall's Wolsey becomes chancellor by politicking his predecessor out of the post: Warham resigns after "perceauing that the Archebyshop of Yorke medled more in his office of Chauncelourship then it became hym to suffer."[64] Likewise, when the papal legate Lorenzo Campeggio comes to England to seek Henry's support for the pope's wars in the 1510s, Wolsey, "whose ambicion was neuer satisfied," insists upon being made legate *a latere* so that he would equal the Italian cardinal.[65] In the early 1520s, Hall's Wolsey squares off with the House of Commons over taxation, earning the enmity of Hall's beloved London merchants. With regard to his dealings with Parliament, Hall represents Wolsey as engaging, at best, in what modern politicians would call spin. Stated more bluntly, Hall represents the cardinal as lying outright when Wolsey claims that it was not just he but the whole privy council that in 1525 had sought an unprecedented "benevolence," the so-called Amicable Grant, to fund war in France. "But the people toke all this for a mocke, and saied God saue the kyng, for the Cardinal is knowen wel inough, the commons would heare no prayse spoke[n] of the Cardinall, they hated hym so muche."[66] As Peter C. Herman has suggested, in Hall's narrative, as in Skelton's satires before it, invoking "the commons," or simply "the people," serves as a literary device for an author to voice personal views without risking the charge of sedition.[67]

The Amicable Grant represents the first downward turn in the fortunes of Hall's Wolsey. Hall reports that the cardinal was roundly ridiculed, for instance being mocked as a "Bochers dogge" living in a royal palace.[68] The *Chronicle* represents Wolsey becoming increasingly paranoid as the years go on, imagining, for instance, that a play performed at Gray's Inn in 1526/27 was an allegory against him, even though the play had been written prior to his rise to power. Hall's mention of this unfortunate entertainment coincides with his first allusion to the prospect of King Henry's annulment. Curiously, however, it is not Wolsey's involvement in the king's "great matter" that led to his downfall but instead his mismanagement of foreign policy. In the late 1520s, Hall's Wolsey becomes a symbol for the excessive involvement of foreign powers in English affairs. First, the cardinal persuades the king to send a substantial sum of money to support the besieged Pope Clement VII, about which Hall comments that "of this charge the realme shall not be one peny the better . . . [the pope] neuer shall do us good."[69] At the same time, Hall argues that Wolsey is too closely identified with France: Indeed, Wolsey "was al Frenche," and in negotiations with the French "ye Cardinal was euer on the French part."[70]

Yet Henry's opinion of Wolsey begins to change decisively only when he is confronted with physical evidence that the cardinal has played him false—miscarried letters to the emperor's ambassadors in which Wolsey had recommended a policy different from the king's. Hall's description of Henry's response to the bearer of this news deserves quotation in full:

> He mused a great while, and saied: O Lord Jesus, he that I trusted moste, tolde me all these thynges co[n]trary, well Clarenseaux, I will be no more of so light credence hereafter, or nowe I see perfectly, that I am made to beleue the thing that was neuer done. Then the kyng sent for the Cardinall and priuily talked with hym, but whatsoeuer he saied to hym, the Cardinal was not very mery, and after that tyme, the Kyng mistrusted hym euer after.[71]

Henry's suspicion only grows when the legatine court investigating his marriage encounters delays. Sensing an opportunity, Wolsey's long-embittered enemies among the nobles present the king with a book listing the cardinal's misdeeds. "When the kyng saw the boke . . . he euidently perceived the high pride and couetousnes of the Cardinal, and saw openlye with what dyssymulacion and clokyng, he had ha[n]deled the Kinges causes."[72] Indicted for praemunire, forced out of his London home at York Place, and in exile at his episcopal residence at Esher, Wolsey appears to accept responsibility for his actions when he pleads guilty to the charges against him.[73] However, either he was dissembling or his repentance was short-lived, for in the last months of his life, Hall's cardinal wages a campaign of retribution and complaint. Wolsey agrees to travel northward and establish himself in his diocese, but even after Henry grants him permission to do so, the cardinal "continued this yere euer grudgying at his fall as you shall here after."[74] Once in York, Wolsey becomes nothing short of seditious: He "wrote to the Court of Rome and to divers other prynces letters in reproche of the kyng. . . . The Cardinal also woulde speake fayre to the people to wynne their heartes, and declared euer, that he was uniustlye and untruely ordered . . . and to gentlemen he gaue great gyftes to allure them unto him."[75] Henry orders Wolsey's arrest, yet the cardinal resists almost to the end, claiming that as papal legate he was not subject to royal authority and that he had already been forgiven his praemunire, a crime into which he only "by negligence fell."[76] Even though Wolsey does eventually submit to arrest, Hall implies but does not state explicitly that the cardinal deliberately frustrates the king's justice by hastening his own death before he could return to London for trial.[77] In the end, Hall opines:

> This Cardinall as you may perceuyue in this story was of a great stomacke, for he compted him selfe egall with princes, and by craftye suggestion gatte into his hands innumerable treasure; He forced little be simony & was not pitiful and stode affeccionate in his owne opinion: In open presence he would lye and say untrueth and was double both in speche and meaning: He would promise much and performe lytle: He was vicious of his body and gaue the clergie euyl example: He hated sore the citie of London and feared it. The authoritie of this Cardinal set the clergie in such a pride that they dysdayned al men, wherefore when he was fallen thei followed after as you shall heare.[78]

The last clause of this passage epitomizes Wolsey's role in *Hall's Chronicle*. Formerly a symbol of the political overreaching of the Roman church, now Wolsey is a harbinger of the church's fate. Wolsey and the pope were greedy for power, both were inimical to London, and both fell once the king came to perceive the true state of affairs.

Even though Hall's narrative contains evangelical as well as nationalistic overtones, his *Chronicle* focuses more on political than theological affairs. In this regard, Hall reflects the standing of the Church of England at the end of Henry VIII's reign: freed from the putative yoke of Rome and under royal control but not substantially reformed in doctrine. However, later evangelical writers went further. Just as Vergil's initial statement of the Catholic case against Wolsey was elaborated upon by Harpsfield and Sander, so also did John Foxe, among others, magnify Hall's criticisms of the cardinal. Felicity Heal reminds us that Foxe, the author of the classic martyrology *Actes and Monuments*, "clothed polemical writing in historical garb, rendering chronicle ideologically charged."[79]

Schwartz-Leeper has persuasively argued that Foxe employed Wolsey "as a vehicle to transmit negative imagery of the Roman church," characterizing the cardinal "as an overproud and clownish hypocrite."[80] Foxe's language about Wolsey is both hyperbolic and repetitive, and Schwartz-Leeper has shown how the *Actes and Monuments* implicitly and explicitly contrasts Wolsey's vices with the virtues of Henrician reformers. In addition, Schwartz-Leeper has established that the characterization of Wolsey evolved strikingly from the first English edition of Foxe's martyrology, published in 1563, through the other three editions that appeared under Foxe's editorship in 1570, 1576, and 1583.[81]

There is not space here for a thorough discussion of Foxe's teleological, providential, and nationalistic account of what he called the restoration of the gospel to England. Indeed, the *Actes and Monuments* has been the subject of a great deal of scholarship, and Schwartz-Leeper has examined in detail the sections of Foxe's lengthy work that refer to Wolsey.[82] However, at the risk of duplicating some of this analysis, it is important for our purposes to highlight some of the ways in which Foxe contributed to a growing reservoir of evangelical representations of the cardinal as well as to note on which subjects Foxe remained conspicuously silent.

The 1563 edition of *Actes and Monuments* pays comparatively little attention to Wolsey. Foxe observes at one point that "it is not greatly pertinente vnto thys history, nor gretly requisit in these so waighty matters, to intreaet much of Thomas Wolsey Cardinall of York."[83] He borrows from Hall a comic story about the arrival of Cardinal Campeggio in London, to which he gives the subtitle "The history of a certaine ridiculous spectacle of the Cardinalles pompe, at London in the yeare of our Lorde 1517."[84] Wolsey had sent his fellow cardinal a train of twelve mules, in addition to the eight Campeggio already had, to carry his supposedly extensive treasure. But as Campeggio's procession moved through London, one of the mules broke free and triggered a stampede. In the ensuing chaos, onlookers discovered that Campeggio's mules were actually carrying "pieces of meat . . . pieces of bread and rosted egges, horse shoes, and olde shoes with suche other baggage."[85] In the 1563 edition, Foxe does not dwell on this anecdote but instead reverts quickly to his original subject: "nowe, we wyll leaue the pompous & proude Cardinalles, and returne agayne to the simple Martyrs of Ihesus Christ."[86] He does go on to refer to Wolsey's role in events such as the ill-fated convocation of clergy of 1523, and he borrows from Hall several anecdotes that disparage the cardinal. However, the 1563 edition does not represent Wolsey's dismissal, exile, or death, apart from a passing reference in connection with the death of another episcopal villain, Stephen Gardiner.

> Wherfore as touchinge the maner and order of his death, how riche
> he dyed, what were his wordes in defieng the honour of this world
> whether he dyed with his tounge swolne and out of his mouth, as
> Thomas Arundell Archbyshop of Caunt. [pag. 276.] or whether he
> stonke before he dyed, as Cardinall Wolsey dyd, (who as he had vsed
> coniuration before, so after he had poysoned hym selfe by the waye at

his buriall was so heauy that they let him fall did geue suche a sauoure that they coulde not abide him, with such a sodain storme & tempest aboute him, that al the torches wente out and coulde beare no light) or whether he died in dispaire. &c. al this I refere either to theire reportes of whō I hard it, or leaue it to the knoledge of them which knowe it better.[87]

A marginal note, in Latin, that appears next to the reference to Wolsey recounts that Foxe had acquired his information from an eyewitness: "from the telling of one who was there, and who held the dying cardinal in his arms."[88] As we will see, Foxe was fond of representing the manner of a person's death as evidence of divine judgment upon the conduct of his or her life.

The three later editions of *Actes and Monuments* contain a fuller characterization of Wolsey. Beginning with the 1570 edition, Foxe interrupts his account of the persecution of "simple men within the dioces of Lincolne" with what he entitles "A briefe discourse concerning the Storye and lyfe of Thomas Wolsey, late Cardinall of Yorke, by way of digression, wherin is to be seene and noted the expresse image of the proud vainglorious church of Rome, how farre it differeth from the true church of Christ Iesus."[89] He justifies his digression by writing that after describing the forced abjurations of followers of the gospel, "we will some thyng speake (God willyng) of the lyfe and doynges of the contrary part, who were their persecutors . . . to þe entent that by those Rulers, it may better be discerned, & iudged, what maner of Church that was, which then so persecuted the true doctrine of Christ."[90] Not without indulging his penchant for repetition, Foxe makes clear that his representation of Wolsey serves the overall purpose of his book, namely to contrast the churches of Christ and Antichrist. In the new section about Wolsey, Foxe characterizes the cardinal as a Roman leader who opposed the progress of the gospel. As he goes on to say explicitly, he features Wolsey in order that the "pompe and pride" of the Roman church "more notoriouslye may appeare to all men."[91]

The narrative that Foxe added to his 1570 edition he reprinted without change in the editions of 1576 and 1583.[92] Some criticisms of Wolsey Foxe borrowed directly from Hall, including Hall's complaints about the sums of money Wolsey had sent from England to Rome. Even Henry's papal title, Defender of the Faith, Foxe claims Wolsey purchased with English money: "it cost more then London and xl. myle about it, considering yᵉ great summes which you haue heard the Cardinall obteyned of the kyng."[93] However, Foxe adds to Hall's account a series of details designed to characterize Wolsey as an agent of Antichrist and to provoke disgust in the godly reader. As Schwartz-Leeper has noted, in the 1570 and ensuing editions Foxe "presents an altogether more serious tone."[94] Foxe dedicates more than two full columns to Wolsey's supposed campaign of vengeance against Richard Pace, representing the cardinal as having drawn Pace, Henry's former secretary, "out of the kinges fauour, and at last also, out of his perfect wyttes."[95] Foxe prints a list of eight of the forty-four charges against Wolsey that were presented to Parliament in 1529, choosing the articles that most characterized Wolsey as having sought equality with the king and having shown greater loyalty to Rome than England.

But it was with reference to Wolsey's death that Foxe most expanded the symbolic breadth of his 1563 narrative.[96] Like Hall's, Foxe's cardinal is unrepentant to the end. Indeed, Foxe borrows directly from Hall the paragraphs in which he narrates Wolsey's begrudging journey to York, his prideful behavior there, and his arrogant invocation of clerical immunity in the face of arrest. But Foxe embellishes Hall's account of Wolsey's final days by adding sensory details. Adopting the strategy of attributing controversial claims to popular rumor, Foxe writes that "men sayd that hee willingly tooke so much quantitie of a strong purgatio[n], that his nature was not able to beare it."[97] As the cardinal grows sicker, "the matter came from hym was so blacke, that the steining therof, could not be gotten out of hys blanckets by any meanes."[98] And when Wolsey dies, Foxe introduces what Schwartz-Leeper has rightly called "grotesque and morally weighted detail":

It is testified by one, yet beyng a lyue, in whose armes the sayd Cardinall dyed, that his body beyng dead, was blacke as pitch, also was so heauy, y^t vi. could scares beare it. Furthermore, it did so stinke aboue the ground, y^t they were co[n]streyned to hasten the burial therof in the night season, before it was day. At the which burial, such a tempest, with such a stinche there arose, that all the torches went out, and so he was throwen into the tombe, and there was layd.[99]

Thus, even—or, perhaps, especially—in death, Foxe's Wolsey symbolizes the decay of late medieval Catholicism, its political bloating and spiritual blackening, and its coming overthrow by the gospel. Many of the details Foxe relates draw consciously, and we might add ironically, on the tropes of medieval hagiography. Wolsey's dark, malodorous corpse constitutes the antithesis of saintly bodies like those of the virgin martyrs Agatha and Cecilia, which remained intact long after death; the remains of other saints were often said to smell of roses.[100]

To sum up, Foxe's characterization of Wolsey innovates in at least three substantial ways. First, as we have just seen, he deploys data from the senses—sight, smell, and touch—to associate Wolsey's body, in both life and death, with the opposite of sanctity. Second, he magnifies and adds detail to earlier charges that Wolsey had served a foreign power, the papacy, more than England and its king. Third, he deliberately represents Wolsey, along with other Roman churchmen like Thomas Arundel and Stephen Gardiner, as representatives of one side in the ongoing battle between Christ and Antichrist. As Foxe writes in the preface to his 1570 edition, the *Actes and Monuments* seeks to show "the image of both Churches, aswell of the one, as of the other: especially of the poore oppressed and persecuted Church of Christ."[101] For Foxe, Wolsey is a perfect emblem of those who are responsible for oppression and persecution, and Foxe's representation of the cardinal is accordingly unsparing, offering his caricature of a papist prelate no opportunity to demonstrate penitence or undergo redemption. After exploring a contrasting perspective in the next section, we will see later in this chapter how some evangelicals who wrote after Foxe combined features of his account with those of other sources in order to produce hybrid representations of Wolsey.

Wolsey the Repentant Sinner

Wolsey as author of the schism and Wolsey as papist are the prototypes that all but monopolized Tudor historical writing. In addition, for at least the first three centuries after Wolsey's death, they shaped the vast majority of literary, historical, and dramatic representations of the cardinal. However, we must consider as well a competing set of ideas and images about Wolsey: those that portrayed him as a flawed man who, toward the end of his life, repented for his sins. Unlike the first two prototypes, which were built up in a series of influential texts written over several decades, the features of our third prototype can be traced largely to one source, the memoirs of Wolsey's gentleman-usher George Cavendish.[102]

Cavendish began to write his two extant texts, the *Metrical Visions* and the *Life of Wolsey*, in 1554, the year after the accession of Mary Tudor had given English Catholics new hope. In the prologue to the *Life of Wolsey*, Cavendish asserts that he was compelled to write the cardinal's biography in order to correct the mistaken impressions that earlier "writers of Cronycles" had maliciously created.[103] As Richard Sylvester, the most recent editor of the *Life*, has argued, these chronicles must have included Hall's, a commercial success that evangelicals had received enthusiastically in the final years of Edward's reign. "It would perhaps be going too far to assert that it was the publication of Hall's work which first prompted Cavendish to begin his *Life*, but there is ample reason to believe both that he knew the *Chronicle* well and that he may have taken some of his material from it."[104] *Hall's Chronicle* appeared on a list of books to be destroyed that Mary's government promulgated in 1555, but it is not unreasonable, as Sylvester has argued, to think that Cavendish found this remedy insufficient.[105] Hall had already done too much to blacken Wolsey's reputation.

Before turning to the longer and more influential *Life*, let us briefly consider Cavendish's earlier work, a collection of poems given the title *Metrical Visions* by S. W. Singer, who first published them in 1825. Cavendish likely composed the bulk of the poems between 1552 and 1554, then putting them aside to begin work on the *Life*. He later returned to the *Visions*, bringing them to a conclusion in 1558 by recording his sorrow at the passing of Queen Mary.[106] The *Metrical Visions* are extant in only three manuscripts, two of which also preserve the *Life*.[107] They feature a parade of specters, each representing a character from the Henrician court. One by one, the ghosts reflect on their lives, accomplishments, and regrets. Most literary scholars have been critical of the *Visions*, with Derek Pearsall, for instance, complaining that "the extraordinary thing about the *Visions* is that Cavendish should have bothered to write them at all."[108] Yet as A. S. G. Edwards has observed, "However limited may be the claims of the *Metrical Visions* to intrinsic merit, it is a work of historical importance," since it contains valuable evidence about how Cavendish, a highly placed domestic associate of Wolsey's who had firsthand experience of the court, perceived some of the most influential actors of the first half of Henry VIII's reign.[109]

The visions take as their overall theme the "ffickkellnes of ffortune / and of the Course of kind," a concern that animates the *Life* as well.[110] Cavendish's interest in the workings of fortune situates him as an heir of the medieval *de casibus* tradition, a style of writing about the fall of influential persons whose origin is usually attributed to Boccaccio's mid–fourteenth century *De casibus virorum illustrium*. Boccaccio's work entered English literature primarily through the fifteenth-century poet John Lydgate's *Fall of Princes*. Among other works, the tradition inspired Tudor poets to assemble the collection of lives entitled *A Mirror for Magistrates*, whose first edition appeared in 1559, shortly after Cavendish finished composing the *Metrical Visions*.[111]

In the *Visions*, as in the *Life*, Cavendish figures fortune as changeable, irresistible, and not a little vengeful.[112] Wolsey is the first specter to appear in the poem, and his character invokes fortune at the beginning of his remarks. Wolsey observes that his fall from power was the almost inevitable consequence of his spectacular rise:

O ffortune / quod he / shold I on the complayn
Or of my necligence that I susteyn this smart
Thy doble visage hathe led me to this trayn
Ffor at my begynnyng / thou dydest ay take my part
Vntill ambysion had puffed vppe my hart
With vaynglory . honor . and vsurped dignyte.
Fforgetting cleane my naturall mendycitie.[113]

For this Wolsey, fortune is an inconstant ally, its "doble visage" first helping him into positions of authority and then taking away his honors when he forgets that he received them by happenstance rather than merit. This conception of fortune animates the *Life* as well, and there are perhaps more similarities between the two works than earlier commentators have recognized.[114] Here as there, fortune works against Wolsey through a particular instrument, namely Anne Boleyn. Wolsey's ghost in the *Visions* charges that "Venus the goddesse / that called is of love / Spared not with spight / to bryng me frome above."[115] Here as there, Cavendish criticizes King Henry for his caprice, lust, and selfishness. Indeed, in the *Visions* Cavendish's critique is sharper, with Henry's ghost declaring that "of my lust / will was my souerayn / My reason was bridelled / so by sensualite / That wyll rewled all / without lawe and equyte."[116] And here as there, Cavendish suggests that Wolsey experienced something of a conversion before he died. As Wolsey's ghost prepares to leave Cavendish's sight, he repeatedly asks "what avayllyth nowe" his earthly glories.[117]

These features—the prominent role that Cavendish assigns to fortune, the identification of Anne as the proximate cause of Wolsey's disgrace, the criticism of Henry's actions and motivations, and Wolsey's conversion— all distinguish our third prototypical representation. In the *Life*, Cavendish expands upon the themes of the *Visions* in a prose narrative that some commentators have designated the first modern biography written in English.[118] The text circulated in manuscript until 1641, when (as we will see in Chapter 2) a badly mangled and ideologically inflected edition appeared. Manuscripts of the *Life* were both numerous—at least thirty-nine separate witnesses remain extant today, many from the sixteenth century—and influential.[119] Cavendish's work was known to the Tudor historical writer John Stow, who incorporated long extracts from it into his *Chronicles of England* (1580) and *Annales of England* (1592), and as we will see, it was through Stow's

Chronicles that Cavendish's words entered the second edition of *Holinshed's Chronicles* (1587). No doubt Stow's appreciation for Cavendish's portrait of Wolsey helps explain why Elizabethan authorities investigated Stow at least once on suspicion of Roman Catholic sympathies.

But what narrative about Wolsey does Cavendish's *Life* contain? Sylvester has asserted that the text "stands out uniquely among sixteenth century accounts of the Cardinal, for it is no exaggeration to say that both Protestant and Catholic writers of the period tend to treat Wolsey as the most despicable of men."[120] The *Life* is a personal as well as a political portrait of its subject, and the rhetorical techniques and hermeneutical lenses that Cavendish employs differ greatly from those of Hall or Foxe. Even though Cavendish was familiar with Hall, his religious and political sympathies were quite different, and his role as one of Wolsey's leading servants afforded him a measure of access that would have been impossible for an evangelical-leaning London MP who was just slightly older than thirty when Wolsey was dismissed as chancellor.[121] Nevertheless, it is essential to stress that only late in Wolsey's life did Cavendish acquire an intimate position in the cardinal's service. As Cavendish himself relates, Wolsey had more than twelve gentleman-ushers and no fewer than forty-six yeomen of his chamber, all part of a total retinue of at least five hundred. And Cavendish's closeness to Wolsey, especially in the months following his dismissal as chancellor, was unlikely to make his representation of the cardinal an impartial one. In fact, his biography has been labeled as "profoundly partisan" as Thomas More's life of Richard III or William Roper's of More.[122] Because Cavendish is our sole source for a significant number of anecdotes about Wolsey, the temptation is strong to treat the *Life* as more truthful than other sources. However, we employ such a hermeneutic at our peril. Cavendish was as committed to his view of the Henrician period as Vergil, Hall, Foxe, and others were to theirs, and the grief he expressed in the *Metrical Visions* over the untimely death of Queen Mary is just one piece of evidence for what Schwartz-Leeper has called his "moderate Romanist" sympathies.[123]

Cavendish's primary interpretive schema for Wolsey's rise and fall is that of fortune's wheel. Warren Wooden has persuasively argued that the *Life* combines elements of the *de casibus* tradition with those of the medieval morality play.[124] Cavendish asserts that fortune "folowyth some whome she lystithe to promote, and evyn so to Somme hyr fauour is contrary thoughe they shold travell neuer so myche wᵗ vrgent diligence & paynfull study that they could device or Imagyn."[125] It is with fortune's aid that Wolsey first rose in the service of King Henry VII, for whom he allegedly completed in three days a mission to the emperor that would have taken another man many more.[126] Likewise, fortune made Wolsey prominent enough by the time of Henry VIII's accession that the young king was able to see him as "a mete Instrume^t for the accomplysssheme^t of his devised wyll & pleasure."[127] But fortune also brings about Wolsey's downfall, for at the time of the cardinal's greatest influence, "ffortune (of whos fauour no man is lenger assured than she is dysposed) began to wexe some thyng wrothe w^t his prosperous estate, thought she wold devyse a mean to abate his hyghe port wherfor she procured Venus the Insaciat goddesse to be hir Instrument to worke hir purpose."[128] It is Anne Boleyn whom fortune uses to bring Wolsey down. Anne's motives are not so much about evangelical commitment as personal jealousy, for Cavendish adds that she resented the cardinal for intervening, at the king's command, to break off her early engagement to Henry Percy, the son of the Earl of Northumberland.[129] The great lords of the council, who in Hall were Wolsey's primary enemies, in Cavendish take advantage of Anne's vindictiveness and her position as the object of the king's affection to drive a wedge between Henry and his chancellor.[130]

Wolsey's fall from power occupies a disproportionately lengthy section of Cavendish's narrative. Indeed, it comprises more than half of the latest edition of the *Life*, a "chronological 'telescoping'" in equal parts moralizing and moving.[131] As critics have routinely noticed, the *Life* pays particular attention to the state of Wolsey's soul, taking not a few cues from the gospel narratives of Christ's passion. Cavendish's fallen Wolsey is most unlike his counterpart in *Hall's Chronicle*. The cardinal asserts his innocence of the charges against him yet deliberately humbles himself by not contesting them before the king. Wolsey's words to his treasurer at the time of the confiscation of his goods are emblematic of his strategy: "I wold all the world knewe and so I confesse to haue no thyng other riches, honour, or dignity that hathe not growen of hyme & by hyme therfore it is my very dewtie to surrender the same to hyme agayn as his very owen w^t all my hart, or elles I ware an onkynd seruaunt."[132] The disgraced cardinal shows other signs of repentance as well: He sheds tears when he cannot compensate his household staff; he does not speak against Henry or Anne until the very last; and he rejoices at any sign that he might be restored to royal favor, as in the memorable scene where he kneels in the dirt before Sir Henry Norris, a member of the king's privy chamber, who has come to bring Wolsey a ring symbolizing Henry's ongoing affection.[133] Cavendish's exiled Wolsey adopts religious practices not previously part of his piety. Before undertaking his journey to York, for instance, Wolsey stays for some weeks at the Charterhouse at Richmond, where every day he attends prayers and where the monks "by ther councell perswayded [him] frome the vaynglory of thys world, and gave hyme dyuers shirtes of heare the w^{che} he often ware after ward."[134]

Some critics have argued that Cavendish was taken in by Wolsey's political subtlety and his intentional self-fashioning as a penitent. In this perspective, the cardinal deliberately abased himself in order to have the greatest chance of being restored to his position or, failing that, to be most favorably remembered by posterity.[135] In the *Life*, Wolsey explains to Cavendish that "it was most best way for me (all thynges consideryd) to do as I haue don, than to stand in triall w^t the kyng ffor he wold haue byn lothe to haue byn noted a wrong doer. And in my submission the kyng (I dought not) had a great remorse of concyence, wherin he wold rather pitie me than malygne me."[136] Whether intentionally or otherwise, Wolsey performs his duties as archbishop of York in such a way as to assure the king that he has learned his lesson. Plans for his installation in York Minster are "not in so sumptuous a wyse as his predecessors did byfore hyme," and en route to York Wolsey spends two days confirming children—the sort of quotidian pastoral duty that at the height of his power would have been beneath him.[137] Especially in the time of the cardinal's political nadir, the differences between Hall's and Cavendish's Wolseys are stark, and it seems especially likely that Cavendish had passages of Hall's in mind as he narrated his master's downfall. Thus, for instance, Cavendish fashions the scene of Wolsey's arrest in glaring contrast to Hall: While Wolsey does ask the Earl of Northumberland to show him a copy of the commission to arrest him, the cardinal neither asserts clerical immunity nor attempts to excuse his actions. Once it is clear that a member of the king's privy chamber has come with the earl, he relents altogether: "you are a sufficyent commyssion yor self in that behalfe in as myche as ye be oon of the kynges privy chamber, ffor the worst person there is a sufficient warraunt to arrest the greattest peere of this realme."[138]

The period from Wolsey's arrest to his death occupies two sentences in Hall but nearly thirty pages in Cavendish. The cardinal's health begins to fail precipitately after he learns that the king has sent Sir William Kingston, constable of the Tower, to conduct him back to the capital. At the same time, Wolsey's conversations with Kingston reveal him to have glimpsed the nature of the master he has served: "rather than he wyll owyther mysse or want any parte of hys wyll or apetite, he wyll put the losse of oon half of hys realme in daynger."[139] Wolsey's famous deathbed words, "if I had serued god as diligently as I haue don the kyng he wold not haue gevyn me ouer in my gray heares," testify to his recognition of the state of affairs between him and Henry.[140] Yet Wolsey is pensive and penitent rather than bitter, and far from committing suicide, in Cavendish's telling his death is a good Christian one. Not unlike Christ before the crucifixion, Wolsey predicts the hour he will die. He confesses, receives the last rites, and passes away with dignity—all marks of the medieval *ars moriendi*. And when servants strip his body for burial, they are surprised to find a hair shirt under his fine linen.[141]

It must be emphasized that for all his sympathy toward the fallen Wolsey, Cavendish is not blind to the cardinal's faults. While there is not space here to multiply examples, many episodes in the *Life* present Wolsey as ambitious, overly concerned for pomp and ostentation, jealous of rivals, arrogant, and greedy—traits not unfamiliar from Hall's or Foxe's representations. For Cavendish, Wolsey tempted fortune with his worldly success, and so, even if he did not *deserve* his end, he risked his fall by trusting too much in fortune's constancy and in the favor of an earthly king—a king who appears in the closing pages of Cavendish's memoir as lustful, indecisive, self-absorbed, and at the end "hated" by the cardinal.[142] Thus, in contrast to Hall, Cavendish's presents a Wolsey who underwent a conversion, if not in the year between his dismissal as chancellor and his arrest, then at least in the short span between his arrest and death.

Just as the first two prototypes that we explored, Cavendish's representation of Wolsey inspired subsequent writers. We will see in the remainder of this chapter and in Chapter 2 that Cavendish's texts provided material for a number of subsequent chroniclers and historians. The *Life* was received in a different fashion by Thomas Storer, a student (which is to say a fellow or tutor) of Christ Church, Oxford, the successor to Wolsey's Cardinal College. In his relatively short life (c. 1571–1604), Storer wrote a number of poems that attracted the attention and praise of his contemporaries.[143] In 1599, a London press brought out Storer's *Life and Death of Thomas Wolsey Cardinall*, an elegy of several hundred stanzas in which Wolsey's spirit, as in Cavendish's *Visions*, reviews and reflects upon the events of his life.[144] Storer adopts from Cavendish not only a string of facts but also an important hermeneutic tool: the invocation of fortune—"cruell Fortune," in the opening stanza—as the great leveler of the mighty.[145] Wolsey moves from a young man anticipating a bright future to a ruler ambivalent about his authority and aware of the risks of royal service. In the face of his enemies' long-simmering disdain, Wolsey contemplates heading north to his diocese before being forced to do so. "Within the honest North I might be free / From scorching hatred: happy is that see / Whose Prelate sees no courtiers, none of these/That come a fleecing in their dioecese."[146] Yet he does not choose that wiser course, deciding instead to erect a monument that no previous archbishop of York had attempted to build, an Oxbridge college.[147]

Storer versifies many of Cavendish's memorable episodes, including Wolsey's revenge on Amias Paulet and the falling cross that injured Edmund Bonner and forewarned Wolsey of his own impending death.[148] But Storer writes from the perspective of some four decades later than Cavendish, at a moment when the Elizabethan religious settlement had both confirmed the Church of England's independence from Rome and prompted new debates about just how reformed that church should be. In this new milieu, one that we will explore further in the next chapter, Storer represents Wolsey as a specifically *English* churchman. In the first section, "Wolseius triumphans," the cardinal's ghost reflects upon the envy he had felt toward Warham, admitting that "my Romish frends" proposed to make him first cardinal, then pope, so that he could outrank his domestic competitor. In the poem's concluding section, "Wolseius moriens," Storer demonstrates his knowledge of England's subsequent religious history, mourning that fortune had brought down not only Wolsey but also Leicester Abbey, the site of his burial. "Paint on the churches wall," says Wolsey's spirit, "Here lies an Abbey, there a Cardinall."[149]

Hybrid Representations

One of the obvious drawbacks to discussing sixteenth-century representations of Wolsey by means of a series of prototypes is that many texts display features of more than one model. This is particularly the case with the compilation known as *Holinshed's Chronicles*. It was published in two substantially different editions, dated 1577 and 1587 respectively, and ascribed to Raphael Holinshed, a onetime assistant to the evangelical printer Reyner Wolfe. The first edition, produced toward the end of Holinshed's life, was a collaboration between Holinshed, his fellow evangelical William Harrison, and the Catholic writer Richard Stanihurst. As Schwartz-Leeper has noted (and we will find confirmed), "In many ways the various spiritual and political positions held by these men aligned when preparing the sections on Wolsey in the 1557 edition; the Protestants . . . could write negatively about Wolsey because he was a Catholic, and the Catholic . . . could do the same because Wolsey had failed to head off the chain of events which led to the split with Rome."[150] The mixed religious and political

allegiances of these men, combined with the extent to which they incorporated into the *Chronicles* material from other sources, render the text
multivocal and often unstable in viewpoint. When Abraham Fleming, the
prominent evangelical preacher-printer, took it upon himself to expand the
Chronicles in 1587, he rewrote some sections, inserted new material, and
added a large number of marginalia, generating a second edition textually
even more complicated than its predecessor.[151] Fleming's editorial activity,
which can be seen throughout the Tudor sections of the chronicles, produced significant changes with regard to the representation of Wolsey. The
hybridization of the cardinal's representation in the *Chronicles* serves to
exemplify a process that, in subsequent chapters, we will find repeated in
countless other contexts.

Schwartz-Leeper has investigated at some length the portrayal of Wolsey in both editions of the *Chronicles*, and it is worth summarizing his conclusions here. First, echoing the distinguished Holinshed scholar Annabel
Patterson, he observes that the 1577 and 1587 editions of the *Chronicles* "are
distinct texts, with different authors, editors, and approaches to historiography."[152] As a corollary, he notes that it is inappropriate to regard the 1587
edition as Holinshed's; it should rather be seen as the product of a different cohort of editors led by Fleming. Next, Schwartz-Leeper finds that in
the 1577 edition, most criticisms of Wolsey are personal rather than structural; the compilers highlight Wolsey's pride, for instance, as an individual failing, rather than attributing it to his status as a Roman prelate.[153]
However, the first edition of the *Chronicles* is not wholly negative in its
representation of Wolsey, primarily by virtue of including a different assessment of the cardinal drawn from the *History of Ireland* by the Jesuit
Edmund Campion, the martyred mentor of editor Stanihurst. In contrast,
the second edition ventures much more serious criticisms both of Wolsey
and the Roman church. Fleming and his collaborators embellish and
render more polemical material from the 1577 edition, and to the same
purpose they introduce new anecdotes from sources as disparate as Hall,
Foxe, and Vergil. Schwartz-Leeper concludes that these changes "turned
Holinshed's 1577 *Chronicles* from an admirable and ambitious framework
occasionally lacking in specifics into a significantly richer and denser text."[154]

All this is true, and Schwartz-Leeper makes his case in detail, at far
greater length than it is possible to recount here. However, it is remarkable that Schwartz-Leeper does not acknowledge Fleming's use of a most
surprising source for his characterization of Wolsey in the 1587 edition,
namely Cavendish's *Life*, at least as it was filtered through the works of John

Stow.[155] Whereas the 1577 edition of the *Chronicles* seems innocent of material from Cavendish, the 1587 edition borrows extensively from the *Life*, splicing it together with hostile material in a manner that produces a confused and certainly hybrid narrative, particularly with regard to the cardinal's fall, exile, and death. After listing some of the charges against Wolsey brought forward in the Parliament of 1529, Fleming quotes verbatim Hall's narrative of Wolsey being sent north to his diocese of York, recounting in particular that Wolsey did not take well to his dismissal but instead was "euer grudging at his fall."[156] Fleming then turns briefly to foreign affairs, coming back to England with the observation that "Now will we leave France, and returne to England, renewing the remembrance of cardinall Wolseie, who after great sute made to the king, was licenced to remooue from Asher to Richmond. . . . The cardinall hauing licence of the king to repaire to Richmond, made hast thither."[157] This is, of course, chronologically jumbled, since Wolsey had begun his journey toward York on the previous page. In a marginal note, Fleming acknowledges that this new material is "ex I.S., p. 968, 969," a reference to pages in the 1580 edition of Stow's *Chronicles of England* that contain the same narrative ("Cardinall Wolsey after great suite made to the King, was licenced to remove from Asher to Richmond. . . . The Cardinall hauing licence of the King to repaire to Richmond, made hast thither . . .").[158] However, what Stow did not indicate in his own marginalia—and what therefore Fleming may not have known at all—is that this passage is originally not Stow's but rather a close adaptation of Cavendish. In the *Life*: "My lord having licence of the kyng to repayer & remove to Richemond wherfore my lord made hast to prepare hyme thetherward."[159] The next two and a half paragraphs in the 1587 *Chronicles* follow Stow verbatim, with all of Stow's material coming from Cavendish.[160]

In the immediately next section, Fleming blends charming details about Wolsey's domestic life from Stow (which is to say, from Cavendish) with new criticisms of Wolsey's pomposity and pride. For instance, Fleming notes that Wolsey "was not abashed" to ask Henry to send him the set of liturgical vestments he had previously used at court.[161] For his narrative of Wolsey's arrest, decline, and death, Fleming relies most upon Stow and Cavendish, including material from the *Life* that represents Wolsey as having undergone a moral conversion.[162] However, Fleming does not fail to include Stow's version of the critical assessment of Wolsey's life that Cavendish offers immediately after describing his master's death. Consider the close similarities between Cavendish and Fleming as shown in the accompanying table.

Cavendish	Fleming
Here is thend and ffal of pryde and Arrogauncye of *suche* men exalted by ffortune to *honour & highe* dygnytes, ffor *I assure you* in hys tyme *of auctoryte & glory* he was the haultest man in all his procedeynges *that than* lyved, hauyng more respect to the *worldly* honor of hys person than he had to his sperytuall profession wherin shold be all meknes, hymylitie, & charitie.[163]	Here is the end and fall of pride and arrogancie of men exalted by fortune to dignitie: for in his time he was the hautiest man in all his proceedings aliue, hauing more respect to the honor of his person, than he had to his spirituall profession, wherin should be *shewed* all meekenes, humlitie, and charitie.[164]

All this might seem to constitute a surprisingly moderate representation of the disgraced and ailing Wolsey, aided unawares by the long reach of Cavendish's *Life*. However, in the next few pages the textual situation becomes even more complicated. Fleming reprints a second assessment of Wolsey's life, the one Holinshed had originally appropriated from the Jesuit martyr Campion. As Schwartz-Leeper has noted, Campion's words frame Wolsey in language that is in places itself almost martyrological. While Campion acknowledges Wolsey's "tendency toward vice, vengefulness, flattery, ambition, and arrogance," he also characterizes the cardinal as "an aduancer of learning, stout in euerie quarrel, neuer happie till this his ouerthrow. Wherein he shewed such moderation, and ended so perfectlie, that the houre of his death did him more honor, than all the pompe of his life passed."[165] Fleming's inclusion of this material from the previous edition of the *Chronicles* undercuts the overall thrust of the 1587 edition's representation of Wolsey. What is more, after reprinting Campion's eulogy Fleming returns to the narrative of "I.S.," which is to say Cavendish's *Life* filtered through Stow, and includes, over the course of six pages, a long adaptation from the *Life* that covers Wolsey's birth up through a banquet at Hampton Court that King Henry attends in disguise. In the next passage, both the tone and quality of the narrative changes sharply:

> *And thus spent this cardinall his time from daie to daie, and yeare to year, in such wealth, ioie, triumph, and glorie, hauing always on his side the kings especiall favour, until fortune* [enuied his prosperitie, and ouerthrew all the foundations of his glorie;] which as they were laid upon sand, so they shroonke and slipt awaie, whereby insued the ruine of his estate, euen to the verie losse of his life, which (as a man of a guiltie conscience, and fearing capitall punishment due by law for his undutiful demeanour against his souereigne) Edward Hall saith (upon report) he partlie procured, willinglie taking so great a quantitie of a strong purgation,

as nature was therewith oppressed, and unable to digest the same; so
that in fine he gaue up the ghost.[166]

Whereas the italicized portion comes directly from Cavendish via Stow
and whereas the phrases in brackets might be said to constitute a summary
of other material from Cavendish, the balance of this passage is of Fleming's own composition. It abruptly reintroduces the circumstances of
Wolsey's death, for which Fleming cites Hall, but at the same time oc-
cludes Cavendish's explanation of the ultimate cause of the cardinal's
downfall. In Cavendish, the italicized passage is followed immediately
by the suggestion that Fortune "procured Venus the Insaciat goddesse to
be hir Instrument to worke hir purpose" by stirring up Henry's love for
Anne.[167] Of course, any narrative that questioned the legitimacy of Anne's
marriage, and in consequence the legitimacy of Elizabeth's birth, was
anathema in late-sixteenth-century England, and it is no surprise that
Fleming made the adjustments he did. The 1587 *Chronicles*' section concerning Wolsey concludes with several paragraphs drawn directly from
Hall's Chronicle, including Hall's overall assessment of Wolsey's life, which
I quoted at length above; the *Chronicles* also reproduce Hall's segue from
Wolsey's crimes to those of the clergy at large.

Conclusions

All these sections of the 1587 edition of *Holinshed's Chronicles* exemplify a
process of representational hybridization in which many Tudor authors engaged. Whether they were aware of it or not, Fleming and his collaborators borrowed from strongly contrasting accounts of Wolsey, and in so
doing they represented the cardinal in a way that defies easy categorization. Since this sort of hybridization was not limited to the *Chronicles*, it is
important to remember that the three prototypes whose contours we have
been tracing in this chapter are tools for analysis rather than historical categories. As a matter of fact, most Tudor representations of Wolsey—and
most representations of Wolsey, full stop—draw upon elements from more
than one of the prototypes I have identified. John Stow, for instance, juxtaposed citations from *Hall's Chronicle* and Cavendish's *Life*, preserving
evangelical criticisms of Wolsey alongside Cavendish's more generous
memories.[168] The pace of hybridization accelerated as the sixteenth century
wore on, for at least three interrelated reasons. First, whereas the earliest
authors of representations of Wolsey, such as Vergil and Hall, relied chiefly
on their memories alongside a relatively small corpus of texts, later authors

had many accounts of Wolsey upon which to draw. Second, later authors lived at a greater chronological remove from Wolsey and from the events of Henry's first divorce: While regimes of censorship discouraged the expression of certain kinds of evangelical opinion under Queen Mary and certain forms of Catholic loyalty under Elizabeth, the representation of Wolsey became less politically fraught over time. And third, related to this, as the long reign of Elizabeth solidified the ecclesiastical independence of England from Rome and confirmed that animosity toward Rome and its partisans was a test as much of national loyalty as of religious commitment, criticisms of Wolsey by Catholics such as Vergil became somewhat more available for evangelical appropriation. It is no surprise, therefore, that later English histories, such as *Holinshed's Chronicles*, quote Catholic authors like Vergil alongside native evangelicals like Hall.

The three prototypes for representing Wolsey outlined in this chapter offer ways of thinking about and characterizing many of the representations we will encounter in the chapters that follow. I hasten to reiterate that these prototypes are conceptual frameworks that I am discerning retroactively, even though the first two of them map broadly onto sixteenth-century Catholic and evangelical identities. Just as Schwartz-Leeper has traced the different sets of images about the cardinal that appear across the sixteenth and early seventeenth centuries, these prototypes capture the three most common political and theological positionings of Wolsey in narratives about the reign of King Henry and the early stages of the English Reformation. We identified, first of all, Wolsey the corrupt author of the schism, whose greed, vengefulness, and ambition opened the door for Henry to separate his realm from communion with Rome; this is the representation that Polydore Vergil inaugurated and that Catholic writers like Nicholas Harpsfield and Nicholas Sander embellished. Second, we saw Wolsey the papist, the symbol of the rapaciousness, pride, and theological errors of the Roman church whose way of life epitomized the need for religious reformation. *Hall's Chronicle* articulated a relatively tame version of this representation, to which John Foxe and Abraham Fleming added new, sometimes quite lurid details. Finally, in the pages of George Cavendish's *Metrical Visions* and *Life* and in a comparatively small number of later texts we encountered Wolsey the repentant sinner, the pompous, flawed, yet ultimately transformed servant of a capricious master. Each of these Wolseys will reappear in the chapters that follow, in ways tailored carefully to the circumstances in which later representations were crafted.

For now, however, let us observe that in the sixteenth century, the primary lens through which writers interpreted Wolsey was that of the dichotomy between what we today call Catholic versus Protestant religious identities. (Sixteenth-century authors would likely have employed the terms "orthodox" or "evangelical" for themselves and "heretical" and "schismatic" for their opponents.) That is to say, in the sixteenth century the choice between competing representations of Wolsey was, at root, a binary choice for or against the claims of Rome. Those who embraced Henry's, Edward's, and Elizabeth's reformations had every incentive to characterize Wolsey negatively, as a representative of both a meddlesome foreign power and a profane religious system. Those who approved of the restoration of Catholicism under Queen Mary or who sought greater tolerance for Catholics under Elizabeth more often tended to highlight Wolsey's redeeming qualities or to condemn his failings as personal rather than institutional ones. As we will see in the next chapter, the evangelical/ Catholic binary did not long remain the primary lens through which English writers looked back at King Henry's cardinal. With the new categories that would emerge out of the political and religious vicissitudes of the early seventeenth century, in the early Stuart period the representation of Wolsey came primarily to be shaped by the terms of internecine Anglican disputes.

CHAPTER 2

Parchment, Pamphlets, and Plays:
Into the Early Stuart Period (c. 1580–1641)

The passing of Queen Elizabeth I in 1603 brought about a sea change in the politics of remembering and representing Wolsey. For the first time since the cardinal's death, the throne would be occupied by a monarch who was not a child of the king Wolsey had served or whose mother's marriage he had been accused of seeking to annul or thwart. The new king, James VI and I, was born three and a half decades after Wolsey's death, and neither of his parents had been involved in Wolsey's rise, administration, down-fall, or exile. The same was true for most of the leading actors in Jacobean government, whether civil or ecclesiastical. As a result, the transition from Tudors to Stuarts made available new discourses about the Henri-cian Reformation. No longer would certain kinds of assertions about Henry VIII, his spouses, or courtiers like Wolsey be liable to interpreta-tion as coded forms of comment on the reigning monarch, as the asper-sions Nicholas Sander had cast on Anne Boleyn were taken to have been aimed at her daughter. No longer, also, did the succession rest on the le-gitimacy of any of Henry's marriages. In short, greater historical distance made it possible for some seventeenth-century writers to produce more nuanced treatments of Henry and his reign. For others, however, the loosening of the boundaries of discourse about Tudor history offered fertile hunting ground in connection with the religious controversies of the early Stuart period. These writers not infrequently returned to Henry's reign in search of moral exemplars and cautionary tales.

This chapter examines Wolsey's fate during roughly the first half of the seventeenth century. It builds upon the previous chapter, which identified three prototypical representations of the cardinal in the poetry, chronicles, and histories of the sixteenth century—Wolsey the author of the schism, Wolsey the papist, and Wolsey the repentant sinner. Here, we will explore how elements of these prototypes, which, as we saw, were already being hybridized toward the end of the Tudor period, provided raw material for Stuart treatments of Wolsey and his king. Perhaps unsurprisingly, the prototype that continued to command the greatest attention was the evangelical one, passed down through beloved writers like Hall and, even more so, Foxe. However, the more sympathetic strand of representation that we identified with Cavendish's *Life* did not die out; in fact, it too remained open for new appropriation. William Shakespeare and John Fletcher, for instance, represented in their *King Henry VIII (All Is True)* a Wolsey who falls victim to unjust accusations and emerges from his downfall morally and spiritually redeemed. But this perspective remained in the minority. Not too many decades after Shakespeare and Fletcher's play was first performed, the earliest printed edition of Cavendish's *Life* bowdlerized and twisted that text to fit a contemporary agenda. Thus, as these and other examples indicate, the first half of the seventeenth century did not see the emergence of wholly new narratives about Wolsey's life and achievements or the discovery of new archival materials. Rather, it witnessed repeated acts of literary, historical, and theological bricolage, with writers assembling accounts of the cardinal by combining, editing, and embellishing the works of their predecessors.

The political and cultural changes that arrived with the Stuart monarchy are too many to enumerate exhaustively.[1] Just as Tudor representations of Wolsey depended in part upon the political situation of the day, in the first half of the seventeenth century Wolsey was represented against the backdrop of contemporary crises. Among them were theological disputes within the Church of England and the imprisonment and execution of King Charles I's leading advisors, including Archbishop of Canterbury William Laud. These events culminated, of course, in civil war and in the king's own trial and beheading. Such conflicts collectively gave greater definition to the competing agendas of rival ecclesial-theological parties. Anti-Laudian writers, in particular, invoked the memory of Wolsey to press their case that Archbishop Laud's administration reflected authoritarian and rapacious—in short, Roman—tendencies that had not been seen since the time of King Henry's cardinal. Other, more moderate writers represented Wolsey as having been a check upon the autocratic and capricious tendencies of his monarch. The events of the first half of the seventeenth century, particularly the failed Gunpowder Plot of 1605, raised to previously unseen heights English distrust of Roman Catholicism and of Catholics, but anti-Roman imagery had been an integral part of stock depictions of Wolsey for decades. What was strikingly new in the early Stuart period, instead, was the invocation of Wolsey's memory in disputes among Anglicans.

A word, only, remains to be said about the chronological parameters of this chapter. By and large, it considers notable works about Wolsey produced between 1603, the year of James I's accession to the English throne, and 1641, the year of Archbishop Laud's execution and the first full year of the Long Parliament. These dates bound a period during which Wolsey's representation served a range of polemical and theological purposes in the crises swirling around the crown and the Church of England. As we will see, the year 1641 in particular was crucial in the history of the anglophone representation of Wolsey, since it witnessed the printing of Cavendish's *Life* and the appearance of a series of puritan pamphlets that sought to associate Laud with the long-dead and much-derided cardinal. However, these dates, like any I might have chosen, are also somewhat artificial, and occasionally, where it helps put early Stuart writings in broader context, I will refer to works produced before 1603 or after 1641. The chapter unfolds with reference to both genre and chronology: After an extended discussion of the manuscript and print reception of Cavendish's *Life*, we will consider representations of Wolsey in pamphlets and stage plays, concluding with influential prose histories.

Remembering Cavendish

George Cavendish's *Life* made its appearance in print in the inauspicious year 1641. Earlier print consumers could access Cavendish's narrative about Wolsey only through the mediation of other authors. As we saw in the previous chapter, John Stow printed lengthy excerpts from the *Life* in the last quarter of the sixteenth century, and those excerpts made their way into better-known works such as *Holinshed's Chronicles*, but the suspicions of Catholic sympathies that dogged Stow's later years reveal that associating oneself with texts like Cavendish's remained dangerous. Indeed, it is not surprising that Cavendish's perspective was represented in late Tudor historical writings rarely; as a rule, it tended to be absent entirely both from evangelical histories such as Foxe's and from Catholic ones such as Sander's.[2]

However, even if direct access to Cavendish's *Life* was limited, the text continued to circulate in manuscript. How widely it was copied and read cannot be determined with any great degree of certainty, but copies were owned by influential establishment figures under Elizabeth I, such as Robert Beale, clerk of the privy council, and likewise by their counterparts under the first two Stuarts, such as Francis Godwin, bishop of Llandaff and Hereford. Indeed, at least twenty-five of the extant complete or partial copies of the *Life* have been dated prior to the publication of the 1641 edition. And even after Cavendish appeared in print, new manuscripts continued to be made.[3] It is not unreasonable to conclude, therefore, that the *Life* remained a text of interest in the late sixteenth and seventeenth centuries and that the story of its consumption, reception, and reproduction constitutes an important and heretofore little explored mechanism for remembering Wolsey.[4]

In other words, for us to account fully for how Wolsey was remembered in the seventeenth century, we must investigate how Cavendish was received. This section proceeds along two parallel lines. First, we will explore the edition of 1641 in the form of an extended case study. Printed by the puritan William Sheares, the edition was, in the words of Cavendish's most recent editor, "undoubtedly issued as a propaganda piece in the Puritan campaign against Archbishop Laud which had been raging openly since the suppression of the Star Chamber in 1640."[5] In this, it was not unlike the many contemporary pamphlets, usually of puritan origin and implicitly or explicitly anti-Laudian in content, that seized upon the memory of Wolsey in order to highlight the failings of King Charles's archbishop. After examining the ways in which Sheares, or an unnamed editor working at his direction, expurgated and reworked Cavendish's text in order to serve a specific theological and political agenda, we will turn to a number of the extant manuscripts of the *Life*.[6] There, we will discover that the emendations, omissions, marginal notes, and drawings in a number of manuscripts testify to ongoing and often conflicting forms of engagement with Wolsey's memory.

Sheares's Cavendish

Let us start with the printed edition (see Plate 7).[7] As we have already seen, it appeared more than eighty years after Cavendish had finished his memoir. The delay can be explained, first, by Queen Mary's death soon after the completion of Cavendish's work; he, not to mention his potential printers, may have judged it inadvisable to publish a text that was both critical of Anne Boleyn and sympathetic toward Wolsey when Anne's daughter was newly on the throne.[8] As the relationship between Rome and the English government deteriorated over the course of Elizabeth's reign, circumstances became increasingly unfavorable for the printing of the *Life*, and when it was finally printed, it had fallen prey to numerous editorial changes. Many of those changes stuck: Sheares's edition of 1641 was reprinted almost verbatim in 1667, 1706, and 1708. A wholly new edition was not prepared until 1825, when the Shakespearean scholar S. W. Singer attempted to restore Cavendish's original text.[9]

While Sheares's redaction "has occasioned a good deal of comment from critics and historians," no recent analysis has considered the impulses that produced such a considerable reworking of Cavendish's text.[10] Some of the changes Sheares made to the *Life* are apparently superficial, including the introduction of chapter divisions, chapter titles, and a table of contents.[11] Other changes may have been unintentional, such as the apparently random omission of occasional words. However, a detailed comparison of Sheares's edition with the critical edition of the original text reveals that the majority of his changes appear to have been made on ideological grounds. Overall, these fall into three broad categories. First, Sheares supplants many of Cavendish's references to fortune with invocations of God's providence; in doing so, he downplays Cavendish's invocation of the medieval *de casibus* tradition. Second, Sheares deletes passages in which Cavendish cultivates his reader's sympathy for Wolsey, especially after the cardinal's fall. Finally, Sheares introduces changes that seek to exonerate Henry from some of the criticisms implicit in Cavendish's narrative.

We saw in the previous chapter that, in both the *Life* and the earlier *Metrical Visions*, Cavendish seeks to interpret Wolsey's life by referring to the operations of fortune. As in the *de casibus* tradition, of which he presents himself as an heir, Cavendish views fortune as capricious and impartial, neither inherently biased toward some persons or groups over others nor susceptible to prayer or appeal. In this regard, we observed, Cavendish's invocation of fortune shares more with late antique and medieval conceptions than with later ideas such as Reformed accounts of the operation of divine providence.[12] However, Sheares's edition shifts Cavendish's discourse in precisely this latter direction, focusing on God's involvement in the events of Wolsey's rise and fall.

While Sheares leaves a few of Cavendish's references to fortune intact, many he excises or amends. For instance, when Cavendish comments that Wolsey's actions against Amias Paulet, his old enemy, were "wonderfull works of god And ffortune," Sheares describes them only as "works of Gods providence."[13] That Sheares is skeptical of Cavendish's ideas about fortune is confirmed a few pages later, where his edition omits entirely a passage in which, after Wolsey has been made almoner to King Henry VII, Cavendish reflects ruefully on the seemingly random operations of fortune: "Here may all men note the chaunces of ffortune that folowyth some whome she lystithe to promote And even so to Somme hyr fauour is contrary thoughe they shold travell neuer so myche w^t urgent diligence & paynfull studye that they could device or Imagyn wherof for my part I haue tasted of thexperience."[14] Again after a few more pages, Sheares substantially condenses another passage warning against the vagaries of fortune. While he leaves intact Cavendish's assertion that Wolsey, under the young Henry VIII, was "clyming up Fortunes wheele," Sheares omits Cavendish's warning against fortune: "to what end she brought hyme ye shall here after Therfore lett all men to whome ffortune extendythe hir grace not to trust to myche to hir fikkyll fauor and plesaunt promysis vnder Colour wherof she Cariethe venemous galle."[15] In both passages, Sheares elides observations by Cavendish that call into question the causal link between hard work and good fortune. The effect is to suggest that Wolsey *earned* his promotions as he ascended the ranks of the court and the church just as he *deserved* his fall, which Sheares figures as a just punishment for his misdeeds.

Perhaps nowhere is Sheares's discontent with Cavendish more obvious than in the manner in which he introduces the character of Anne Boleyn. As we have seen, Cavendish presents Anne largely as fortune's unwitting instrument: It is Anne's anger at Wolsey after he breaks off her engagement with Henry Percy that fortune uses, over time, to bring about the cardinal's downfall. Cavendish's first reference to Anne explicitly situates her within the context of fortune's operations against Wolsey. (Anne is not given a distinct identity, or even her full name, until the following paragraph.)

Thus passed the Cardynall hys lyfe & tyme frome day to day And yere to yere in such great welthe, Ioy tryhumphe & glory hauyng allwayes on his syde the kynges especyall fauour vntill ffortune (of whos fauour no man is lenger assured than she is disposed) began to wexe some thing wrothe w^t his prosperous estate thought she wold devyse a mean to abate his hyghe port wherfor she procured Venus the Insaciat goddesse to be hir Instrument to worke hir purpose She brought the kyng in love w^t a gentillwoman . . . . [16]

Sheares omits these lines entirely, instead introducing Anne by way of the young Henry Percy. In perhaps a passing concession to Cavendish, Sheares entitles this chapter of the *Life* "Of the originall *Instrument* of the Cardinalls fall: Mistris Anne Bullen."[17] The edition retains Anne's displeasure at Wolsey for having intervened to break off her engagement with Percy, but here, Anne's desire for revenge is at least as much her own and God's as it is fortune's. While Sheares does retain one of Cavendish's subsequent references to fortune,[18] he inserts in the middle of one of Cavendish's paragraphs a chapter heading, "Of Mistris Anne Bullen her favour with the King," which has the effect of highlighting one of the few passages in which Cavendish had offered explicit commentary about God's providence:

> Oh Lord, what a great God art thou, that workest thy wonders so secretly, that they are not perceived, untill they bee brought to passe and finished.
>
> Attend now good Reader to this story following, and note every circumstance, and thou shalt at the end perceive a wonderfull worke of God against such as forget him and his benefits.[19]

We could multiply additional examples of changes introduced by Sheares that replace Cavendish's primary interpretive device, the fickleness of fortune, with a more morally weighty emphasis on divine intervention and judgment. But let us fast forward: As Schwartz-Leeper has suggested, the most significant interpretive moments in the various lives of Wolsey typically occur in connection with his death.[20] Here are Cavendish's and Sheares's versions of a passage in which Cavendish assesses the significance of Wolsey's death, with text not common to both italicized:

Cavendish	*Sheares*
Here is thend and ffall of pride *and Arrogauncye of suche men exalted by ffortune to honour & highe dygnytes*/ffor I assure you in hys tyme *of auctortye & glory* he was the haultest man *in all his procedynges* that than lyved/hauyng more respect to the *worldly* honor of hys person than he had to his sperytuall *profession*/wherin shold be all meekness, hymylitie, *& charitie*/the *processe wherof I leave to theme that be learned & seen in the dyvyn lawes.*[21]	Here is the end and fall of pride, for I assure you he was in his time the proudest man alive, having more regard to the honour of his Person than to his spirituall *function*, wherein he should have expressed more meekenesse and humility: *For Pride and Ambition are both linked together; and Ambition is like Choller, which is an humor that makes men active, earnest, and full of alacrity and stirring, if it bee not stopped or hindred in its course: But if it be stopped, and cannot have its way, it becommeth dust, and thereby maligne and venomous. So Ambitious and proud men, if they find the way open for their rising and advancement, and still get forwards; they are rather busie then dangerous: But if they bee checked in their desires, they become secretly discontent, and look upon men and matters with an evill eye, and are best pleased when things goe backewards: but I forbeare to speak any further herein.*[22]

In his recasting of this crucial passage, not only does Sheares once again omit Cavendish's reference to fortune, but he also adds an extended denunciation of Wolsey's pride, strongly hinting that Wolsey began acting treasonously because Henry and Anne had "checked" his desire for dominance and further advancement—perhaps, by implication, even to the papacy.

These emendations disavowing fortune as the ruling force of the world, usually but not always in favor of God's providence, point to the influence of Sheares's puritan beliefs. But Sheares changed Cavendish's text in other ways as well. Through a second set of alterations, he sought to discredit Wolsey by substantially telescoping or omitting altogether passages in which Cavendish had demonstrated sympathy with his former patron. Indeed, in Sheares's hands, the balanced symmetry of Cavendish's text, as we described it in the previous chapter, is all but destroyed. The first half of the *Life* traces Wolsey's rise and triumph up to the point of his dismissal as chancellor, whereas the second half depicts his gradual downfall and conversion. Sylvester's edition of the *Life* takes ninety-six pages to tell Wolsey's story up to his dismissal, then ninety-one pages to continue and conclude the text. In Sheares's edition, however, Wolsey surrenders the Great Seal on page 79 of only 118. The highly compressed second half of Sheares's version omits many of the episodes that render Cavendish's fallen Wolsey a sympathetic character.[23] Gone, among many other moving scenes, are those in which the cardinal kneels in the dirt before Sir Henry Norris, takes consolation from a midnight visit from Sir John Russell, conducts an amiable conversation with the Duke of Norfolk, carries out well-regarded pastoral work in the north of England, and expresses his desire that his installation as archbishop of York be simple rather than ostentatious.[24] At the same time, Sheares inserts a new claim, making explicit what Hall and Foxe only rumored, that when Wolsey fell ill on his journey back to London, "it was apparant that he had poisoned himself."[25]

Finally, if Sheares sought through his editorial practices to diminish readers' sympathy for Wolsey, in a third set of changes he also seems to have aimed at moderating Cavendish's criticisms of Henry. Perhaps most significantly, Sheares wholly reworked Cavendish's epilogue to the *Life*, which, as we saw in the previous chapter, quotes Ecclesiastes to the effect that Henry, whom Cavendish presents Wolsey as having "hated in his life," had willfully seized the cardinal's riches and treated him dishonorably.[26] Sheares prints approximately half of the epilogue as an "Advertisement to the Reader" that appears between the prologue and the beginning of the main text. But he omits Cavendish's heartfelt cries, "O madnes, O folyshe desier, O fond hope, O gredy desier of vayn honors, dignyties, and Ryches, O what inconstant trust And assuraunce is in Rollyng ffortune!", and perhaps most significantly, he deletes the Ecclesiastes reference that disparaged Henry.[27] At the same time, many of the changes that Sheares introduced in order to present Wolsey as a less sympathetic character redound to the king's credit. The same deletions that make Wolsey appear to have been treated justly render Henry as a consistent, responsible monarch. Whereas in Cavendish's original, the stream of secret communications that Henry sends to the fallen cardinal leaves the reader uncertain about the king's motivations and surprised when Wolsey is finally arrested, in Sheares's edition Henry acts unambiguously and unwaveringly to bring about Wolsey's just downfall.

All these changes—the invocation of God's providence as a primary explanation for the fall of an ambitious prelate; the deletion of some of the passages that render Wolsey as a human and, ultimately, contrite character; and the deflection of blame for Wolsey's treatment away from King

Henry—combine to produce a Wolsey who is a very different man from
the one his gentleman-usher had originally remembered. For Sheares's
readers, Wolsey appears to be a prideful, unrepentant man who received
what he deserved and against whose sins God acted in providential judgment. Sheares's edition transforms the prototype of Wolsey the repentant sinner into someone more sinister: not quite the papist Wolsey of
Hall and Foxe but a character not inconsistent with such evangelical
representations.

Cavendish in Manuscript

However, Sheares's was not the only version of Cavendish's *Life* that circulated in the late Tudor and Stuart periods. A manuscript tradition also
flourished, including several instances of critical engagement with, and in
some cases reassessment of, the *Life*. Approximately a quarter of the extant manuscripts of Cavendish's work contain substantial, often theologically weighted, marginalia and amendments.[28] Interpolations and marks
of use appear across all three centuries for which we have extant manuscripts, and they occur in similar numbers in contexts favorable and unfavorable to the cardinal. Collectively, they testify to the existence of ongoing
contestation about Wolsey's legacy.

Like Cavendish himself, some manuscripts attempt to draw moral
lessons from Wolsey's rise and fall. Thus Washington, Folger Shakespeare Library V.b.111, a relatively plain manuscript dated c. 1600 and
signed by one of its owners, Roger Bradhaigh, in 1659, appends to the *Life*
a short poem whose text appears to be drawn from *King Richard III* and
King Henry VIII:

> O momentary state of worldly men,
> which they more hunt for then the grace of heauen
> Lyvinge like drunken sayliors on a Mast
> ready with euerie nod to tumble downe
> into the fatall bowells of the deepe
>
> Adieu deceiptfull world thy pleasures I detest
> Now others w[i]th thy ioyes delude, my hopes in heaven shall rest.[29]

The first five lines occur in the speech of Lord Hastings that concludes
Act III, scene 4, of *Richard III*. Hastings, discovering that he is about to
lose his life as a result of Richard's treachery, muses upon the "momentary
state of worldly men," a theme hardly foreign to Cavendish. The remain-

ing lines echo the sense, if not exactly the text, of Wolsey's final words in *Henry VIII*: "Farewell, / The hopes of court: my hopes in heaven do dwell."[30] The concatenation of lines from these two plays perhaps seeks to invoke a historical coincidence: that Wolsey was buried near the reputed site of Richard's grave in Leicester Abbey, in a space that even shortly after Wolsey's death was being called the Tyrants' Sepulcher.[31]

While the intent of the Folger scribe is not entirely transparent—he could be echoing Cavendish's warnings about fortune or else seeking to link Wolsey with one of Shakespeare's greatest villains—material in other manuscripts of the *Life* is unambiguously favorable to the cardinal. Oxford, Bodleian Library Jones 14, a mid-seventeenth-century manuscript, interrupts the course of the *Life* with the text of a letter from Wolsey to the masters of his ill-fated school in Ipswich. The insertion of this document presents Wolsey as a caring, perhaps overly involved patron of one of his educational institutions.[32] Oxford, Christ Church CLIV, from the late sixteenth or early seventeenth centuries, contains on its front board an advertisement for two other works concerning Wolsey: "See Anthony Woods acc^t of the Cardinal wherein is drawn up a Better acct than in this Author as I think. Note A Wood in his Athenae P 280 vol 11us says that Tho: Storer Student of Xt Church wrote the Cardinals life in 10 sheets in q^{rto} in English verse & printed it in 1599."[33] Both Storer, whose elegy we encountered briefly in the previous chapter, and Wood, whom we will meet in Chapter 3, represented Wolsey in terms at least as favorable as Cavendish's, although it is unclear on what grounds this annotator, who was perhaps the Oxford historian Thomas Tanner, judged Wood's work to be "Better."[34] Another manuscript from Wolsey's college, Christ Church CLV, is a later, eighteenth-century copy of the *Life* bearing a number of annotations. Most of these correct the text of the manuscript against Sheares's printed edition, but one of them, in a different hand from the rest, reflects a distinctively pro-Wolsey bias.[35] Next to the passage in which Anne, after having her engagement with Percy canceled, pledges to "worke much displeasure to the Cardinall, as after Shee did indeede," the annotator sought to justify the cardinal's actions: "But yet was he not in blame altogether, for he did nothing byt ye Kinges advised comaundement; & even as my Lorde Percye was comaunde^d to avoyde her companye, soe was shee discharged of ye Courte, & sente home to her Father for a Season, whereat shee fretted: for all this while shee knewe nothinge of ye Kinges intended purpose."[36]

Some manuscripts contain direct evidence of disagreements over Cavendish's assessment of Wolsey. Oxford, Bodleian Library MS Laud Misc.

591 contains multiple corrections to the closing passage of the *Life*, the same passage that, as we just saw, Sheares also significantly edited. The scribe, perhaps the William Langham whose name and the year 1613 appear on the manuscript's first page, copied out the start of Cavendish's epilogue: "Here is the end and fall of pryde and arrogancie of men, exalted by fortune to dignities; ffor I assure you in his tyme, he was the haughtiest man in all his proceedings aliyve." A second, likely contemporary hand corrected this passage, via strikethrough and interlinear additions, to "Here is the end and fall of *a miserable* man, exalted by fortune to dignities; ffor I assure you in his tyme, he was the *mightiest* man in all this *kingdome and by nature very much ambitious*." However, in the margin, a third, almost certainly later hand has resupplied some of the original wording, namely "pride and arrogancie," "haughtieste," and "proceedings alive" (see Plate 8).[37] Even among this manuscript's users, therefore, there appears to have been disagreement about how best to remember Wolsey.

Another manuscript, London, British Library Additional MS 48066, was owned by Robert Beale, a puritan who served from 1572 to 1601 as a clerk of the privy council under Elizabeth I. The manuscript appears to bear witness to Elizabethan anxieties about the queen's mother's place in Cavendish's narrative. At six points in Beale's copy of the *Life*, small Greek letters appear in the margins of what is otherwise a mostly unannotated text. These letters indicate the excision of six passages that run from one to four folios each. While there is nothing in the text apart from the small marginal letters to indicate that material has been removed, Beale copied out the missing passages in full in another section of his manuscript. Whereas the *Life* runs from fols. 90 to 165v, this appendix follows a few leaves later, at fols. 175 to 182v. Such an arrangement of the text is of course unusual, although the content of the omitted passages offers a likely explanation. Each of them deals in some way with an aspect or consequence of Henry's first divorce that might have been thought to reflect poorly on Anne Boleyn or on the legitimacy of her marriage or offspring. Anne's love interest in Henry Percy and Wolsey's intervention to break off their engagement, the suggestion that the king's commissioners who were sent to European universities to obtain their opinions on the divorce had bribed the scholars there, and a reference to the martyrdom of John Fisher are all absent from the main text.[38] Although Beale clearly thought these stories worthy of preservation in some form, he seems to have taken care that they not be part of the main body of Wolsey's life. Another possible explanation, that Beale copied his manuscript from one missing the controversial passages and later found a second manuscript that included them, would evidence similar anxiety, but on the part of the earlier scribe rather than that of Beale.

By far, the manuscript with the greatest volume of annotation and interpolated material is Oxford, Bodleian Library Douce 363. It contains marginalia on almost every folio of the *Life*, along with a commentary on Wolsey's legacy that appears on the folio following the conclusion of Cavendish's text. In addition, Douce contains six large drawings, each of which occupies approximately half a folio. Three of these, depicting one of Wolsey's processions at the height of his power, one of his journeys via sail barge, and his surrender of the Great Seal, have been colored in with red and black inks. The other three, which show Wolsey setting forth on one of his journeys to France, the fallen cardinal on his sick bed, and his funeral, are line drawings only. We have already had cause to comment on this manuscript in the Introduction, since all five of the drawings that portray the living Wolsey show him as an older man of fairly ordinary girth, wearing a long beard.

It is fortunate that the copyist of Douce 363 concluded the *Life* with his initials, "S.B.," and the date that he finished his labors: September 1, 1578. This allows us to date the manuscript to roughly the same period as Beale's. A note on the first folio identifies S.B. as Stephen Batman, an Anglican clergyman, bibliophile, and at the time of the copying of the manuscript chaplain to Archbishop of Canterbury Matthew Parker.[39] Batman appears to have copied the text and composed its concluding commentary, but it is unclear how many of the annotations are his. Most are in an italic hand that resembles the hand of the main text, but there are enough inconsistencies between them that it is not possible to state with certainty that Batman and the annotator are the same person. Other marginalia are most certainly not Batman's: Some are recognizably in the hand of a later owner, the antiquarian Francis Douce, and still others are quite clearly in a third hand, whose apparent haste makes it hard to decipher all his scribblings.

To the extent that they express opinions rather than simply summarize the main text, the annotations convey a significantly less favorable view of Wolsey than Cavendish's.[40] Next to the discussion of Wolsey's revenge against Paulet, for instance, the main annotator has added, with no small irony, a quotation from the Lord's Prayer: "remitte nobis debita / sicut et nos demittemus" ("forgive us our sins, just as we forgive"). Bishop Richard Fox's service as Lord Privy Seal is greeted with the comment "the office of prelacy in both govermentes is dangerous yf the religion be not good."[41] Next to the ostentatious ceremonies with which Wolsey received his cardinal's hat: "Yf a pore christian sholde haue browgth the bible &

testament he sholde scarcely had such rewarde."[42] And at what the main
annotator takes to have been Wolsey's seizure of the chancellorship from
his fellow archbishop William Warham: "this is schare brotherly charitie
to take from an other haueng inowgh him selfe."[43]

The theological proclivities of this annotator are not always easy to discern. In one place, he condemns Henry's government for offering bribes
to foreign universities in order that they would support the king's divorce:
"forsed friendship bredes dissembling cortesy: Where by is nourished
partiality then good condemned for ill: and ill allowed for good. O indig-
nitie."[44] In this regard, the annotator echoes Batman's concluding commentary, which criticizes Wolsey and by extension Henry, for disendowing
monasteries, including those whose revenues were used to found Cardinal
College. "O the pitefull disorder of good lawis that Money is Master
over nobilitie (when nothing taketh plais that is set downe for good/But
all geven to privat co[m]odie what shall folowe god knoweth assuredly). It
is a wicked reformation of the Religious when then is destroyed the mayn-
tainanc for Religion."[45] However, much as these comments on the *Life* suggest a pro-Roman orientation on the part of the annotator, others, set next
to Wolsey's deathbed words, take a more critical view. In one place, the
same annotator observes that "Here in maye easely be perceyued of what
religion, the Cardinall was. a wolfe a gennste the lawe of Christe: and a
lambe in soffering temporall ewells: who in pleasing the king before God:
fell in to both there displeasures." The second half of this annotation echoes
Cavendish's characterization of Wolsey as someone who accepted his fall
with dignity and only late in life discovered that he had been serving the
wrong master, but the first half is strongly antipapist. The likely evangelical provenance of these ideas is confirmed by another annotation on
the same page, in the same hand, where next to Wolsey's deathbed warning against Wycliffite heresies, the annotator retorts: "Wyklyfe was a
foe, to supersticion; and an opener of Christian religion: no raisar of y^e
com[m]ons &c."[46]

Douce 363, like Laud Misc. 591 before it, testifies to the mixed reception not only of Wolsey's memory but also that of Cavendish's *Life*. Manuscripts such as these, as well as surviving copies of early printed editions
of Cavendish that bear annotations and corrections, reveal that strong feelings about the proper representation of Wolsey persisted well into the
Stuart period.[47] As we have seen, some manuscript readers reinforced Cavendish's representation of Wolsey through their annotations, corrections,
and additions. Others sought to correct Cavendish's version, intervening
textually in ways that sought to embrace the evangelical representation of

the cardinal. However, it was not only Cavendish's version of Wolsey's life that was contested: Stuart writers, especially in the years leading up to the outbreak of civil war, employed a variety of rhetorical and narrative devices to recruit Wolsey as a partisan in the conflicts of their time. The following section explores a series of pamphlets that, like the manuscripts we have been studying, confirm that the invocation of Wolsey remained potent more than a century after his death.

The Pamphlet War

Both Sheares and the owners of the manuscripts that we have been examining employed Cavendish's *Life* as a medium through which to comment upon, and draw lessons from, the life of Wolsey. Around the time that Sheares was making his version of Cavendish's biography available to the reading public, however, other writers and printers were appropriating Wolsey's reputation for their own ends. Three pamphlets produced in 1641 all invoked the cardinal's memory in order to comment on contemporary events and, in particular, to draw unfavorable comparisons between him and the controversial archbishop of Canterbury, William Laud.

It is no coincidence that these pamphlets appeared in 1641, the year that followed the convocation of the Long Parliament. Assembled by Charles I to obtain revenue for his wars in Scotland, the Parliament derives its epithet from the fact that it was not, officially at least, dissolved until after the restoration of the monarchy in 1660. It was, however, purged by Oliver Cromwell's New Model Army in 1648, and between then and the end of Cromwell's protectorate, it existed primarily to give legislative sanction to his regime. The Long Parliament directly inspired at least one of the events commemorated in the 1641 pamphlets featuring Wolsey. In the first months of its sitting, the Parliament asserted its authority by impeaching Laud for a series of crimes. It accused him of taking bribes and subverting justice, monopolizing ecclesiastical appointments for his own ends, provoking King Charles into war with his Scottish subjects, arrogating to himself powers rightly vested in the crown, and, perhaps most notoriously, seeking to reconcile England with Rome.[48] In a number of ways, the charges against Laud resemble the forty-four articles presented against Wolsey in the Parliament of 1529; pamphleteers certainly lost no time in pointing out the similarities.

At the same time as parliamentarians indicted Laud, they also sought to impeach Thomas Wentworth on a charge of high treason. Wentworth was the first Earl of Strafford and a leading counselor of the king's.

Parliament's treatment of the two men differed sharply: Legislators were initially content to leave Laud in the custody of Black Rod, although he was later moved to the Tower of London; in Strafford's case, on the other hand, they moved rapidly. Strafford's impeachment trial failed on April 10, 1641, but the House of Commons moved three days later to pass a bill of attainder against him. The Lords approved his attainder on May 5, and although he had originally vowed not to condemn his ally, Charles capitulated on May 10. Strafford was beheaded two days later, on Tower Hill, after receiving Laud's blessing; he died in the same location where Laud would eventually be beheaded in 1645.

Strafford's execution provided the immediate context for the first of our three pamphlets, entitled *Canterburies Dreame: in which the Apparition of Cardinall Wolsey did present himself unto him on the fourtenth of May last past: it being the third night after my Lord of Strafford had taken his fare-well to the World* (see Plate 9).[49] The pamphlet was not the only recent work to feature a ghostly spirit that returns to earth to provide political advice: In 1640, the Stationers' Company had recorded the publication of a book entitled *Machavills Ghost as he lately appeared to his deare soone the Moderne Proiector, divulged for the pr[e]tended good of the kingddomes of England, Scotland, and Ireland.*[50] The pamphlet about Laud, which may have been written by the prolific Richard Overton, opens in Laud's prison cell, where the archbishop sees "the reverend shadow of Cardinall Wolsey . . . with a gracefull and Majesticke gate, accoutered with those habiliments which did become his honours."[51]

The pamphlet employs two rhetorical tactics to link Laud with Wolsey. On the one hand, it directly identifies similarities and explicitly draws comparisons between the two men. Wolsey's ghost observes that he and Laud came from similar backgrounds: "my parentage was as low as yours, my education in the University was in Magdalen Colledge of Oxford, as yours of Saint Johns."[52] But, the ghost is quick to point out, in many ways Laud has gone beyond Wolsey. Wolsey's spirit observes that he had visited personal revenge only on the unlucky Sir Amias Paulet, his antagonist from his Somerset days, whereas Laud has "made more then one man suffer, and have put them to a harder if not a longer durance."[53] Likewise, Wolsey admits to taking "many barrells gold and silver" to help the pope, but he adds, "I doubt not but you have found new waies to raise as great sums, and for what ends (my Lord) your selfe best know."[54] Perhaps most interestingly, when Wolsey's ghost declares that "The hatred of the Commons hath beene unto us alike, and some great men in both our times have grievously accused us," he then draws an important contrast: Laud had the "happinesse to meete with a Prince of a most excellent and a more constant temper."[55] This last observation performs several varieties of political work simultaneously: asserting the author's loyalty to King Charles, casting Laud's actions as the betrayal of a morally upright monarch and therefore denouncing Laud as a greater betrayer of his king than Wolsey ever was, and in the process implicitly criticizing Henry VIII for his caprice.

The other strategy of *Canterburies Dreame*, like that of so many medieval and early modern stories involving the spirits of the dead, is to frame Wolsey's life as a cautionary tale. Explaining his appearance at Laud's bedside, the cardinal's ghost declares that "the newes of your greatnesse, and the noyse of the falling Episcopacie, hath rouz'd me from the sloath of death."[56] Thus awakened, the ghost sought to "understand what new ambition could prompt againe the Miter to aspire unto a parity with the Crowne."[57] Wolsey specifically invokes the memory of his misdeeds, which he takes to be known well enough to Laud—and, therefore, also to the reader—as not to require enumeration. "My Lord, I had thought after my fate, that no man would againe adventure to preferre the pomp of this vaine world to the service of Almighty God, and the care by him injoyned to his charge."[58] In making this case, Wolsey's ghost goes so far as to invoke another historical exemplar, Thomas à Becket, warning that both he and Becket had been "blowne up by Fortune" and that their examples should not have tempted Laud "in your pride of heart to magnifie your Grace with mine."[59]

The self-presentation of Wolsey's spirit in *Canterburies Dreame* draws extensively upon the depiction of the cardinal in Cavendish's *Life*. It appropriates details known only through Cavendish, such as Wolsey's harsh treatment of Amias Paulet and the circumstances of his early life as a student and tutor in Oxford. By portraying the ghost of Wolsey as repentant and self-aware, the pamphlet also echoes Cavendish's cardinal's words on his deathbed; indeed, perhaps to evoke the parallel more clearly, the generic image that the printer chose for the cover of the pamphlet is that of a sick or dying man being visited by a bishop in his bedroom.[60] However, if *Canterburies Dreame* borrows from Cavendish in these regards, its overall thrust is somewhat different from that of the *Life*, namely to condemn Laud for the same sins that Wolsey had committed during his time in power. In taking Wolsey (and, therefore, Laud) to be guilty of extortion, vengeance, and embezzlement, among other crimes, the pamphlet echoes the anti-Wolsey texts of the Tudor period at least as much as it does Cavendish's more measured treatment of the cardinal.

The pamphlet's juxtaposition of Wolsey and Laud was, as Thomas Kranidas has shown, by no means unusual in the years leading up to civil war.
"Cardinal Wolsey became the classic example of prelatical hybris [*sic*], and
the Puritans compared Laud and Wolsey again and again for their disastrous mingling of Church and State."[61] Another 1641 pamphlet, printed
only weeks after Cavendish's *Life*, contains an exposition of the similarities between the two ecclesiastics.[62] This work, *A True Description, or rather
a Parallel between Cardinall Wolsey, Arch-Bishop of York, and William Laud,
Arch-Bishop of Canterbury*, sets Wolsey and Laud within a broader context,
that of the abuse of power by the Roman church and its prelates. After
reciting a litany of instances of clerical ambition and misgovernment from
the time of England's King Henry I through that of the near-contemporary
French Cardinal Richelieu, the author admits that "I could continue the
pride of the Prelacie, and their great Tyrannie through all the Kings
Reignes."[63] However, he turns instead to a set of detailed comparisons of
Wolsey and Laud. He begins with their physical attributes: "as they were
of different times, so they were of different statures; yet either of them well
shapt according to their proportions: Wolsey was of a competent tallnesse,
Laud of a lesse size, but might be called a prettie man, as the other a proper
man."[64] It is worth observing that the author does not follow many other
critics of Wolsey in representing the cardinal as a man of substantial girth.
Although imagery about Wolsey's size was certainly available to the
author in sources ranging from Holinshed through Shakespeare and Fletcher,
perhaps he believed that Laud's diminutive stature would suffer more in
comparison with an ordinarily sized rather than a bulky body. *A True Comparison* continues by tracing both men's academic careers and their rise to
high ecclesiastical office. Here again, perhaps surprisingly, the author is
willing to make some small allowances in regard to Wolsey's behavior
as chancellor. He observes that Wolsey exceeded Laud "in his numerous
Traine, and the noblenesse thereof," and he also notes that the cardinal
"spent more Coyne in the service of his King, for the honour of his Coun-
trie, and to uphold the credit of his Cardinals Cap, than would (for the
time) have paid an Armie Royal."[65] The first two of these motives—
exhibiting ostentation to promote monarch and country—are creditable
to a chief minister, but the third, "to uphold the credit of his Cardinals
Cap," associates Wolsey firmly with Rome and, therefore, with Laud's
allegedly Romanist sympathies.

Apart from these moments of moderation, the author of *A True Description* is not willing to excuse much else about Wolsey or, for that matter,
Laud. He calls their conduct in church courts "tyrannous." He declares

straightforwardly about their religious allegiance: "They both favoured the Sea [*sic*] of Rome, and respected his Holinesse in it. The Cardinall did professe it publickly, the Arch-Bishop did reverence it privately." Whereas Wolsey openly sought the papacy, Laud "strove to bee Patriarch," likely a reference to Laud's ecclesiology.[66] Laud had opined, in his *Conference with Fisher*, that in the ancient church, "every patriarch was alike supreme in his own patriarchate. Therefore the pope then had no supremacy over the whole church." Laud continued, applying the argument to later church history: "Now, the Britons having a primate of their own (which is greater than a metropolitan,) yea, a patriarch, if you will, he could not be appealed from to Rome."[67] Perhaps, in alluding to this line of Laud's thought, the pamphleteer was accusing the archbishop of setting himself up, if not as a Roman prelate, than as an Anglican one who believed that he owed no obedience to the king. Yet, the author continues, both Laud and Wolsey met their due end, ironically, because of measures they had taken for their own preservation and aggrandizement:

> And as the Cardinall by plucking downe of some small Abbies, to prepare stone for the greater Structures, opened a gap for the King, by which he took the advantage utterly to raze and demolish the rest: so Canterburie by giving way for one Bishop to have a temporall Triall, and to be convicted, not by the Clergie, but the Laitie, so he left the same path open both for himselfe, and the rest of the Episcopacie.[68]

In the end, of course, both men lost their power, and the pamphlet concludes on a foreboding tone, quoting Ecclesiastes. "The Cardinall dyed at Leicester some say of a Flux; Canterburie remaines still in the Tower, onely sick of a fever. *Vanitas vanitatum omnia vanitas.*"[69] The phrase "some say" in the author's description of Wolsey's death is suggestive; it alludes to, without repeating outright, the accusation that the cardinal took his own life. Likewise, the word "onely" in the description of Laud's imprisonment suggests that the archbishop is due more severe punishment.

In contrast to these two pamphlets, *Canterburies Dreame* and *A True Description*, which represented Wolsey as a harbinger of the clerical misgovernment that their authors identified with Laud, a third pamphlet from 1641 highlighted other elements of Wolsey's legacy. *The Prophesie of Mother Shipton* (see Plate 10) was one among many pamphlets from the years of civil war that featured prophecies and predictions about the future. Such prophecies, as Harry Rusche has argued, "were popular among all classes. . . . Rich and poor, educated and uneducated, read them, circulated them orally, and sometimes even acted upon them."[70] Andrew Crome has added that the "remarkable renaissance" in the publication of pamphlets, especially prophetic ones, in the early 1640s was due to a breakdown in the processes of censorship. Texts that might not have been approved for publication under the Elizabethan or Jacobean regimes more easily entered into circulation during the years of civil war.[71]

Amid this frenzy of political prophecy, the character of Mother Shipton stands out vividly. While it is uncertain if Ursula Shipton, who supposedly was the daughter of a witch and the devil and lived in Yorkshire during the reign of Henry VIII, was in fact a historical figure, she became the protagonist of a series of pamphlets that were published beginning in 1641.[72] *The Prophesie of Mother Shipton*, set in the 1520s, opens by quoting Shipton's claim that "Cardinall Wolsey should never come to Yorke with the King." In the pamphlet Wolsey is incensed by the prediction and dispatches the Duke of Suffolk and Lords Percy and Dacre to meet with Shipton. The next scene appears to confirm her powers of foresight:

> She bade them welcome, calling them all by their names, and sent
> for some Cakes and Ale, and they drunke and were very merry.
> Mother Shipton, said the Duke, if you knew what wee come about, you
> would not make us so welcome, and shee said the messenger should
> not be hang'd; Mother Shipton, said the Duke, you said the Cardinall
> should never see Yorke; Yea, said shee, I said hee might see Yorke, but
> never come at it; But said the Duke, when he comes to Yorke thou
> shalt be burned; Wee shall see that, said shee, and plucking her
> Handkerchieffe off her head shee threw it into the fire, and it would
> not burne; then she took her staffe and turned it into the fire, and it
> would not burne, then she tooke it and put it on againe.[73]

Shipton proceeds to prophesy about the future of her three interlocutors, accurately predicting the manner of their deaths. The reader hears no more of Suffolk, Percy, and Dacre, though, as the pamphlet suddenly shifts to Wolsey's arrival at Cawood Castle outside of York. The cardinal climbs the tower and asks where the city is, knowing that Shipton has prophesied that he would see it but not reach it. Although Wolsey proudly pronounces "that he will be soone there," he is promptly arrested and Shipton's prediction vindicated.

The thrust of *The Prophesie of Mother Shipton* is much less obvious than that of *Canterburies Dreame* or *A True Description*, and the pamphlet's characterization of Wolsey appears to mistake a number of historical details. Wolsey's apparent skepticism about Shipton's prophecy is somewhat at odds with several Tudor portraits of the cardinal, especially Cavendish's *Life*, where Wolsey repeats a prophecy that he believes foretells his fall and, later, treats as an evil omen the falling of his processional cross when one of his chaplains accidentally bumps into it.[74] Even more so, the threats to burn Shipton are out of character for the historical Wolsey, who did not hand suspected heretics over for burning. What, then, was the anonymous author's purpose in ascribing to Mother Shipton an accurate prophecy concerning the fate of Cardinal Wolsey? Perhaps the import of the story was to confirm Shipton's prophetic powers, validating her as a person who is equally capable of prophesying about later events. Both the 1641 pamphlet and the other Shipton texts that followed it featured predictions that were not only about the past but also about the contemporary world. In this view, Shipton's success in predicting accurately the futures of Wolsey, Suffolk, and other historical actors gave readers in the Stuart era a good reason to pay attention to her predictions about future events.[75] In the *Shipton* pamphlet, therefore, Wolsey is less an independent actor than a character witness.

Each of our pamphlets from the fateful year 1641 invoked Wolsey's memory for a different purpose: in *Canterburies Dreame*, to offer words of reproach and caution against the churchmanship of Laud; in *A True Comparison*, to stand as an example of the corruption of the clergy; and in *The Prophesie of Mother Shipton*, to verify the protagonist's prophetic powers. It is worth noting that in each of these pamphlets, Wolsey is introduced simply by name; none of the authors provide any of the contextual details that might have been necessary to situate a less well-known character in the minds of their readers. Wolsey, therefore, remained a name to conjure with in the 1640s: Each pamphleteer was able to assume that the broad lines of the cardinal's biography, which are necessary to an informed reading of the pamphlets, would have been familiar to his audience. Here is further evidence that the memory of Wolsey was alive and available for appropriation around the outbreak of the English civil war.

Wolsey on Stage

The previous two sections have established that Wolsey retained a place in the collective historical and theological memory in 1641, more than a century after his deposition and death. The commercial success of Sheares's edition of Cavendish, the continuing circulation of that text in manuscript, and the availability of Wolsey as a character for pamphlets and prophecies all suggest that he was known well enough to be employed rhetorically and symbolically in the internecine conflicts of mid-seventeenth-century

England. Both in this chapter and in the previous one, we have pointed to some of the mechanisms through which Wolsey's memory was kept alive, especially the polemical histories of Foxe, Holinshed, and Holinshed's successors, on the one hand, and the ongoing use of and contestation over Cavendish's biography, on the other. These mechanisms did not preserve only a single strand of memory about Wolsey but rather gave continued life to two of our prototypical representations: Wolsey the papist in the pamphlets and Wolsey the repentant sinner in Cavendish. However, we have not thus far explored two of the most prominent media through which representations of Wolsey were transmitted during the late Tudor and the Stuart periods, namely the theater and the growing professionalization of the craft of historiography. The last two sections of this chapter therefore examine some seventeenth-century dramatic productions that featured Wolsey, as well as a few influential histories of Tudor England.

The Stuarts were not alone in using theater to advance political and theological agendas. As Rainer Pineas has shown, the English history play—in equal parts didactic, controversial, and moralizing—dates back at least to John Bale's *King Johan*, written during the reign of Henry VIII.[76] Subsequently, the *Actes and Monuments*, that great work of Bale's close friend and collaborator John Foxe, inspired a cohort of plays that "invoked a providential historiography" and dramatized many of the accounts in Foxe's book.[77] Among these are at least two plays that directly advance Foxe's interpretation of Cardinal Wolsey as well as a third, more famous play, Shakespeare and Fletcher's *King Henry VIII (All Is True)*, which offers a more nuanced treatment.[78]

FOXEAN HISTORY PLAYS

The True Chronicle Historie of the Whole Life and Death of Thomas Lord Cromwell appeared from the press of William Jones in 1602, but it was likely written and first performed in the 1590s.[79] Pineas has argued that the play served two ends: first, to depict Cromwell as the prototypical "Tudor Protestant hero, who is pictured not only as the perfect Protestant but also as the perfect man," and second, to defend the dissolution of the monasteries and advance the slander that "Catholics consider the murder of opposing monarchs meritorious, an accusation made timely by Catholic attempts on the life of Elizabeth."[80] While the play features Wolsey, it does not focus on him to any great extent. However, it explicitly frames Cromwell's downfall in contrast to the end both of the cardinal and of Thomas More. A speech of Stephen Gardiner casts Cromwell in terms of what Marsha

Robinson has called "a *de casibus* script—the decline of ambitious and faith-less chancellors," but, Robinson continues, "that construction of the past is countered by the play's representation of the fall as *providential*—the per-secution of a martyr at the hands of Antichrist."[81] Whereas Wolsey and More deserved their ends, Cromwell's demise is figured instead as an in-stance of the temporary victory of Antichrist over the saints. In this way, *Thomas Lord Cromwell* presents a polemically charged history that enacts the favorable assessments of Cromwell that populated many Tudor evan-gelical texts.

A second evangelically inspired play offers a more fanciful account of Wolsey's demise. Its writer, Samuel Rowley, remains a somewhat obscure figure in the world of the Tudor-Stuart stage; we know for certain that he acted in at least three companies in the late sixteenth and early seventeenth centuries, and he likely contributed to the writing of several plays now at-tributed to Shakespeare or Marlowe.[82] We can be almost certain that Rowley's play *When You See Me, You Know Me* premiered in 1604; a pub-lished edition followed the next year, appearing in the Stationers' Register on February 12, 1605, as "the enterlude of King Henry the 8th."[83] The play depicts the circumstances of Henry's break from Rome in terms that are as comic as they are anachronistic. Among its many chronological incon-sistencies, the play leaves Wolsey alive to witness the birth of the future King Edward VI and has Henry marry Katherine Parr, rather than Anne of Cleves, upon the death of Jane Seymour. In doing so, as Robinson has argued, the play "foregrounds historiographic patterns and suppresses his-torical differences" in order to make an ideological and theological case against Rome.[84]

Within these manipulations of chronological time, *When You See Me, You Know Me* presents the main lines of the conflict between Wolsey and Henry as Foxe, Hall, and their fellow evangelical writers understood them. Early in the play, Wolsey is exceedingly confident of his influence over the king, even to the point of declaring openly that "Great England's lord have I so won with words, / That, under colour of advising him, / I overrule both council, court, and king."[85] The cardinal's chief concerns are to combat the Lutheran views that he associates with Anne Boleyn, Katherine Parr, and Thomas Cranmer and, equally, to advance his candidacy for the papacy. Wolsey gloats over Anne's fall yet worries that Katherine "is the hope of Luther's heresy / If she be queen, the protestants will swell, / And Cranmer, tutor to the prince of Wales, / Will boldly speak 'gainst Rome's religion."[86]

In contrast, the evangelical point of view is advanced by the king's fool, Will Summers, who is an unlikely hero only if we forget the royal fool's

ability to tell truths too unpopular to be spoken by anyone else and if, likewise, we neglect St. Paul's characterization of Christ's wisdom as foolish-
ness.[87] Summers at one point directly reminds Wolsey of his unpopularity
with the commons: "If you should die,/There's none would cry,/Though
your neck should break."[88] The action comes to a head when Wolsey and
his fellow bishops, in an epitome of Roman overreaching, attempt to arrest Queen Katherine. In the ensuing fracas, Summers reveals to Henry
that he has, quite by accident, discovered the extent of Wolsey's hidden
wealth.[89] The king briefly defends his minister but then dramatically re-
verses course, charging Wolsey with a list of misdeeds and banishing
him from court: "Durst thou presume so, base-born cardinal,/Without
our knowledge to abuse our name? . . . Belike thou meanst to level at a
crown,/But thy ambitious crown shall hurl thee down."[90] The accusations
for which Henry lambasts the cardinal—that he placed his hat on the royal
coinage, that he negotiated with foreign potentates without the king's permission, that he made himself equal to the king by using the phrase *Ego et
rex meus*, and that he seized religious properties to enrich himself—all appear in the indictment against Wolsey that historically was presented to
Parliament in 1529; all but one occur in Hall's summary of that indictment.[91] Rowley's play also echoes Hall in omitting any reference to Wolsey undergoing repentance: Indeed, as in Hall, Rowley's Wolsey remains
obstinate to the end: "Yet will I proudly pass as cardinal,/Although this
day define my heavy fall."[92]

King Henry VIII (All Is True)

Whereas Rowley's Wolsey is a papist villain in the evangelical mold, the
cardinal of William Shakespeare and John Fletcher's play *King Henry VIII
(All Is True)* is morally more ambiguous.[93] Their play does not adopt
wholesale any of our prototypes about Wolsey.[94] Perhaps this is an artifact
of the collaboration between Shakespeare and Fletcher—some have suggested that the latter sought to sentimentalize and tidy up the play's action at the expense of consistent characterization—but, as Schwartz-Leeper
has recently argued, it may also be because the playwrights deliberately
sought to craft a character who "continually unsettles stock images," "undercuts decades of negative imagery," and can be, and has been, played in
a variety of conflicting ways.[95]

The double title of the play suggests that its objectives are at least two:
to present an account of some of the events of Henry's reign and at the
same time to weigh up, in a self-reflexive way, competing modes of his-

torical narrative and claims to historical truth. Recent critics, who have been divided with regard to the play's merits as a work of drama, have registered substantially different opinions about the theory or theories of history that it embraces. L. S. Champion, for instance, has argued that *King Henry VIII* ought to be understood within the framework of evangelical or, to use Marsha Robinson's term, "Foxean" history. The play at first "seems to lack narrative coherence," but by the end it is clear that "the central thrust . . . is the birth of Elizabeth and the prophecy of the culmination of Tudor greatness."[96] However, others have suggested that the incoherence Champion identified is intentional. Rather than simply reenacting Foxe's version of Tudor history, as it is clear that the *Cromwell* playwright and Rowley did, Shakespeare and Fletcher's play may represent "a self-conscious recapitulation of the historiographic reformation undertaken by Bale and Foxe." On this account, it "addresses Foxean history without embracing it."[97] Episodes in the play such as Cranmer's prophecy in Act V illustrate how *King Henry VIII* "draws attention to itself *as* a historiographical representation."[98] This latter, more nuanced approach helps explain why Shakespeare and Fletcher drew upon a variety of source materials: Their play quotes from or alludes to Cavendish's *Life* as well as to Holinshed and Foxe. Such an interpretation also permits us, as Schwartz-Leeper has suggested, to understand why "Shakespeare and Fletcher's Wolsey does not sit comfortably with Wolsey's overwhelmingly negative public image."[99]

One of the first performances of *King Henry VIII* occurred on June 29, 1613; the date is famous because, according to contemporary accounts, a cannon used in the production to announce the arrival of visitors at Wolsey's palace in Act I, scene 4, ended up setting fire to the theater.[100] The play was one among a number of historical dramas that were written or revived around the time of the marriage of Princess Elizabeth, the eldest daughter of King James, to Fredrick V, the Elector Palatine. *Thomas Lord Cromwell* and *When You See Me, You Know Me*, each more than a decade old, had been restaged in the year leading up to the premiere of Shakespeare and Fletcher's play.[101] There is some debate about the relationship between Rowley's play and *King Henry VIII*: Many have asserted that the playwrights deliberately fashioned a serious drama as a riposte to what they viewed as Rowley's more flippant production. Hence, the argument goes, these lines from the Prologue: "Only they / That come to hear a merry, bawdy play, / A noise of targets, or to see a fellow / In a long motley coat guarded with yellow, / Will be deceived."[102] The post-1641 performance history of *King Henry VIII* must wait until later chapters, but one production

is worth noting briefly: the play's revival, on June 29, 1628, at the rebuilt
Globe Theatre. In attendance was George Villiers, Duke of Buckingham
and royal favorite, deeply unpopular and destined to be assassinated by
the end of the summer. As prominent as Villiers's attendance was his
abrupt departure at the end of the first scene of Act II, just after the play's
Duke of Buckingham had been taken away to his execution. Thomas
Cogswell and Peter Lake have persuasively argued that Villiers's sudden
and highly visible departure was an instance of his ongoing "image making and message sending." Specifically, they suggested, Villiers sought
to associate himself visually with his historical namesake, who in the play
is sent to an unjust end, rather than with Wolsey, another unpopular royal
favorite who appears to receive his just reward.[103]

In their play, Shakespeare and Fletcher represent Wolsey's political
glory and the tragedy of his fall with equal poignancy. The first two acts
portray Wolsey as a powerful enemy of the nobility. However, as Schwartz-
Leeper has emphasized, Wolsey's power does not prevent him from behaving hospitably and solicitously toward his friends, and his conduct does
not merit the insults and harsh characterizations directed at him.[104] Admittedly, Wolsey does procure the downfall of Buckingham by paying the
duke's servants to testify against him, and the cardinal seeks his own advantage when Henry decides to repeal the Amicable Grant. Yet the Wolsey of these scenes is also the king's trusted confidant, one who "acts only
with the allowance of his master."[105] The playwrights have Henry enter the
second scene "leaning on the Cardinal's shoulder . . . the Cardinal places
himself under the King's feet on his right side"; as Stuart Kurland has
noted, "the gesture signals Henry's dependence on Wolsey while also sug-
gesting King James I's habit, reported by various sources, of leaning on
his courtiers' shoulders."[106] In addition to his trusting relationship with the
king, Wolsey appears to be an excellent host: His generosity toward his
guests is described as "noble" and "liberal," and by noblemen no less; their
remarks contrast sharply with the disparaging epithets about Wolsey's
birth that punctuate the play's opening conversation between Buckingham
and Norfolk.[107] In Act II, the cardinal continues to hold a place at Henry's
right hand: He procures the papal commission for him and Campeggio to
judge the king's marriage, and Henry, joyful to see him ("O my Wolsey, / The quiet of my wounded conscience, / Thou art a cure fit for a
king"), abruptly dismisses Norfolk and Suffolk from his presence.[108] Shakespeare and Fletcher borrow from Holinshed much of their narrative of
the legatine court, but they imaginatively expand upon Holinshed's report,
drawn from Cavendish, that Wolsey asked the king to put to rest publicly

any rumor that the cardinal had provoked him to seek an annulment. Significantly, the play devotes more than sixty lines to this exchange between king and cardinal, lines that Schwartz-Leeper has argued undercut strongly the representation of Wolsey as the instigator of Henry's divorce.[109]

Wolsey's dominance, which some scholars have characterized as Machiavellian, comes to an abrupt end when Henry mistakenly receives a damning cache of documents, including an inventory of the cardinal's wealth and a letter to the pope arguing against his divorce.[110] Sources for this scene abound: Holinshed had presented a similar episode featuring King Henry VII and the then-bishop of Durham, and the most recent editor of *King Henry VIII* has noted another parallel with a scene in Foxe; to these we might also add Hall's account of Henry's discovery of Wolsey's deceptiveness in his correspondence.[111] Whatever their inspiration, Shakespeare and Fletcher stage a vigorous confrontation between Henry and Wolsey, at the end of which the king leaves Wolsey with the miscarried documents. Almost immediately the cardinal, admitting that he had sought to use his resources "for mine own ends—indeed to gain the popedom," perceives that his career has run its course: "I have touched the high point of all my greatness,/And from that full meridian of my glory/I haste now to my setting."[112] The confiscation of the Great Seal, a rehearsal of charges against the cardinal, and news of the king's marriage to Anne all follow in short order.

How exactly do the playwrights represent Wolsey's reaction to the reversal of his fortunes? Noting that Wolsey is "sharply depicted within the play as villain and regenerate," Champion has wondered whether the cardinal experiences a real, internal transformation as opposed to simply displaying "a keen sensitivity toward his loss of power and possession."[113] However, other critics have argued that Wolsey's conversion is more than merely rational. In a conversation between Wolsey and Cromwell, based loosely on Cavendish's account of their exchanges during the cardinal's exile, the tenor of Wolsey's repentance comes fully into view.[114] The cardinal recognizes that "My high-blown pride/At length broke under me and now has left me,/Weary and old with service, to the mercy/Of a rude stream that must for ever hide me."[115] Wolsey confesses that he "falls like Lucifer,/Never to hope again," in an allusion not only to his former glory but also, perhaps, to Holinshed's characterization of him as "luciferian."[116] Strangely, even though Wolsey knows that it was his own writings that furnished Henry with evidence against him, he attributes his fall to Anne Boleyn in a passage that could easily have come from the pen of Cavendish: "All my glories/In that one woman I have lost for ever."[117] These comments suggest that there is more to Wolsey's response than the discovery that he had miscalculated; instead, he recognizes that his former way of life was unsustainable both morally and politically, and he urges Cromwell to take a different path:[118]

> Mark but my fall and that that ruined me.
> Cromwell, I charge thee, fling away ambition.
> By that sin fell the angels. How can man then,
> The image of his maker, hope to win by it?
> Love thyself last; cherish those hearts that hate thee.
> Corruption wins not more than honesty.[119]

Wolsey's last words—"Farewell, / The hopes of court: my hopes in heaven do dwell"—mark the completeness of his conversion and gesture toward the religious practices that Cavendish's Wolsey takes up in exile. Unlike the Wolsey of Foxean historiography, the cardinal of *King Henry VIII* does not die unrepentant. Yet, unlike Cavendish's Wolsey, he does not dwell for more than a few lines on his treatment by the king. Instead, Shakespeare and Fletcher's cardinal acknowledges his faults and accepts his fate with a greater degree of equanimity, advising Cromwell to "Let all the ends thou aimest at be thy country's / Thy God's, and truth's."[120]

Robinson has made perhaps the most compelling argument that Wolsey's conversion is thoroughgoing. She has identified the structural similarities among the four downfalls Shakespeare and Fletcher stage: those of Buckingham, Wolsey, Katherine, and, almost, Cranmer. In these cases, she has argued, "each falls 'a blessed martyr,' exhibiting patience in suffering, a charity which blesses its enemies, and a joy in escaping the snares of the world—all marks of the redeemed."[121] If Robinson is right—and the passages I have quoted above suggest that she is—it is striking that the fall of Wolsey, who in the eyes of so many of his contemporaries epitomized all that was wrong with Catholicism, receives the same moral treatment as the fall of characters who were situated at other points on the spectrum of Tudor religious and political positions.

But not only do Shakespeare and Fletcher appear willing to allow Wolsey a greater capacity for repentance than their evangelical sources.[122] They also call into being an alternative manner in which the cardinal might be remembered. In Act IV, the dying Katherine of Aragon and her trusted usher, Griffiths, both offer eulogies for Wolsey. Katherine gives voice to many of the criticisms of Wolsey advanced by his enemies in the play and by hostile writers throughout the sixteenth century. To her, Wolsey is "a man / Of an unbounded stomach," and in this Katherine echoes the many corporeal insults we have identified both inside and outside the play.[123] Katherine reiterates key charges in the indictment against Wolsey, claiming for instance that he was "ever ranking / Himself with princes."[124] She accuses him of simony, deceit, and, at least implicitly, sexual immorality. Yet Griffiths pleads another case—perhaps, if we follow Schwartz-Leeper's argument, the case of the playwrights themselves. Katherine's usher, like Wolsey's usher Cavendish, offers a generous assessment of the cardinal's life. He lifts up Wolsey's scholarship, eloquence, and charity, praising him especially for his educational foundations in Ipswich and Oxford. For Griffiths, just as for Cavendish and the cardinal of Act III, Wolsey's fall from power marks a new beginning in grace:

> His overthrow heaped happiness upon him,
> For then, and not till then, he felt himself,
> And found the blessedness of being little
> And, to add greater honours to his age
> Than man could give him, he died fearing God.[125]

Griffiths thus undercuts traditional characterizations of Wolsey: For instance, "little" constitutes no subtle response to the accusations of gluttony and obesity in Act I or even to Katherine's "unbounded stomach" jibe of a few lines earlier. In the play's last speech about Wolsey, Griffiths offers a counter-reminiscence of the cardinal, envisioning a different way in which he might be remembered and commemorated in the years to come. As we will see in Chapter 4, in the early twentieth century the citizens of Ipswich took Griffiths up on his invitation.

Early Stuart Historiography

Before carrying forward into those future centuries our examination of Wolsey's commemoration and representation, however, we must briefly backtrack. The final section of this chapter considers how the cardinal was represented in a few works of Stuart historical prose. Subsequent chapters continue this historiographical analysis well past the outbreak of the civil wars, but here I stop in 1641 in order to privilege those historians who wrote during the years when Cavendish's manuscripts were continuing to circulate; the anti-Laudian pamphlets we have analyzed were being written; and Rowley, Shakespeare, Fletcher, and others were producing their history plays.

With regard to Wolsey, Stuart historians undertook a different set of historiographical tasks than their Tudor predecessors. First, the burden of approaching the recent past with extraordinary caution lifted after the accession of King James, who of course descended from neither Anne nor Elizabeth. As a result, histories of the English Reformation produced during the Stuart period grappled more openly with the circumstances that had brought about the establishment of the Church of England. Second, whereas many of the writers we encountered in Chapter 1 used the various genres of historical prose to construct narratives about Wolsey that had not previously been articulated quite so systematically, seventeenth-century historians tended to combine elements from existing narratives. And third, the ideological spectrum along which later historians worked was somewhat narrower. In the previous chapter, our writers tended to identify themselves as proponents for the cause of evangelicalism against popery or else, for those authors who were more sympathetic to Rome, as advocates for catholicity against schism. In the seventeenth century, by way of contrast, historians more often situated themselves amid the internecine struggles of the Church of England, a body that was still seeking consensus about key elements of its identity. This trend only intensified after the resolution of the civil wars, which had left such debates prominently unfinished.[126] In this new ecclesiological context, Francis Godwin and Edward, Lord Herbert both engaged extensively with Wolsey's legacy, reaching strikingly different conclusions.

Godwin was an alumnus of Christ Church, and although his record of service as bishop of Llandaff and Hereford has been characterized as middling at best, he was an eager student of history.[127] His *Rerum Anglicarum Henrico VIII. Edwardo VI. et Maria regnantibus*, published in Latin (1616) and in English translation as *Annales of England* (1630), offers an example of Stuart historians' willingness to break with some of the narratives they had inherited from their predecessors. *Annales of England*, like its Latin original, opens by taking aim at the historical method of Polydore Vergil, whom Godwin charges with writing in a way "so false and misbeseeming the ingenuitie of an Historian, that he seemeth to have aimed at no other end, then by bitter invectives against Henry the Eighth and Cardinall Wolsey to demerit the favour of Queene Mary, already more then befitted incensed against both for the Divorce of her Mother."[128] Few of the late Tudor sources we have reviewed took Vergil as a primary interlocutor, and Godwin's willingness to engage in invective against Vergil suggests two conclusions. First, writing in Latin for an audience likely intended to extend outside of England, Godwin seems to have found it necessary to rebut the accusations of at least one prominent earlier Latin writer. Second, his willingness to criticize Vergil in Wolsey's defense reveals how the boundaries of acceptable historical discourse had begun to shift by Godwin's time.

Indeed, Godwin is more sympathetic, or at least more balanced, in his treatment of the cardinal than many of those who came before him. This is in part unsurprising: He does, after all, dub himself a "Foster-childe" of Christ Church, and his chief source for his material about Wolsey appears to have been Cavendish's *Life*, which must have been available to him in manuscript form.[129] But even though Godwin borrows from Cavendish the interpretive device of fortune's wheel, and though he joins Cavendish in seeking to absolve Wolsey from responsibility for such episodes as the execution of the Duke of Buckingham, his *Annales* does not whitewash the cardinal's memory.[130] Instead, Godwin notes with some distaste Wolsey's "first rising and immoderate power," he claims that Wolsey had questioned the legitimacy of Princess Mary's birth in order to drive a wedge between Henry and Charles V, and he admits that Wolsey eventually grew more powerful and wealthy than was proper for a subject.[131] Yet, whatever the cardinal's faults may have been, in Godwin's telling the king's were far greater. Calling Henry "a raging King," Godwin presents Wolsey as the man who, in his time, saved Henry from himself:

> For as often as I consider how laudably Henry had hitherto ruled, and behold the calamities of ensuing times, I cannot but accord with them, who ascribe the sway which he did beare over all the Princes of Christendome to the excellency of Wolsey his counsailes. But Wolsey being taken away, to whom shall we impute those effects of Lust, Tyrannie, and Avarice, two Wives killed, two put away, so many (and among them many of the greater sort) put to death for their Religion only, extremitie only differing in the manner used by Hanging against Papists, by Fire against Heretiques, (these were the termes of those dayes) & the Church (or rather the Common-wealth) horribly spoiled and robbed of her Patrimony? Certainly had Wolsey sate at the Sterne, the King had never like a Ship destitute of a Pilot, beene carried to and fro with such contrary and uncertaine motions.[132]

This powerful passage, the sense of which we will discover being echoed in numerous subsequent works, introduces Godwin's lengthy treatment of Wolsey's fall. For many of his details Godwin depends on Cavendish, but toward the end of his narrative he imagines two speeches by Wolsey, one to a group of judges sent by Henry to hear his plea to the charge of praemunire and the other to the men gathered around his deathbed. In both, Wolsey is calm, self-aware, and occasionally quite pointed. To his judges, Wolsey observes that he had exercised his legatine power only with the king's permission, yet he pleads guilty and surrenders his goods because he considers "it good reason, that he should revoke his gifts, if he thinke me vnworthy of them."[133] On his deathbed, Godwin ascribes to Wolsey words of regret and repentance that go well beyond Cavendish's:

> God hath iustly rewarded mee for neglecting my due service to him, and wholy applying my selfe to his Maiesties pleasure. Woe is me wretch and sot that I am, who have beene ungratefull to the King of Kings, whom if I had served with that due devout observance that befits a Christian, hee would not have forsaken me in the evening of my age.[134]

In light of his failures, Wolsey offers himself as a "generall example (even to the King himself) how sliperily they stand in this world, who do not above all things rely upon the same support of Gods Favour and Providence."[135]

As we will see in the next chapter, Godwin's view regained currency near the end of the seventeenth century, above all in the celebrated history of Bishop Gilbert Burnet. Closer to the middle of the century, however, the demands of politics and polemic inspired at least one less forgiving account of Wolsey. In 1639, Edward, Lord Herbert of Cherbury completed a major historical work on the Henrician Reformation, *The Life and Raigne of King Henry the Eighth*.[136] Herbert was a former associate of George Villiers, the Duke of Buckingham and royal favorite who had been assassinated in 1628, and Herbert sought, unsuccessfully, to gain Charles I's favor through his historical work.[137] The *Life*, perhaps unusually for a text written to please an autocratic monarch, begins with an ambivalent assessment of its subject:

> I shall labour with this Difficulty in King *Henry* VIII. not so much for the general observation (among Politicks) that the Government of Princes rarely grows milder towards their latter end; but because this King in particular, (being about his declining Age, so diverse in many of his Desires, that he knew not well how either to command or obey them) interverted all, falling at last into such violent Courses, as in common Opinion derogated not a little from those Vertues which at first made him one of the most renown'd Princes of Christendom.[138]

Wolsey figures prominently in Herbert's narrative, and although Herbert admires his loyalty to the king, he finds no shortage of faults in the cardinal. Citing many of the hostile authors whom we have encountered—

Vergil, Hall, Holinshed, and most frequently Sander—Herbert remarks upon Wolsey's wealth, his ambition, his willingness to cut ties with his friends and accept bribes from England's enemies, and his vengefulness. Editorial comment on Wolsey is largely absent from Herbert's account of the years when he flourished as Henry's minister, but when Herbert comes to the period of Wolsey's dismissal, he returns to the cardinal at some length. He borrows from Hall and others the dramatic device of a miscarried letter, sent by Wolsey to a third party, which inadvertently ends up in the hands of the king. As a result, "the King was observ'd to mistrust him ever afterwards."[139] Herbert borrows at length from "a Manuscript of one Master *George Cavendish*," including Cavendish's accounts of the relationship between Anne Boleyn and Henry Percy; Wolsey's actions around the time of his dismissal as chancellor; the cardinal's journey north; and his arrest, final illness, and death. However, while Herbert echoes the censures of earlier writers, he occasionally also critiques them. As in Godwin's *Annales*, in Herbert's work Polydore Vergil comes in for the greatest disapproval: Herbert observes that Vergil had cause to hate Wolsey personally and charges him with fabricating the accusation that Wolsey had been the driving force behind Henry's annulment.[140] Likewise, Herbert dismisses Sander's "foul Calumnies" about Anne Boleyn's parentage, rejecting at some length the theory that Anne was Henry's illegitimate daughter.[141]

The histories of Godwin and Herbert share several features, some of them quite distinctive in comparison with the Tudor histories we studied in the previous chapter. First, these writers were not afraid to venture explicit criticism of Henry VIII, especially with reference to the second half of his reign. Herbert differs somewhat from Godwin in not explicitly linking Henry's increasing capriciousness with Wolsey's departure as chief minister, but both men's works demonstrate a degree of dissatisfaction with Henry's administration that their predecessors only hinted at. Second, they engage in explicit criticism of early historians, especially Vergil and Sander, whose assessments they judge to be biased, their methods faulty, or both. As a result, the representations of both Henry and Wolsey in these early Stuart histories are somewhat more judicious, albeit with Godwin inclining toward excusing Wolsey's faults and Herbert taking a less lenient stance. It is important to note, however, that neither historian benefited from access to many of the archival materials that allowed their successors to nuance their accounts of Wolsey further still. In the chapters that follow, we will trace how the availability of increasing numbers of primary documents shaped later representations of the cardinal.

Conclusions

But first, to sum up the findings of this chapter: If writers of the sixteenth century forged and embellished competing narratives about the cardinal, those of the seventeenth century tended instead to engage in bricolage and interpretation. In the preceding pages, we have traced the ways in which early Stuart writers received, refashioned, and retold the narratives about Wolsey and the Henrician Reformation that they had inherited from their Tudor predecessors. The prototypical representations of Wolsey we identified in Chapter 1 continued to shape seventeenth-century texts about the cardinal, but more often than not, these later authors wove together elements from multiple prototypes. At the same time, these writers were more interested in, and responsive to, internecine disputes within the realm and the Church of England, as opposed to the conflict between evangelicalism and Roman obedience that had attracted the attention of earlier commentators. With a few exceptions, the sources we have been examining in this chapter take the *independence* of the Church of England as a given; for them, the more important question was what *form* the church should take. To the extent that a churchman or doctrine reminded their authors of Wolsey, it reminded them of Rome, and that, almost always, portended danger.

Against the backdrop of the events leading up to the civil wars, engagement with and contestation over the memory of Wolsey took a variety of forms. On the one hand, there were conflicts over the interpretation—and even the text—of sixteenth-century sources, most notably Cavendish's *Life*. The late Tudor and early Stuart reception of Cavendish's distinctive narrative about Wolsey was, as we have seen, something of a mixed bag: Puritans expurgated Cavendish's account in order to bring it into line with their own ideas about divine providence and to foreground Wolsey's sins rather than his conversion. The manuscript tradition, which perhaps because of this censorship continued to flourish even after the appearance of the first printed edition, also gives evidence of ongoing disagreements about Wolsey's legacy. While some manuscript owners sought to downplay the role that Anne Boleyn and her allies at court had played in procuring the cardinal's fall, others used marginal annotations to censure Wolsey for his misdeeds in terms far stronger than those his gentleman-usher had used. However, on the other hand seventeenth-century debates about Wolsey's legacy were not limited to the reception and revision of older texts. The plays we have examined in this chapter reveal that the cardinal was presented on the late Elizabethan and Stuart stage in a range of substantially different guises—for instance, as the Roman villain of Rowley's *When You See Me, You Know Me* and as the complex and maligned historical actor of Shakespeare and Fletcher's *King Henry VIII*. Puritan pamphlets sought explicitly to tie Wolsey to the hated William Laud in the crucial years leading up to the civil wars (and, of course, to Laud's, and then King Charles I's, trial and execution). Finally, historical writers combined and criticized existing sources to produce their own accounts of Wolsey's life.

Thus, over the course of the seventeenth century, the three representations of Wolsey that had been constructed in the Tudor period splintered into a host of competing assessments of the cardinal and his place in the Henrician Reformation, with not a few of these assessments reflecting their authors' verdict on the success or failure of reformation itself. Only in the second half of the century, as we will see in the next chapter, did new documents about the cardinal's life inform this ongoing debate, a fact that limited the breadth of conclusions that earlier historians could reasonably reach, even if their counterparts among playwrights and pamphleteers felt no such compunction. In every medium, however, Wolsey remained a name to conjure with—a name, more precisely, with which to conjure *up* and further vilify England's discredited Catholic past. But, as we will see in the chapters that follow, little of this was unique to the first half of the seventeenth century.

CHAPTER 3

From Restoration to Catholic Emancipation: Texts and Places (1641–c. 1860)

In the previous two chapters, we traced how Tudor and early Stuart authors represented Wolsey in ways that advanced their political and theological agendas. While sixteenth-century authors invoked Wolsey primarily in the context of the ongoing controversy between the churches of England and Rome, seventeenth-century writers more often represented him in order to intervene in internecine Anglican debates about the extent to which the Church of England had been and should be reformed. In both periods, we observed how the writers who called upon Wolsey engaged in a form of interpretive bricolage, bringing together elements from multiple clusters of images and ideas, what we have called prototypes. These acts of bricolage were often carefully attuned to the circumstances within which our authors were working.

This chapter and the two that follow it take the history of the representation and commemoration of Wolsey up to the present day. Before we resume our chronological narrative, however, several observations are in order. First, between the commencement of the English civil wars and our own day, not only did new texts about Wolsey continue to be written, but some texts that we have already encountered were reprinted, performed anew, and adapted to the needs of latter-day audiences. We must therefore attend both to new representations of the cardinal, whether in print, on stage, or on screen, and to new appropriations of earlier representations. Second, even though the production of texts about Wolsey in the seventeenth through early nineteenth centuries continued at a pace roughly consistent with the preceding century and a half, the speed of cultural production accelerated dramatically in the second half of the nineteenth century. As we will find in chapters 4 and 5, both the professionalization of the historical guild and the publication of primary sources contributed to a proliferation of studies of Tudor England starting around the time of Queen Victoria's accession. Third, amid the appearance of these new accounts of Wolsey, earlier representations experienced periods both of neglect and of renewed popularity. For instance, Shakespeare and Fletcher's *King Henry VIII (All Is True)* became, in Stella Fletcher's words, "a patriotic staple of the London stage" in the eighteenth century before entering something of a drought in the first half of the nineteenth.[1]

The present chapter covers a period of approximately two centuries, starting with the outbreak of the civil wars and concluding just prior to the appearance of the first volume of *Letters and Papers, Foreign and Domestic, of the Reign of Henry VIII* in 1862. As in all the chapters of this book, to describe every representation of Wolsey during the years under consideration would be impossible. Therefore, I have carefully selected a small number of works for analysis, choosing those that have exerted the greatest influence, those that have advanced the most innovative representations, and those that deserve more extensive attention than they have received thus far from scholars. The notes identify some additional sources, particularly those that derive closely from the leading texts I will be exploring. The chapter begins with representations of Wolsey in historical works published during and immediately after the civil wars. A brief excursus describes one of the few new plays that featured Wolsey during the Restoration period. Then, as we turn to the eighteenth and early nineteenth centuries, the chapter introduces a whole host of new scholarly and literary treatments of the cardinal, beginning with the first modern Wolsey biography, published in 1724 by the Anglican clergyman Richard Fiddes, and concluding with histories produced by partisans on both sides of the nineteenth-century controversy over Catholic emancipation. We conclude with an event that helped shape the popular memory of Wolsey, namely Queen Victoria's decision to open Hampton Court Palace to the public free of charge. The queen's gesture, denounced by not a few establishment figures as an invitation for the supposedly unwashed masses to dirty a national treasure, sparked renewed interest in Wolsey's palace and its history—interest that persists to the time of this writing.

From the Civil War to the Glorious Revolution

Relatively few works of historical scholarship appeared during the years of the civil wars. The exceptions included Edward, Lord Herbert's survey of the reign of Henry VIII (which, as we noted toward the end of the previous chapter, had been composed before the conflict commenced) and Thomas Fuller's *Church History of Britain*, published in 1655. Fuller was the scion of a prominent episcopalian clerical family: His father was a Northamptonshire rector, his uncle a theology professor at Cambridge and president of Queens' College, and his mother's brother-in-law a bishop of Salisbury.[2] In religious matters Fuller was a moderate: He opposed the strictness of Archbishop Laud's proceedings against religious dissenters but nevertheless subscribed his name to the Laudian canons adopted in the 1640 convocation of Canterbury province, an action for which he and other signatories were fined by the Long Parliament. Fuller took the royalist side in the civil wars but fortunately was able to find religious employment during the interregnum, when he also published a series of scholarly texts on biblical and English history. His *Church History*, which W. B. Patterson has called "the first comprehensive English protestant account of Christianity in the island from the earliest times," appeared in the middle of Oliver Cromwell's tenure as Lord Protector.[3]

As Rosemary O'Day and Joseph Preston have argued, Fuller explicitly positioned his *Church History* as a successor to and a continuation of Foxe's *Actes and Monuments*. However, much as the volume "bore witness to the continued strength of the Foxian apocalyptic vision," it did so with "toleration" and served as a "model of moderation."[4] Among other differences, Fuller did not identify late medieval heretics such as Waldensians and Wycliffites as the forerunners of sixteenth-century reformers. Instead, harking back to a line of argument that Henry VIII's advisers had employed in making their case for his first annulment, Fuller emphasized the historical independence of the English church from that of Rome. He endorsed the legend that Joseph of Arimathea had brought Christianity to the British Isles long before the first Roman missionaries arrived, and he presented evidence that purported to show that Eleutherius, the second-century bishop of Rome, had communicated with the early British ruler Lucius.[5]

Fuller's treatment of Wolsey stands as a notable exception to the overall tone of his work. Embracing the prototype of Wolsey the papist, the *Church History* characterizes him chiefly as a man of ambition. However, his ambition was a double-edged sword. On the one hand, when Wolsey was successful in elevating himself to a higher degree than any subject had previously achieved, he found himself the subject of criticism. For instance, Fuller reports that at Cardinal College, "King Henry took just offence that the Cardinal set his own Arms above the Kings, on the Gate-house, at the entrance into the Colledg. This was no verbal but a real *Ego & Rex meus*, excusable by no plea in Manners or Grammer." Indeed, Fuller notes, "to humble the Cardinals pride, some afterwards set up on a window, a painted Mastiff-dog, gnawing the spate-bone of a shoulder of Mutton, to mind the Cardinal of his extraction, being the Son of a Butcher."[6] On the other hand, in the few instances where Wolsey failed to achieve his goals, he resorted to vengeance. In making this latter case, Fuller echoes many of the writers who came before him. He claims that Wolsey had inordinately desired to be elected pope, and when he concluded that Charles V was blocking his path to the papal throne, he instigated Henry to seek the annulment of his marriage in order to take vengeance. Perhaps having Godwin's *Annales of England* in mind, Fuller avers, "And this is affirmed by the generality of our Historians, though some of late have endeavoured to acquit Wolsey, as not the first perswader of the King['s] divorce."[7]

Fuller's distaste for the cardinal was so strong even to trump his generally critical attitude toward traditional religion. The *Church History* employs a biblical metaphor to castigate Wolsey for disendowing the monasteries whose revenues he used to found Cardinal College. Figuring Wolsey as King David, Fuller writes, "The more the pitty, that having of his own such a flock of preferments, nothing but the poor mans Ewe-lamb would please him, so that being to Found two Colledges, he seised on no fewer than fourty small Monasteries, turning their inhabitants out of house and home, and converting their means principally to a Colledg in Oxford."[8] Fuller's religious preferences included no sympathy for monastic life, yet his disgust at Wolsey led him to mourn the loss of institutions for which he did not have great love.

Again embracing our evangelical prototype, Fuller's depiction of Wolsey's downfall broadly follows Foxe's. Wolsey prepares for a "princely" installation as archbishop of York, "attracting envie from such as beheld it. All is told unto the King, and all made worse by telling it, complaining Wolsey would never leave his pride, till life first left him. His old faults

are revived and aggravated, and the King incensed afresh against him."[9]
Yet Fuller departs somewhat from Foxe regarding the particulars of Wolsey's death, which Fuller characterizes as a result of "the dysentery, the pain
lying much in his guts, more in his heart. . . . Coming to Leicester he died,
being buried almost as obscurely as he was born." Absent here are Foxe's
gory particulars, which Fuller replaces with a set of details we have not yet
come across:

> I know not whether or not it be worth the mentioning here, (however
> we will put it on the adventure) that Cardinal Wolsey, in his life time
> was inform'd by some Fortune-tellers, that he should have his end at
> Kingston. This credulity interpreted of Kingston on Thames, which
> made him always to avoid the riding through that Town, though the
> nearest way from his house to the Court. Afterwards understanding
> that he was to be committed by the Kings express order to the charge
> of Sr Anthony [sic] Kingston, it struck to his heart, too late perceiving
> himself deluded by that Father of Lies in his homonymous
> prediction.[10]

Wolsey's paranoid fear of "Kingston" appears plainly, at the end of his life,
to be as superstitious as it is misguided. Fuller figures the cardinal as an
object lesson about the dangers of prophecy, a practice that Fuller's contemporaries associated with Rome. At the same time, Fuller's account of
Wolsey's confusion associates the cardinal with the devil—a common antipapist trope that was to be carried forward, as we will see, in many Restoration accounts.

The return of the monarchy in 1660 brought with it yet another set of
reconfigurations in English politics and ecclesiology. In particular, as
Jeffrey R. Collins has argued, Restoration bishops eagerly embraced a
"two-sphere" model of spiritual and temporal authority, in which the episcopacy, conceived of as existing *jure divino* (by divine law), enjoyed a
greater degree of independence from the monarch than had historically
been the case. Collins traces the roots of this model back to Laud, who
had sought to magnify royal authority and establish episcopacy as an institution of divine origin. Following the Restoration, however, "Laud's vision of monarchy had been abandoned in favor of his vision of episcopacy."[11]
A new danger accompanied this shift: If the prewar Church of England
had been too much a creature of the monarch, the increasing independence of the Restoration church risked it being perceived too near to Roman
models for the division of spiritual and temporal power.[12]

Peter Heylyn and Gilbert Burnet each wrote substantial works of church history amid the uncertainties of the period between the restoration of the monarchy and the so-called Glorious Revolution of 1689. Whereas Fuller had brought forward traditional elements of evangelical historiography, these writers—both episcopalians and royalists—advanced different interpretations of the Henrician reformation. Heylyn was an Oxford scholar, as skilled in natural philosophy as in theology and history, who had been an ardent defender of Archbishop Laud and the royalist cause both during and after the civil wars.[13] With the Restoration, he resumed the church positions he had lost during the interregnum, but despite his hopes to the contrary, he received no further preferments. In the last few years of his life, he produced a series of influential historical works, including a laudatory (if the reader will pardon the pun) biography of Laud published in 1668 under the title *Cyprianus Anglicus*. Heylyn's *Ecclesia Restaurata* (1660–61) likewise "provides an emphatically Laudian view of the Reformation, withering in its attacks on the excesses of the Edwardian reformation" and on subsequent puritan writers, including Fuller.[14] Heylyn's account figures the early years of the English reformation as inadvertent and halting. Henry VIII may have laid the groundwork for a religious settlement under his daughter Elizabeth, but Henry's actions were "accidental only, and by the by, rather designed on private ends, than out of any settled purpose to restore the Church."[15] Heylyn did agree with Fuller, however, about the prehistory of the reformation. For both of them, reform had emerged not from the ongoing presence of a "secret multitude of true professors," such as late medieval lollards or Wycliffites. Instead, they "stressed the continuity between the Catholic church and the Church of England," at least as the latter had been configured in the early years of Elizabeth's reign.[16]

Given Heylyn's high regard for Laud, whom we saw in the previous chapter being depicted by puritan writers as a latter-day Wolsey, it is unsurprising that *Ecclesia Restaurata* spares the cardinal some of the criticisms of Fuller's *Church History*. In Heylyn's telling, King Henry's scruples about the legitimacy of his marriage were at first entirely his own. Longland, the royal confessor, urged the king to share his concerns with Wolsey, "on whose judgment he relied in most other matters." While Wolsey was therefore not the *origin* of the divorce, in Heylyn's account he did not fail to wield the king's scruples in order to exact vengeance upon Charles V. "The Emperor had lately crossed him in his suit for the Popedom, and since denied him the Archbishoprick of Toledo, with the promise whereof he had before bound him to his side."[17] Wolsey's plan, however, goes amiss: With "the return of Viscount Rochford [i.e., Thomas Boleyn] and the planting of Anne Bollen in the court," Anne gains an opportunity to take her own revenge for the failure of her engagement with Henry Percy, and she exploits her closeness with the king to bring about the cardinal's ruin.[18] Heylyn explicitly cites Cavendish as the source for these elements of his narrative, yet he also borrows elements from the Catholic prototype that figured Wolsey as the malicious author of schism.

Heylyn was not the only seventeenth-century author to rely, at least in part, on Cavendish's *Life*. So also did Gilbert Burnet, the Scottish-born bishop of Salisbury and author of the widely disseminated *History of the Reformation of the Church of England*. The first volume of Burnet's history, published in 1679, constituted the opening salvo in his extensive response to a new French translation of Sander's *Schismatis Anglicani*.[19] As John Spurr has argued, Sander was not Burnet's only target: "Burnet used the opportunity to draw some unflattering parallels between the sixteenth century and the pretensions of the Restoration church and the Stuart dynasty," especially targeting James, Duke of York.[20] In fact, Burnet went so far as to claim that James's conversion to Catholicism had come in part from reading Heylyn.[21]

Joseph R. Preston has praised Burnet for appreciating more than many of his contemporaries the effect of religious bias on historiography. More than simply promising impartiality, as many of his predecessors had done, Burnet offered his readers direct access to the documents upon which he had relied, printing them *in extenso* as appendices. In the preface to the first volume of his *History of the Reformation*, he makes an assertion that later positivist researchers, such as Lord Acton, would find congenial:

> For I shall vouch my warrants for what I say, and tell where they may
> be found. And having copied out of the records and MSS many papers
> of great importance, I shall not only insert the substance of them in
> the following work, but at the end of it shall give a collection of them
> at their full length.[22]

Among the sources Burnet employed to construct his representation of Wolsey was Cavendish's *Life*, which at one point he asserts he is quoting from manuscript.[23] Burnet cites Cavendish on Wolsey's rise, on the relationship between Anne and Henry Percy, and on Wolsey's behavior after his exile; he also leans upon Cavendish's invocation of fortune as a hermeneutic for Wolsey's rise and fall.[24] Yet, like Heylyn, Burnet did not share Cavendish's ambivalent respect for Wolsey the repentant sinner. Instead, Burnet's assessment of the cardinal distinguishes sharply between Wolsey's work as a statesman and his role as a church leader. In the former capacity, "he was a very extraordinary Person," the bishop-author allows. "But as he was a Churchman, he was the disgrace of his Profession."[25] Burnet alludes to Wolsey's relationship with Joan Larke, calling the cardinal "lewd and vicious," and his *History* likewise accepts at face value one of the more prurient charges brought against Wolsey at the time of his dismissal, namely that he had contracted syphilis, the "French pox."[26]

Perhaps influenced by Cavendish's characterization of the relationship between Wolsey and Henry, Burnet was more forthright than many of his predecessors in acknowledging the king's faults. His preface divides Henry's reign into three periods: the first from his accession through the commencement of the annulment proceedings, the second from then until the separation of the English church from Rome, and the third from the schism until the king's death. Godwin had previously dated Henry's slide into caprice and tyranny from the time of Wolsey's dismissal, but Burnet, far from absolving Wolsey from Henry's misdeeds, blames the cardinal directly for the king's autocratic tendencies: "Cardinal Wolsey had so dissolved his mind into pleasures, and puffed him up with Flattery and servile Compliances, that it was not an easie thing to serve him."[27] However, Burnet argues that even if the king had been unfit, he was an agent of God's providence, however unwitting: "But if we consider the great things that were done by him, we must acknowledge that there was a signal Providence of God, in raising up a King of his temper, for clearing the way to that blessed Work that followed."[28]

Let us pause to recall that historians such as Fuller, Heylyn, and Burnet were not writing biographies of Wolsey. They were less prone than their sixteenth-century predecessors to sacrifice accuracy about the specific details of Wolsey's life in order to pursue polemical agendas, true, but none of them set out to produce an independent account of the cardinal's life. Instead, they represented him chiefly as a leading actor in the events of the Henrician Reformation.

Two late-seventeenth-century antiquarians, John Aubrey and Anthony Wood, had a different purpose in mind when they wrote short biographies of Wolsey for their collections. Both Wood's *Athenae Oxonienses*, a catalogue of the achievements of notable alumni of the University of Oxford (1691), and the compilation that came to be known as Aubrey's *Brief Lives* (1693) include entries on Wolsey.[29] The two texts are closely linked, since Aubrey served as Wood's research assistant until they parted ways when Wood was prosecuted for libel as a result of sloppy research Aubrey allegedly had conducted.[30]

For Wood, few of the traditional criticisms of Wolsey held water. What others had called Wolsey's pride, Wood dubbed his "vast mind, and a great sense of regulation, and glory." Wolsey's ostentation Wood celebrated as "great splendor," noting that he "left the most lasting and most noble Monuments of his Bounty." Wolsey's ambition for the papacy Wood considered to have been stillborn from the beginning, owing to his age and his refusal to move to Rome if elected.[31] It is not surprising that Wood concluded his encomium of the cardinal with a plea for more sympathetic analysis:

> Many Historians of that time, whether out of envy of his Order, or contempt of his Birth, or hatred of his Religion, have not been very favourable to his fame, and the traditionary reporters since, who have pretended to an exact account of his actions, have, upon too slight enquiries, and with too great confidence, transcribed the former narratives. So that we yet want an exact and faithful History of the greatest, most noble, and most disinterested Clergyman of that age.[32]

Aubrey, likewise, praised Wolsey as "a great Builder" whose architectural achievements included the tower of Magdalen College, York Place (the later Whitehall Palace), Hampton Court Palace, and of course Christ Church. Dubbing the cardinal "a most magnificent spirit," Aubrey included in his short biography several episodes from Cavendish's *Life*, among them the story of the falling cross that injured one of Wolsey's chaplains and was thought to have foretold the cardinal's arrest.[33] Perhaps most memorably, Aubrey's biography features six lines from an elegiac section of a lengthy poem, "Iter Boreale," by the early Stuart bishop Richard Corbet, who cited Wolsey as an example of the transience of earthly authority. Aubrey does not attribute the poem to Corbet but introduces it by describing the circumstances of Wolsey's death and entombment in Leicester, where along with Richard III "he lies buried (to the shame of Christ-church men) yet without any monument":

> And though, from his owne store, Wolsey might have
> A Palace or a Colledge for his Grave,
> Yet here he lies interr'd, as if that all
> Of him to be remembered were his Fall.
> If thou art thus neglected, what shall wee
> Hope after Death that are but Shreds of thee?[34]

A Restoration Drama

Before we move into the eighteenth century, let us pause briefly to return to the theater. The previous chapter analyzed several late Tudor and early Stuart history plays, discussing how they depicted the cardinal. We discovered that while Samuel Rowley's *When You See Me, You Know Me* and the anonymous *Thomas, Lord Cromwell* represented Wolsey along the lines of the evangelical prototype, Shakespeare and Fletcher nuanced his character somewhat after the fashion of Cavendish.[35] However, if the prototype of Wolsey the repentant sinner that originated with Cavendish received only limited attention in Stuart drama, the prototype we traced through Catholic sources like Vergil, Harpsfield, and Sander received hardly any attention at all. Instances of its survival into the seventeenth century can be found only on the European continent, such as in the play *Henricus Octavus* by Nicholas Vernulaeus, the rector of the University of Louvain.[36]

Neither during nor after the years of civil war did any English Catholic playwright dare to produce a drama like Vernulaeus's. Instead, after the restoration of the monarchy and the frenzy over the so-called Popish Plot of the late 1670s and early 1680s, the dramatic portrayal of Catholics on the English stage became even more polemical.[37] Space permits mention of only one example: *Vertue Betray'd; or, Anna Bullen*, which in 1682 John Banks added to the many anti-Catholic dramas that had been appearing in London.[38] The play, the first in a number of years to take the Henrician court as its setting, became an instant dramatic and commercial success. It was printed immediately, with fourteen further editions following through 1800.[39] While little is known about Banks personally, his play tightly embraces contemporary antipapist sentiments. In *Vertue Betray'd*, Wolsey is the "consummate villain" who schemes, quite anachronistically, to bring about Anne Boleyn's downfall by fabricating allegations of adultery against her. Equally anachronistically, Banks assigns as Wolsey's accomplice Elizabeth Blunt, Henry VIII's onetime mistress, who begrudges the king his infatuation with Anne. As Diane Dreher has pointed out, the play's historical inaccuracies and its diabolical caricatures of Wolsey cannot be put down to Banks's ignorance, since the publication of even a highly expurgated version of Cavendish's *Life* had "made the story too familiar for that." Instead, "by combining the villainy of Wolsey with that of Thomas Cromwell and further emphasizing his degeneracy by giving him a liaison with Blunt and proud ranting speeches in which he boasts of his ability to manipulate the King, Banks made the Cardinal an evil caricature of the Catholic Church itself."[40]

A close examination of Banks's text reveals that he depicted perhaps the most villainous Wolsey to date. Both Wolsey's speeches and those of other characters associate the cardinal with two places of horrific repute: Rome and hell. News of Anne's coronation, Henry Percy announces in the play's first scene, was suppressed, "so long kept secret,/[By] our great Cardinal's Delays, and Tricks/Of *Rome*, which *Harry* has with Frowns discover'd."[41] Wolsey demonstrates throughout the play that he owes greater allegiance to Rome than to England; even in his earliest appearance, he expostulates against Anne in language that goes well beyond the "spleeny Lutheran" epithet that Shakespeare and Fletcher's cardinal had spat out. "A *Lutheran* Queen upon the Throne of *England*!/She to lye in the Bosom of our Prince!/A Buxom King, that for a wanton Smile/Will pawn his Faith, and turn an Heretick!"[42] Plotting with Blunt, Wolsey does not hesitate to invoke, even if conditionally, the powers of the devil: "I will retire, and leave him to your Care,/To mannage him with all the Art of Woman;/And Hell, if Heaven wont [*sic*], inspire your Wit/and Malice."[43] Toward the end of the play, it is the young Princess Elizabeth, whom Banks represents as the hero of the Protestant cause, who sees the truth about Wolsey most clearly:

> *Child* [i.e., Elizabeth]. Cause I love none so well as you——
> But oh you'l never hear me what I have to say,
> As long as He, that Devil there, stands by
> Your Elbow.
>   *King*. Ha! what Devil?
>   *Child*. That Red Thing there.
>   *King*. Oh Child; He is no Devil, he's a Cardinal.
>   *Child*. Why does he wear that huge, long Coat then?
> Unless it be to hide his Cloven Feet.[44]

Banks's identification of Wolsey with the devil caps off his thoroughgoing embrace of the evangelical prototype.

Eighteenth-Century Historians

We will return in the next two chapters to Wolsey's appearances in plays, pageants, and eventually film and television productions. As we will see in Chapter 5, with very few exceptions, it was not for at least two hundred years that more sympathetic portrayals of the cardinal appeared on the stage and (eventually) the screen. In the closing years of the seventeenth century through the end of the eighteenth, however, Wolsey was represented almost exclusively in the pages of prose works of history. Among them was the *Ecclesiastical History of Great Britain* by Jeremy Collier, an Anglican clergyman who, following the 1689 accession of King William III and Queen Mary II had lost his church offices as a nonjuror (that is, for refusing to swear fealty to the new monarchs on the grounds that their predecessor, James II, had never officially abdicated). Collier, perhaps more famous as a moralistic critic of the theater than as a historian, was among the most prominent nonjurors. He famously granted absolution to two of his fellows just before they were executed for allegedly participating in a plot to assassinate King William.[45] In the 1710s he began to pastor a nonjuring congregation in London; in 1713 he was consecrated a bishop; and in 1716 he became primus, first among equals, of the nonjuring episcopal bench. Collier published his *Ecclesiastical History of Great Britain* in two substantial folio volumes in 1708 and 1714. As J. Hopes and Eric Salmon have characterized it, the *Ecclesiastical History* upheld the church's independence from the crown and presented nonjurors like Collier "as the representatives of an unchanging ecclesiastical tradition handed down from the early church," in comparison with which royal authority was of much more recent vintage.[46]

Collier's second volume opens with the accession of Henry VIII. Collier characterizes one of Henry's earliest decisions—marrying Katherine of Aragon against his father's deathbed wishes—in unflattering terms. "When he came into his own Conduct, his Fancy govern'd the matter, and made him forget his Father's Instructions."[47] Here and elsewhere, Collier frames the king as governed more by emotion than by rationality. As in Herbert's and Burnet's accounts, these dimensions of Henry's character offered Wolsey an opportunity to rise to power. In Collier's terms, the future cardinal "charg'd to make his Interest with the King with too much Art, to apply to his Inclination, and gratify his Fancy, without regard to the Merit of the Case. The King being young was govern'd by his Diversions: Wolsey perceiving the bent of his Humour, undertook to ease him of the Fatigues of Business."[48] However, as Collier's narrative develops, Henry's unpredictability eventually costs Wolsey his position and his life: "To speak softly," Collier admits, "the King crush'd this Minister with a very indifferent Grace."[49]

Collier explicitly weighs the opinions of earlier writers against one another as well as against original documents. For instance, with regard to the origins of Henry's annulment, he notes that whereas Herbert had argued that Henry desired more than anything else to become head of the English clergy, and whereas Sander had attributed Henry's scruples to

Wolsey's vengeance and manipulation, Cavendish, "who seems to have been much in his Secrets, gives another Account of the Matter."[50] In another passage, Collier criticizes Cavendish for blaming Wolsey's fall too much on Anne's ill will. He argues that Wolsey "was very sincere in the King's Business; and prosecuted the Divorce with all the Heartiness and Application imaginable."[51] Using Anne's flattering letters to the cardinal as evidence, he somewhat naively claims that Cavendish and Herbert were incorrect that Anne helped bring Wolsey down in retribution for his having broken off her engagement to Percy.

Overall, Collier represents Wolsey as a loyal servant, one whom the king unfairly punished for the failure of his annulment. The terms in which Collier describes Wolsey pay tribute to his abilities as an administrator: He was "a Person of great Industry and Dispatch," a "Person of great Parts and Industry," who "had deservedly the Reputation of an Able minister and was courted by the Greatest Princes."[52] With regard to the monasteries he dissolved to found his colleges, Collier both praises monastic life ("the Monks deserved a fairer Character than is sometimes given them. . . . They were far from being Enemies to Learning") and notes that Wolsey, "govern'd by the Principles of the Age," did nothing especially unusual in transferring the goods of monastic houses to the equally religious purposes of his educational establishments. In implicit contrast to the later dissolutions under Cromwell, Wolsey "did not alienate the Revenues from *religious* Service, but only made a Change in the Disposal."[53] Collier denies the substance of many of the charges against Wolsey that were presented in the Parliament of 1529, and he explicitly rejects Foxe's characterization of Wolsey as an image for the Roman clergy. Foxe, Collier writes, "makes the Cardinal a sort of Pattern, by which we are to judge the rest of the Hierarchy. . . . Can any thing be more injudicious, and lean-temper'd, than to throw the Blemishes of a single Person, upon a whole Order of Men?"[54] Nevertheless, Collier is not reticent about identifying Wolsey's faults. Specifically, the cardinal relied too much on his status as a papal legate; he cared too much for "Pomp and secular Grandeur"; and, as we have already noted, he was too ready to facilitate the king's desires.[55]

Collier, like most writers before him, assessed Wolsey in the course of his narrative of Henry's reign and reformation. As we have seen, such texts demonstrate less interest in Wolsey as an individual than as a character, or even a caricature, in a broader story. It was not until the decade after the publication of Collier's history that an author set out to produce a detailed *biography* of Wolsey—a different kind of text, one that placed the cardinal, rather than the king, the monarchy, the church, or any other individual or institution, at its center. The author of *The Life of Cardinal Wolsey* (1724), the first book-length prose biography since Cavendish's *Life* and the most extensive treatment of Wolsey since Storer's little-known elegy, was Richard Fiddes, an Anglican clergyman from Yorkshire. His Wolsey biography appeared in the year before his death and constituted, as Richard Sharp has argued, "a work of notable originality" that "attracted much interest." Like Burnet's *History*, it "was supported by 260 pages of original documents."[56]

In his preface, Fiddes states that he has written Wolsey's biography for three interconnected reasons. First, he wishes to commemorate Wolsey as a patron of learning and literature, particularly in connection with his foundations in Ipswich and Oxford.[57] Fiddes was himself an Oxford man, matriculating at Corpus Christi College and taking his BA in 1691 as a member of University College.[58] The second of his stated purposes is historiographically the most significant: "a Desire of doing Justice to his injured Memory." Fiddes explains himself in these terms:

> There have been few Persons, if any, to whom Mankind has been
> obliged for any considerable Benefactions, that have met with such
> ungrateful Usage in Return of them, as Cardinal Wolsey. . . . The
> Historians, on both Sides, have in general transmitted his Name down
> to Posterity, with equal Rancour, and Bigotry to the Party, which they
> professed to espouse. Those of the Romish Persuasion hated him, as
> he had promoted the Divorce with much Zeal and Assiduity. . . . The
> Reformed, on the other Hand, were his Enemies for adhering strictly
> to the Doctrine and Communion of the Church of Rome.[59]

According to Fiddes, reformers and traditionalists alike had allowed their religious convictions to prohibit them from taking a fuller view of Wolsey's character. He argues that "certain authentick Monuments, relating to him, which do not depend on the Credit of either Party" have been neglected, and in the *Life* he seeks explicitly to rehabilitate the cardinal's character by reference to documents such as these.[60] For his own part, however, Fiddes is clear about his religious allegiance, and the third reason he gives for writing is to demonstrate that the English Reformation was "a regular, and ecclesiastical Method of Procedure; according to the primitive Constitution, and true Rights of the christian Church."[61] While in the *Life* Fiddes seeks to rescue Wolsey from some of the criticisms his reputation had suffered, he is not shy about criticizing the church of Rome or defending episcopalianism as a divinely authorized form of church polity.[62] However, he still rejects strongly what he calls the tendency of previous historians to ransack Wolsey's life for evidence of the corruption of Rome. Indeed, "it was with a false View of doing some Service to the reformed Religion, that the Memory of Cardinal Wolsey, whose Power and Post in that Church which opposed it was so great, has been most injuriously treated."[63]

Fiddes's desire to restore Wolsey's good name strongly inflects the content and method of his book. At several points, he explicitly employs what we might call a hermeneutic of charity. He articulates this dimension of his method most explicitly in the context of the cardinal's negotiations with France. Rejecting Polydore Vergil's characterization of Wolsey's foreign policy, Fiddes writes:

> To what has been said before, I only beg Leave to add the following Observation, That this Writer [i.e., Vergil] ascribes the whole Conduct of the Cardinal, in transacting this Affair, to ill and unworthy Motives: If Historians had a Right, where they have any personal Prejudice, to take such a Liberty, how easy might they often find it to resolve the best Actions, upon one Pretence or other, into the worst Principles. *But certainly Reasons both of common Justice and Humanity require, That, where the natural Appearances of Things will admit, and there is no good or certain Evidence to the contrary, we should rather ascribe the Counsels and Conduct of Men, to honourable, or at least to innocent Motives.*[64]

Fiddes employs this interpretive tool repeatedly in the *Life*. For example, he excuses Wolsey's vengeance upon Amias Paulet by claiming that the cardinal was defending the rights of the clergy against lay incursion. With regard to the execution of the Duke of Buckingham, he argues that Wolsey had simply been doing his duty as "Prime Minister" and that the duke's conviction by his peers demonstrated that he was indeed guilty.[65] In only a few cases does Fiddes admit that he cannot defend Wolsey's conduct, for instance with regard to the ongoing rivalry between the cardinal and Archbishop Warham.[66] More often, Fiddes's hyperbole tends in the opposite direction, and his charity leads him to reach conclusions that are more than a little exaggerated. Praising Wolsey for his generosity toward Oxford, Fiddes declares that "History affordeth us very few equal, but scarce any superior Characters" and that Wolsey's benefactions in support of learning "will ever transmit his Name with Honour to Posterity; and be an excellent Precedent, whereby, they, who are invested with the same Powers in the Church, may be taught to regulate the Use and Application of them."[67] By comparing Wolsey favorably, and at length, to his Spanish contemporary

Cardinal Francisco Ximenes de Cisneros, Fiddes introduces a new analogy into anglophone discourse about Wolsey. In terms opposite those of the Stuart puritans who compared Wolsey and Laud in order to taint Laud with Wolsey's poor reputation, Fiddes associates Wolsey with a pre-Reformation Spanish cardinal known for his learning, generosity, and statesmanship.[68]

Overall, Fiddes characterizes Wolsey as an indirect cause of what he considers to have been the speedy reception of the English Reformation. Far from treating Wolsey as a typical example of Roman corruption, Fiddes seeks to mitigate some charges about the cardinal's personal conduct—the *Life* never mentions Joan Larke by name and largely demurs in discussing the cardinal's children, for instance.[69] Instead, Fiddes represents Wolsey chiefly as a Catholic reformer, one who, while "averse to any Innovation in Religion," still employed "his best Efforts, in order to a Reformation of Manners, and especially of all scandalous Disorders, whether among the regular or secular Clergy."[70] Because Wolsey's attempts to reform the clergy shone a light on clerical corruption and thereby converted many to the evangelical cause, Fiddes argues, "he may, in this respect, be considered as one of the occasional Causes at least of the surprising Progress, which in a short time after the Reformation made in Great Britain."[71]

Fiddes's admiration for Wolsey contrasts strongly with his assessment of Henry VIII. About the king, Fiddes writes: "Without descending into the Detail of his Character, there was found so great a Variety in it, of good and less commendable Qualities, that it sometimes appears hard to determine . . . which of them operated with more Force."[72] However, like Herbert and Burnet, Fiddes observes that Henry's cruelty showed itself more after Wolsey's dismissal, when the cardinal was no longer there to restrain it. Fiddes represents Wolsey as a hesitant but publicly unequivocal champion of Henry's annulment. His narrative of the interaction between the king and cardinal in the fateful years 1529 and 1530 closely follows Cavendish, and Fiddes is the first of our authors to note explicitly that the printed editions of Cavendish's *Life*, which descended from Sheares's 1641 version, omit crucial material such as Cavendish's ascription of Wolsey's fall to the vengeance of Anne Boleyn.[73] But Fiddes adds to and departs from Cavendish in several instances. Like Collier before him, Fiddes hypothesizes that Wolsey's death may have been hastened not by the cardinal but by someone who intended him ill.[74] And Fiddes takes the final words that Cavendish ascribes to Wolsey—the famous quip about God having abandoned him in his gray hairs—to apply not to the overall conduct of his life but instead only to the way in which "he exceeded in too obsequious a

Compliance with the Will of a Prince, who rewarded him after the Manner we have mentioned."[75] In the end, Fiddes argues that Wolsey's actions in his final years are the best evidence of his character:

> Therefore the inflexible Vertue and Constancy of Cardinal Wolsey, during so great and severe a Trial, and over which he finally triumphed, is what I would leave an Impression of upon the Reader's Mind. For if it do not prove, what it is not intended to do, that he was a Man of consummate Vertue, it must be admitted at least . . . that he was a Man of Honour and Probity.[76]

Fiddes's *Life of Cardinal Wolsey* attracted a large number of subscribers, many of whom, as Richard Sharp has noted, were "high-church, high-tory, and nonjuring in character."[77] A second, corrected edition appeared in 1726, and Fiddes's biography remained a standard work for some time, even though few modern scholars have studied it in detail. It certainly inspired Fiddes's near-contemporary Joseph Grove, an Oxfordshire attorney, to write his *History of the Life and Times of Cardinal Wolsey, Prime Minister to King Henry VIII*, which was published in four volumes in 1742. Grove specifically positions his study as a successor to and enlargement upon Fiddes's biography, arguing that "the Doctor himself seemed to hint, that the History of the Affairs of Europe ought to accompany that of the Life of the Cardinal."[78] In many ways, this is an understatement: Grove's volumes treat European affairs at far greater length than Wolsey's life. Grove's books are also textually unusual: He reprints the entirety of the 1641 edition of Cavendish's *Life* on the bottom half of the first few dozen pages of each volume; in the third volume, he does the same with long excerpts from *King Henry VIII*. In the preface to his work, Grove avers that he has implemented this idiosyncratic design in order to demonstrate what is and is not included in Cavendish's narrative, but the result is an unusual and confusing visual layout.[79] Moreover, since Grove reprints the 1641 edition of the *Life* but refers in his text to episodes missing from that highly expurgated edition, there are striking incongruities between what Grove says about the *Life* and the version of that text he prints.[80]

There is little original material in Grove's biography: The *History* tends to repeat and amplify themes from Fiddes's more substantial work, such as his comparison between Wolsey and Ximenes, but one of the few ways in which Grove differs from Fiddes is in his avowed purpose for writing.[81] Fiddes stated that one of his goals in writing the *Life* was to rescue Wolsey from the charges of those who had unjustly slandered him. Grove, on the other hand, is concerned to seem impartial, and he articulates a rationale for writing that has more to do with exemplarity than with the attempt to right a perceived historiographical injustice:

> The Character of a bad Minister, stigmatiz'd in History for giving such Counsels, and pursuing such Measures, as were most injurious to the publick Good, must have a Tendency in it to deter all that are in the same high Trusts, from a shameful Misapplication of their Talents. . . . As, on the contrary, the Life of a good minister . . . will help to Infuse into the Hearts of others such an Emulation as to follow his great Example.[82]

But Grove's assertions of impartiality notwithstanding, in almost all of the instances where writers had previously called Wolsey's conduct into question, Grove seeks to excuse the cardinal. He strives most commonly to defend Wolsey's reputation from the attacks of a recent French Protestant, Paul de Rapin, whose *Histoire de l'Angleterre* (1724) he cites repeatedly.[83] Where Rapin had inveighed against Wolsey's love for pomp and ceremony, for instance, Grove responds that not only did other leading churchmen go in procession with their crosses but also employed temporal lords to serve them at mass.[84] Likewise, Grove endorses Fiddes's account of Wolsey's role in the trial of the Duke of Buckingham, quoting his predecessor: "If the Duke was really guilty, wherein did Wolsey do amiss?"[85] With regard to the supposed rivalry between Wolsey and Warham, however, Grove is somewhat more circumspect, repeating the claims of other writers more often than venturing his own opinions. He does, however, print a 1528 letter from Warham to Wolsey in which the aged archbishop thanked the cardinal for permitting him to have an apartment at Hampton Court.[86]

Wolsey and Catholic Emancipation: The Early Nineteenth Century

Throughout this book, we have seen that political and social crises such as the English civil wars and the Glorious Revolution have shaped representations of Wolsey. As Rosemary O'Day has rightly observed, the early nineteenth century witnessed new controversies that affected Reformation historiography, namely "the debate about Roman Catholic emancipation which culminated in the passing of the Emancipation Act in 1829."[87] English Catholics had gradually been restored their civil and political freedoms starting in the last quarter of the eighteenth century: Their rights of inheritance were guaranteed in 1778 and their freedom of worship in 1791.[88] However, full emancipation and civil equality, including the right to sit in Parliament, to attend the English universities, and to celebrate marriages and funerals in public, continued to be stoutly resisted by the Anglican establishment. Some Anglican historians invoked specters from the sixteenth century—Catholic persecution under Mary Tudor and Catholic treason under Elizabeth—to justify the continued denial of political rights to their countrymen.

Both Anglican and Catholic histories of the English Reformation—the former far outnumbering the latter—appeared in the decades leading up to full emancipation. As a rule, historiographical controversy focused more on the reigns of Edward, Mary, and Elizabeth than that of Henry: The later reigns, after all, had featured religious policies with more consistent theological underpinnings. But historians did not neglect Henry's reign, and they continued to employ Wolsey as a foil. In this section, we will examine three representative works from this period—the Protestant writer John Galt's biography of Wolsey, the long-form history of the Catholic priest John Lingard, and the counterhistory published by the anti-Roman Anglican controversialist Henry Soames.[89]

Galt's *Life and Administration of Cardinal Wolsey* (1811) was his first book and the first biography of Wolsey to appear since Grove's. Recognized more as a novelist than a historian, Galt was born in 1779 in Irvine, on the west coast of Scotland, and came of age as a writer amid the surge of interest in historical fiction inaugurated by his fellow countryman Walter Scott.[90] Galt's book on Wolsey was his only major work of nonfiction, and it is not without its deficiencies. Among other substantial mistakes, Galt characterizes the famously ascetic bishop of Rochester, John Fisher, as opulent, and he claims that Wolsey's onetime usher was the same Cavendish who founded the modern line of dukes of Devonshire.[91]

One might charitably call Galt's treatment of Wolsey ambivalent, but to speak more plainly, Galt's book presents a muddled and confused picture of its subject. From his opening pages, it is evident that Galt's sympathies are against the Roman church. He alleges that in the later Middle Ages, "the means by which the papal power was upheld and exercised, were as wonderful as the alleged extent of its prerogatives." Galt calls clerical liberties "pernicious," argues that the Roman priesthood required people to "slavishly obey its authority," and characterized the age as one of "the fulness of the ecclesiastical usurpation."[92] Galt sprinkles similar characterizations of Wolsey throughout his biography. Discussing the marriage of Henry's sister Mary with the Duke of Suffolk, for instance, Galt repeats a contemporary rumor that Wolsey and Suffolk "have dealings with Satan, by which they rule the king for their own ends."[93] Galt alleges that as chancellor, Wolsey "may be regarded as the dictator of England," and although he admits that the cardinal had many intellectual and political gifts, Galt avers that Wolsey used those gifts in a way that "seemed then only calculated to acquire and secure respect."[94] In addition, while Galt depends on Cavendish for many details of Wolsey's life, especially the circumstances of his exile and death, Galt assigns different moral weight to the events that Cavendish described. As an example, Galt repeats Cavendish's claim that the fallen Wolsey had taken up traditional religious practices—such as wearing a hair shirt, consulting a confessor at the Charterhouse in Richmond, and relying on prophesies and omens—but Galt character-izes Wolsey's transformation quite differently. "Like many other great men in adversity, his mind took a superstitious turn, and seemed to dis-cover, in accidents certainly trivial, an ominous and fatal meaning."[95] Galt thus associates the cardinal's newfound devotion with practices that had been characterized as superstitious by Protestants from the sixteenth century down to Galt's own day.

Yet at the same time, Galt's *Life and Administration* seeks to defend the cardinal from many of the criticisms that we have seen being made against him. Galt asserts that Wolsey did not accept bribes from foreign powers and was not influenced by the gifts he did receive: Instead, the cardinal's aim was ever to "restore the equilibrium of Europe," a goal so lofty that both Wolsey's contemporaries and later historians failed to understand it.[96] The trial of Buckingham was a fair process, and while Londoners genuinely mourned the duke's execution, this was "rather a proof of the generosity of the people and of his own popularity, than evidence of innocence, or of the machiavelism [*sic*] ascribed by contemporary historians to the cardi-nal."[97] With regard to Wolsey's religious policy, Galt, like Fiddes before him, describes the cardinal as a Catholic reformer. He even goes so far as to suggest that had it not been for Wolsey, the full corruption of the Roman system might not have become known: "To disclose the whole tur-pitude of the ecclesiastical abodes of England, and to propose a system of gradual reformation, was reserved for cardinal Wolsey."[98] However, for Galt, Wolsey's purpose was to improve clerical morals without precipitat-ing the overthrow of the Roman system, and Galt characterizes Wolsey's pursuit of legatine powers, the establishment of his legatine court, and the ways in which he visually linked the prerogatives he had received from the pope with those he held from the king as attempts on the cardinal's part to shore up devotion to Rome. As his argument advances, Galt even goes so far as to compare Wolsey with Ignatius of Loyola, the founder of the Society of Jesus: "The aim of his designs was, to obtain for the priesthood, generally, the same kind of influence which the institutes of Loyola, afterward, so wonderfully ministered to procure for the famous society of the Jesuits. It was calculated to render them entitled to possess superiority, although directed to preserve their exclusive privileges."[99] For Galt, Wolsey had sought reform, but only within the confines of a papal system that Galt takes on its face to be dictatorial and corrupt.

John Lingard shared Galt's assessments of certain episodes in Wolsey's career, but he interpreted the overall significance of the cardinal's life in a substantially different fashion. Lingard, the first "Roman Catholic in modern times to write a comprehensive history of England," began publishing his *History of England* in 1819.[100] It was a commercial success, with more than five hundred copies of the first three volumes selling out in a week. A secular priest, Lingard faced almost immediate criticism from Protestant commentators for allowing his religious beliefs to affect his historiographical judgment; in contrast, and predictably, many of his fellow Catholics showered him with praise. Lingard produced the volumes of his history that dealt with the Reformation at the height of the debate over Catholic emancipation, when English Catholics represented no more than 1 percent of the British population.[101] He wrote in the face of an almost entirely Protestant, mostly Anglican, historical guild whose overall conclusions were not much different from Galt's. He also worked amid intra-Catholic debates between Jesuit and secular clergy, and his works were frequently thought to have the goal of bringing about full emancipation. John Vidmar has argued, however, that Lingard subordinated politics to scholarship: "Whether Catholics gained their freedom or not, the Reformation story still needed to be told. . . . He wanted to tell a true story. Then Emancipation would come."[102]

In some respects, Lingard's account of the English Reformation resembles those of Tudor Catholic historian-polemicists. Like Harpsfield and Sander, Lingard did not scruple to name Henry VIII's failings, including by cataloguing the mistresses who had preceded Anne Boleyn. Lingard echoes as well those Anglican historians such as Godwin who had argued that the king's proclivities had been kept in check only by Wolsey's careful ministrations. Indeed, Lingard concludes his treatment of Wolsey with the observation that "The best eulogy on his character is to be found in the contrast between the conduct of Henry before, and after the cardinal's fall. As long as Wolsey continued in favor, the royal passions were confined within certain bounds; the moment his influence was extinguished, they burst through every restraint."[103]

Lingard represents Wolsey as a wholly capable, deeply loyal, but appropriately unassertive servant of a royal master who was very much in charge. This representation is in keeping with one of the aims of Lingard's *History*, namely to present Catholicism as something other than "a disloyal, seditious, and 'foreign' force in Britain."[104] In contrast to Cavendish, Lingard rejects the notion that Wolsey had lulled Henry into a benign neglect of his royal duties. Instead, "the king himself devoted a considerable portion of his time and attention to the cares of government," and in the few cases where Wolsey disagreed with Henry, he was sufficiently dutiful as to defend royal decisions as his own.[105] Thus, Lingard insists that it was not Wolsey who had schemed to bring down the Duke of Buckingham: Buckingham had instead caused his own undoing.[106] And when Henry first broached with the cardinal the possibility of annulling his marriage, according to Lingard, "the royal wish was no sooner communicated to Wolsey, than he offered his aid, and ventured to promise complete success."[107] However, Lingard claims that Wolsey was unaware of the king's desire to marry Anne Boleyn, and the more that Wolsey learned about the king's intentions, the more hesitant he became. Wolsey's about-face angered Henry, but it angered Anne more, and following Cavendish, Lingard presents the queen-to-be as Wolsey's primary enemy. She engineers the abrupt termination of Wolsey's final interview with Henry, and it is at her urging that Wolsey is charged with violating the statute of praemunire. "Nothing could be more iniquitous than this prosecution," Lingard asserts, since it was clear that Wolsey had always acted with the king's permission.[108] Lingard closely follows Cavendish for the final year of Wolsey's life, representing the cardinal's despair at his dismissal, his pastoral work in the north of England, the unexpected shock of his arrest, and his declining health all along the lines of the *Life*.

In sharp contrast to Lingard, opponents of Catholic emancipation reiterated many of the criticisms of Wolsey they had inherited from Tudor evangelicals. Characteristic of this historiographical approach was the work of Henry Soames, an Essex clergyman who ended his career as chancellor of St. Paul's Cathedral. In Soames's *History of the Reformation of the Church of England* (1828) and *Reasons for Opposing the Romish Claims* (1829), he explicitly rejected political freedom for Catholics on the grounds that they would seek to restore "the lost ascendancy of their sect." Although he did not refer to Lingard by name, Soames likely had him in mind when he charged that "as one step towards the attainment of this object, they have industriously revived various calumnies and misrepresentations by which opponents of a former day sought to render the Reformers odious and contemptible."[109] In response, Soames recited a litany of the crimes and misrepresentations of the Roman church, going all the way back to the arrival of Christianity in the British Isles. Romans burned lollards, the predecessors of latter-day Anglicans. Henry VIII was in such thrall to Rome that even after his break from the papacy he continued to burn people for denying transubstantiation.[110] And Henry relied so much on Wolsey, who in Soames's narrative exemplifies the ostentation and corruption of Rome, that the cardinal was able to plant in Henry's mind scruples about his marriage. While Soames takes from our Tudor Catholic prototype the charge that Wolsey sought the annulment of Henry's marriage as a form of vengeance, Soames appropriates his account of Wolsey's fall from evangelical histories instead. Wolsey "wholly ruined himself by his double dealing as to the king's matrimonial cause," Soames charges, and even in his exile in Yorkshire, the cardinal "was forming conspiracies against the government both in England, and with Rome."[111] Soames's historical works all but explicitly contend that Catholicism goes hand in hand with falsehood and treason; consequently, it would be foolish for England to offer a civil or political foothold to such subjects as Wolsey had been.

Remembering Wolsey at Hampton Court Palace

Soames did not get his way. And not more than a decade after Parliament approved the Roman Catholic Relief Act of 1829, Queen Victoria opened Hampton Court Palace to the public, free of charge. Her decision was both novel and controversial: As Adrian Tinniswood has observed, "Nothing like this had ever happened before, and not surprisingly, such a radical move provoked strong opposition and dire warnings of vandalism, drunkenness, and violent behavior."[112] But before we consider further Victoria's generosity with one of the most storied of her palaces, we must pause to address briefly the manner in which historic sites and their material contents can commemorate and represent Wolsey's life—a manner that both resembles and differs from the textual representations we have been discussing thus far. One difference, of course, is of audience: Some of the works we have encountered, such as Burnet's *History of the Reformation*, reached a wide enough readership, but the majority of them enjoyed only limited circulation. In contrast, in the 1840s and 1850s more than two hundred thousand visitors, many of them from the working classes, made visits to Wolsey's former palace. Today, nearly six hundred thousand tourists from around the world stream through its gates annually.[113]

The French historiographer Pierre Nora has written compellingly of what he calls *lieux de mémoire*—places that, by virtue of their historical or cultural significance, possess a particular capacity to preserve and pass on memories of earlier times.[114] More recently, Marius Kwint has catalogued the various ways in which material objects, whether as large as a palace or as small as a coin in a museum exhibit, can shape memory. Some objects deliberately serve the purpose of memory: Both a monument in a town square and a souvenir brought back from a special vacation have memorialization as an express aim. But other objects create the possibility for "serendipitious encounter, bringing back experiences which otherwise would have remained dormant, repressed, or forgotten."[115] Therefore, "objects have consequences. . . . Human memory has undergone a mutual evolution with the objects that inform it. . . . The relationship between them is dialectical."[116] We must therefore consider how material objects have played a role in the representation and commemoration of Wolsey.

There are relatively few items of Wolsey's that remain extant. With a few exceptions, his clothes, his books, and his devotional paraphernalia have all been lost. Even the location of his bones is uncertain, and the monument to him in the grounds of Leicester's Abbey Park only approximates the whereabouts of his gravesite.[117] Many of Wolsey's papers, which tend to be more of an administrative than a personal nature, do survive, and in the next chapter we will explore how the publication of them in the middle of the nineteenth century substantially influenced scholarly treatments of the cardinal and the English Reformation. But just as in the case of Christopher Wren, whose monument in the crypt of St. Paul's Cathedral bears the inscription "*Lector, si monumentum requiris, circumspice*" (Reader, if you seek his memorial, look around you), the most notable *lieux de mémoire* for Wolsey are his large-scale building projects, especially Christ Church (formerly Cardinal College) and Magdalen College Tower in Oxford and Hampton Court Palace in Surrey.

Hampton Court has experienced the historical vicissitudes of Wolsey's representation and commemoration perhaps more than any other place, and this section therefore takes the palace as a case study.[118] Since the royal family left in the mid–eighteenth century, Hampton Court has existed in a variety of guises: as a semiprivate art gallery, a residence for courtiers, a site for archaeological and historical research, and most recently a historical attraction that, in its present incarnation, understands itself more as a heritage site than a museum.[119] The palace memorializes other individuals besides the cardinal, of course, but from the time of Victoria's opening of the palace, Wolsey has never been far from the minds of curators and visitors. As the civil servant and renovator Edward Jesse wrote in the first guidebook that was published after the palace's public opening, "Spacious

and splendid, however, as the palace may be, it is on that account more calculated to convey a striking lesson on the mutability of human greatness.
That lesson is laid before us in the life of the founder of this enormous
pile of building, and that founder was the celebrated Cardinal Wolsey."[120]
The writers of subsequent guidebooks likewise tied Hampton Court to
Wolsey, and by 1890, the palace had acquired at least one new legend ce-
menting this mnemonic link. Ernest Law, a barrister and Hampton Court
resident who devoted much of his later life to the palace, wrote about the
"Cardinal Spider":

> This enormous insect, with its fat, reddish-brown body and long
> jointed hairy legs, often attains the size of five inches in width; and,
> when seen crawling about a bed-room at night, will startle even
> persons of tolerably composed nerves. It is alleged to be a kind of
> spider peculiar to Wolsey's palace, and being in some mysterious way
> connected with his disastrous fate, to be destined for ever to haunt the
> scene of his former greatness.[121]

Law hastened to add that the spider, *Tegenaria guyonii* or *domestica*, while
present in surprisingly large numbers at Hampton Court, is not unique to
the site. It is not surprising, however, that at the palace this unusual speci-
men is associated with Wolsey, whom Skelton, as well as Shakespeare and
Fletcher, had represented as a spider spinning a web in which to ensnare
the kingdom of England.[122]

Not a few questions about Hampton Court's architectural history remain unanswered, and there has been a vigorous technical debate about
the circumstances of its construction and reconstruction.[123] We know that
Wolsey leased the site in 1514 from the Order of St. John of Jerusalem,
who had held the land since the first half of the thirteenth century.[124]
Located up the Thames from Westminster, Hampton Court held a series
of attractions for the cardinal: distance from the capital, access to the river,
clear air and drinking water, and a sizeable plot. Around the year 1525,
Wolsey formally granted the palace to Henry, who returned the favor by
licensing the cardinal to reside there.[125] By the time of Wolsey's dismissal,
Henry had made the palace his own, and in the year of the cardinal's exile
the king undertook a substantial program of rebuilding.[126]

Henry's renovations remade Wolsey's palace in the king's image. The
hall was demolished and a larger structure built; the chapel was lavishly
redecorated; and royal iconography was added throughout, including statues of majestic beasts like griffons and lions.[127] Perhaps most significantly
for our purposes, Henry's workmen defaced or hid reminders of the

cardinal's ownership. Among them was a terracotta representation of Wolsey's arms that had been placed above the gateway of Clock Court, the second of the palace's courtyards. Henry's builders covered up Wolsey's iconography and replaced it with the royal arms; the original stonework was uncovered only in 1879, in the course of a series of renovations to the gatehouse (see Plate 11).[128] Those renovations were so skillfully done that when Law wrote his history of the palace ten years later, he mistook the display as having never been altered: "It is strange it should have remained undisturbed by Henry VIII, who afterwards substituted his own arms and cognizances everywhere."[129] Law is correct, of course, that Henry was famous for obliterating the memory of those who he believed had betrayed him, for instance ordering the destruction of countless Anne Boleyn monograms after the queen's execution.[130] As we will see in Chapter 5, Hilary Mantel's *Wolf Hall* novels reflect at some length on how Henry shaped his court's memory of the past.

Hampton Court remained an active palace through the middle of the eighteenth century, witnessing such major events as the Hampton Court Conference, which led to the production of the Authorized Version of the Bible. Parliament assigned the palace to be Oliver Cromwell's chief residence as Lord Protector, and after the revolutions of the seventeenth century, Hampton Court was substantially expanded under William and Mary. Wren, the royal architect, sought to replace almost all of the Tudor portions of the palace, but a financial shortfall meant that he had to leave much of the original site intact, including rooms used by Wolsey's guests and senior retainers.[131] Upon the death of George II's daughter Caroline in 1757, the royal family ceased to use the palace, and by the early nineteenth century it had fallen into disrepair.[132] It continued to house a number of "grace and favor" apartments for widows, veterans, and aristocrats. Some residents offered tours for a fee.

Victoria's decision to open the palace to the public brought substantial changes. A site that previously had been the preserve of royalty and the upper classes now began to witness the influx of substantial numbers of tourists, many of them day-trippers from London who, to the scandal of their social superiors, spread picnic blankets in the palace gardens. As Peter Mandler has demonstrated, these Victorian visitors were part of a new (and much misunderstood) phenomenon, that of mass historical tourism. "There was not much contemporary comment on the mass touristic experience, and what there was tended to be snide, uncomprehending condescension from above."[133] Indeed, elite publications such as London's *The Gentleman's Magazine* called the opening of Hampton Court "an unmitigated

disaster," and high-church clergymen complained that the tourists who
flocked to the palace on Sundays were violating the Sabbath.[134] However,
mass tourism constituted "a particularly populist form of respectability,"
and those who journeyed to Hampton Court often did so out of a passion
for specifically English (as opposed to British or European) history, focusing especially on the so-called Olden Time between the Wars of the Roses
and the civil wars. For many, a visit to Hampton Court was one element of
"a dense web of representation that we might today call a multimedia experience." Some tourists had read guidebooks to the site or historical novels
set there; others had viewed paintings or attended dramatic performances
with Tudor themes. During their visits, such well-informed tourists could
integrate the site they saw in front of them with knowledge from these
other sources.[135]

But where in this touristic frenzy was Wolsey? The few guidebooks
and pamphlets about the palace published prior to the 1838 opening had
expressed divided opinions about his legacy. George Bickham's *Deliciae
Brittanicae* (1742) characterized Wolsey the builder of Hampton Court as
"that imperious Prelate, who knew no Bounds to his Avarice, till he was
overthrown at once, by incurring the Displeasure of his Royal, and mu-
nificent Benefactor."[136] A 1778 poem by F. Streeter took a more sympathetic position:

> This stately palace, which learn'd Woolsey rais'd,
> By env'ous tongues to Harry oft was prais'd!
> The jealous King then cast a wishful eye,
> And for the mansion breathes an ardent sigh;
> Soon cashiers Woolsey, and the palace seiz'd,
> (All acts were right, which furious Harry pleas'd!)
> The fallen Prelate found this truth, tho' late,
> "No woman 'scap'd his lust—nor man his hate!"[137]

The tenor of these lines is reminiscent of Cavendish's *Life*, and W. H.
Pyne's *History of the Royal Residences* (1819) amplified Streeter's critique, representing Wolsey as "the last of the enlightened churchmen of old" and
characterizing Henry as sadistic and mendacious. Pyne repeated Cavendish's story of the token of favor that Henry sent Wolsey soon after his
dismissal. This gesture, according to Pyne, "was only intended to deceive:
the monarch debased himself not more by the injustice of the act, than the
ungracious manner in which he discarded his minister."[138]

Once Victoria opened Hampton Court to the public, guidebooks proliferated; in Mandler's terms, these often served as aides-mémoires for mass

tourists, who would prepare for their visits to the palace by learning about its history.[139] Perhaps because they sought to commemorate Wolsey more as an architectural visionary than as a religious or political actor, the majority of those who wrote such publications demonstrated sympathy toward him. Jesse's guide of 1840 sought explicitly to rescue Wolsey from the calumnies of critical historians. Reciting a series of anecdotes from Cavendish, Jesse excused the cardinal in terms that his gentleman-usher would almost certainly have recognized as his own. "Whatever faults Wolsey may have had, it is impossible not to feel for him in his reverse of fortune. . . . We may add that historians appear to have loaded his memory with violent reproaches, unmindful of the obstinate, rapacious, and arbitrary disposition of the master he served, whose reign was much more criminal after the death of his former favorite."[140] Felix Summerly's *Handbook for the Architecture, Tapestries, Paintings, Gardens, and Grounds of Hampton Court* (1843) censured Henry for the "narrow, selfish sensuality" with which he took the palace from its builder, contrasting the king with Wolsey, "the last political priest, bold practical reformer of monastic corruption, (too ripe for his age,) and promoter of learning and of art!"[141] Later, when Ernest Law came to occupy a place of prominence at Hampton Court, his characterizations of Wolsey were outright enthusiastic. The cardinal was "one of the most remarkable figures in our national story," "the real founder of England's Imperial greatness," and, in the title of Law's 1916 biography, *England's First Great War Minister.*[142] Law's many publications, including his three-volume *History of Hampton Court*, helped not only to burnish Wolsey's legacy but also to cement his palace in the English touristic imagination.

Hampton Court's opening inspired a new round of renovation. Attention was particularly paid to the great hall, which Jesse, a surveyor in the Department of Works and Public Buildings, sought to restore beginning in 1840. Jesse added to the hall chivalric banners featuring "the devices of Henry VIII and the arms of Wolsey, and of his several benefices." He hung Tudor tapestries and commissioned Thomas Willement, a noted stained-glass artist, to fill the hall's windows with Tudor iconography. An 1843 guidebook noted that Willement's work included "the arms of the archbishopric of York, and the private arms of the illustrious Cardinal . . . [and] the badges, ciphers, and armorial bearings of Henry VIII, beneath which, in the center of the upper range of lights, is placed a full-length portrait of that monarch . . . [and] the arms, devices and mottos proper to his six queens."[143] In short, Jesse and Willement turned the Great Hall into a symbolically rich shrine to the leading figures of Tudor England (see Plate 12). They did so under very little supervision, whether from Jesse's superiors in government or from the historical and architectural guilds. Their method, as Julia Parker has described it, comprised a "'scattergun' approach to the decorative scheme which incorporated many different Tudor motifs . . . in an apparently indiscriminate explosion of 'Tudor-ness.'"[144] Jesse's and Willement's work did not return the hall to a state in which it had ever historically appeared (indeed, at no point during Henry's reign did the monarch suffer the arms of his former wives, much less his former chancellor, to be displayed alongside his own). Jesse's and Willement's design reflected one nineteenth-century school of thought about historic restoration, one that, in Parker's words, "allowed for the imaginative embellishment (and, in some cases, wholesale recreation) of historical buildings on the basis of an eclectic mix of influences, some architectural precedents and some imagined inventions."[145]

Jesse's and Willement's renovations sparked debate both in their own time and thereafter. We might call them debates about the shape and the limits of commemoration. For these nineteenth-century enthusiasts, the goal of restoration was to provide visitors with a multisensory experience of history, not "to recreate Henry's hall exactly as it would have been. Instead [Jesse] enjoyed the flexibility of picking and choosing elements from the Tudor period, irrespective of whether they were actually displayed there."[146] To this manner of thinking, even if as a matter of historical fact Henry's, Wolsey's, Anne's, and Jane Seymour's arms never appeared simultaneously in the great hall, their display there still conveys to visitors the sense that each of these persons had once occupied the space. By way of contrast, Jesse's and Willement's contemporary Henry Clarke, the author of an 1843 guidebook, argued that to be successful, restorations must "place things *as they were*, and not in accordance with our own notions of *how they should have been*."[147] The former model of commemoration is symbolic and evocative; the latter, literal and realistic.

Debates of this sort have shaped scholarship on curatorship and museum design in the twentieth and early twenty-first centuries as well. As what Parker and Hewison have dubbed the "heritage industry" has undergone professionalization, museums centered on the display of historic objects have given way to heritage sites centered on the experience of visitors.[148] At Hampton Court, the five-hundredth anniversary of Henry's accession to the throne prompted curators to reimagine the display of rooms closely associated with Wolsey in light of a shift to what the Hampton Court curator Brett Dolman has called a "biographic-led approach."[149] Whereas these rooms had previously presented a collection of artworks from the Royal Collection displayed chronologically, beginning in 2007 they were repurposed for the new "Young Henry VIII Exhibition." The exhibition chronicles the years leading up to Henry's first divorce; to design it, Hampton Court curators hired a Dutch firm, Opera, which proposed to frame the exhibit around the life stories of Henry, Wolsey, and Katherine. The designers placed in each room three modern high-backed chairs, on each of which they printed descriptions of how one of the characters might have experienced the events being described in that particular room. For instance, text on a chair in the first room introduces Wolsey in these terms: "Thomas Wolsey was a rising star at the court of Henry VIII. He was a brilliant administrator with one eye for detail and another for opportunity. He knew how to make friends and influence them. Henry was a dynamic new king. Surely there would be splendid rewards for such a loyal and industrious servant?"[150] The exhibit retains some traditional features, for instance displaying the famous Royal Collection paintings of the Battle of the Spurs and the Field of the Cloth of Gold. But, as the palace's internal guide for docents describes it, unequivocally the Young Henry exhibit "is a bold departure from the rest of the palace. It is informed by the Cause with the visitor firmly at the center of the interpretative approach. We have used the storytelling principle as our main guidance."[151] The guide, like the exhibit itself, employs affective as well as intellectual language, and it seeks to use "the natural drama of the spaces and the story to help provide different emotional moments for the visitor."[152]

According to Parker and Dolman, the nonprofit organization Historic Royal Palaces has prized "stories over stones" in making decisions about its presentation of Hampton Court. In refashioning what were previously known as the Wolsey Rooms into the somewhat misleadingly titled Young Henry exhibit (the king was, as Dolman noted, in his mid-thirties for most of the events described there), curators sought "to breathe some sense of empathy into the decisions that were made by these individuals and how their relationships changed over time."[153] They did so against the backdrop of changes in scholarly opinion as well as the appearance of new historical fictions, especially the television series *The Tudors*. We will see in Chapter 5 that fictions can shape popular understandings of history to a surprising degree; in the case of Hampton Court, which experienced a substantial increase in visitors after the premiere of *The Tudors*, they can also affect the public's choice of historical sites and the presentation of those sites to visitors.[154]

Of course, Hampton Court is not the only location where Wolsey has been commemorated or where his memory has been contested. In the next chapter, we will investigate the ways in which Wolsey was remembered in

Ipswich and Oxford in the nineteenth and twentieth centuries. Though limitations of space do not permit, we might also look to Leicester, where Abbey Park contains a statue of the cardinal and a humble stone edifice that, since the 1930s, has stood in for his tomb. However, our study of the treatment of Wolsey at Hampton Court illustrates how one of the cardinal's primary *lieux de mémoire* has served as a vehicle for his representation and commemoration over several centuries. Not only have those who have written about Hampton Court taken different positions on how Wolsey should be remembered, but so also have those responsible for the palace's preservation, renovation, and display as a historic site. Thus the palace demonstrates the close connection between historical memory and the exercise of power. In the cardinal's own century, King Henry made changes to the fabric of the palace in order to suppress the memory of Wolsey, not to mention several of his spouses. In the nineteenth century, civil servants shaped parts of the palace into an eclectic, ahistorical memorial to "Tudor-ness," and even today, as Dolman acknowledged when I interviewed him, curators ponder how best to strike the appropriate balance between commemorating Wolsey, Henry, and the palace's later inhabitants. Wolsey's role in shaping Hampton Court has given rise both to staid scholarly inquiry and to curious local myths such as that of the Cardinal Spider. Likewise, the manner in which the cardinal has been represented has been informed by academic research as well as popular culture. Wren ordered his epitaph to read "*Lector, si monumentum requiris, circumspice,*" but if we are interested in finding a monument to many of the currents of mnemohistory that this book has been addressing, we need look no further than Hampton Court.

Conclusions

This chapter has covered a wide swath of time, indeed the longest stretch of any of the chapters of this book. For much of this period, it is not unfair to say that Wolsey was a topic primarily of antiquarian interest; however, his capacity to serve political and theological agendas remained, and as new religious controversies flared, writers continued to find in Wolsey a historical foil. As in earlier chapters, the manner in which Wolsey was represented during these decades depended to no small extent on broader social, political, and theological circumstances. During and immediately after the civil wars, advocates for and against episcopalianism, like Fuller and Heylyn, cited Wolsey to buttress their positions on *iure divino* episcopacy and the relationship between church and crown. Later, during the debate over Catholic emancipation, the question of whether Wolsey had been a malign influence on a king whom he had kept in the dark about the details of policy or instead a dutiful servant who went along with Henry's quest for an annulment even when he believed otherwise became a matter on which the loyalty of Catholic subjects turned. It would be reductive, of course, to claim that every writer's representation of Wolsey matches his (and it is worth noting that, with notable exceptions like Jane Austen's humorous *History of England*, those who wrote about history in this period were men) political and theological presuppositions. This is not an ironclad rule— Collier, for instance, depicted a Wolsey more subservient to Henry than his nonjuring convictions might have led him to think appropriate. However, more often than not, those who represented Wolsey in the course of larger historical narratives did so in ways consistent with their overall theological and ecclesiological orientations.

There are some interesting differences in Wolsey's representation across various genres. For those who produced sweeping works of history, Wolsey was largely a dramatic foil or an emblem of the Roman church. But those who wrote the cardinal's biography often had a different set of goals in view. Wood, Aubrey, and Fiddes, for instance, all articulated a certain degree of regret that Wolsey had not been appropriately treated by church historians; their biographical works therefore emerged explicitly, in Fiddes's words, from "a Desire of doing Justice to his injured Memory." Such works, along with Galt's, often depended to a greater extent on Cavendish's *Life* than on other sources, and they are often less easy to classify in terms of a writer's religious or political outlook. And the writers of guidebooks and histories of Hampton Court Palace approached the representation of Wolsey with still other purposes in mind, many of them wishing to commemorate the cardinal as an outstanding builder and architectural patron.

By the middle of the nineteenth century, a kind of stasis had set in with regard to the representation of Wolsey. The three prototypical narratives we identified in Chapter 1 had been whittled down, effectively, to two: a critical narrative incorporating the calumnies of both Catholic and evangelical writers and a sympathetic one leaning chiefly upon Cavendish and his later interpreters. Few innovations extended either narrative in the eighteenth and early nineteenth centuries, and the growing cultural and chronological distance between industrial England and its Tudor past took Wolsey increasingly further out of the collective anglophone memory. However, as we will see in the next chapter, the century after 1850 witnessed renewed interest in the cardinal—interest generated by the appearance of new historical documents, new genres of fiction, and new methods of civic commemoration.

CHAPTER 4

Historical Fiction, Academic History, and Civic Pageantry (c. 1850–c. 1960)

The opening of Hampton Court was only one instance of the renewed interest in Tudor history, and English history more generally, that characterized the long reign of Queen Victoria. Another was the appearance of more than twenty volumes of *Letters and Papers, Foreign and Domestic, of the Reign of King Henry VIII*. With primary documents newly available for analysis, works of historical scholarship proliferated. So also did debates about the proper boundaries of the discipline of history, and advocates for what they called scientific or empirical history employed new methods to challenge commonplace ideas that they had inherited from their predecessors. Outside the academy, local communities began to commemorate their past in new ways, especially, toward the end of the nineteenth century, in the form of the historical pageant. And blurring the boundaries between history and literature, the historical novel and short story emerged as genres in which writers and readers could imaginatively explore the past.

All of these trends shaped the commemoration and representation of Thomas Wolsey. This chapter explores a series of sites for remembering Wolsey during the century beginning approximately in 1850. Like the previous chapter, but even more so, our account of these years will necessarily be selective: Far more works about Wolsey appeared during this century than in any before it. These publications were spurred on by the (contested) professionalization of the historical guild, the establishment of learned journals, and the modernization of university presses—all mechanisms that shaped what "counted" as reputable history. Such mechanisms also promoted the production of detailed studies of specific episodes in the cardinal's biography as well as close textual analyses and new editions of works such as Cavendish's *Life*.

This chapter begins a decade before the appearance of the first volume of *Letters and Papers* and concludes just prior to the premiere of Robert Bolt's influential play about the life of Thomas More, *A Man for All Seasons*. As we will see throughout the chapter, the intervening century witnessed the continuation and elaboration of debates about Wolsey's role in the early English Reformation—debates in which the availability of a greater number of primary sources now permitted the cardinal's partisans, and likewise his detractors, to argue their cases more fully. Our analysis also goes beyond the textual, as the century witnessed the appearance of new works of art depicting scenes from Wolsey's life and multiple treatments of the cardinal by fiction writers, whose works employed his life as a moral exemplar. Throughout the chapter, we will trace the fortunes of our three prototypes in each of these genres, noting that some new forms of representation, like the civic pageant, eschewed the traditional prototypes altogether.

Early Historical Fictions

Before turning to the texts themselves, I must offer some initial remarks about historical fictions and endeavor to explain their presence in this book about the representation and commemoration of Wolsey. These remarks begin from a premise that we will explore over the course of this chapter and the next: that the boundary between history and fiction has shifted over time and, more often than not, has been fuzzy rather than well defined. Beverley Southgate has observed about the twentieth-century debates on this question that "historical theorists, or philosophers of history, have . . . questioned historians' own claims to be able to represent the '*truth*' about the past; and at their most extreme, these critics have likened histories to fictions."[1] Indeed, historians and fiction writers have often sought to accomplish a similar task: that of imposing order on the limited source material that survives from the past. For Hayden White, whose criticisms of quasi-scientific historiography are well known, historians and the creators of historical fictions are in much the same boat. They share "'the problem' of the too much and not enough," "the question of what to leave out in their treatment of real events and processes in the past," and the need for "art as well as information."[2] Hilary Mantel, whose critically acclaimed novels about Tudor England we will be exploring in the next chapter, has offered similar reflections, observing: "The past is not dead ground, and to traverse it is not a sterile exercise. History is always changing behind us, and the past changes a little every time we retell it." Once the biases of and institutional pressures on academic historians are made explicit, "the trade of the historical novelist doesn't seem so reprehensible or dubious."[3]

For Mantel, even if historians and fiction writers confront similar methodological challenges, their relationship has more often than not been contentious. To an even greater extent than so-called popular historical works, historical fictions have frequently come in for criticism from the writers of scholarly prose. As Shannon McSheffrey has commented, "conventionally, historians have decried the inaccuracies in historical films and television programs, acting as 'historian-cops' in pointing out the errors, big and small, in screen treatments of the past."[4] Professional historical research, to the contrary, has often claimed to constitute a gold standard for accuracy and objectivity. The gatekeeping institutions of the historical guild—academic departments, learned journals, and university presses (such as the one that published the book you are reading right now!)— function in large part to enforce this standard. However, in recent years a number of critics have sought to reposition the various genres of historical fiction, arguing that they can (and, for many people, do) serve as effective vehicles for the representation and commemoration of the past. Most prominent among these scholars have been Southgate, White, Ludmilla Jordanova, and Jerome De Groot.

As De Groot, in particular, has sought to demonstrate in a series of monographs, historical fictions can help us contextualize and reassess more standard forms of historiography. Building upon the seminal work of the Marxist critic Georg Lukács, whose 1937 study *The Historical Novel* was one of the first and most influential of its kind, De Groot has suggested that historical fictions "provide a means to critique, conceptualize, engage with, and reject the processes of representation or narrativization. These works provide their audience with a historiographical toolkit that allows them to remark upon the discourse of 'making' history."[5] Historical fictions accomplish this through a queer sense of time—what Lukács dubbed their "necessary anachronism."[6] As we will see, fictions often self-consciously highlight how they depart from the "historical record," that is, from facts that can be established from original documents.[7] Fictions also communicate the "indeterminacy and unknowability of history to the reader," whom they ask simultaneously to accept an author's version of past events and to be aware that other versions, potentially none of them identical with the past, could be substituted in its place.[8] Historical fictions thereby permit authors and readers to engage in playful "thought experiments" about the past, either by starting from premises that scholarship cannot verify or by exploring counterfactual alternatives to the historical sequence of events.[9] They also permit the articulation of voices that are silent in the evidence available to historians: When writers engage with periods of time when women or those assigned to certain racial categories were not able to write or when their writings were suppressed, their fictions can imagine what subaltern individuals and communities might have said or experienced.[10]

Yet these are not the only reasons for this book to engage with the many historical fictions that have included Wolsey as a character. Not only do these fictions perform the epistemological work I just described, but the most influential of them have profoundly shaped anglophone cultural memories of Tudor England. To again quote De Groot, while "scholarly work regularly ignores the contribution to the historical imaginary and to popular historiography" of historical fictions, most nonspecialists—which is to say the vast majority of the general public—encounter history "outside an academic or professional framework. Indeed, in popular culture, the professional historian is at best one of a range of voices contributing to an awareness of things that happened in the past."[11] While it may be impossible to justify this assessment quantitatively, we will discover in this chapter and the next that some historical fictions about Wolsey and the Tudors have circulated widely and enjoyed a significant measure of social currency.[12] Anecdotally, in the years that I have been working on the history of Wolsey's representation and commemoration, the most common response I have heard from those who learned I was writing a book on the cardinal has come in the form of reference to one or more of three twentieth- or twenty-first-century fictions, *A Man for All Seasons*, *The Tudors*, and *Wolf Hall*.

The earliest historical fictions about Wolsey were the Tudor and Stuart history plays we encountered in Chapters 2 and 3. Although they would not have understood themselves as producing "historical fiction," playwrights like Rowley, Shakespeare, Fletcher, and Banks all portrayed events at the court of Henry VIII in ways that went beyond, and in some cases contradicted, records that were available. So also, to very different effect, did the authors of early modern pamphlets like *Canterburies Dreame* (1641). While representations of Wolsey that we might call fictional were occasionally produced prior to the early nineteenth century, it was in the middle of that century that they, like anglophone historical fictions in general, began to be crafted in greater numbers.[13] These later fictions, too, were in general more exploratory and interpretive than outright polemical, although it is easy to identify exceptions to this rule both in the Tudor-Stuart period (for example, Shakespeare and Fletcher's *King Henry VIII*) and in the modern period (as we will see immediately below).

Authors of historical novels, plays, and more recently screen productions have regularly set them during the reign of Henry VIII, who remains one of England's most recognizable monarchs.[14] A number of nineteenth-century authors wrote specifically about Wolsey, most often choosing to explore dimensions of his biography about which historical documents are silent. For instance, an 1845 play, *Wolsey! Or, the Secret Witness*, first performed at the Royal Surrey Theatre in London, depicts the cardinal coming to the aid of a woman unjustly accused of murder. Incongruous in comparison with the representations of the historical Wolsey we have encountered thus far, here the cardinal surreptitiously observes the murder while disguised as a peripatetic friar; later, he appears in court, resplendent in his robes, to proclaim the defendant's innocence and denounce the guilty party.[15] The play appears to be almost deliberately ignorant of existing discourses about Wolsey and, thereby, detaches him from his original context. There is little here that reflects, much less endorses, any of our prototypes for the cardinal.

When we turn to works that *do* seek to advance one or more of the traditional representations of Wolsey, we discover that the nineteenth-century historical fictions in which he appears were disproportionately interested in his childhood and adolescence. Like early Christians whose extracanonical gospels recounted Jesus's deeds before the start of his public ministry, fiction writers sought to fill in details about Wolsey's private life. Their stories draw moral lessons from the future cardinal's supposed achievements and disappointments as well as provide frameworks that may explain his later actions. Particularly representative of such texts are two from the middle of the nineteenth century, the three-volume novel *Freston Tower* (1850) and a short story that appeared under several titles, including "Wolsey Bridge" (1849).

The titles of both these works point to landmarks in Wolsey's county of birth, Suffolk. Both are still extant today: Freston Tower, a charming folly, or free-standing tower built for aesthetic purposes, marks the skyline of a village of the same name located approximately three miles south of Ipswich proper (see Plate 13), while Wolsey Bridge spans a small creek near Southwold, slightly more than thirty miles northeast of Ipswich. Much as our fiction writers endeavored to claim the contrary, neither structure is contemporary with the cardinal: The tower was likely raised in the mid–sixteenth century, whereas the bridge is an eighteenth-century construction.[16] Yet both, as we will see in this section, inspired Victorian representations of one of Suffolk's most famous sons.[17]

Freston Tower was one of seven historical novels by the Anglican clergyman Richard Cobbold, almost all of which are set in Suffolk. It achieved substantial enough notoriety that an 1875 critic of Cobbold's work described it as being "widely circulated," and two meetings of the Suffolk Institute of Archaeology, in 1856 and 1909, featured papers that rebutted the novel's most unlikely historical claims.[18] Cobbold's book depicts Wolsey first as a young man, a protégé of a noble Suffolk family, the de Frestons, who provide him with books and help pave his way to Oxford. The adolescent Wolsey develops a romantic interest in Lord de Freston's daughter, Ellen, and is bitterly disappointed when she chooses for her husband another Oxford scholar, William Latimer. (The historical Latimer, a priest unlike the lay scholar of the novel, was likely Wolsey's contemporary at Oxford.)[19] Jealousy and despair over the loss of Ellen prompt Wolsey to enter the priesthood, but not before composing a twelve-page lament that Cobbold prints, claiming that the original "is in the possession of a gentleman who will doubtless preserve it, if he does not publish it."[20] For Cobbold, who employs fiercely anti-Catholic rhetoric throughout the novel, Wolsey's embrace of the priesthood and its prerogatives changes him very much for the worse. When he returns to Suffolk for the painful duty of presiding at Ellen's wedding to Latimer, Cobbold recounts the effect Wolsey has upon his old friends. It seems to Lord de Freston, in particular, that "an Ambassador from Rome had arrived, in the place of that cheerful friend who was once the delight of his hall."[21] Later, as a cardinal, Wolsey exacts some measure of revenge when he suppresses one of the monasteries of which de Freston is a patron.

In his preface, Cobbold declares that his aim is twofold: first, to "afford an entertaining and instructive record of [the] origin of Freston Tower," which he takes to have been a medieval construction, and second, "to afford a lesson to readers, of both sexes, of the punishment of haughtiness, and the reward of true nobility and patience."[22] A third and perhaps overriding purpose lurks not far beneath the surface. Cobbold's novel appeared in the year of the restoration of the Catholic hierarchy in England, during the heyday of the catholicizing Oxford movement in the Church of England. We traced in the previous chapter how the debate over Catholic emancipation influenced representations of Wolsey by writers like Lingard and Soames; in similar fashion, the strongly anti-Roman sentiments of Cobbold's novel may reflect his unease at the newest inroads that Catholicism had made in England. Yet if the first two volumes of *Freston Tower* depict the disappointed Wolsey embracing the pride and haughtiness that Cobbold believed was endemic to the Roman church, the third narrates something of Wolsey's redemption. Lord de Freston, who articulates evangelical convictions increasingly prominently as the novel goes on, is imprisoned for heresy by Cuthbert Tunstall, the bishop of London; his daughter, now Latimer's wife, pleads to Wolsey for her father's freedom. Cobbold telescopes history so that these events occur just as the cardinal is about to be dismissed from the chancellorship. "Wolsey's heart was softened by his coming fall," Cobbold writes, and he proceeds to narrate a touching reconciliation between Wolsey, de Freston, and the Latimers that ends with the cardinal liberating Ellen's father. (Naturally, the novel's Wolsey admonishes Cavendish to let this matter "be unrecorded among the transactions of my career, which you have undertaken to set down.")[23] Changed as a result of this encounter and reconciled with his friends, Wolsey goes on to suffer his exile and death patiently, while de Freston and his family return to Suffolk. In short order, their manor house is destroyed in a plot orchestrated by local Catholic rivals, with assistance from a most anachronistic Jesuit, but in the novel's final pages, even the Jesuit confesses and receives forgiveness.

Cobbold's clumsy attempts to explain the absence of his novel's events from the historical record aside, *Freston Tower* is fanciful in the extreme. The tower itself, which in the book symbolizes the family's love of learning and by extension their evangelical leanings, was constructed decades after the historical Wolsey's last known visit to Suffolk. Almost all of Cobbold's characters, with the exception of Cavendish, are fabricated out of whole cloth or have basic elements of their biographies altered. Yet, if in these and other ways Cobbold's novel fails at the first of its stated goals, it does offer a moral lesson. *Freston Tower* represents Wolsey as a case study in the corruption of Rome as well as in the redemption that comes through the gospel and the practice of forgiveness and friendship. The novel also reflects on the nature of commemoration. Wolsey masterminds the construction of the tower of Magdalen College, Oxford, in order to outshine Freston Tower, so that "I will be remembered when he [Latimer] shall be forgotten. His tower may grace the banks of the Orwell, and please his fair mistress's eye, but this . . . shall astonish even the eyes of the university."[24] Toward the end of the book, Latimer echoes Wolsey's sentiment in a more altruistic key, sharing with Ellen his insight that Freston Tower will stand, for the rest of their lives, as what we might call a *lieu de mémoire* for her father, Wolsey, and their friendship.[25]

Like *Freston Tower*, the short story "Wolsey Bridge" is framed as a lesson in morality. It first appeared in the collection *The Youth's Historical Cabinet* (1849) and was reprinted at least three times in the 1850s and 1860s.[26] One of its appearances is in *Merry's Book of Tales*, another collection of historical short stories published in 1860, which reflects in its preface upon the kinds of truths it seeks to represent:

> We do not mean to say that all the stories in this volume are true in all their details; but they are true in this, that they speak truly of the habits and feelings of children and youth, and illustrate truly the temptations to which they are exposed, and the duties they are required to perform, or they relate some interesting fact in natural history. We think that no story can be truly amusing even which has not some good lesson in it.[27]

When "Wolsey Bridge" was reprinted eight years later, in *Tales from English History: For Children*, the new volume's editor, Agnes Strickland, was even more explicit about her didactic purpose: "It is the object of the present work to offer to the Young a series of moral and instructive tales, each founded on some striking authentic fact in the annals of English History." Strickland added to each of her stories a "historical summary" that seeks to provide context for the events narrated.[28]

However, if *Freston Tower* and "Wolsey Bridge" are both didactic, the morals they seek to impart differ substantially. Whereas Cobbold wrote *Freston Tower* as a warning against the dangers of Catholicism, "Wolsey Bridge" foregrounds the relationship between hard work and worldly achievement. Here, Wolsey's father (inaccurately presented as Thomas Wolsey the elder) wishes his son to follow him in his trade as a butcher. Young Thomas, however, has more ambitious plans for himself: "The idea of such servilely earned pelf was revolting to the excited imagination of the youthful student, whose mind was full of classic imagery, and intent on the attainment of academic honors, the steps by which he projected to ascend to the more elevated objects of his ambition."[29] In this story, the church is the source not of Wolsey's corruption but of his advancement, "the only avenue through which talented persons of obscure birth might hope to arrive at greatness."[30] Wolsey therefore strikes out almost alone on his academic and ecclesiastical career. When his father warns him that "the end which you propose is *impossible*," he sharply retorts, "Sir . . . I have blotted *that word* out of MY dictionary."[31]

In representing how the future cardinal's hard work allowed him to rise above the circumstances of his birth, "Wolsey Bridge" seeks to valorize achievement through diligent and uncomplaining labor. Through the episode to which its title alludes, the story also holds up as a model Wolsey's generosity toward his native county. One day, when riding home with his companions from a local monastery, the future cardinal encounters a swollen, muddy stream in which he is nearly drowned. Turning to his companions, he urges them to follow him, "unless ye choose to stay where ye art till I am a Cardinal, when it is my intention to build a bridge over this sweet stream, to prevent other travellers from incurring the peril which I have done in endeavoring to ford such a bottomless abyss of mud."[32] True to his word, the story concludes, Wolsey did in fact order the construction of the bridge that bears his name. "The name of the bridge, and the local tradition thereunto belonging, will long, I trust, exist to preserve the memory of an action of pure benevolence to future ages," concludes the tale.[33]

Freston Tower and "Wolsey Bridge" share a number of features, both with each other and with most other early fictional representations of the cardinal. Rather than seeking to advance an account of Wolsey's involvement in public affairs, they focus instead on his inner life and motivations. Both texts highlight Wolsey's intelligence and represent him as someone who was capable, at least sometimes, of great generosity. In remembering Wolsey as a builder, whether of the tower of Magdalen College or of Wolsey Bridge, they simultaneously reflect on the ways in which landmarks exercise commemorative functions, as in Nora's later notion of *lieux de mémoire*.

Marking the Boundaries of Historical Scholarship

But at the same time that the authors of fictions like these were deploying Wolsey as a moral symbol, some historians were starting to use newly published materials and newly minted techniques to represent the cardinal in ways that would have been impossible for their predecessors. There is not space here to recount all of the many changes that European historiography underwent over the course of the nineteenth century. Among them were new structures for training historians and measuring their scholarly achievements, many of them borrowed from the German academic system; the influence of scientific insights from thinkers such as Lyell and Darwin; the continuation and intensification of forms of political, economic, and intellectual colonialism; and, perhaps most significantly, the opening of state archives and the publication of vast quantities of primary sources. This last factor fueled the confidence of some historians, most famously the German scholar Leopold von Ranke, that with enough documents in hand, it might be possible to write history "as it essentially was."[34]

Ranke explicitly disclaimed "the office of judging the past and of instructing the present for the benefit of future ages."[35] Those following in his footsteps, including the English Catholic historian Lord Acton, reiterated Ranke's call to rely carefully upon documents and practice disinterested analysis. For Acton, the publication of materials from European state and church archives marked "the beginning of the documentary age, which will tend to make history independent of historians."[36] The task of the historian, as he pronounced in his inaugural lecture as Regius Professor of Modern History at Cambridge, is to sift through documents, "discerning truth from falsehood and certainty from doubt," rather than relying uncritically upon earlier writers who likely wrote with partisan ends in mind.[37]

While neither Ranke nor Acton specialized primarily in the history of Tudor England, their disciples cheered the extent to which English primary sources appeared in print from the mid–nineteenth century onward. Starting in 1830, the Royal Commission for State Papers brought out eleven volumes of the *State Papers of Henry VIII*, and between 1858 and 1911 the "Rolls Series," officially *The Chronicles and Memorials of Great Britain and Ireland during the Middle Ages*, printed critical editions of ninety-nine medieval historical works. English scholars generated calendars of state papers and bishops' registers, along with critical editions of literary and polemical works. Most important for our purposes, twenty-one volumes of *Letters and Papers of the Reign of Henry VIII* were published between 1862 and 1932, with the four volumes covering the years of Wolsey's influence appearing between 1862 and 1876 under the editorship of the Anglican clergyman-scholar J. S. Brewer.[38] Brewer's successor, James Gairdner, collated the prefaces Brewer had written for each of these volumes and published them in 1884 as a two-volume work, *The Reign of Henry VIII from His Accession to the Death of Wolsey*.[39]

As we will see throughout this section, it is difficult to overestimate the impact of the publication of the *Letters and Papers*. While the volumes assembled by Brewer and his successors were not without their flaws, they made accessible in a single location the contents of thousands of manuscript letters, memoranda, and other documents; these allowed scholars to trace the history of Henry's reign as it was experienced year by year and, sometimes, day by day. Recognizing the significance of the documents being published, Acton wrote in a review of the first four volumes that "Mr. Brewer has done more than any other man to dispel the dark tradition, and to pour light upon an epoch which will always interest every description of educated men."[40] Admittedly, Acton's review also took Brewer to task for going too far toward rehabilitating the memory of Wolsey, whom Acton dubbed "a Minister of tyranny . . . a pensioner of foreign potentates, [and] a priest of immoral life."[41]

About Brewer's praise of Wolsey we shall say more in a moment. First, however, we must pause to observe that not all historians of Tudor England working in the second half of the nineteenth century availed themselves of the newly published materials, much less reached conclusions as revisionist as Brewer's. Indeed, some continued to produce accounts of the English Reformation and of Wolsey's role in its origins that echoed the prototype of Wolsey the papist that we have seen favored by evangelical writers going back to Hall and Foxe. Among the best read of these writers was Jean Henri Merle d'Aubigné, a Genevan historian with a distinguished family pedigree and strongly Reformed theological convictions.[42] His *History of the Reformation in the Sixteenth Century* was published in Paris in five volumes (1835–1853), with each volume appearing in English translation a few years later. Merle, as he preferred to be known, has received comparatively little attention from historiographers, at least in proportion to the extraordinary popularity of his works among both francophone and anglophone readers; it is for this reason I include him here. In the words of S. M. Houghton, the most recent editor of *History of the Reformation*, Merle attracted a broad readership because he wrote "for the ordinary Christian public" and focused on the stories of individuals rather than those of institutions.[43] Houghton's denomination of Merle's audience as a specifically Christian one is essential for understanding the assumptions that governed his work. The *History* takes as its central theme God's involvement in religious reformation, a theme that put Merle's books at odds with much of the self-avowedly scientific historiography of his day. As J. H. M. Salmon has noted, "with his dramatic and sensationalist style and his invented dialog (which he defended as a paraphrase of documentary sources), Merle often resembles a Romantic historical novelist rather than the school of Augustin Thierry."[44]

Unsurprisingly for a historian working from Reformed theological principles, Merle characterizes the first thirteen centuries of Christianity in England as marked by the increasing domination of the Roman church. The early years of the reign of Henry VIII provided no indication of the reform that was to come, since "at heart the king cared more about the victories of Alexander than of Jesus Christ."[45] Wolsey first appears in Merle's narrative amid Henry's French campaigns of 1512–13, introduced only by a series of epithets that associate him with sexual, and hence moral, depravity: "Wolsey, the father of several illegitimate children, and . . . suffering the penalty of his irregularities."[46] In the next few pages, Merle draws the character of Wolsey in greater detail, identifying the cardinal as a man whose combination of "extreme ability with notorious immorality" made him a roadblock to reformation.[47] Merle represents Wolsey as a master of political intrigue and possibly a patron of darker arts still: He repeats without qualification Tyndale's claim that the cardinal, in order to secure his dominance over the king, "cast Henry's nativity, and procured an amulet which he wore constantly, in order to charm his master by its magic properties."[48]

Between the authority that the Roman church had amassed over the centuries and Wolsey's own personal talents, by the time the cardinal achieved his highest offices, the prospects for reformation were dim. To explain the ensuing course of events, Merle advances a set of theological distinctions: "It was within the province of four powers in the sixteenth century to effect a reformation of the church: these were the papacy, the episcopate, the monarchy, and Holy Scripture. The Reformation in England was essentially the work of Scripture."[49] That reform did not come from either the papacy or the episcopate is obvious, but in contrast to other historians we will encounter, Merle argues that the English Reformation was not driven by the crown, either. However, he does distinguish between what he calls the reformation "in the name of the king" and the reformation "in the name of the Scriptures." The former—the severing of communion between the Church of England and that of Rome—was necessary, but it was not sufficient, since Henry VIII was not himself wholly committed to the theological and ecclesiological changes that Merle believes constitute true reform. Instead, God "had already decided the victory along the whole line of operations" and brought about a reformation in the hearts of the people by raising up preachers, translators, and theologians.[50] The balance of Merle's history alternates between one story of limited and limping ecclesiological reform engineered through Henry's divorce and another story of the enthusiastic spread of the gospel by such figures as Tyndale, Miles Coverdale, and Thomas Cranmer.

According to Merle, Wolsey played an unwitting role in bringing about Henry's reformation. Throughout the *History*, Wolsey is deeply ambitious for the papal throne. Yet far from denying Wolsey's talents, Merle permits himself to imagine what Wolsey's papacy might have looked like:

> At length he would no longer be the favorite only, but the arbiter of the kings of the earth, and his genius, for which England was too narrow, would have Europe and the world for its stage. Already revolving gigantic projects in his mind, the future pope dreamt of the destruction of heresy in the west, and in the east the cessation of the Greek schism, and new crusades to replant the cross on the walls of Constantinople. There is nothing that Wolsey would not have dared undertake when seated on the throne of catholicism, and the pontificates of Gregory VII and Innocent III would have been eclipsed by that of the Ipswich butcher's son.[51]

But according to Merle, however expansive were Wolsey's intentions, equally sizeable were the despair and the desire for vengeance that he felt upon being denied the papacy. Throughout the *History* Merle composes speeches that he imagines his historical actors might have made, and the words he assigns Wolsey upon hearing of the election of Clement VII are particularly sharp: "They laugh at me, and thrust me into the second rank. . . . So be it! I will create such a confusion in the world as has not been seen for ages. . . . I will do it, even should England be swallowed up in the tempest!"[52] Henceforth, Wolsey seeks to exact vengeance upon Charles V, whom he blames for not being elected, as well as upon Katherine of Aragon, whose criticisms of his worldly lifestyle he resents.[53]

Merle's stress on Wolsey's desire for vengeance belongs more to the Tudor Catholic prototype of Wolsey the author of schism than to the prototype favored by Tudor evangelicals. However, Merle does borrow from his evangelical predecessors much of his narrative of Wolsey's dismissal and death, including an episode in which King Henry receives miscarried letters that demonstrate that the cardinal has been playing him false.[54] Merle criticizes Wolsey for taking comfort from the tokens of affection that Henry sends him during his exile, claiming that the cardinal never sought God's forgiveness with equal fervor. While Merle admits that Wolsey may not have been culpable for the exact crimes for which he was finally charged, he maintains that the cardinal was guilty of seeking to maintain "the sacerdotal prerogative" and "the Roman primacy," even to the point of encouraging the persecution of evangelicals on his deathbed.[55] Many of the features of Merle's representation recur in other partisan Protestant histories of the same period. Samuel Martin, in a lecture he gave at the London Young Men's Christian Association in 1849, asserted that "It does not appear . . . that Wolsey had any religious principle. His own confession on his deathbed is proof of this. And, on one point, all agree— in attributing to Wolsey excessive, unlawful ambition."[56] J. A. Wylie, in his *History of Protestantism* (1878), dwells at length on Wolsey's desire for the papacy and emphasizes that the cardinal, on his deathbed, was still calling for the destruction of Lutheranism.[57] Lindley Murray, in a brief biographical summary from 1875, represents Wolsey as an "evil mastermind advisor duping the King," one who offers "a memorable instance of the vanity and inconstancy of human things, both in his rise and fall."[58] Many of these criticisms fall along the lines of the evangelical prototype we first encountered in Chapter 1, with the notable exception of Martin's assertion that Wolsey was not motivated by religion.

While all these authors, and more besides them, repeated time-honored criticisms of Wolsey, the publication of documents such as the *State Papers* and *Letters and Papers* led other scholars to produce more generous accounts of the cardinal and his achievements. Already in 1858, historians such as J. A. Froude had begun to reconsider some longstanding assessments of Wolsey. Froude was the scion of a prominent clerical family: His father was the archdeacon of Totnes, and his elder brother, Richard Hurrell Froude, was a major contributor to the Oxford movement before his untimely death.[59] But much as Froude cherished the memory of his brother, his theological views came to diverge substantially.[60] As Llewelyn Williams has argued, "the Church before 1828 remained to him the model of what an established religion should be. He was a thorough Erastian, who believed in the subordination of the Church to the state. He detested theological doctrinalism of all kinds."[61] Thus, when Froude wrote his *History of England* in 1858, he not only cast Henry VIII in a heroic light but also demonstrated sympathy for Catholics including Fisher, More, Warham, and Wolsey.[62]

Froude was at the center of many of the controversies that attended the emergence of history as an academic discipline. Repeatedly attacked by many of his contemporaries over inaccuracies in his works and routinely savaged in reviews for a style of writing that his critics took to be too popular and too literary, Froude's works represented a sharp divergence from the empirical forms of historiography championed by Ranke and his disciples.[63] As Ian Hesketh has suggested, the viciousness of criticism directed against Froude represented a kind of disciplinary "boundary work" on the part of his critics, who in rejecting his methods were attempting to distinguish history as a "scientific pursuit" from the writing of historical fiction. By contrast, in an 1864 lecture Froude himself expressed skepticism about his opponents' supposed empiricism, arguing that historical facts are not quite the same as scientific ones.[64]

Unlike many of the long-form histories that we have been studying, Froude's does not include an extensive biographical sketch of Wolsey. In his earliest references to the cardinal, however, Froude begins to develop two themes that recur throughout his *History*. First, Froude represents Wolsey as "essentially a transition minister," one who served as a bridge between the ecclesiastical statesmen of the late Middle Ages and the lay ministers of state who dominated the remainder of the Tudor period. One element of Wolsey's transitional role was that he, "by a combination of talent, honesty, and arrogance," was able to pose, but not to answer, questions that would reshape the English church.[65] To cite two examples, both in accepting papal authority to reform religious houses and in urging Henry to seek his annulment in Rome Wolsey opened for debate, and in so doing made vulnerable to revision, longstanding assumptions about the relationship between the crown and the papacy. For Froude, Wolsey was aware of the danger that he was courting: "He knew well that Henry's connivance, or even expressed permission, could not avail him if his conduct was challenged."[66] The cardinal took a calculated series of risks to reform the church from within, but his loyalty to Rome blinded him from recognizing that the old religious system had in fact had its day. In Froude's evocative metaphor, "He could not read the signs of the times; and confounded the barrenness of death with the barrenness of a winter which might be followed by a new spring or summer."[67] Mistaken though Wolsey may have been, Froude was not prepared to pronounce him either disloyal or ill-intentioned. Quoting a letter in which Wolsey begged Pope Clement to grant the king's annulment or else put England in danger of schism, Froude comments, "These were the words of a man who loved England well, but who loved Rome better; and Wolsey has received but scanty justice from catholic writers, since he sacrificed himself for the catholic cause."[68]

Froude was not the only midcentury Anglican historian to express regret about the representation of Wolsey by earlier writers. Charles Martin, who published a prize-winning essay on the cardinal in 1862, averred that "It is difficult to find in history another instance of so great a man, who left absolutely no party behind him."[69] Like Froude, Martin applauded

Wolsey's desire to reform the religious houses and praised him for his lenient attitude toward heresy, which Martin says Wolsey "reproved . . . as folly without punishing it as crime."[70] Then, in his 1869 work *The Reformation of the Church of England*, J. H. Blunt repeated the favorable comparisons between Wolsey and Cardinal Ximenes of Spain advanced by some of the eighteenth-century writers we met in Chapter 3.[71] Following Froude and Martin, Blunt cast Wolsey as the source of the "first effective impulse" of the reformation, but Blunt went further, identifying seven characteristics of the reformation that Wolsey would have sought to mastermind had he been given the opportunity. These included improvements in clerical education; a general visitation of the clergy and monastic houses; the creation of new bishoprics centered on major monasteries; toleration and conversion rather than persecution of reformers; the promotion of the study of Greek; and, ultimately, a concerted campaign to gain the papacy, so that England's reforms might be extended to the worldwide church.[72] In Blunt's estimation, Wolsey's plan for reformation constituted "the most comprehensive view of Church reform that was ever contemplated, and one before which the actual Reformation shrinks into a confused mass of half accomplished good and unobstructed evil. Perhaps the very magnitude of Wolsey's plans was one element in their failure; and with all his far-sightedness, he had not made sufficient allowance for human weakness."[73]

Several of these writers explicitly cited the *State Papers*, which (as we have seen) began to appear in 1830. In Blunt's words, Wolsey's deeds "were grossly misrepresented by most writers who had to deal with the events of his age, until the publication of the State Papers revealed their true character."[74] For both Martin and Blunt, the *State Papers* revealed that King Henry was very much his own master and that he became increasingly so as the tortuous legal processes concerning his annulment dragged on.[75] Wolsey, by contrast, appeared to these writers to be a dutiful instrument of the king's: "He idolized the King, and loved to bow before him. . . . And so he came to regard himself as a privileged servant; above the level of ordinary subjects; associated with the King in every act of legislation, and almost enjoying a share of the kingly office itself."[76]

But if the publication of the *State Papers* encouraged historians to begin to revisit some longstanding commonplaces about Wolsey, the subsequent appearance of the far more extensive *Letters and Papers of the Reign of Henry VIII* accelerated that process dramatically. Wolsey found one of his most enthusiastic and eloquent defenders in J. S. Brewer, the first editor of the *Letters and Papers*, whose prefaces abound with expressions of admiration at many of the cardinal's deeds, grief at his ultimate fate, and revulsion at those around Henry who encouraged him to discard his most loyal servant. For Brewer, the opprobrium Wolsey unjustly suffered, in both life and death, was without parallel in English history. Two quotations from Brewer's assessment of Wolsey's legacy capture the tone of the rest: "No man ever met with harder measure from his contemporaries; and never was the verdict of contemporaries less challenged than in his case by subsequent inquirers."[77] "No statesman of such eminence ever died less lamented. On no one did his own contemporaries pile a greater load of obloquy; not one stone of which has posterity seriously attempted to remove."[78]

Given Brewer's service as editor of the *Letters and Papers*, it should be unsurprising that his prefaces cite original documents extensively, either to confirm, or more often to contradict, the conclusions of earlier historians. Often, Brewer explicitly weighs their claims against one another. He particularly criticizes Polydore Vergil, taking pains to demonstrate that the calumnies Vergil directed at Wolsey were motivated by a personal vendetta more than by any sense of historical accuracy. For Brewer, Wolsey had acted justly in imprisoning Vergil for what amounted to disloyalty and treachery. Vergil, on his part, "took immortal revenge" once he was safely out of Wolsey's reach. "He sneered at the Cardinal's birth, sneered at his ingratitude, sneered at his buildings, sneered at his administration of justice, sneered at his cardinal's hat. He painted Wolsey, in his history, as an ambitious priest, successful only because he was unscrupulous."[79] Whereas Vergil emerges from Brewer's prefaces as a thoroughly disreputable source of information, *Hall's Chronicle* fares substantially better. Brewer does identify instances where he believes that Hall's treatment of the cardinal was inaccurate: He concludes, for example, that Hall attributed the Amicable Grant too much to Wolsey and not enough to the king, and he thinks that Hall underestimated Wolsey's willingness to help Henry procure his annulment.[80] But at least as often, Brewer finds himself in agreement with Hall. He accepts Hall's story about Wolsey supplementing Cardinal Campeggio's baggage with the "treasure" of rotten groceries and old clothing that spills onto the streets of London when the visiting legate's mules are spooked.[81] He affirms Hall for not attributing the Duke of Buckingham's downfall to ill will on Wolsey's part—noting, in a backhanded compliment, that Hall had strong ideological motivation to blame Wolsey for the duke's destruction but chose not to do so.[82] He also favors Hall's circumspect account of the confrontation between the cardinal and Thomas More in the Parliament of 1523 over the more dramatic version offered by More's son-in-law and biographer, William Roper.[83] About the testimony of Cavendish's *Life*, Brewer is largely skeptical, even though as we will see Brewer largely embraces Cavendish's prototypical representation of Wolsey. Cavendish may have "painted the last days of the fallen statesman with unrivalled pathos and fidelity," Brewer writes, but he "was clearly unversed in politics, and knew nothing, except by vague report, of Wolsey's earlier and more active years."[84]

Even though Brewer was the editor of volumes entitled *Letters and Papers . . . of the Reign of Henry VIII*, and even though his collected prefaces appeared under the title *The Reign of Henry VIII*, the hero of his narrative was in fact Wolsey.[85] For Brewer, it was the cardinal whose careful conduct of foreign policy catapulted England into a position of disproportionate influence in Europe. Wolsey "contrived by his individual energy to raise this country from a third-rate State into the highest circle of European politics."[86] For Brewer, and as we will see later in this chapter for many early-twentieth-century historians, England under Wolsey held the so-called balance of power between France and the Holy Roman Empire. The cost, or at least the consequence, of Wolsey's involvement in foreign policy and European affairs was the relative inattention that the cardinal devoted to domestic policy and the state of the church.[87] Brewer's Wolsey was not the great dispenser of justice, pacifier of the realm, or religious reformer that other writers have made him to be. Instead, perhaps having Froude's *History of England* or Blunt's *Reformation of the Church of England* in mind, Brewer is skeptical about the work that Wolsey might have accomplished had he been elected pope. "If such had been his lot, though he might have retarded the progress of the Reformation, he could never have prevented it."[88]

If in Brewer's work Wolsey appears in an unusually heroic guise, it will come as little surprise that Brewer reserved the role of villain for his title character, King Henry, as well as for the collection of nobles who sought to hound Wolsey from authority. Despite his evident patriotism and his preference for the evangelical Hall over the Catholic writers Vergil and Cavendish, Brewer saves his sharpest language for the king's pursuit of his first annulment. "I would gladly have passed over in silence this dark and revolting page of history, could it be done with justice," Brewer admits. "It is not pleasant to have to chronicle the artifices, the dissimulation, the fraud, the intimidation employed to hunt down a forlorn and defenseless woman."[89] He portrays Katherine as the primary victim of Henry's willfulness, casting Wolsey as an unintended casualty. Once it became clear that Henry, who never before had had an objective so bluntly denied him, would brook no opposition to the annulment, Wolsey knew that his position would be untenable and his life endangered if he could not meet the king's demands.[90] And indeed, that was how it happened—despite that Wolsey had sincerely attempted to procure the king's annulment, employing a flexible and nimble style of negotiation with the curia far superior to the approaches the king and his counselors had tried.[91] Brewer's narrative of Wolsey's downfall is poignant and pathetic. Defending the cardinal against the accusations that led to his arrest for treason, Brewer emphasizes that Wolsey's enemies were not content with his ruin and death but continued to intrigue against him even after he was gone. "Cruel to him in life, the age was not less cruel to his memory."[92]

Does Brewer admit any of Wolsey's faults? He portrays the cardinal as a dutiful servant unfairly hounded by his enemies and eventually even by the king whose wishes he sought to obey. Not unlike Cavendish, Brewer waxes lyrical about Wolsey's work ethic, his capacity for managing complex negotiations, and his unwillingness to meet reformers with violent persecution. But criticisms do appear, sprinkled throughout the praise. Brewer notes that Wolsey did not enjoy delegating his authority, especially to those outside his immediate circle of trust. Over time, the volume of work that came across his desk multiplied beyond his talents, to the frustration of the king and his clients. "That he was peremptory, unceremonious, and sometimes lost his temper, must be admitted," Brewer also confesses, representing Wolsey as behaving impatiently toward those who did not share his expansive view of the European political terrain.[93] As his narrative moves into the years of the annulment crisis, however, Brewer's primary criticism of Wolsey comes clearly into view: The cardinal treated the king as an "idol." Brewer discerns Wolsey's idolatry in his pattern of histrionic responses as his relationship with the king began to change. His letters to Henry during their dispute over the nomination of a new abbess for Wilton, as well as in the days immediately following his dismissal, Brewer writes, are "at variance with our modern notions of manliness and independence," revealing hopelessness, self-effacement, and exuberance inappropriate for such a person as the cardinal.[94] Brewer characterizes Wolsey's groveling response to Henry Norris as equally unfitting, although he does admit that the excesses in the cardinal's behavior, however different from the staid demeanor of a stereotypical Victorian statesman, were not necessarily unusual for a sixteenth-century courtier.[95]

Brewer's praise of Wolsey's conduct of diplomacy, his anguish at Wolsey's treatment by the king, and his anger at the cardinal's representation by hostile writers were not universally shared. As we saw, Lord Acton questioned what he described as Brewer's overly laudatory treatment of the cardinal. According to Acton, for all the documents Brewer cited, he failed to demonstrate satisfactorily that Wolsey was not the source of Henry's scruples about his marriage. Moreover, Acton blamed Brewer for downplaying or even deliberately omitting unflattering details about the cardinal's life. According to Acton, Brewer refused to admit that Wolsey had fathered an illegitimate son, Thomas Winter; that he had sought to transfer the see of Durham to Winter upon being nominated to Winchester; and that he had "caused Protestants to be burnt in the day of his power."[96] Brewer may indeed have expressed unwarranted skepticism about Winter's paternity, but this last charge of Acton's is overstated: Wolsey never handed heresy defendants over to the secular authorities for burning.

But even if Acton was unconvinced by Brewer's representation, we can discern the influence of Brewer's perspective in two book-length biographies published around the turn of the twentieth century. First, in 1888 Mandell Creighton, a Cambridge historian who was soon to be nominated bishop of Peterborough, published a slim biography entitled *Cardinal Wolsey*, in which he, crediting Brewer, characterized the cardinal as "probably the greatest political genius whom England has ever produced."[97] Like most historians working in the wake of the publication of the *Letters and Papers*, Creighton took Henry to be the master of his own affairs, one who did not scruple to claim credit for successes while allowing his cardinal-minister to be blamed for failures.[98] Despite Wolsey's faithful service, in the end he ceased to be useful to the king: He "had served his master only too well, and met with the basest ingratitude for all the sacrifices of his own wishes and his own principles."[99] Creighton, like Brewer before him, argues that Henry's treatment of Wolsey was succeeded by the ingratitude of posterity. However unfairly, Wolsey came to be "regarded only as the type of the arrogant ecclesiastic whom it was the great work of the Reformation to have rendered impossible in the future." He was "branded as the minion of the Pope, and the upholder of a foreign despotism," and when sympathetic writers such as Fiddes sought to rehabilitate his reputation, their efforts met with accusations of disloyalty and popery.[100]

Our second turn-of-the-century biography, Ethelred Taunton's 1901 *Thomas Wolsey: Legate and Reformer*, approached Wolsey's career from a different vantage point. Taunton, a Catholic priest and historian, believed that Wolsey's career as a churchman, as opposed to a statesman, had suffered from inattention.[101] Taunton's claims were somewhat overstated—as we have seen, both friendly writers like Blunt and hostile ones like Merle had indeed attended to Wolsey's ecclesiastical leadership. However, Taunton's biography offered an enthusiastic representation of Wolsey as an agent of reform. Taunton was quick to defend the cardinal from charges of corruption and ambition—both Wolsey's practice of holding multiple benefices and his ambition for the papacy were typical of the great prelates of his day, and "neither is there anything wrong in aspiring to a position which affords capabilities of doing good."[102] For Taunton, as the subtitle of his book indicates, Wolsey amassed authority primarily in order to effect a thorough reformation of the English church.[103] The cardinal was "a born administrator" who had mapped out a scheme of Catholic reform that would have addressed the church's worst abuses and saved it from heresy. Like Blunt before him, Taunton imagined that Wolsey's reforms would have included a general visitation of the clergy and especially the monasteries, the foundation of new institutions for clerical education, the establishment of new bishoprics centered on great abbeys, and the conversion of Lutheran sympathizers through effective preaching rather than by the threat of fire or the sword.[104]

During the period when Creighton and Taunton were writing, historical scholarship blossomed and became increasingly specialized. The *English Historical Review*, which identifies itself as the oldest historical journal in the language, was founded in 1886, and many of its early numbers carried articles about the cardinal, as did learned journals of local history.[105] At least four essays published between 1888 and 1918 investigated the cardinal's early life and family history, concluding that his father, far from being the lowly butcher of hostile representations, was a landowner, civic personage, and occasional troublemaker.[106] James Gairdner, in a landmark article of 1899, explored the circumstances of Wolsey's dismissal and parliamentary impeachment, and other historians attempted to unpack the canonical issues involved in Henry's annulment.[107] Last but not least, a series of writers, architectural historians and archaeologists prominent among them, discussed Wolsey's building projects.[108] This last group included the Hampton Court enthusiast Ernest Law, who amid the chaos of World War I published in 1916 an enthusiastic study of Wolsey's involvement in Henry's military exploits, *England's First Great War Minister.*[109]

In 1930 came the four hundredth anniversary of Wolsey's death, which was marked by public commemorations and two new book-length studies. The earlier and the more scholarly of these volumes was Alfred Frederick Pollard's *Wolsey* (1929), an expanded version of the Ford lectures that he had delivered at Oxford in 1927–28; the latter, the more impressionistic, was a book of the same title by the Catholic essayist Hilaire Belloc (1930). The volumes differ strikingly in method as well as content, and it may have been as a result of Pollard's dismay that Belloc had covered the same historical territory as him, without employing the conventions of academic historiography or engaging at nearly the same depth with primary documents, that he savaged Belloc's book in a review in the *Observer*, claiming that it "teems with dogmatic statements for which there is not a tittle of evidence."[110]

As the founder of both the Institute of Historical Research at the University of London and its still influential journal, the *Bulletin of the Institute of Historical Research* (now simply *Historical Research*), Pollard shaped the field of Tudor history to an extent that Patrick Collinson, writing in 2008, dubbed "unrivalled."[111] Pollard's first major book, a 1902 biography of Henry VIII, was a landmark treatment of the king that influenced subsequent interpretations through at least the 1950s. A constitutional historian, Pollard consistently saw the English Reformation not as a conflict over doctrine but rather as an episode in the perennial conflict between church and state.[112] For him, Henry's reign falls fundamentally into two halves: the period from the king's accession through 1529, when for the most part Wolsey governed with Henry's permission, and the period from Wolsey's fall through the end of the reign, when Henry was his own prime minister.[113] Pollard attributed to Henry a long list of positive leadership traits, summarized by Collinson as "superb judgement, great subtlety, long vision and deep insight, and virtually invariable success, profoundly at one with the nation's destiny."[114] But, for Pollard, Henry could never have governed alone nor alone wrested control of England's religious allegiance away from the Roman church: He was able to do so only with the consent of the people, whose representatives in Parliament he may sometimes have pressured but never outright ignored.[115]

Pollard's *Wolsey*, which Rosemary O'Day has characterized as his "masterpiece," is no celebration of the cardinal's legacy but rather a cautious and often critical assessment of his political achievements and their consequences. Pollard argued that while Wolsey had attempted to maintain, if not expand, the church's sphere of autonomy, the powers he concentrated in himself provided Henry with a blueprint for the royal supremacy:

> Henry was heir to much more than Wolsey's wealth, and Wolsey had taught him other things than to dissolve monasteries, build palaces, and grasp at riches. He had shown him a vision of that unity of jurisdiction and monopoly of power, which, whether vested in a single person, in a popular assembly, or in that composite entity, "the crown in parliament," is the essence of our ideas of sovereignty and of the modern state. Wolsey, indeed, had no conception of parliamentary

government; but, with that fundamental exception, Henry's royal
supremacy was Wolsey's work.[116]

The breadth of Wolsey's legacy, in Pollard's telling, was an anomaly: Never
before had a subject been appointed not simply *legatus natus* but *legatus a
latere*, and the powers Wolsey procured were so extensive that "they were
almost bound to provoke a constitutional breach between the English
crown and the papacy."[117] But Wolsey, committed as he was to papal polity
and the papacy itself, neither foresaw nor intended the consequences of his
actions. For Pollard, Wolsey was no ideologue. Never fully committed to
the reform of the church, or to the constitutional role of Parliament, or
even to any consistent vision of the balance of power in Europe, the aims
the cardinal pursued were those that benefited him personally.[118]

Critical appraisals dominate the chapter that Pollard dedicated to Wolsey's character. Pollard lambasts the cardinal for the unseemly patronage
he directed toward his illegitimate son, Thomas Winter, saying that his
"nepotism, like his legatine authority, almost attained to papal proportions."[119] Wolsey possessed an "inferiority complex" and, like Napoleon,
"did not know when or even how to stop." He combined these unflattering traits with a lack of respect for Parliament, and he depended for his
self-worth upon external pomp.[120] His vices, above all his ambition, ruined
the career that Wolsey's "superiority of intellectual vigor and vitality" had
promised, and he himself was responsible for the circumstances that
brought about his downfall. Rather than demonstrating in Yorkshire the
posture of contrition that Cavendish attributed to him and that his friends
had urged him to take, for Pollard Wolsey instead "wad[ed] deeper and
deeper into the treacherous stream of political opposition and intrigue,"
even going so far as to offer advice to Katherine about the prospect of her
restoration.[121] When he announced his enthronement as archbishop of
York without having sought royal permission to proceed with the ceremony, it was to flaunt his authority—a threat the government could not
tolerate and would not permit. Thus, despite whatever limited praise he
offers, Pollard argues that Wolsey was his own worst enemy, choosing
courses of action that neither achieved his goals nor permitted him to
escape condemnation.

Turning now to the second biography of 1930, it is worth observing that
as much as Pollard criticized Belloc for the quality of his book, the two
men shared not a few assessments of the cardinal.[122] Belloc, a prolific essayist, Catholic apologist, and "public literary personality" in the first half
of the twentieth century, produced numerous books on English and French

history (he had been born outside of Paris to an English mother and French father and performed French military service, although he ultimately became a British subject).[123] Like most of his books, his *Wolsey* billed itself not as an exhaustive biography or a critique of Pollard's research but as an essayistic account designed "to establish character and motive in him and his contemporaries."[124] Belloc identified two primary defects in Wolsey's character, "one of the intelligence, the other of the will." With regard to the former, Belloc argued that the cardinal never developed a "vision." "The thing of the moment absorbed him; he was concerned solely with the events of day to day." As to the latter, "the defect of will was fatal. It was the defect of ambition," which for Belloc meant Wolsey's habit of placing his own desires above the tasks that needed to be accomplished.[125] Belloc agreed with Pollard that Wolsey was a man of great potential, but by concentrating authority in his own person and thereby showing what royal supremacy might look like, he sowed the seeds for the destruction of the ecclesiastical system that had facilitated his rise. Belloc departed from Pollard, though, in casting Wolsey's story explicitly in the form of a tragedy. Pollard had argued that the cardinal contributed to his own undoing, but in Belloc's telling Wolsey's disgrace and demise were hastened by the betrayal of his associate Cromwell.[126] What's more, Belloc lays greater stress than Pollard on the antagonism Anne Boleyn directed toward the cardinal and on the extent to which Anne, rather than Henry, guided royal policy. Belloc's treatment of the king is far from the hero worship that some critics attributed to Pollard (as to Froude before him). Henry was diseased; "his caprice increased; with it went a nervous violence; and with that nervous violence what was not at all incompatible with it, but rather a consequence of it, namely his offering even greater opportunity than of old to be influenced by whoever was for the moment his director; and his director now was Anne."[127] So for Belloc, the combination of the cardinal's own substantial flaws, the careerism that prompted Cromwell's betrayal, and Anne's relentless hostility together brought about Wolsey's fall. Wolsey appears, in Belloc's book, neither a hero nor a villain but a man of great limitations and few defenses against his eventual destruction.

Remembering Wolsey in Public, 1846–1946

We will return to Wolsey's representation in historical writings in Chapter 5. For now, we must observe that the century that this chapter covers witnessed not only the emergence of historical fiction and the professionalization of the historical guild. It also saw some of the most extensive public commemorations of Wolsey, which, because they were highly local in character, may have served to lodge the cardinal more firmly in the collective memories of some of the places with which he is most closely associated.[128] In some ways, the appearance of these local celebrations in a chapter dedicated to the Victorian period and its aftermath is not surprising. As Mark Freeman has shown, the first half of the twentieth century constituted a heyday for the British public's engagement with history, particularly in the form of historical pageants, "in which successive episodes from a community's history were depicted, involving large numbers of local people." Some forty such events were produced in the single decade from 1905 to 1914.[129] The chronological and geographical patterns for commemorations of Wolsey are unsurprising: The cities most closely associated with Wolsey's largesse, Oxford and Ipswich, are also those that mounted the most extensive commemorations of him. Likewise, commemorations were most often timed to coincide with significant anniversaries, those of Wolsey's death and the foundation year(s) of his Oxford college. In this section, we will see that both Ipswich and Oxford commemorated a Wolsey largely abstracted from his original historical context (and our prototypes for his representation). This is a Wolsey who was a generous patron rather than a player in the politics of the Henrician court and European diplomacy.

Let us begin in Ipswich, which even today celebrates Wolsey as its most famous son. Of course, very few remnants of the town he knew remain extant; the exceptions include a Tudor house near the site of Wolsey's reputed birthplace and a gate that marked one of the side entrances to his short-lived Cardinal's College. Nevertheless, as of this writing, he is commemorated in the names of several streets (Wolsey Street, Cardinal Street, New Cardinal Street), two theaters (the New Wolsey Theatre and New Wolsey Studio), the Wolsey Art Gallery, a shopping mall (Cardinal Park), at least one pub (The Thomas Wolsey), two upscale housing developments (Cardinal House and Wolsey House), and a school for pupils with special needs (Thomas Wolsey School), among other features of the civic landscape. A bust of the cardinal stands next to the entrance to the main Borough Council chamber in the Town Hall, although it is partially obscured by a recently installed bar. He figures in the permanent exhibit of the Ipswich Museum, which admiringly claims that Wolsey "showed an interest in developing his home town right up until his fall from power," and his arms are proudly featured in the fourth of eight embroidered panels depicting the history of Ipswich that were commissioned in 2000 to mark the eight hundredth anniversary of King John's royal charter.[130] Most recently, in 2011 the town erected a public memorial to the cardinal, following a competition that attracted more than fifty proposed designs. We will return to this memorial, which depicts Wolsey sitting and teaching, in the Conclusion.

Ipswich's most extensive commemorations of Wolsey occurred in 1930, marking the fourth centenary of the cardinal's death. For six evenings in June, the town treated residents and guests to a fully staged "Wolsey Pageant." The pageant was widely advertised (see Plate 14), and its proceedings went to pay for the construction of the Wolsey Art Gallery at the back of Christchurch Mansion, a local landmark and Tudor home that stands on the site of the Holy Trinity Priory suppressed by Henry VIII in 1536. (One of those who helped acquire the mansion for public use in 1894 was Felix Cobbold, a relative of the Anglican clergyman Richard Cobbold, whose portrayal of Wolsey in *Freston Tower* we have already discussed.)[131]

In the souvenir program distributed to pageant audiences, Ipswich's mayor and the pageant's organizer lauded Wolsey as "a remarkable personality, one of the greatest statesmen England has produced, the most acute master of diplomacy of his time, a reformer and educationist, a man who raised himself, by his own ability, from humble origins to the exercise of power second only to that of his Royal master, King Henry VIII."[132] They asserted that the pageant offered an opportunity "to show both his greatness and his weaknesses, and to realize the romance and the tragedy of his rise and fall." In addition, they remarked that Wolsey himself had been a master of pageantry, such that "at a time when the display of magnificence was of high concern to monarchs and noblemen, Wolsey outbid all with his splendor."[133] The program refers audience members who wish to learn more to Cavendish's *Life* and the modern biographies by Creighton and Pollard. However, few of Pollard's criticisms of the cardinal were on display during the pageant. Even local merchants stretched the limits of credulity to show their admiration by employing Wolsey as a spokesman for their wares. An advertisement for one store borrowed lines from Shakespeare and Fletcher's *King Henry VIII*: "If we shall stand still / In fear, our motion will be mocked at, or carped at, / We should take root here where we set." The advertisement went on to announce that "The Ipswich Industrial Co-Operative Society Ltd. never stands still—but goes forward boldly. . . . Join the Great Pageant which is marching to the Co-operative Commonwealth."[134]

The pageant consisted largely of edited scenes from *King Henry VIII*, interspersed with a few newly written sketches that connected the action of the play and the events of Wolsey's life back to Ipswich. Lifted directly

from Shakespeare and Fletcher were the scenes (or portions of scenes) featuring the nobles' criticisms of Wolsey (I.1), Wolsey's first appearance at
Henry's side (I.2), his revels at Hampton Court (I.4), Buckingham's fare-
well (II.2), the arrival of Campeggio (II.2), Anne Boleyn's conversation with
the Old Lady (II.3), the annulment hearing (II.4), Wolsey's and Campeggio's confrontation with Katherine (III.1), Wolsey's dismissal (III.2), his
farewells to Cromwell and courtly life (III.3), Katherine's assessment of
Wolsey and her death (IV.2), and Anne's coronation procession (IV.1), the
visual climax with which the pageant concluded. Of the new scenes, the
first represents Wolsey, as a boy, being sent to Oxford at the behest of his
parish priest. Young Tom, "nearly crying," as the stage direction has
it, avers that he would rather stay home, and in response to his parents'
rejoinder that Ipswich claims no suitable institution of learning, he complains, "Well, there should be one."[135] After Tom and his parents watch a
mystery play about the Epiphany—the scene is set on the feast of Corpus
Christi, when such plays were usually performed—a neighbor asks whether
Tom wishes to be a king like the ones in the play. He declares instead, "I'd
rather be the Pope/For he's above all Kings and rules their hearts."[136] The
pageant next returns to Ipswich after the conclusion of Shakespeare and
Fletcher's II.2, this time to commemorate the foundation of Cardinal College. Townspeople gather excitedly to await Wolsey's triumphant return
but are disappointed when Cromwell appears in his stead. Later, after Wolsey's farewells in III.3, the pageant stages his burial at Leicester Abbey.
Two monks regret the speed and secrecy of Wolsey's entombment, with
one of them commenting presciently on the ways in which the enmity of
powerful figures has shaped the cardinal's memory:

> A fallen man is but a felon to
> His enemies, remembering the wrongs
> He did supposedly against them. Now
> There's not a friend may show him much respect
> Since mighty ones would have him much debased.[137]

The other monk praises Wolsey's service to the church, affirming his
ambition for the papacy and commending his involvement in temporal
affairs. Not even Cavendish had offered such a full-throated defense of his
master's aspirations as this monk's:

> He was a man who kept, by divers ways,
> Steadily on the journey t'wards that goal
> The Papal Crown. He served the Church with all

His strength, yea fiercely wrenching pow'r with both
His hands to make Her seem more glorious.
He labored day and night to circumvent
Her enemies and for reward took
Such dignities as best would honour Her.
His was not saintly war of prayer or fast;
He fought with worldly weapons, and his fall
Came when those weapons broke. God rest his soul.[138]

After the monks watch the cardinal's funeral procession, the first monk concludes the scene with a speech drawn largely from the one Shakespeare and Fletcher had placed in the mouth of Griffith, Katherine's gentleman-usher. Italicized here are the portions that the Ipswich pageant masters re-wrote for their own purposes:

This Cardinal
Though from an humble stock undoubtedly
Was fashioned to much honour from his cradle.
He was a scholar, and a ripe and good one;
Exceeding wise, fair-spoken, and persuading:
Lofty and sour to those who loved him not,
But to those men who sought him, sweet as summer.
And though he were unsatisfied in getting
Which was a sin, yet in bestowing, *brother*
He was most princely: ever witness for him
Those twins of learning that he raised in *stone,*
Ipswich and Oxford, *and though worms corrode*
And stones shall crumble, his memorial
Built in the hearts of scholars cannot fall
But stands for ever to uphold his name.[139]

These emendations rectify what the pageant writers might have considered Shakespeare and Fletcher's overemphasis on the dissolution of Cardinal College, Ipswich (which, in Griffith's speech, "fell with him, / Unwilling to outlive the good that did it"); they also accentuate and seek to enact Wolsey's enduring place in the local collective memory. At the same time, in the course of attributing these speeches to the monks rather than to Griffith in dialogue with Katherine, the writers invisibly omit Katherine's speech in IV.2, which recapitulates criticisms of Wolsey that almost certainly would have been judged too hostile for reproduction in a pageant honoring Ipswich's favorite son. The focus, therefore, is not squarely on any of our prototypes, Wolsey the papist, Wolsey the author of the schism, or Wolsey the repentant sinner. Instead it is Wolsey the hometown hero who comes to the fore, in ways that displace other characterizations of the cardinal.

Like the Ipswich pageant of 1930, commemorations of Wolsey in Oxford, the other place that has been a leading recipient of his patronage, have almost uniformly been celebratory. In 1907, amid what some contemporaries dubbed a national outbreak of "pageantitis," the city of Oxford, with the support of the university, sponsored an "Oxford Historical Pageant" featuring scenes from local history.[140] The spectacle, directed by master pageanteer Frank Lascelles, was performed daily for a week. The company included more than a thousand participants; the stands had room for five times as many spectators. As Deborah Sugg Ryan has observed, all of Lascelles's pageants "explored the process of remembering," and his Oxford production "set a particular precedent that shaped the whole direction of the modern pageant movement."[141] Of the pageant's fifteen major scenes, the seventh was entitled "Wolsey Receives Henry VIII at Oxford" and is set in 1518, according to the *Book of Words*, a commemorative edition of the script that sold more than 17,000 copies. The scene depicts Wolsey showing Henry and Katherine the site for Cardinal College (see Plate 15). As a matter of historical fact, Wolsey did visit Oxford in Katherine's company around the time the scene envisions, although Henry, afraid of contracting the notorious sweating sickness, did not join them.[142] In the pageant, after Wolsey has explained his scheme to enhance the university with a new foundation, the king asks how his college would be paid for. Wolsey announces that "out of decay springs life" and presents Henry with a list of monasteries to be dissolved. Thomas More and Richard Pace, who have accompanied the king, are appalled by this suggestion, and at first Henry joins in their skepticism, but Wolsey's assurance that everything has been done with papal approval puts the king at ease.[143] Still, Henry declares, he would rather rely on his sword "than all/Your colleges and clerks in Christendom." The lengthy speech Wolsey makes in response appears to replace the principles of early modern humanism with a modern, secular defense of the value of higher learning:

> I pray your Grace
> Forget that here are colleges or clerks;
> Only remember here be men who think,
> And even as the brain is master to the hand,

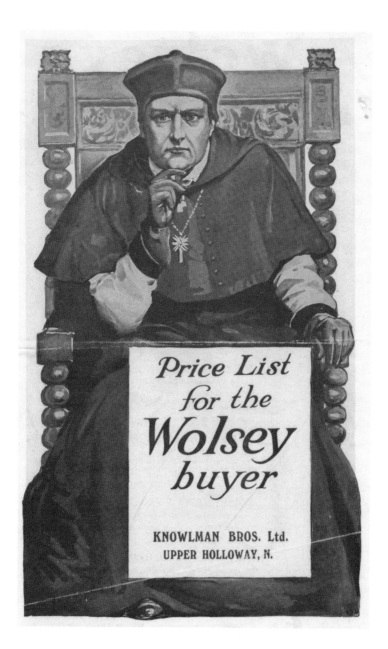

PLATE 1. Wolsey's image has been used not only for polemical but also for commercial purposes. The Wolsey clothing brand has used the cardinal's likeness since 1897, including in this undated advertisement for underwear.
Source: The Bodleian Libraries, The University of Oxford, John Johnson Collection: Men's Clothing 1 (71).

CARDINAL   WOOLSEY

PLATE 2. The oldest extant color portrait of Wolsey, this anonymous likeness was likely executed between 1589 and 1595 and now resides in the National Portrait Gallery, London. *Source*: © National Portrait Gallery, London.

PLATE 3. Vivian Forbes's oil painting *Sir Thomas More Refusing to Grant Wolsey a Subsidy, 1523* (1925) was commissioned as part of a series celebrating key moments in the development of British democracy. Thomas More, as speaker of the House of Commons, confronts Wolsey, the representative of the pre-Reformation church.

Source: © Parliamentary Art Collection, WOA 2596. www.parliament.uk/art.

257 Wᵘ Lee

Thomas Woolsey Cardinal Dyork autheur du schisme

PLATE 4. This early line drawing, likely from the 1510s, represents a cardinal-to-be who does not conform to later stereotypes about his girth. A subsequent hand has added the epithet "autheur du schisme," reflecting one of our three prototypical representations of Wolsey. *Source*: Bibliothèque d'Arras, France.

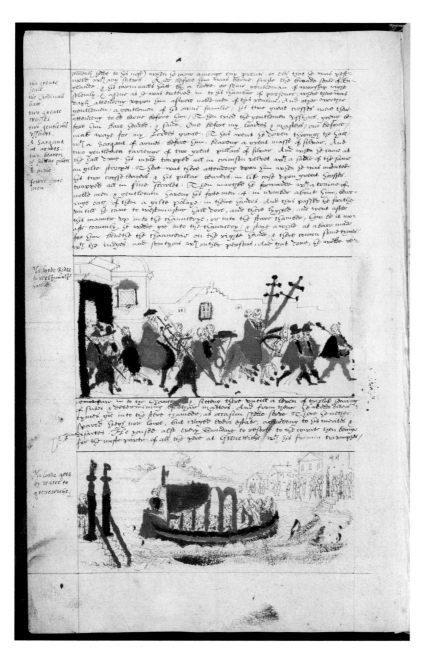

PLATE 5. The drawings in Oxford, Bodleian Library MS Douce 363, a manuscript of Cavendish's *Life* that dates from the last quarter of the sixteenth century, represent a thin, bearded cardinal.
Source: The Bodleian Libraries, The University of Oxford, MS. Douce 363, fol. 52v.

CANTERBVRIES
DREAME:
IN WHICH
The Apparition of Cardinall *Wolfey* did
prefent himfelfe unto him on the fourteenth
of May laft paft:

It being

The third night after my Lord of STRAFFORD had
taken his fare-well to the WORLD.

Printed in the yeare 1641.

PLATE 9. *Canterburies Dreame* was one of several puritan pamphlets published in the critical year 1641 that took Wolsey as a parallel or cautionary tale for King Charles's controversial Archbishop of Canterbury, William Laud. *Source*: Early English Books Online.

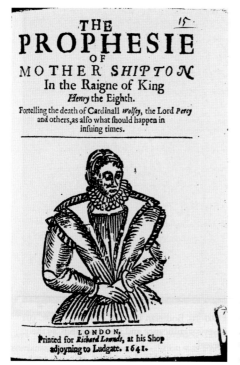

THE
PROPHESIE
OF
MOTHER SHIPTON
In the Raigne of King
Henry the Eighth.

Foretelling the death of Cardinall *Wolfey*, the Lord *Percy*
and others, as alfo what fhould happen in
infuing times.

LONDON,
Printed for *Richard Lownds*, at his Shop
adjoyning to Ludgate. 1641.

PLATE 10. One among a number of Stuart pamphlets that took the quasi-fictional character Mother Shipton as their protagonist, *The Prophesie of Mother Shipton* (1641) has its title character foretell Wolsey's downfall. *Source*: Early English Books Online.

PLATE 11. The many renovations that Henry VIII undertook at Hampton Court Palace upon Wolsey's exile included plastering over the cardinal's arms above the gateway to Clock Court. The plaster was so skillfully removed in the mid–nineteenth century that a Victorian historian of Hampton Court imagined that King Henry had in fact left Wolsey's arms in place.
Source: Author's photograph.

PLATE 12. As part of the restoration of Hampton Court Palace that followed Queen Victoria's opening of the site to the public free of charge, architects and surveyors sought to create in the palace's great hall a sense of what they thought it had looked like under Wolsey's ownership. *Source:* Joseph Nash, *The Mansions of England in the Olden Time*, vol. 3 (London: Sotheran, 1871).

PLATE 13. A contemporary view of Freston Tower, which stands outside the village of the same name some three miles south of Ipswich. Unlike its counterpart in Richard Cobbold's historical novel, the tower was constructed well after Wolsey's lifetime.
Source: Author's photograph.

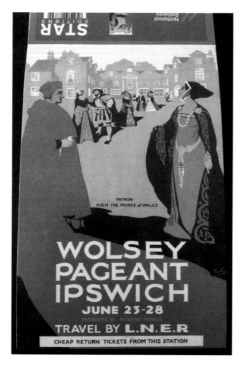

PLATE 14. To commemorate the fourth centenary of Wolsey's death in 1930, the town of Ipswich produced and broadly advertised a "Wolsey Pageant," which featured scenes adapted from William Shakespeare and John Fletcher's *King Henry VIII*, along with episodes of the pageanteers' own composition.
Source: Author's photograph of historic postcard sold at Christchurch Mansion, Ipswich.

PLATE 15. The "Oxford Historical Pageant," a model of its kind, was performed in 1907 and featured episodes from the history of the town and university. One scene, captured here in two commemorative postcards, depicts Wolsey showing King Henry and Queen Katherine the site for his planned Cardinal College.

Source: The Bodleian Libraries, The University of Oxford, John Johnson Collection: Pageants 6.

PLATE 16. Alumni of Christ Church, Oxford, presented the college in 1898 with a hat that tradition holds to have been Wolsey's galero. Since that time and to this day, it is proudly displayed in the college's Upper Library.
SOURCE: © The Governing Body of Christ Church, Oxford, 2018

PLATE 17. Orson Welles, who portrayed Wolsey in the 1966 film *A Man for All Seasons*, has been called "arguably the definitive Wolsey."

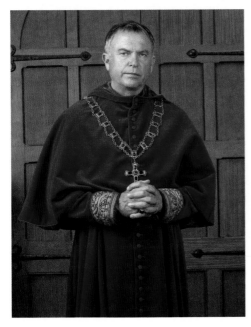

PLATE 18. Sam Neill's more recent portrayal of the cardinal in the controversial television production *The Tudors* is highly revisionist yet also takes cues from the representation of Wolsey in Cavendish's *Life*.

PLATE 19. The most recent public commemoration of Wolsey's life and legacy, this statue by the Scottish sculptor David Annand was unveiled in Ipswich's town center in 2011. Annand's unconventional design beat out nearly fifty competitors.
Source: Author's photograph.

PLATE 20. This somewhat grotesque statue of Wolsey stands near the site of his tomb in Leicester's Abbey Park. It was commissioned and donated to the city by the Wolsey international clothing firm, which took the cardinal's name when established in 1755.
Source: Author's photograph.

The master of the nation's task is here.
Here let us build, but not with stones alone;
Let's build with courage, faith, and enterprise,
With daring and a challenge to the unknown,
And most with honesty. Let's build a house
Wherein by spirit-subtle alchemy
Men may transform the wise high thoughts of old
To new and golden deeds. Then shall we build
As I have dreamed we built.[144]

The Oxford pageant, unlike its counterpart in Ipswich, does not develop Wolsey's character to any significant extent. It commemorates him as the founder of one of Oxford's great colleges, Christ Church (whose nickname, "the House," features subtly in the lines just quoted), and largely skirts the controversies associated with Wolsey, with the obvious exception of his decision to dissolve a number of religious houses to fund his new establishment. Also absent here, as in the Ipswich production, are allusions to Wolsey's role in the royal annulment crisis and subsequent schism—a topic on which the pageant is conspicuously silent.

For more extensive commemorations of Wolsey in Oxford, we must turn to his college. "His," of course, is a contested term, since Wolsey's Cardinal College was suppressed following his dismissal; it was formally refounded as King Henry VIII's College in 1532. That institution, in turn, was dissolved in 1545 and then finally established in something like its current form in 1546, a shared foundation uniting the cathedral of the newly created diocese of Oxford with a college of the university, under the official title of the Cathedral Church of Christ in Oxford of the Foundation of King Henry VIII. However, Henry's death halted the drafting of statutes for the new foundation, and as Judith Curthoys has noted in her magisterial history, "The foundation charter, strangely, describes only the ecclesiastical establishment with a mere hint of the academic side of life which was assumed and, to a certain extent, already established."[145] Wolsey's statutes for Cardinal College guided Christ Church de facto for much of its history, and it was not until 1867, after a significant reorganization and much political wrangling both inside and outside the college, that Christ Church acquired a full set of statutes.

Who, though, is the founder of Christ Church? Legally, the answer is Henry VIII. Within weeks of Wolsey's fall, the word at court was that Henry would seek both to possess the college and to obliterate all references to its first founder. As Chapuys wrote to Charles V:

Now it is rumored that the King has very lately issued orders for all priests and ecclesiastics appointed by the Cardinal to quit the place forthwith, as part of it is to be demolished, were it for no other purpose than that of removing the Cardinal's escutcheon, which will be no easy work, as there is hardly a stone from the top of the building to the very foundations where his blazoned armorial is not sculptured.[146]

We have already seen that Henry engaged in similar efforts to expunge Wolsey's memory at Hampton Court, but even though he proceeded to dissolve completely the college in Ipswich, it is unclear whether Henry took similar steps at the foundation that eventually became Christ Church. We have no evidence to show what Henry envisioned would become of some of the devotional practices mandated in Wolsey's statutes, which called upon college members to pray daily for "Thomas, Cardinal, Legate *de latere*, and our Founder" and his parents, Robert and Joan.[147] Unsurprisingly, the college archives for the transitional period 1530 through 1546 are thin, and we have even less evidence as to how the members of the foundation regarded the cardinal during those years of anxiety.

In practice, over the course of its history Christ Church has commemorated Wolsey at least as often, and at least as glowingly, as Henry. In particular, it has taken as its most prominent symbol Wolsey's galero, which Curthoys, the current college archivist, points out "has been used on headed paper, on oars, on tankards, etc., from the earliest times that these things appeared."[148] The college proudly claims ownership of what it takes to be the cardinal's actual hat, presented around 1898 by a group of devoted alumni (see Plate 16); it also boasts no fewer than seven paintings, two busts, and two full-length statues of Wolsey.[149] Of the paintings, the most famous is the portrait by Sampson Strong that hangs immediately to the right of King Henry VIII in the dining hall and depicts the cardinal in profile, with Christ Church in the background.[150] Of the statues, the earlier of the two stands over the main gate and was donated in 1719 by an Anglican bishop, Jonathan Trelawney, who identified himself in the accompanying inscription as Wolsey's successor in Winchester.[151] The other, placed on the "Wolsey Tower" that was constructed in the late nineteenth century above the staircase to the dining hall, was given by the theologian Henry Parry Liddon.[152] One can therefore find statues of Wolsey on two of the four sides of the college's main quadrangle, Tom Quad, which is also home to Christopher Wren's Tom Tower, an imposing belfry which in turn holds Great Tom, the college's largest bell. All of these references to "Tom," of course, are in Wolsey's honor.

Christ Church has staged substantial commemorations of its history in 1846, 1925, and 1946, making the three and four hundredth anniversaries of the present foundation and the four hundredth anniversary of the foundation of Cardinal College. These competing anniversary dates serve as reminders of the college's multiple foundations, and it is worthwhile to consider, if only briefly, how with each commemoration the institution situated itself in reference to the two men it honors as founders.

The 1846 commemoration appears to have been the first centenary celebration the college hosted. As a contemporary newspaper article noted, 1646 and 1746 were inauspicious years to call the college's history to mind, given "the troubles of the great rebellion in the one century, and the unsettled state of political parties in the other."[153] The commemoration occurred on November 4, the precise date of Henry VIII's letters patent that created the current foundation; celebrations included "the usual Choir service," a commemorative address, and a dinner hosted by the dean and chapter.[154] The address, delivered by an S. Stokes, celebrated "the great results, which during three centuries have flowed from the munificence of the Royal Founder."[155] The celebration, therefore, was a commemoration of Henry's generosity, and Wolsey appears to have been remembered primarily as a matter of historical interest. The *Guardian* described Henry's establishment as having been built "upon the ruins of Cardinal Wolsey's magnificent foundation."[156]

Even by choosing to commemorate 1925 as a centenary year, Christ Church disavowed this Henry-centric narrative. In contrast to the limited evidence available from 1846, a brief history that the college commissioned for its 1925 celebrations gives Wolsey pride of place, noting that "the early years of the sixteenth century saw great enthusiasm for the New Learning, and Wolsey, who, on the testimony of Shakespeare, 'was a scholar, and a ripe and good one,' was only one among many who were determined to promote it."[157] The booklet invisibly downplays Henry's involvement by using the passive voice to describe the college's evolution in the 1530s and 1540s: It "was re-founded" and later "founded for the third time." Christ Church staged a concert on May 23 and a more formal celebration, a garden party followed by a church service, on June 24. King George V and Queen Mary attended the latter events, giving tacit sanction to the equally tacit displacement of their royal predecessor as the college's sole founder. Choral evensong that afternoon included a prayer of plural thanksgiving: "for our founders, Thomas Wolsey, Cardinal, Archbishop of York, and

King Henry the Eighth, by whose munificence we are here brought up to godliness and the studies of good learning."[158]

Press reports from 1925 likewise highlighted Wolsey's role in the establishment of Christ Church. One contemporary account of the celebrations observed that "the present generation is more loyal to the essential truth of things. It is doing homage now, defying the pains of *praemunire*, not to the King but to the Cardinal. Wolsey is the man stamped on the imagination of the House. He first conceived its existence, he secured the site, he built the hall and the great quadrangle."[159] Christopher Hussey, who had attended Christ Church and went on to become editor of *Country Life*, applauded Wolsey in his article for the magazine. "The idea of Cardinal College fertilised in Wolsey's brain, out of the 'No Greek' agitations of 1515–20. When an obscure Bursar of Magdalen, he had known Grocyn, Linacre, More and the rest of that circle of humanists which delighted Erasmus." Hussey linked his praise of Wolsey with contrasting sentiments about his royal master:

> Cardinal College was the first and only great institution produced
> by the Renaissance—one can almost say by the Reformation—in
> England. . . . Had Henry VIII been able to control his sexual lusts, not
> only would Cardinal College be the finest monument of the early
> Renaissance in this country, but the sixteenth century might have
> been the most splendid, instead of the most dreary epoch in English
> history.[160]

By 1946, a pattern for centenary commemorations had been set, and the successful conclusion of the Second World War provided Christ Church with additional reason to celebrate its four hundredth anniversary. The 1925 order of service for evensong was duly updated, with the prayer for Wolsey and Henry retained verbatim. Plans were laid for another royal visit, this time from King George VI and Queen Elizabeth, and caterers prepared for another garden party. For this anniversary, the college resurrected its early tradition of performing plays for royal guests, and it chose, appropriately enough, Shakespeare and Fletcher's *King Henry VIII*.[161] Press coverage again sought to adjudicate Wolsey's and Henry's claims to the title of founder. The *Times Literary Supplement* observed, somewhat ambivalently, that Henry "is entitled to his place among Oxford founders," but Wolsey's title is by far better attested in practice:

> Though [Henry's] portrait hangs in hall, it is the Cardinal's arms that
> confront St. Aldate's from the outer bastions of Tom Quad, the

Cardinal's Hat that stands as the emblem of Christ Church on stationery and athletic colors, the Cardinal's name or title that the college clubs generally prefer to the King's. Left in his age "naked to his enemies," Wolsey in his reputation has had his revenge upon the master who cast him down, and that in the very place where Henry had most honorable reason to vaunt his victory. "The fabric of Christ Church," writes Mr. Hiscock, in his opening sentence, "is a collaboration of Wolsey, the long line of Deans, the benefactors, and the artists they commanded"—he does not find it necessary to say a word of Henry Tudor.[162]

The critic's reference here was to W. G. Hiscock, the college's deputy librarian, who in the centenary year had published his research on the college's fabric, history, and archives under the title *A Christ Church Miscellany*. Hiscock was only one in a series of college librarians and archivists who have promoted Wolsey's claims; the title of the magisterial history written by the current archivist Curthoys, *The Cardinal's College*, continues this tradition. Perhaps in response to Hiscock's work, when the Christ Church historian Hugh Trevor-Roper proposed in 1950 to write a brief history of the institution for visitors and newcomers, he gave greater prominence to Henry than Wolsey, arguing that the king "made practical the idea and used the materials of Cardinal Wolsey, building more firmly and permanently upon his frustrated foundation."[163] Trevor-Roper went on to describe Henry in the most laudatory of terms, calling him "the greatest patron of learning that ever sat on the English throne" and expressing regret that Christ Church has no statue of its royal founder.

However one seeks to balance Wolsey's and Henry's claims to the title of founder, commemorations of Wolsey in Oxford, as in Ipswich, have represented him as a benefactor more than a political or ecclesiastical leader. We might say that these commemorations constitute something of an additional prototype for the representation of Wolsey: as a favorite and loyal son of his hometown, a visionary alumnus and patron of his university, and an innovator in the history of English education. Almost of necessity, civic and university commemorations have chosen to dodge the most complicated questions that Wolsey's life presents; that is, they have sought quietly to extract him from his role in late medieval English Catholicism and the events that led up to the religious break with Rome. Pageants, prayer services, and commemorative publications have been able to perform this work of extraction with some ease. Only with regard to one phase of Wolsey's life do they generally encounter difficulties: These Ipswich and

Oxford commemorations had to find creative ways of grappling with Wolsey's dismissal as chancellor and the subsequent dissolution and refoundation of his colleges. In the Ipswich pageant, the scene of Wolsey's burial and the dialogue between the two monks of Leicester Abbey created space for pageanteers to defend Wolsey against claims of ambition and worldliness. The Oxford pageant, the twentieth-century Christ Church commemorations, and the day-to-day practices of the college have taken a different tack, seeking almost willfully to forget Wolsey's disgrace and to remember him in the place of his royal master. These competing strategies of representation and commemoration serve substantially different purposes from many of those we have been tracing throughout this book.

Conclusions

This chapter has surveyed three substantially different contexts in which Wolsey was remembered over the course of the century that began around 1850: fictions, historical scholarship, and public commemorations. Historians, pageanteers, and others working in these contexts employed distinctive strategies for representing the cardinal, strategies often tied to the demands of their particular medium, the theological and political convictions with which they approached their task, and their investment in contemporary debates like those about the discipline of history and the place of Catholicism in English life. Yet it is important to resist the sort of reductionist analysis that seeks to reduce any specific representation of Wolsey to a neat function of its creator's religious and political allegiances. To take but one contrary example, the staunch patriot and Anglican Brewer depicted Wolsey in perhaps the most laudatory terms of all the historians we have encountered, embracing an exaggerated version of Cavendish's prototype while at the same time disavowing Cavendish himself. Nevertheless, Brewer's is an exceptional case, and more often than not, Wolsey continued to serve as a foil for writers' preconceived narratives about the Reformation, Catholicism, and the Church of England.

Each of our three contexts involved the representation of Wolsey for distinctive reasons. For the writers of early historical fictions, the cardinal more often than not served as a moral exemplar. Curiously, these authors drew lessons primarily from episodes in Wolsey's life that they either imagined out of whole cloth or embellished substantially. They tended not to engage with Wolsey's more complex and contested legacy as a participant in the political machinations that preceded the break between England

and Rome. While they may have demonstrated anti-Roman biases, as in the case of *Freston Tower*, their narratives diverged sharply from those of earlier antipapists. Indeed, as we will see in the next chapter, it was not until the second half of the twentieth century that fiction writers engaged more directly with Wolsey's involvement in the annulment; when they began to do so, they produced works whose attitudes toward the cardinal were as divided as those we have encountered here.

The period of this chapter provided space for experimentation by fiction writers, but for professional historians, it offered instead space for self-definition. As the debate between scientific and literary models of historical scholarship intensified, scholars of both stripes continued to write about the reign of Henry VIII and the early years of the independent Church of England. We found that a number of historians, such as Merle, followed closely in the footsteps of their predecessors. Others, however, took advantage of the burgeoning number of original documents to craft new, often more complimentary, narratives about Wolsey. However, authors like Brewer, Creighton, and Taunton were not the successors of Cavendish in the same way that Merle was of Foxe. Instead, their assessments derived from newly printed materials that identified weaknesses in the cardinal about which Cavendish was reticent or unaware, yet they also freed Wolsey from some of the criticisms that his gentleman-usher had articulated.

With regard to these nonfiction works, there are substantial differences between biographies and works that represented Wolsey in the course of larger narratives, whether about English history or the history of the Reformation. With the sole exception of Pollard's monograph, the cardinal's biographers have almost always sought to rehabilitate Wolsey more than to perpetuate criticisms of him. Writers of general histories, however, have articulated both positive and negative assessments—verdicts often driven, as in the cases of Froude and Brewer, by their opinions about King Henry.

The final set of representations that we considered, including civic performances and Wolsey's remembrance at Christ Church, served yet another set of purposes. Where historical fictions tended to present Wolsey as a study in morality and historical scholarship largely continued to operate within the bounds of our time-honored prototypes, public and semipublic events remembering the cardinal have instead been commemorative. In the sense that we distinguished between representations and commemorations in the Introduction, events such as those in Ipswich and Oxford held up the cardinal for recollection and celebration as a local boy made good and a generous patron of learning. As the historical fictions did, but in a different way, these commemorations skirted some of the most challenging questions about the cardinal's life and legacy.

Yet, even though it is helpful to distinguish between these three sets of representations—fictions, histories, and commemorations—the boundaries between them are not entirely so clear. We have seen that as the historical guild sought to achieve consensus about the norms of history as a discipline, techniques that Ian Hesketh has called "boundary work" were employed to exclude certain styles of historical writing, particularly those represented in this chapter by Merle and Froude, because they appeared to be too similar to literature. But the theoretical questions we encountered at the beginning of this chapter—about the limitations of history as well as those of fiction—certainly did not vanish with the establishment of the *English Historical Review*, and they became increasingly complex in the latter half of the twentieth century. To the most recent chapter in the history of Wolsey's representation, then, we must at last turn.

CHAPTER 5

From *A Man for All Seasons* to *Wolf Hall* (c. 1960–present)

A. F. Pollard's representation of Henry VIII and his associated representation of Wolsey remained influential throughout the first half of the twentieth century. Pollard's depiction of a king who fully controlled policy and of a cardinal whose constitutionally anomalous role prepared the way for the royal supremacy laid the groundwork for subsequent accounts of the Henrician Reformation. For instance, Maurice Powicke's famous dictum in *The Reformation in England* (1941), that "the one definite thing which can be said about the Reformation in England is that it was an act of State," echoed the emphasis Pollard had placed on the king's role as chief agent of change.[1]

We saw in the previous chapter that the Victorian period witnessed several innovations in the representation of the Tudor past. At an elite level, university-trained historians sought to demarcate the boundaries of their discipline; closer to the ground, historical fictions and civic pageants offered ordinary consumers of history a new set of media for understanding the past. When these trends intersected, controversies often resulted. The critics of J. A. Froude, for example, alleged that he was writing literature rather than so-called empirical history; on that basis, they sought to bar him both from ascending to a professorial chair and from contributing to the most distinguished academic journals.

By the middle of the twentieth century, the range of possibilities for the representation of Wolsey had expanded still further. The invention of motion pictures, followed by that of television broadcasting, created entirely new ways for audiences to engage with history. The first motion picture to depict Wolsey was a silent film featuring five scenes from the 1910 London production of Shakespeare and Fletcher's *King Henry VIII.* Not long after, a nine-minute silent short entitled *Cardinal Wolsey* was filmed in the United States; it was a brief representation of Wolsey's fall from power that, remarkably, showed the cardinal excommunicating the king and, even more remarkably, being permitted to live out his old age.[2] A few other films about Henry, Wolsey, Anne Boleyn, and the English Reformation appeared starting in the 1920s. They, along with their successors, pose interpretive challenges similar to those of the historical novels and short stories we examined in Chapter 4. In the first section of this chapter, we will explore some of these challenges through two classic film representations of Wolsey, *A Man for All Seasons* (1966) and *Anne of the Thousand Days* (1969). Toward the end of the chapter, we will discover how two more recent television productions, *The Tudors* (2007–2010) and *Wolf Hall* (2015), interpreted the cardinal differently than their midcentury predecessors and, in so doing, contributed new insights about historical representation.

However, it should go without saying that twentieth- and twenty-first-century innovations in the representation of Wolsey have not been limited to the screen. In the middle section of the chapter, therefore, we will investigate some prominent developments in the burgeoning field of English Reformation historiography. Beginning with the revision of Pollard's conclusions by historians such as Geoffrey Elton, we will turn to the famous debate between A. G. Dickens and his revisionist critics, including Christopher Haigh and Eamon Duffy. Curiously, revisionists had little to say about Wolsey, whose pluralism and ostentation created a conundrum for their attempts to rehabilitate late medieval Catholicism. In the period this chapter covers, advances in the scholarly representation of Wolsey have come less in the form of biographies—the few such works that have been produced have generally not been the most innovative—than in the form of narrowly focused studies published in niche journals. With the increasing specialization of scholarship, along with the heightened suspicion of master narratives that has been promoted in contemporary critical theory, has come a splintering of the academic conversation about Wolsey, so that political historians, art historians, church historians, and literary scholars do not share assumptions about which texts, or even which sorts of texts, "matter" enough to be read and discussed. As we will see, this sense of indeterminacy maps closely onto the methodological and epistemological questions posed by a number of the latest historical fictions. However, the recent history of Wolsey's representation is not simply one of disintegration. As we will see toward the end of the chapter, many fictional and scholarly accounts of the cardinal produced during the last half-century point toward the emergence of a new and final representation, that of Wolsey as Henry's dutiful but ill-treated servant.

Midcentury Plays and Their Film Adaptations

In the previous chapter, we examined several historical novels and short stories from the nineteenth century. Wolsey appeared occasionally in historical fictions in the first half of the twentieth century, but it was only after the midpoint of the century that portrayals of the cardinal gained broad cultural currency. Robert Bolt's play *A Man for All Seasons* (1960) was first adapted for film in 1966. In 1969 premiered the film *Anne of the Thousand Days*, based on a 1948 play by Maxwell Anderson that had previously escaped wider recognition on account of its "frank talk about bastards, incest, and adultery."[3] Both films received Academy Awards, *A Man for All Seasons* being recognized as Best Picture of its year; it was later remade in 1988, with Charlton Heston playing the title role. Neither drama, of course, has Wolsey as its protagonist, but in each the cardinal serves as a dramatic foil to, and creates a sharp contrast with, a heroic figure, whether Thomas More or Anne Boleyn. The unflattering portrayal of Wolsey in both dramas contributed to the way he has been remembered in the second half of the twentieth century.

A number of commentators have observed that *A Man for All Seasons* represented a sea change in the portrayal of Thomas More. In its wake, John Guy has observed, "his reputation becomes almost a transferable skill. His name is invoked in national assemblies, the law courts or the media less to help us understand things about the past than to win arguments or prove points about religious faith or the rule of law in the present."[4] Examples are too numerous to multiply, but Guy has identified many instances in which the memory of More has been invoked in the aftermath of Bolt's version of his life, whether in the impeachment trial of President Bill Clinton, the pages of the journal *Moreana*, or special exhibitions in major museums.[5] We might add to Guy's list More's more recent appearance, along with John Fisher, as one of the patron saints of the US Catholic bishops'

"Fortnight for Freedom," a series of annual demonstrations to protest what the bishops take to be US government efforts to curtail religious liberty.[6]

Bolt's play, informed primarily by R. W. Chambers's 1935 biography, presents More as a defender of conscience against the tyranny of an oppressive monarchy.[7] As Anthony Kenny demonstrated in 1983, the historical More would likely *not* have understood conscience as an individual's private possession but instead as something objective, the recognition of God's will and the revealed order of things, which, for More, included the authority of the pope.[8] Bolt's preface indicates explicitly that his More is not meant to be identical to the historical lord chancellor:

> This brings me to something for which I feel the need to explain, perhaps apologize. More was a very orthodox Catholic and for him an oath was something perfectly specific; it was an invitation to God. . . . So for More the issue was simple (though remembering the outcome it can hardly have been easy). But I am not a Catholic nor even in the meaningful sense of the word a Christian. So by what right do I appropriate a Christian saint to my purposes?[9]

Indeed, Bolt proceeds to apologize "for treating Thomas More, a Christian saint, as a hero of selfhood."[10]

More could be said about the genesis of Bolt's representation, and Peter Marshall has chronicled the ways in which Bolt's play gave rise to a "veritable flood" of scholarly writings on an individual who had been neglected in earlier studies of Tudor England. In the decades following Bolt's play, works on More multiplied in an unprecedented way: "This kind of reciprocal dialogue between scholarship and representation, history and drama, is decidedly unusual. In the field of early-modern and medieval history, it is virtually unique."[11]

The extraordinary visibility of *A Man for All Seasons* helped shape the reputation not only of More but also of Wolsey, who appears in the play as his antagonist.[12] The cardinal speaks in only one scene, but the contrast between the outgoing and soon-to-be-incoming lord chancellors serves a series of dramatic functions: to illustrate the corruption of the medieval church, to highlight More's idealism, and to lay out the political stakes for the play's subsequent action. Here, in ways that Wolsey's early critics like John Skelton would have appreciated, the cardinal appears as a spider, sitting at the middle of a political web through which he seeks to capture the king's annulment. Bolt makes much of More's summons to see Wolsey, and the 1988 film remake, channeling Cavendish's description of the approach to Wolsey's audience chamber, dwells on the various rooms and passages

More must traverse to reach the lair of the cardinal, here played by John Gielgud.[13] Bolt's brief character sketch of Wolsey employs language from a similar register. For Bolt, the cardinal is "Old. A big decayed body in scarlet. An almost megalomaniac ambition unhappily matched by an excelling intellect, he now inhabits a lonely den of self-indulgence and contempt."[14]

Stella Fletcher lauded Orson Welles's performance opposite Paul Scofield in the 1966 *A Man for All Seasons* as "arguably the definitive Wolsey."[15] Certainly Welles matches Bolt's sketch: He is obese, world-weary, perceptive, pragmatic, and determined, a man who knows what needs to happen and possesses the willpower to make it so (see Plate 17). His conversation with More highlights the differences in their worldviews. In the original play, Bolt makes clear that More sometimes differs from Wolsey on style rather than substance. For instance, when the cardinal declares that he has appointed a "ninny" as English ambassador to Rome precisely "so that I can write to Cardinal Campeggio!", the stage directions that precede More's response contain an important distinction: "(*Won't respond; with aesthetic distaste—not moral disapproval*) It's devious."[16] Yet soon, Wolsey perceives that More is entertaining reservations of a more serious sort—and his criticism of More, which both films reproduce verbatim, goes to the heart of their differences. "You're a constant regret to me, Thomas. If you could just see facts flat on, without that horrible moral squint; with just a little common sense, you could have been a statesman."[17]

For Bolt's Wolsey, the king's need for an heir who will secure the Tudor dynasty outweighs all else. Wolsey badgers More about the consequences of not meeting Henry's demands. "D'you think two Tudors is sufficient?" "Do you *remember* the Yorkist Wars?" "Let him die without an heir and this 'peace' you think so much of will go out like that!" Ultimately, according to Wolsey, More cannot "explain how you as Councilor of England can obstruct those measures for the sake of your own, private, conscience."[18] For More, on the other hand, "when statesmen forsake their own private conscience for the sake of their public duties . . . they lead their country by a short route to chaos."[19] This is, of course, the nub of the play, and Bolt's stage direction for Wolsey is pointed: "*Looks back at him, hard-faced, harsh; for the first time we see this is a carnivore.*" When he reminds More to "come down to earth. . . . And until you do, bear in mind you have an enemy," he could be referring as much to Henry as to himself.[20] But it is More who gets the final word. As he leaves, Wolsey avers, "More! You should have been a cleric!" And More responds, "(*Amused . . .*) Like yourself, Your Grace?"[21] The 1988 film emphasizes More's point by showing Wolsey taking a long drink from an ornate chalice.[22]

One curious line in the play, changed in or omitted from the films, adds further evidence that Bolt might not have intended the contrast between More and Wolsey to be entirely stark. When More's wife informs him that the Duke of Norfolk had spoken of him as a future chancellor, More responds: "He's a dangerous friend then. Wolsey's Chancellor, God help him. We don't want another." The 1966 film omits the line "We don't want another" altogether, whereas the 1988 remake changes it to "We don't *need* another."[23] Much as Bolt's original More may be repulsed by Wolsey's pragmatism, he also judges it a necessary evil. More does not seek the chancellorship, and it appears that he recognizes Wolsey's skills to be well suited to his position. If so, there is more to the Wolsey of *A Man for All Seasons* than a simple contrast with the title character. Perhaps this ambiguity is why the directors of both films omitted the line in question; if so, its absence deprived audiences of the opportunity to encounter a slightly more complex representation of Wolsey. Instead, they got a caricature of a cardinal who is substantially different from the traditional prototypes for representing him. This Wolsey is not the vengeful author of the divorce, nor is he a fanatic papist. He may somewhat resemble the proud cardinal of the first half of Cavendish's *Life*, but Bolt, following the dominant historiography of his day, casts Wolsey primarily as a ruthless political servant dedicated to his master's desires.

As Marshall suggested, in the wake of *A Man for All Seasons*, it was difficult for dramatic productions set at the Henrician court to sideline Wolsey. Certainly this is true of *Anne of the Thousand Days*, the 1969 film adaptation of Maxwell Anderson's play about Henry's second queen. The third of Anderson's "Tudor trilogy"—his other two plays, on Elizabeth I and Mary, Queen of Scots, were also made into films—*Anne of the Thousand Days* comprised what some critics took to be a distinctively American representation of Tudor England.[24] Produced by the Hollywood stalwart Hal Wallis, it premiered to mixed reviews.[25] However, in the decades since its appearance, the critical consensus has turned mostly in its favor, with Glenn Richardson writing in 2005, for instance, that it "at least tries to be faithful to evidence as analyzed by historians and it presents a version of events that is broadly consistent with the record, interpreting them in an emotionally engaging way."[26]

Even those critics who found *Anne of the Thousand Days* inaccurate, hackneyed, or overly laden with emotional content have usually found room to praise Anthony Quayle's performance as Wolsey. For the first half of the film, Quayle's Wolsey is as visible a presence as Richard Burton's Henry and Genevieve Bujold's Anne. Clothed consistently in scarlet regalia (with, occasionally, his galero on his head instead of being carried before him), Wolsey is the consummate fixer of Henry's court. In Anderson's telling, Henry's mercurial temper requires particularly careful management, and in a knowing conversation with Cromwell, Wolsey alludes to the danger of awakening the king's darker instincts. "Let sleeping kings lie, Thomas, and we'll see to the government of the country."[27] The pattern for the film's depiction of Wolsey appears to be Cavendish's *Life*: Central to the dramatic action here is Anne's desire for revenge on Wolsey for breaking off, at the king's behest, her engagement with Henry Percy. The film includes several scenes that suggest how Anne planted in Henry's mind the seeds of his minister's destruction. In one, Anne describes for Henry how the ladies of the court reckon that Wolsey has both more titles and more wealth than him, forcing Wolsey to express his willingness to part with his possessions. Yet, curiously, the film hedges on the question of Wolsey's ultimate fate. When Campeggio dissolves the Blackfriars court, Henry dismisses Wolsey as chancellor, declaring, "I do not forgive you. I spare you for your past services." In a touching scene that follows, the cardinal makes his peace with Henry and Anne. To the king, he declares, "Your Majesty has taken from my shoulders a load that would sink a navy"; to Anne, he offers a written inventory of his goods at York Place, yet she responds, "I've been your enemy, but I can't take it from you."[28] Both Henry and, a few minutes later, More use identical words to say farewell to the fallen cardinal. "I'm sorry to see you go" is a far cry from the historical More's denunciation of Wolsey in the Parliament of 1529, not to mention the historical Henry's treatment of his onetime minister.[29] Whether this Wolsey ever meets the fate of his real-life counterpart is left ambiguous.

There are not a few similarities between the Wolseys of *A Man for All Seasons* and *Anne of the Thousand Days*. Both versions of the cardinal take an outsized role in directing the king's affairs; both rely heavily on Cromwell, who in each of the films moves quickly to take his master's place; both are criticized for their wealth. Neither is a particularly sympathetic character, although Quayle's dignified departure from office permits him to show a grace in defeat that Cavendish would have recognized. This morally censorious style of representing Wolsey was not of course unique to the two midcentury films we have been discussing here; indeed, it shaped the majority of historical novels and films produced in the twentieth century.[30]

Recent Historiography

But let us take a brief step backward. In the previous chapter, our survey of historiographical representations of Wolsey concluded with two biographies, those of A. F. Pollard (1929) and Hilaire Belloc (1930). The two books did not duel directly with each other but instead posed different sets of questions. Both criticized the cardinal for lacking vision in the areas of foreign policy and church reform as well as for being driven too much by personal ambition, but whereas Pollard depended largely on analyzing primary documents, Belloc wrote a book that, like many of his studies, was impressionistic.

As Rosemary O'Day has demonstrated, Pollard's interpretation of Tudor England, particularly as articulated in his *Henry VIII*, cast a long shadow over the next half-century of scholarship.[31] By the middle of the twentieth century, however, a variety of developments combined to make a different set of arguments possible. On the one hand, history had established itself more firmly as an academic discipline, "in no small part due to Pollard's own endeavors" as founder and director of the Institute of Historical Research.[32] Postgraduate degree programs and what today we would call undergraduate research projects appeared at many British universities. Debates about historical method were expanding as well, whether in the Marxist scholarship of Christopher Hill or the critiques of "Whiggish" historiography advanced by Herbert Butterfield.[33] On the other hand, with a greater sense of security, historians began to incorporate into their work methods and insights from other fields, some of which had been evolving at the same pace. They integrated sociological, anthropological, econometric, statistical, and eventually psychological ideas into works of historical scholarship in ways that would have been impossible or been considered inappropriate a few decades earlier.[34]

The debate on the English Reformation continued amid these disciplinary revolutions. In the 1940s and 1950s, most historians who worked on the religious changes of the sixteenth century saw their subject through the lens of politics rather than theology. Among them was the Cambridge constitutional historian Geoffrey Elton, who for all his many contributions to the study of the Reformation had little to say about Wolsey. Elton departed from Pollard's interpretation of the reign of Henry VIII in a number of ways. He challenged Pollard's two-phase theory: While Wolsey did dominate the first half of the reign, Elton believed that it was an oversimplification to argue that there was anything like similar consistency in policy between 1529 and 1547. He rejected Pollard's thesis that Henry became his own "prime minister" after Wolsey's downfall, arguing instead that the king, who was never the sole mover in policy or politics, was instead influenced by a succession of ministers and councilors, each with a distinctive set of political and religious priorities.[35] For Elton, the great innovator during Henry's reign and the "architect, the builder, and the master craftsman of the English Reformation" was neither the king nor the cardinal but instead Cromwell.[36] In contrast to the emphasis that Pollard, and Froude before him, had placed on Henry's personal rule, Elton situated Cromwell center stage, demonstrating that Cromwell's Wolsey, far from being the labor of a submissive servant carrying out his master's directions, had transformed Tudor government and its once-antiquated bureaucracy.[37] In Elton's telling, Cromwell was the first of a new breed of technocratic ministers, many of them with evangelical religious leanings, whereas Wolsey had been the last ecclesiastical statesman of the Middle Ages.

The work of A. G. Dickens comprises the most notable exception to the dominance of political history in mid–twentieth century scholarship. Dickens began from the presupposition that historians had ignored, at their peril, the appeal of Protestant theological ideas. Holding a series of professorial chairs in English universities, Dickens eventually became one of Pollard's successors as director of the Institute of Historical Research. His 1964 monograph *The English Reformation* quickly became the standard account of the period, continuing to be assigned in English school and university classrooms through at least the end of the twentieth century. Dickens's earlier book, *Lollards and Protestants in the Diocese of York* (1959), "articulated themes that ran through the rest of his work on England: that pre-Reformation criticism of the church was important even in the 'frozen' north; that there were continuities between old dissent and new protestantism; that the arrival of the latter could be traced from an early date and had considerable impact, at least in urban communities."[38]

Dickens's account of the Reformation proved to be as controversial as it was influential, and his monograph, despite its wide adoption as a textbook, became a favorite punching bag for historians who identified themselves as revisionists. These critics complained that Dickens had naively appropriated too many of the assumptions of an older, Foxean historiography—especially its emphasis on the corruption and unpopularity of the late medieval church, the roles of Wyclif and lollardy as precursors of the Reformation, and the speed with which ordinary English people accepted change.[39] Dickens's book is not quite as simplistic as has been claimed: For instance, he distinguished the "Henrician Schism," the top-down, politico-ecclesiological break, from the "English Reformation," the reception of Protestant theology by the clergy and commons, in an interpretive move reminiscent of Merle's work.[40] However, Dickens's representations of late medieval clergy in general and Wolsey in particular are among his least subtle. Foxe would surely have recognized these comments on Wolsey, typical of Dickens's overall approach:

> His tactlessness and financial demands in Parliament, his repression of the nobility, his development of Chancery jurisdiction at the expense of the influential common lawyers, his costly and ineffective foreign policy, his failure to execute radical reforms in the Church, his voracious appetite for other clergymen's privileges, the Roman basis of his authority as Legate, each of these features attracted powerful enemies. Above all, his personal arrogance, his enormous wealth and splendid ostentation was resented and freely contrasted with his origin as the butcher's son from East Anglia.[41]

Dickens represented Wolsey as a target of and an inspiration for what he labeled anticlericalism—a capacious term that, as Christopher Haigh, Robert Swanson, and others have argued, may be too diffuse to do much analytical work.[42] Specifically, Dickens claimed that what most drove Wolsey's contemporaries' hatred was his conspicuous use of legatine authority. Because he relied so visibly on prerogatives delegated to him by the pope, Wolsey embodied Roman authority in a way that few English prelates had done. This "undoubtedly stirred the dislike of his fellow Englishmen for Roman jurisdiction. When Wolsey was hated, inevitably some measure of that hatred became directed against Rome."[43] The echoes of the evangelical prototype we identified in Chapter 1 are clear.

However, for Dickens it was not enough that the clergy were inept and poorly educated, that the religious houses were sites of corruption more than holiness, and that Wolsey epitomized the rapacity and foreign allegiance of Roman prelates. All of these things had been the case in the late fourteenth century, yet John Wyclif and his followers had not achieved the kind of reform that they intended.[44] What was different in the first quarter of the sixteenth century was the appearance of new, attractive religious ideas. "Like the old Lollardy before it, the new Lutheranism floated upon a tide of negative criticisms, yet its positive affirmations were well trimmed to catch the winds blowing through the sixteenth century."[45] Dickens therefore included in *The English Reformation* a long section on Luther's theology, its relationship to pre-Reformation humanism, and its dissemination in England.[46]

Dickens's account of the Reformation echoed elements of Pollard's, especially in his emphasis on Henry's role in the genesis of the state reformation that Dickens dubbed the Henrician Schism. But Dickens did not agree with Pollard in every particular, and he gave wider berth to competition among theological ideas. Thus, whereas for Pollard Henry undertook the break from Rome with the more or less passive consent of Parliament, for Dickens the commons and their parliamentary representatives had already been prepared for schism by the activity of lollard and Lutheran preachers and welcomed a change from the incompetence and corruption of Roman clergy. In addition, Dickens's Wolsey explicitly represents all that was wrong with the Roman church, and Dickens criticizes the cardinal's use of legatine authority primarily on the grounds that it reminded people of the extent to which Rome had a say in English affairs. Pollard's Wolsey was no less ambitious than Dickens's and no less committed to the independence of Rome, but Pollard treated Wolsey's legatine authority as a model for Henry's supremacy rather than as a mechanism by which Wolsey the legate had fanned the flames of anticlericalism.

I alluded earlier to the criticisms that Dickens's interpretation suffered. Beginning in the late 1970s and accelerating through the 1990s, revisionist historians—especially Haigh, J. J. Scarisbrick, and Eamon Duffy—vocally argued that Dickens had produced an account of the Reformation that, unintentionally or otherwise, was indebted more to the presuppositions of Tudor evangelicals than to modern canons of historical inquiry. For revisionists, lollardy had not in fact survived into the early sixteenth century, and even if it did, it had become moribund. The late medieval church was not nearly as unpopular as Dickens had made it out to be, the clergy not so uneducated, the people not so frustrated. And the Reformation had not nearly been so rapidly or broadly received: In traditionalist counties, such as Lancashire and Yorkshire, people resisted reforming ideas and practices at least as often as they accepted them.[47] Therefore, for revisionists it was preferable to speak not of *the* English Reformation but instead of multiple English reformation*s*.[48] England's break from Rome was largely unwelcome and at first had to be enforced coercively, rather than being initiated by the crown with either the tacit (as in Pollard) or enthusiastic (as in Dickens) support of Parliament. (The conflict between Dickens and his critics became quite heated at times, and when Dickens published a second edition of *The English Reformation* in 1989, he left his most controversial claims largely intact. His biographer, Felicity Heal, has noted that "this was a bruising controversy and left a legacy of some bitterness.")[49]

Among the earliest revisionist monographs was Scarisbrick's *The Reformation and the English People* (1984), which argued that in the early sixteenth century, most English people were not dissatisfied with the church and that reform, when it came, was largely unwanted.[50] Scarisbrick's book built upon his earlier biography, *Henry VIII* (1968), which contains his most extensive comments on Wolsey. Scarisbrick explicitly rejected our Tudor Catholic prototype for the cardinal, commenting that "Wolsey as 'author of the schism' is scarcely more convincing than Wolsey as 'author of the divorce.'"[51]

Who, then, was Scarisbrick's Wolsey? In his description of the cardinal's rise to power, Scarisbrick followed Cavendish more closely than other Tudor sources. He adopted Cavendish's representation of Henry, at least early in his reign, as a king more interested in amusements than affairs of state. Consequently, "for much of the time, as, week after week, Henry hawked and hunted, jousted and tilted, diced and bowled, played tennis and made music, danced and banqueted, it must have seemed that an indolent, self-indulgent king had wholly surrendered the cares of state into the cardinal's hands."[52] Wolsey assembled an extensive ministerial portfolio by the middle of the 1510s through his capacity for hard work and attention to detail, the patronage he received from senior councilors like Richard Fox, and most of all, the king's willingness to accept his assistance. In Scarisbrick's telling, during Wolsey's greatest period of influence he often dictated English policy, especially foreign policy, even to the point of giving Henry letters to sign or copy out in his own hand.[53]

Scarisbrick differed markedly from Pollard and Dickens in imagining a king who was, at least at first, not entirely the master of his own affairs. He also rejected Pollard's assessment that Wolsey's policy was, first and foremost, to "hitch" England to Rome. On the one hand, even though Wolsey had his hand on the rudder of the ship of state from the middle of the 1510s, the cardinal could not operate without Henry's tacit approval. On the other hand, in Scarisbrick's analysis Wolsey did not often show Rome signs of his loyalty, much less his obedience. Papal officials complained about the sluggishness of English correspondence, they chastised Henry and Wolsey for promising but not delivering financial support, and Wolsey notoriously failed to deploy sufficiently skilled agents at the papal curia.[54] All of this was strange behavior, Scarisbrick concluded, for a cardinal supposedly ambitious for the papacy.[55] Instead, Scarisbrick argued that the goal of Wolsey's policy was peace, arbitrated officially by England but personally by himself, on a scale that Western Europe had not previously known. Wolsey's pleas for peace, and related initiatives such as the Treaty of London (1518), clashed at times with Henry's desire for military glory. Ultimately, of course, the cardinal was unsuccessful.

When it came to the saga of Henry's annulment, Scarisbrick again represented Wolsey in ways that align most closely with Cavendish's prototype. Unlike Cavendish, however, Scarisbrick buttressed his narrative with thorough analysis of the canonical issues at stake in the divorce. Arguing that Henry's desire for an annulment emerged from both diplomatic and dynastic necessity, Scarisbrick contended that Henry most likely developed his scruples about his marriage to Katherine on his own: Among other factors, "it is difficult to imagine that anyone would have dared to question the validity of the royal marriage without being prompted by the king."[56] But by the time Henry broached the possibility of an annulment with Wolsey, their relationship had already begun to deteriorate. On several occasions, Wolsey suggested legal strategies that, had Henry followed them, might have achieved the king's goals. However, Henry's suspicions about Wolsey's loyalties led him to ignore his minister's advice, with disastrous consequences. "At the very moment when Henry needed him most, when (perhaps) he had most to offer Henry, the latter, by a supreme irony, turned away."[57]

Wolsey's fall, when it came, follows the lines laid down by Cavendish. Scarisbrick represents Anne Boleyn and her noble allies as the cardinal's chief opponents. Anne struck the "decisive blow" by cutting short Henry's and Wolsey's conversations at Grafton House in 1529, and her Howard and Boleyn supporters continued to press for the cardinal's final destruction. Henry, on Scarisbrick's account, was "unable to forget either his failures or how remarkable a servant he had been and might be."[58] The king might not have wished to see Wolsey restored, but he might have imagined the cardinal, like Archbishop Warham, living out a modest retirement in his archdiocese. Unfortunately for Wolsey, Anne and her allies had the upper hand in 1530, although, in retrospect, only temporarily.

Scarisbrick was the only prominent revisionist to engage at length with Wolsey's legacy. For others, like Haigh and Duffy, Wolsey presented a historiographical conundrum. As we have seen, the heart of the revisionists' program was to argue that the medieval church was not as dissolute or disliked, nor was the Reformation as well prepared for or joyously received, as Foxean-Dickensian historiography had suggested. Wolsey's contemporary reputation was uniformly poor, as we saw in Chapter 1 and as Schwartz-Leeper and others have revealed through their work on writers like John Skelton. The cardinal's extraordinary pluralism, the scale of his palaces and the sumptuousness of his goods, and the pomp with which he carried himself—all of these made him anything but a helpful datum for revisionist arguments. Haigh conceded that Wolsey epitomized the failings reformers sought to associate with the Roman clergy, but he argued in a 1983 article that Wolsey was atypical. "For every Cardinal Wolsey . . . there were hundreds of poorly-paid and hard-working curates." "While no charge against Wolsey was too gross to be possible, Wolsey was not the church."[59] In his 1993 textbook *English Reformations*, Haigh described at some length Wolsey's role in the contest with Lutheran reformers. He also narrated the part that Wolsey played in conflicts between church and crown, such as the case of Richard Hunne and, of course, Henry's annulment suit. But Haigh did not seek to flesh out either Wolsey's character or the details of his relationship with Henry as Scarisbrick had done, and in *English Reformations* the cardinal appears less frequently than in more traditional accounts of the Henrician period. Even where Wolsey does appear in *English Reformations*, Haigh represents him primarily as a functionary.

His scant treatment of Wolsey notwithstanding, Haigh was significantly more forthcoming about Wolsey's role than his fellow revisionist Eamon Duffy, who emerged in the 1990s as one of the most effective scholarly advocates for the enduring appeal of what he dubbed "traditional religion." Wolsey does not appear in the index of Duffy's seminal 1992 monograph *The Stripping of the Altars*—a notable and surprising absence that indicates just how tricky the unpopular, worldly cardinal was for revisionist representations of the Reformation. Whether revisionists sought to demonstrate that Wolsey's failings were exceptional or whether they aimed instead to show that the religious system he represented remained vibrant despite his obvious moral shortcomings, their silence about him was both telling and problematic.

It was unlikely, therefore, that innovative interpretations of Wolsey would come from the pens of Dickens or his revisionist critics. For Dickens, as we have seen, no one illustrated the corruption of the late medieval church better than Wolsey, and therefore Dickens seemed quite content to resurrect, without much in the way of nuance, some of the earliest evangelical attacks on the cardinal. For Haigh and Duffy, Wolsey presented an inconvenient counterexample, and they, too, found little advantage in delving deeply into the minutiae of the cardinal's life and actions. To the extent that they chose to represent him at all, they figured him as a particularly bad apple in a church that was flourishing more than withering.

Five book-length biographies of Wolsey appeared during the decades of the clash between Dickens and revisionists. Of them, only one—Peter Gwyn's *The King's Cardinal* (1990)—included a full complement of scholarly apparatus. The others were produced for popular rather than academic audiences; one of them, Nancy Lenz Harvey's *Thomas Cardinal Wolsey* (1980), contains so many frank errors that it does not merit extended treatment.[60] However, as the earliest of these books demonstrates, a work for a popular audience is not necessarily an oversimplified or inaccurate one. Indeed, the boundary between popular and learned works is a porous one that often, but not always, has marginalized those who are writing for audiences outside the academy. Charles W. Ferguson, who served for many years as an editor at *Reader's Digest*, published in 1958 his *Naked to Mine Enemies*, a cogently written biography that engages in detail with primary documents, especially the *Letters and Papers*. Ferguson's account incorporated and responded to many of the insights about Wolsey that had emerged from the research of his predecessors. His Wolsey is in some ways an admirable man: a hard worker who took many years to win a position at court, a diligent servant who enjoyed the details of governing in a way his royal master did not, an excellent judge, and a reformer of the church who all too often exempted himself from his own decrees.

For Ferguson, the great dilemma of Wolsey's life was the inevitable conflict between what Ferguson dubbed his two masters: the king and the pope. In this regard, Wolsey was not exceptional: "This followed hallowed custom, and Wolsey was not one to question procedure or depart from order."[61] Instead, Wolsey's extraordinary talent made it possible for him to serve both king and pope and to do so with distinction, for quite some time, until the circumstances of Henry's annulment petition forced him to choose decisively. Ferguson represents the moment in the Blackfriars proceedings immediately after Campeggio declared an extended recess as the pivotal moment in Wolsey's conflict of loyalties:

> Wolsey's hour of decision had struck, and the sound of it reverberated
> with tones of doom. The failure of the legatine court to grant the
> King's wish would mean the end of Wolsey's power. Yet the court need
> not have failed, for under the commission wrung from the Pope
> Thomas Cardinal Wolsey had the full right to pronounce judgment
> himself; he could have pronounced it, if he had had a mind to, in favor
> of the King. If he had done so, he might have saved his station and his
> powers. In an atmosphere crackling with hostility and before an
> audience expecting a verdict favorable to the royal will, Wolsey had
> spoken plainly and he had spoken in defense of Rome. He had made
> his choice, and what so many had suspected and alleged now proved to
> be true: when the chips were down, the Cardinal was playing against
> the King.[62]

Ferguson thus figured Wolsey's decision as consistent with his loyalty to the church, perhaps not so much as the bearer of a theological system but instead as "the ideal of a kingdom above kingdoms, of a united Christendom over and beyond the state and the individual."[63]

Two subsequent biographies published during the last quarter of the century each sought to compare Wolsey with another major figure of his day. Where Neville Williams's *The Cardinal and the Secretary* (1976) juxtaposed Wolsey and Cromwell, Jasper Ridley's *Statesman and Saint* (1982) set Wolsey against More. Williams took a perspective similar to Elton's, labeling Wolsey "the last ecclesiastical statesman in the medieval tradition" in contrast to Cromwell, whom he styles the "layman who broke the power of the church to shape the modern English state."[64] Williams distinguishes between the two men in reference to their style of governance as well as to the extent that they delivered practical action. He repeatedly juxtaposes Wolsey's ostentation, and the extent to which he alienated his contemporaries by the manner in which he wielded authority, with Cromwell's "formal, serious, but never pompous" demeanor.[65] Williams also criticizes Wolsey for acquiring the authority necessary to reshape the late medieval church but then failing to undertake reform. By comparison, whereas Wolsey "had never had a plan beyond saving the old order," Cromwell sought to remake the church and kingdom altogether, wielding his authority in order to implement structural change.[66]

Whereas Wolsey came off poorly in Williams's evaluation, he fared far better in the comparisons that Ridley, a practiced writer of historical works for a broad educated audience, drew between the cardinal and Thomas More. As we saw earlier, the first two-thirds of the twentieth century witnessed the acceleration of a historiographical rehabilitation of More that may have begun as early as the mid-1700s.[67] Between Chambers's biography of More and Bolt's *A Man for All Seasons*, More's reputation had risen dramatically, but Ridley's book bucked the trend. He employed an extended comparison between More and Wolsey—"two very intelligent children" born in the 1470s who both "grew up to be men of outstanding ability."[68] Whereas for Ridley Wolsey was a "great statesman," More was an "intolerant fanatic."[69] Ridley treats both men's biographies at some length, but he bases his judgments primarily on how Wolsey and More approached the problem of heresy. It is significant for Ridley that Wolsey did not authorize the execution of any convicted heretics. During the years between his appointment and his dismissal as chancellor, no more than eight heretics were burned in all of England, and their executions were sanctioned by local bishops, not Wolsey. Therefore, "his policy toward heretics was relatively tolerant. He may have been responsible for the deaths of many soldiers killed in wars and of women and children left to starve to death in their devastated villages . . . but he was not responsible for the deaths of heretics."[70] Ridley held Wolsey up as an English statesman, not the fervent papist of Dickens's telling or the self-interested counselor of Pollard's. The cardinal fell, on this account, because Henry was willing to sacrifice his long-serving chancellor in order to break decisively from Rome.

Ridley's representation of More is less glowing in every respect. If Wolsey had been "tolerant and merciful" toward heretics, More asserted that their burning "was 'lawful, necessary and well done.'"[71] Ridley chronicles More's treatment of heresy suspects, and he extends his criticism to More's family life as well. Far from the saintly, solicitous father and husband of *A Man for All Seasons*, Ridley's More believed that "the object of family life was . . . duty, service to God, and the subjugation of the lusts of the flesh." He severely restricted the leisure-time activities of his family, flagellated his body, and continually wore a hair shirt next to his skin. It was perhaps especially with Bolt's play in mind that Ridley also asserted that the actions More took in the months leading up to his execution were not those of a virtuous, or even consistent, defender of the rights of conscience. As chancellor, More had "made statements in the House of Lords in favor of the divorce which he knew were untrue; he had refused to give any encouragement to opponents of the divorce, or even to read their books; and he had promised not to do anything against the divorce. But he would not swear to uphold it. On this issue More, who had so often compromised and lied, would not compromise and would not lie."[72] Instead, he "rested his defense on a legal quibble."[73] In Ridley's assessment, this was not the courageous act of a saint but a legal nicety that contradicted More's own track record as a prosecutor of heresy suspects. If he had refused defendants the liberty to obey their consciences in religious matters, on what ground did he seek that right for himself?

Whereas Williams's and Ridley's books positioned the cardinal in comparison with his contemporaries, in 1990 a biography appeared dedicated solely to Wolsey, Peter Gwyn's *The King's Cardinal*. Gwyn's tome, weighing in at more than 650 pages, is among the most sympathetic treatments of its kind. Gwyn argues that Wolsey was always the king's servant, a man who, in the book's closing words, "loved his master more than himself."[74] In a critical review of the book, Richard Rex somewhat disparagingly contrasted Gwyn, a former schoolteacher and "dedicated amateur," with the professional historians whose conclusions he sought to overturn. "The list of those with whom Mr. Gwyn has major interpretative disagreements over

Wolsey reads like a roll of honor of Tudor historiography: A. F. Pollard, A. G. Dickens, G. R. Elton, J. J. Scarisbrick, E. W. Ives, D. R. Starkey, J. Guy, and G. Bernard."[75] The long-held suppositions that Rex believed Gwyn's book had failed to rebut include the idea that Wolsey's rise and fall were due primarily to the operation of factions at Henry's court. Out of his detailed archival explorations, Gwyn presents a Wolsey whose foreign policy was pragmatic and not nearly as consistent as earlier historians had believed. Gwyn's book, which identifies itself as a "political biography," concentrates more on Wolsey's secular than his religious activities, although Gwyn critiques at some length the notion that the cardinal was more tolerant of heresy than his contemporaries.[76] Instead, Gwyn argues, the heresy defendants whom Wolsey encountered tended to come from within, rather than outside, the walls of the universities; they abjured rather than defended their beliefs; and there were relatively few of them to start with. It was not therefore out of conviction that Wolsey did not burn anyone for heresy; it was because circumstances did not ever demand that he do so. *The King's Cardinal* contends that Wolsey was interested in reforming abuses in the church, even if at first he did not have a specific plan. But Wolsey's reforms would have been orthodox: Gwyn writes at greater length about Wolsey's personal piety than other historians, taking at least some of Wolsey's public religious acts to signify his internal commitment to traditional beliefs and practices. Nevertheless, Gwyn asserts, for Wolsey the king's wishes always came first, and "Wolsey would have followed his monarch into schism but he would have hated doing so."[77]

While Rex may have queried Gwyn's scholarly bona fides, *The King's Cardinal* remains the most recent book on Wolsey to rely extensively on original documents. But academic representations of Wolsey in the second half of the twentieth century were not limited to book-length monographs. Between 1960 and the present day more than three hundred essays, appearing as journal articles and book chapters, have featured Wolsey. Collectively, they testify both to the ongoing popularity of Tudor England as a research topic and to the increasing specialization of scholarly inquiry. While it is impossible to treat each of these contributions individually, and while they do not always lend themselves to easy categorization, several trends in the study of Wolsey during the past sixty years deserve our attention.

First, it has been during this period that the *historiography* of Wolsey has explicitly become the subject of detailed analysis. Several writers of master's theses and doctoral dissertations have explored the representation of Wolsey in historical writings and literary texts, particularly *Hall's Chronicle*, Cavendish's *Life*, Foxe's *Actes and Monuments*, Holinshed's *Chronicles*, and Shakespeare and Fletcher's *King Henry VIII*.[78] In the twenty-first century, Gavin Schwartz-Leeper's doctoral thesis was published as *From Princes to Pages: The Literary Lives of Cardinal Wolsey, Tudor England's "Other King"* (2016).[79] (Chapter 1 and part of Chapter 2 of this book relied heavily upon Schwartz-Leeper's analysis of the prominent Tudor and early Stuart representations of the cardinal.) All these historiographical works have reached roughly similar conclusions, namely that early representations of Wolsey were shaped to a great extent by writers' theological commitments and by the literary forms within which they were operating. At the same time, our awareness of the conventions of early modern literary genres has been advanced by specialized research on the satires of John Skelton, on Cavendish's memoir, and on the dramatic strategies of *King Henry VIII*.[80]

Second, while Gwyn's biography focused primarily on Wolsey's work as chancellor and maker of English foreign policy, other historians have sought to add detail to our knowledge of the cardinal's involvement in legal and constitutional matters. In this area, John Guy's studies of the court of Star Chamber during Wolsey's tenure are particularly invaluable.[81] Guy and other constitutional historians have also considered Wolsey's interaction, or more accurately lack of interaction, with Parliament.[82] His role in the king's council and his relationships with fellow councilors have been analyzed.[83] Some of these essays, following the pattern set down by Elton and Williams, compare Wolsey's stewardship of government with that of Thomas Cromwell.[84]

Wolsey's achievements as a patron of education and the creative arts have been the subject of scholarship as well. We reviewed recent work on Hampton Court and Christ Church in Chapters 3 and 4, respectively, but important essays on Wolsey's involvement in the reform of the universities of Oxford and Cambridge;[85] on the works of art, sculpture, and music he commissioned;[86] and on the architectural innovations he inspired have all appeared in the past half-century.[87] These studies have confirmed or corrected previous assertions about Wolsey's relationship with education and the arts, but they have not, by and large, contributed to overall interpretations of the cardinal's life.

Next, scholars have offered new light on the circumstances surrounding Wolsey's downfall. In 1975, E. A. Hammond penned an essay on Augustine de Augustinis, Wolsey's physician during his brief sojourn in the north of England. He established that Dr. Augustine, as the physician was commonly known, had been a faithful servant of the cardinal's up until the night of his arrest at Cawood Castle. Subsequently, however, Augustine appears to have provided Wolsey's enemies with evidence sufficient to secure his conviction for treason: It was on account of Augustine's evidence that the king authorized sending Sir William Kingston to escort Wolsey to the Tower of London.[88] L. R. Gardiner, in a 1984 study, adduced new details about the manner in which Henry had communicated with France's King Francis about Wolsey's ostensible treachery, and Gardiner concluded that indeed "an extensive and desperate conspiracy seems to have been in Wolsey's mind."[89]

For Eric Ives, writing in 1991 about Wolsey's dismissal, the best explanation for the cardinal's downfall was faction, a concept that has guided much of Ives's work on the Henrician court.[90] Ives argued that a group of aristocrats led by Anne Boleyn and Thomas Darcy had been putting pressure on Henry to dismiss Wolsey as early as January 1529. By the time of the king's move against the cardinal in October, Wolsey's opponents had coalesced into what Ives dubbed an instance of "the phenomenon of 'grand faction' . . . the coming together of disparate groups and individuals to pursue one single objective, in this case the removal of the minister from power."[91] At first, they were only partially successful: Henry was content to permit his fallen minister "a remarkably soft landing," and even within weeks of Wolsey's dismissal, "the king was secretly back-tracking."[92] But Anne and her allies kept up the pressure on Henry until Wolsey himself, for reasons Ives is unable to explain, initiated treasonous exchanges with foreign powers. In Ives's telling, while factions could and did shift, their operation was central to Tudor politics. Not so for G. W. Bernard, who rejected Ives's analysis in a cogent article in 1996.[93] Faction may be an attractive explanation for Wolsey's downfall, Bernard wrote, but Ives erred in minimizing Henry's decisive role in the events unfolding at his court. Rather than being willing to permit Wolsey a dignified retreat, for Bernard the king was in no forgiving mood. The relationship between Henry and his minister had begun to deteriorate in 1527, and the king had lost confidence in Wolsey even before the conclusion of the Blackfriars proceedings in mid-1529. Thereafter, "Wolsey was no longer in charge of business," and Henry went out of his way not to see him. Wolsey's dismissal, far from being the result of a concerted effort to shift the king's mind, was directed by Henry himself.[94]

A final, if somewhat neglected, area of research has to do with Wolsey's work as a diocesan bishop and metropolitan of the ecclesiastical province of York. As we have seen, historians have primarily analyzed the cardinal's legateship in terms of its significance for the reputation of the English clergy and for England's foreign policy. However, a few studies have considered Wolsey as a church reformer, including Keith Brown's work on his proposed visitation of the Observant Franciscans at Greenwich, Tim Thornton's essay on Wolsey's confrontation with the abbot of Chester over the latter's palatinate jurisdiction, and several articles on the so-called little dissolution of monasteries whose lands went to support Wolsey's colleges in Oxford and Ipswich.[95] Jonathan Arnold has compared John Colet's vision of ecclesiastical reform with Wolsey's actual accomplishments.[96] Peter Clarke's study of the dispensations granted by archbishops of Canterbury after the 1532 Act in Restraint of Appeals also contains commentary on Wolsey's legatine administration.[97]

As even this cursory summary reveals, scholarship on Wolsey in the late twentieth and early twenty-first centuries has become increasingly detailed, reflecting an overall trend toward specialization in historical research. This work has immeasurably increased our knowledge of individual episodes in Wolsey's life and specific aspects of his administration. Correspondingly, however, it has become rarer to find overall assessments of him as a statesman, an ecclesiastic, or even simply a person. It is no surprise that Gwyn's remains the most recent fully documented biography of Wolsey—yet, as we noted above, even Gwyn found it necessary to prioritize Wolsey's political achievements at the cost of discussing his character and motivations.

It would be remiss not to note briefly in conclusion the two most recent biographies of the cardinal, *Cardinal Wolsey: A Life in Renaissance Europe*, by Stella Fletcher (2009), and *Wolsey: The Life of King Henry VIII's Cardinal*, by John Matusiak (2014). Fletcher's biography, in many ways the more creative of the two, situates Wolsey in the context of several other great cardinal-statesmen of the fifteenth and sixteenth centuries, including the French prelate George d'Amboise and the Spanish cardinal and humanist patron Ximenes de Cisneros. She represents Wolsey primarily as a diplomat and a faithful servant of his king, although she cautions against attributing to Henry too much dependence on Wolsey. In particular, she points to the disagreement between the two men over the appointment of Henry Standish, the king's choice for bishop of St. Asaph in 1518, as evidence that even early on, Henry did not hesitate to disregard Wolsey's counsel.[98] Fletcher follows Gwyn on a number of controversial points, including his assertion that Wolsey was not as lenient with regard to heresy as has often been supposed.[99] It is in her book's final chapter, "At the Sign of the Red Hat, 1530–2009," that Fletcher breaks the newest ground, providing a rapid-fire survey of the cardinal's appearance in works of historical scholarship, literature, drama, and art—a survey that in this volume I have attempted to expand and nuance. In contrast, Matusiak's biography contains little in the way of evidence-based argumentation, instead presenting a reader-friendly, psychologically oriented narrative that represents Wolsey as a "benevolent despot," "one of the first great political propagandists," and a sufferer from what modern clinicians might call anxiety and panic disorders.[100] For Matusiak, Wolsey was "addicted to status and stricken by a dreamlike self-confidence that was, in his case, a feature of this addiction."[101] His inability to remain on the sidelines when Henry spared his life and sent him into retirement ultimately turned the king against him and resulted in his downfall.

Memory and Fictions of the Twenty-First Century

Lacey Baldwin Smith memorably observed in an essay of 1960 that a "taste for Tudors" had characterized literary and historical scholarship throughout the twentieth century.[102] The previous section sought to demonstrate that the "taste" Smith identified grew more insistent in the second half of the century and the first two decades of the twenty-first. But at the same time that scholarship on Henry's reign has proliferated, historical fictions have multiplied as well. According to Jerome De Groot, the seemingly perennial popularity of Tudor historical novels is epitomized in the success of Philippa Gregory's *The Other Boleyn Girl* (2001), which sold more than eight hundred thousand copies and inspired a major film. For De Groot, Gregory's novel and its counterparts embody the conceptual problems that afflict the categories of historical fiction, genre fiction, and popular fiction. Gregory holds a doctorate in history yet does not write scholarly prose; her books include notes on documentary sources, yet they simultaneously engage issues from our own day, particularly modern and postmodern discourses about gender roles and patriarchy.[103]

De Groot situates novels like *The Other Boleyn Girl* within what he describes as the contemporary British fascination with multimedia "biog-history," quasi-fictional renditions of the past that permit readers (or, at least as often, viewers) to approach the inner lives of those who lived long before them.[104] In a similar vein, two recent productions, occupying very different cultural terrains, have offered new vantages on the lived experience of Wolsey: the critically derided, long-running television series *The Tudors*, on the one hand, and, on the other, the award-winning literary fiction of Hilary Mantel's novel *Wolf Hall* and its adaptation for the stage and screen.[105] In this closing section, we will explore how both of these productions have self-consciously facilitated new representations of Wolsey, while at the same time reflecting on the process of collective memorialization.

The Tudors

It is fair to say that *The Tudors* is a production of extremes. Broadcast in four seasons from 2007 to 2010, Michael Hirst's series is "by far the longest filmic event ever to deal with the Tudor dynasty," clocking in at more than thirty-five hours of screen time.[106] However, it is also one of the least accurate representations of the court of Henry VIII. Among the many deviations in its first season alone, the series marries the wrong sister of Henry to the wrong foreign monarch, conflates the Treaty of London with the Field of the Cloth of Gold, and promotes Thomas Cromwell into a position of authority well before his time. Many of the series' inaccuracies involve Wolsey.[107]

Criticism of *The Tudors* came swiftly after its premiere. David Starkey, the British television historian, compared the series with *A Man for All Seasons*, noting that Bolt's drama is "terrible history, but at least it has a point. . . . *The Tudors* is terrible history with no point. It's wrong for no purpose. I've got no problem with getting history wrong for a purpose—Shakespeare often got things wrong for a reason. But it's the randomized arrogance of ignorance of *The Tudors*. Shame on the BBC for producing it."[108] If Starkey's judgment was especially blunt, it was by no means uncharacteristic of the reactions of the anglophone scholarly and literary establishments, who subjected *The Tudors* to a degree of fact checking unseen in connection with other fictionalizations of the Tudor past. In an interview with the *New York Times*, Hirst appeared unfazed by the criticism. "Showtime commissioned me to write an entertainment, a soap opera, and not history. . . . And we wanted people to watch it."[109] In another interview, Hirst made explicit his criticism of academic historiography: "It's not like any of the historians were actually there. So what you read in history books, is that historically accurate? Not necessarily. *And in any case I'm not writing a documentary*."[110]

Yet as we have seen throughout this book, just because a text (or, in this instance, a television series) is inaccurate does not mean that it cannot be successful in creating or disseminating forms of historical memory. As Starkey just reminded us, consider the ways in which Shakespeare and Fletcher, or even more so Samuel Rowley, adjusted chronology for their respective purposes. De Groot and Ramona Wray have both argued that *The Tudors* is historiographically self-aware, deliberately evoking the possibility of events that might have transpired had historical actors chosen differently.[111] After the pilot, each of the episodes in the first season begins with a voiceover by the actor Jonathan Rhys-Meyers, who plays Henry:

"You think you know the story, but you only know how it ends. To get to the heart of the story, you have to go back to the beginning." While "the beginning" is an odd way to characterize the first season of the series, which begins in the tenth year of the Henry's reign, the disclaimer invites the audience, "you," into an exercise of historical imagination, a universe of alternate memory. It suggests that the seeds of events many years distant, such as Henry's treatment of all of his wives, were planted in his early, less well-known relationships. For this reason, perhaps, the characters that the first season develops at greatest length, apart from Henry, are Wolsey, Cromwell, and More—the individuals historically and dramatically best placed to shape the king's thinking and decision making. That Rhys-Meyers's Henry increasingly chooses not to heed their counsel and instead becomes the tyrant of popular memory provides an opportunity for viewers to reflect on what might have been while at the same time witnessing, as Thomas Freeman has put it, "Rhys-Meyers gradually (very gradually) change into Holbein's Henry—as we know he will."[112]

Most importantly for our purposes, *The Tudors* foregrounds Wolsey's role in the early Henrician court, with the Irish actor Sam Neill "offering the most fully realized onscreen Cardinal Wolsey yet seen—intelligent, subtle, worldly, ambitious, yet sincerely dedicated to peace, justice, and the welfare of his young royal protégé" (see Plate 18).[113] Neill's Wolsey, like (as we shall shortly see) Jonathan Pryce's in *Wolf Hall*, subverts our early modern prototypes for the cardinal even as his portrayal embraces a host of details from early modern texts like Cavendish's *Life*. To mention just three examples: When in the first episode Wolsey goes in procession to the royal chambers, his ushers use Cavendish's exact salutation to clear the way ("on my lordes & maysters make way for my lordes grace");[114] in several episodes the cardinal clutches tight the "very fayer Orrynge wherof the mete or substaunce wᵗ in was taken owt and fylled vppe agayn wᵗ the part of a Sponge";[115] and when Thomas Boleyn plots Wolsey's downfall, he uses a phrase that could have come directly from Cavendish's pen: "When the wheel of Fortune reaches its zenith, there is only one way for it to go."[116]

Wolsey is omnipresent in the first season of *The Tudors* in his role as the king's chief advisor. He displays two interrelated traits: on the one hand, his political pragmatism, and, on the other, his awareness of his dependence upon Henry's continuing favor, which is he willing to maintain even at the cost of violence. In a manner that parallels Bolt's *A Man for All Seasons*, the series contrasts Wolsey's almost entirely secular realpolitik with the religiously informed idealism of Thomas More. The first season pairs Wolsey and More for at least eight extended conversations, in almost all of which More appears as a foil to Wolsey's pragmatism. For instance, when More expresses surprise about the betrayal (that of the French cardinals rather than Charles V) that cost Wolsey the papacy, Wolsey retorts, "You think too highly of me. Perhaps you think too highly of the whole human race."[117] Discussing Henry's desire for a divorce, Wolsey observes casually, and to More's horror, that "kings get divorced all the time."[118] And as Henry's impatience with his annulment intensifies, More expresses disappointment in the king, to which Wolsey responds, "If you are not with me now, you are against me. . . . You don't want to get your hands dirty, but you have no choice."[119]

What most distinguishes Neill's Wolsey from that of Orson Welles is that whereas Welles embodied only Wolsey's arrogant self-assurance, Neill appears simultaneously confident and utterly dependent upon his prince. His awareness that his privileges are in the king's gift punctuates the early episodes; he counsels others, especially More, to follow him in fulfilling the king's desires, whatever they may be. Explaining his relationship with Henry to the king's pregnant mistress Elizabeth Blount, Wolsey avers that "I only do his bidding."[120] As tensions rise, the length to which the cardinal is willing to go to preserve Henry's friendship is increasingly on display: He presents Henry with Hampton Court Palace, manhandles Campeggio's servant and eventually the visiting cardinal himself, and publicly insults Campeggio when he revokes the annulment proceedings to Rome. At the same time as the series casts Wolsey as a bare-knuckled fighter, however, it also invites an imaginative entrée into the cardinal's private life, staging a sequence of scenes with Joan Larke, Wolsey's mistress, whom the historical cardinal had married off well before the years of the series. Larke tells Wolsey that he works too much, she nurses him back to health when he contracts the dreaded sweating sickness (a fatal disease of unknown origin that was prevalent in Tudor England), and she wails when he is arrested. His loyalty to her is equally clear, even to the extent of his refusing King Francis's offer of a woman: one of the few moments in the series in which any character turns down an opportunity for on-screen sex.

The Tudors's treatment of Wolsey's arrest and death departs most widely from the historical record yet draws most poignantly upon historical sources to craft an alternative representation of the cardinal's final moments. Cromwell, who in a previous episode had abandoned Wolsey, informs Henry that the cardinal, in exile in Yorkshire, is plotting against him. Wolsey is arrested by Charles Brandon and taken away in chains, a far cry from the dignified treatment that Cavendish's cardinal received at the hands of William Walsh and Henry Percy. (Curiously, *The Tudors* omits entirely Cavendish's subplot concerning Anne Boleyn's early infatuation with Percy, Wolsey's role in breaking off their relationship, and Anne's vengeance.) Imprisoned in an unidentified location, Neill's Wolsey offers a prayer—perhaps his character's only personally felt religious act—then takes up a knife left for him to carve his food and slits his own throat. The words of his prayer, which do not draw upon any earlier source, are worth quoting at length:

> Lord, we have not spoken as long or as often as we should. I've often been about other business. If I wanted forgiveness I should ask for it, but for all that I have done, and for all I am yet to do, there can be no forgiveness. And yet I think I'm not an evil man. Evil men pray louder and seek penance and think themselves closer to heaven than I am. . . . I know myself for what I am, and I throw my poor soul upon your forgiveness, in the full knowledge that I deserve none at your loving hands.[121]

The scene of Wolsey's suicide is intercut with footage of a court masque celebrating his descent into hell, which serves to heighten the contrast between the cardinal's repentance and the malice of those who sought his downfall. In depicting Wolsey's suicide sympathetically, *The Tudors* reclaims one of the anti-Wolsey tropes that we identified in early modern evangelical texts. Wolsey's turn toward God in his final moments and his articulation of his own limitations render him at least partially redeemed in the eyes of Neill's twenty-first-century audience, just as the same actions, as alleged by Foxe and others, had produced disgust in Tudor readers. By performing such a reversal, as Wray has noted, the series appears to be aware of its ironic relationship with sixteenth-century depictions of Wolsey, an awareness cheekily most manifest when Henry insists to Cromwell that no one is to know of the cardinal's suicide. Is *The Tudors* articulating what Wray calls a kind of historical conspiracy theory?[122] Is it simply pursuing the storyline best calculated to produce shock value? That there is no clear answer only underscores the inherent instability of historical fictions.

WOLF HALL

A year after *The Tudors* screened Wolsey's suicide, our final fictional representation of the cardinal appeared: that of the multiplatform *Wolf Hall* novels, stage plays, and television miniseries.[123] *Wolf Hall* is the brainchild of the English Catholic writer Hilary Mantel, a formidable theorist of historical fiction whose two novels about Cromwell and the Tudor court both won the prestigious Booker Prize.[124] The series takes its name from the ancestral home of the Seymour family, where the action of the first novel (2009) culminates. Its sequel, *Bring Up the Bodies* (2012), alludes to the saying that Tower of London guards used when charged to deliver condemned criminals to the executioner. Mantel's third and final novel, *The Mirror and the Light*, is forthcoming.

In *Wolf Hall*, Mantel's chapter "An Occult History of Britain, 1521–1529" includes in its opening section a phrase set off as a paragraph. Framed as a thought of Cromwell's—the novels employ a complicated third-person narrative form that privileges and renders legible the inner life of Cromwell, the ambiguous "he" of Mantel's prose—the idea is a simple one: "Beneath every history, another history."[125] In the book, Cromwell's thought concludes his musings on the competing claimants to the English throne; it also neatly captures Mantel's approach to the craft of historical fiction. De Groot has characterized *Wolf Hall* as "a very self-aware book, written by an author who has thought deeply about the problems inherent in writing historical novels, and the issues it raises are clearly applicable to the genre as a whole."[126] Elsewhere, De Groot has cited Virginia Woolf's aphorism that "Life is not a series of gig lamps symmetrically arranged; but a luminous halo" to suggest that historical novels permit their authors and readers to break free of conventional chronology, and *Wolf Hall*, across its different media, takes Woolf up on her invitation.[127] Scenes in the novel careen from Cromwell's childhood in Putney forward to the heyday of his work with Wolsey, forward again to the cardinal's downfall, and back to Anne Boleyn's first appearance at Henry's court. The television series, produced in 2015, abruptly cuts between scenes in similar fashion. The overall effect is to accentuate the artificiality of the novel and the television miniseries; in so doing, it highlights the agency of the author and suggests causal connections between events.[128]

The theme of memory figures centrally in *Wolf Hall*.[129] While the action of the novels transpires in the first-person present, Mantel's books constantly allude to both the mechanics and the power of memory. Cromwell's system of remembering—which he informs Cavendish he learned during his sojourn in Italy—is the source of much of his authority, albeit a tool with unwelcome consequences. "The ghosts are gathering," Mantel writes of Cromwell around the time of Wolsey's exile, "he feels cold, his position is irretrievable. In Italy he learned a memory system, so he can remember everything: every stage of how he got here."[130] Yet it is his remarkable memory that ingratiates Cromwell first with

Wolsey and then with Henry. At the same time, Mantel foregrounds the memories of other members of her "Cast of Characters." Despite Wolsey's centrality to the action of the novel, the reader does not witness his last moments directly but rather only through Cavendish's recollections. Mantel's characterization of the distraught gentleman-usher reflects her own assessment of the historical Cavendish's prose: "George Cavendish comes to Austin Friars. He cries as he talks. Sometimes he dries his tears and moralizes. But mostly he cries."[131] As we will see, it is Cavendish's recollection of what he takes to be the unjust treatment of the fallen cardinal that serves as the proximate inspiration for Cromwell's revenge against those he deems responsible.

However, before we turn to Mantel's treatment of the relationship between Cromwell and Wolsey, it is important to note that in *Wolf Hall*, memory is more than a frequently used motif or medium. It also bears a strong connection with power. Mantel's Cromwell derives power from his ability to recall facts and convey information to his patrons. For characters who already have power, especially Henry and Wolsey, memory becomes something that can be fashioned, created, altered, and if necessary destroyed; contemporary theorists like Kansteiner might recognize here their notion of the power of "memory makers who selectively adopt and manipulate . . . traditions."[132] This capacity of powerful people's memory appears in the very first scene in which Wolsey and Cromwell appear together. Set in 1527, this conversation concerns what Mantel dubs "the cardinal's project": the foundation of Cardinal College, Oxford, and its feeder school in Ipswich. Mantel frames the colleges as Wolsey's "breathing monument, working and living long after he is gone," in contrast with Wolsey's great marble tomb, "designed already, by a sculptor from Florence."[133] For Wolsey, to set up his colleges is to ensure he is perpetually remembered, and remembered just as he intends to be. Mantel juxtaposes Wolsey's desire to master the future memory of himself with the ways in which he shapes his contemporaries' sense of their past. When Cromwell and Wolsey recall Katherine's arrival in England, Cromwell muses: "Wolsey talks as if he himself had witnessed everything, eyewitnessed it, and in a sense he has, for the recent past arranges itself *only* in the patterns acknowledged by his superior mind, and agreeable to his eye."[134] Wolsey's sense of the past, of course, is not his alone: It is the basis for much of his diplomatic work on Henry's behalf, and with the judicious word "only," Mantel hints that Wolsey has the capacity to enforce his recollections upon others. Perhaps it is not too much of a stretch to suggest that just as the cardinal might transubstantiate the elements of bread and wine into the body and blood of Christ, he might also transubstantiate the messy events of the past into an authorized, official memory.

Except, as Mantel's Stephen Gardiner would say, he didn't. In the end, the cardinal comes to recognize what the twenty-first-century reader has known all along: Not only is Wolsey unable to deliver the king's annulment, but among the casualties is his vaunted "project," the colleges that were to secure his perpetual commemoration in stone and scholarship. As long as Wolsey has the king's favor, it appears, he is able to shape the memories of others as much as his own; once that favor vanishes, so also does his quasi-sacramental role as a memory maker. It is, instead, Henry's memories—those of his elder brother Arthur's marriage, his own wedding night, his pangs of conscience—that win out. Mantel hints early on that the king's memories have a power both more violent and more authoritative than the cardinal's. Even in 1527, in the same conversation we have been tracing, Cromwell articulates the king's changing recollections of his wife and the circumstances of his marriage:

> She always loved me, the king would say. Seven years or so of diplomacy, if you can call it that, kept me from her side. But now I need fear no one. Rome has dispensed. The papers are in order. The alliances are set in place. I have married a virgin, since my poor brother did not touch her; I have married an alliance, her Spanish relatives; but, above all, I have married for love.
>
> And now? Gone. Or as good as gone: half a lifetime waiting *to be expunged, erased from the record.*[135]

Where Wolsey is not able to effect a wholesale rewriting of the past, Henry brings about what his minister could not. Mantel's language—"expunged, erased"—conjures up the historical Henry, for whom, as we saw in Chapter 3, it was not out of character to order that reminders of Anne Boleyn at Hampton Court be destroyed. Yet perhaps ironically, Mantel's Henry does not wage such a wholesale campaign against the memory of Wolsey—the cardinal's coat of arms remains on the stonework of his Oxford college, and in the miniseries, Cromwell orders one of his own servants to repaint Wolsey's device in his home.[136]

Commentators have observed that *Wolf Hall* departs most strongly from recent literary recollections of the Tudor period by reversing the moral qualities assigned Cromwell and More in works such as *A Man for All Seasons*.[137] Certainly, More emerges from the pages of Mantel's novels more a fanatic than a statesman, to echo the title of Ridley's 1982 study.[138] Yet equally important contrasts with previous representations are to be found in Mantel's treatment of the relationship between Wolsey and Cromwell as well as in Mantel's characterization of Wolsey himself.

In the novel, and even more so the miniseries, Cromwell and Wolsey share an evolving paternal-filial bond, the nature of which shifts from Wolsey being Cromwell's patron to Cromwell becoming Wolsey's defender and, eventually, avenger.[139] Cromwell's loyalty to his master is one of the recurring tropes of *Wolf Hall*: Henry notices it, Wolsey's servants notice it, Cromwell's family notices it, and Cromwell's retinue notices it—even to the point of asking him to leave the cardinal to his fate. "I will say this for you," Henry observes to Cromwell, "You stick by your man." "I have never had anything from the cardinal other than kindness. Why would I not?" Cromwell replies.[140] For his part, Wolsey frets when Cromwell does not come to see him in exile and, in Cavendish's telling, calls out for Cromwell on his deathbed. As I just hinted, Cromwell's loyalty outlives Wolsey, and when he discovers how the cardinal had died and later witnesses the court celebrating Wolsey's demise, he swears vengeance on those responsible.[141] "God need not trouble, he thinks: I shall take it in hand."[142] The passages surrounding Wolsey's death are resplendent with allusions to Cromwell's memory of Wolsey, and Cromwell rapidly steps into his late master's shoes. A ring Wolsey gave him before his departure for Yorkshire "fits as if it had been made for him." Thinking of the cardinal, Cromwell adopts his authoritative countenance: "The red of a carpet's ground, the flush of the robin's breast or the chaffinch, the red of a wax seal or the heart of the rose: implanted in his landscape, cered[143] in his inner eye, and caught in the glint of a ruby, in the color of blood, the cardinal is alive and speaking. Look at my face: I am not afraid of any man alive."[144]

These words—which repeat those that Cavendish recalls Wolsey saying on the night of his arrest—capture Mantel's characterization of the cardinal. She puts in the mouths of Wolsey's opponents many of the slurs that, as we saw in Chapter 1, were in common use in the sixteenth century. Thomas Boleyn calls the cardinal a "butcher's boy"; the Duke of Suffolk taunts Cromwell about his "fat priest." Yet Mantel's direct descriptions of Wolsey make him something else entirely. "The cardinal, at fifty-five, is still as handsome as he was in his prime. . . . His height impresses; his belly, which should in justice belong to a more sedentary man, is merely another princely aspect of his being."[145] This Wolsey, especially as played by Pryce in the miniseries, is courtly, frequently amused, spry, cognizant of his power, but not tyrannical. In the stage productions of *Wolf Hall*, which premiered in Stratford in 2014 and transferred to New York in 2015, Wolsey's role as Cromwell's foster-father continues from beyond the grave, as his spirit returns repeatedly to give advice or allow Cromwell to explain himself.[146] True to Cavendish's account, all the *Wolf Hall* Wolseys are especially aware of omens; in the miniseries in particular, the cardinal and Cromwell debate the significance of kittens born under his bed at Esher.

Thus Mantel's Wolsey, like her Cromwell, is "a textbook 21st century antihero," as *Time*'s review of the miniseries put it. James Poniewozik, writing for *Time*, compared Mantel's Cromwell to other recent television characters whose moral ambiguity is part of their appeal, such as Frank Underwood in the political drama *House of Cards*, or Tyrion and Jaime Lannister in the *Game of Thrones* franchise.[147] The same, as we have already seen, might be said of the Wolsey and Cromwell of *The Tudors*, with at least one most important difference: In *Wolf Hall*, Cromwell is a deeply devoted adopted son who brings about the fall of Henry's second queen and her allies in order to avenge the dead cardinal, rather than a self-serving, ambitious man who discards his patron in order to take his place. Whether in *The Tudors* or *Wolf Hall*, however, few of the twentieth century's commonplaces about Wolsey have survived unquestioned in recent fictions. As we have seen, playwrights like Anderson and Bolt had used Wolsey as a foil for their representations of Henry and More. Whereas Anderson's Wolsey aids and abets the king's violent caprice until he himself falls victim to it, Bolt's Wolsey stands in stark contrast to his More, the cardinal as corrupt and pragmatic as More is pious and idealistic. Early-twenty-first-century renditions in *The Tudors* and *Wolf Hall* offer highly sympathetic reimaginations of Wolsey and Cromwell that serve as vehicles for reflection on the processes of writing and remembering history.

As we bring this survey of recent fictions to a close, it is worth noting a paradox: Many of the representations of Wolsey that have achieved the broadest circulation have also been those that have taken the greatest liberties with the historical record. More research remains to be done, as De Groot has suggested, on why audiences find historical fictions, with their "necessary anachronism" and their commitment to the "indeterminacy and unknowability of history," to be both compelling and entertaining.[148] Nevertheless, especially in the era of mass media, such fictions remain one of the primary mechanisms through which the memory of Wolsey (and, no doubt, other historical actors) is kept alive, refashioned, communicated, and consumed.

Conclusions

It says something about the contemporary sociology of knowledge that, during the period covered by this final chapter, historical fictions came to exert greater influence on the dominant cultural representation of a figure like Wolsey. As I observed in Chapter 4, during the years in which I have been writing this book, colleagues, friends, and casual acquaintances have repeatedly told me that their knowledge of Wolsey derives largely, if not entirely, from fictional portrayals in sources like *A Man for All Seasons* and *The Tudors*. Perhaps this was true in earlier periods as well—certainly Shakespeare and Fletcher's *King Henry VIII*, which is no less fictional than Mantel's novels, was performed frequently throughout the seventeenth and eighteenth centuries and may well have reached a broader audience than the learned tomes of historians such as Heylyn or Burnet. However, it is likely no accident that fictional versions of Tudor England have achieved cultural dominance just as the theoretical boundaries separating literature from academic historiography have grown more porous.

This chapter's account of the most recent representations of Wolsey has been divided almost evenly between fiction and nonfiction sources. Whereas fictions such as *The Tudors* and *Wolf Hall* have delivered some of the most epistemologically sophisticated accounts of the cardinal and of historical memory, in recent years academic engagement with the cardinal's biography has slowed, due at least in part to a trend toward specialization in scholarly endeavors that is sometimes so thorough that practitioners find themselves speaking past rather than to one another. Beyond the challenge of acquiring sufficient expertise in all the fields of activity in which the cardinal was involved, we observed that the revisionists of the 1980s and 1990s had good reason not to feature Wolsey too prominently. Even a generous reading of Tudor sources about the cardinal shows that he was an eminent counterexample to revisionist claims about the popularity of traditional religion on the eve of the Reformation. However, as revisionism has given way to what some historians have called postrevisionism and others have sought simply not to label, few new attempts to produce overall accounts of Wolsey's life have been made.[149] Peter Gwyn's *The King's Cardinal*, whatever its excessive enthusiasm for its subject, remains the most recent biography of the cardinal; it turns twenty-nine this year. The criticism Gwyn's book received from at least one reviewer turned on an issue we encountered among Victorian historians as well, namely that it was written by a "dedicated amateur" rather than a professional historian. It remains to be seen whether the sorts of concerns that motivated some

Victorians to deny membership in their guild to scholars such as J. A. Froude will continue to operate in the twenty-first century, where for different reasons historians have similar motivation to police the boundaries of their discipline.

If we turn to the substance of what has been said about Wolsey in the past half-century or so, both literary and historiographical representations of the cardinal have ventured what we might designate a final representation, that of Wolsey as dutiful (and sometimes maltreated) servant.[150] Building upon ideas articulated by historians like A. F. Pollard in the first half of the twentieth century and by Froude in the half-century before that, many recent representations have stressed the role that Henry played in the formulation of secular as well as religious policy. We have seen this in fictional representations—the Henrys of *Anne of the Thousand Days*, *The Tudors*, and *Wolf Hall* are all decisive to the point of authoritarian—as well as in some but by no means all recent academic works. While for Scarisbrick Henry remained the "self-indulgent," cavalier monarch of Cavendish's *Life*, for many later writers, including Gwyn, Bernard, and Fletcher, decisions depended entirely on the king's word even early in his reign, and Wolsey, far from being the power behind the throne, was Henry's dutiful servant. To the extent that this representation of the king is accurate, Wolsey becomes both a less independent and a less significant character in the spectacle of the Henrician court, more a scarlet functionary than an éminence grise. His fall also becomes something other than it has traditionally been represented to be: not the deserved reward of treachery or ill will (as in many Tudor accounts, whether evangelical or Catholic) or the arbitrary operation of fortune (as in Cavendish's *Life*) but rather the almost inevitable consequence of failing to achieve a tyrant's wishes. A growing consensus about the limitations on Wolsey's agency may, in turn, explain something of the deceleration in wholesale representations of Wolsey—a matter about which I shall have more to say in the Conclusion. The dutiful cardinal of this last representation is neither hero nor villain—less dramatic, but perhaps on that account more tragic and certainly less deserving of the calumnies the centuries have visited upon him.

Conclusion

June 29, 2011, was a festive day in the town of Ipswich. It was the annual Ipswich Charter Day, a local celebration commemorating a grant of liberties made by King John in 1200, but this year, Charter Day had particular significance. As an actor dressed as Wolsey strolled about and musicians played Tudor melodies, a new statue of the cardinal was unveiled near the most likely site of his birth. The sculpture had been commissioned by a group of enthusiasts organized by John Blatchly, a local schoolmaster and historian who told the press that Ipswich had not sufficiently honored its most famous son.[1] The Scottish sculptor David Annand had been chosen out of a field of more than fifty artists who applied to execute the work, and as the cloth covering the finished product was pulled back, members of the three-hundred-strong audience "gasped," according to one news report.[2] Most likely gasped in delight—those in attendance generally gave the sculpture positive reviews—but others were displeased by Annand's representation of Wolsey sitting and teaching from a book, with his galero hanging behind his chair and a cat peering around its side (see Plate 19).[3]

Like so many of the representations of Wolsey that this book has been tracing, Annand's design was controversial both for what it included and for what it left out. Annand depicted Wolsey more as an educator than a statesman or ecclesiastic, representing him in the words inscribed around the statue's base as a "cardinal archbishop[,] chancellor[,] and teacher who believed that pleasure should mingle with study so that the child may think learning an amusement rather than a toil."[4] The second half of the inscription, adapted from the preface Wolsey wrote for the edition of William Lily's grammar textbook he intended to be used at Cardinal College, Ipswich, complements the statue's gesture of invitation, with its open book and outstretched hand.[5] Yet while Annand's sculpture emphasizes how deeply Wolsey was invested in his educational institutions and how desperately eager he was to see them outlive him, it silently passes over many of the interpretive debates about Wolsey's life that we have been exploring. Like the 1930 Ipswich pageant, absent here are any of the longstanding prototypes for the cardinal: He is neither the author of schism, nor a corrupt papist, nor even the flawed but well-intentioned statesman of Cavendish's *Life*. Absent too is any indication that Wolsey had fallen from power or that he had died in disgrace. Instead, with a local audience apparently at the front of the sculptor's mind, the statue hones in on Wolsey's most immediate link to Ipswich and serves up a generous patron of education and a hometown boy made good.

All this, of course, is understandable. Blatchly and his fellow contributors made it clear that Annand's sculpture was to be a work of homage rather than a historical, much less a theological, commentary.[6] Like so many of their predecessors, they sought to remember Wolsey in the way that seemed most appropriate to them, highlighting the elements of his biography that best aligned with the purposes for which they undertook the work, and shouldered the cost, of representing the cardinal.

Annand's statue is but one of the most recent of the long series of representations and commemorations of Wolsey that this book has surveyed. We have encountered representations spanning most of the major textual genres known in early modern England—memoir, biography, elegy, history play, political pamphlet—and have observed how writers took advantage of the appearance of new genres, such as the historical novel, to depict Wolsey afresh. At the same time, we have discovered that writers and artists have chosen to represent Wolsey in the service of a wide spectrum of political and theological positions. He has functioned as a warning against the dangers of foreign influence, a cautionary tale about the spiritual corruption of Roman clergy, and an argument against Catholic emancipation. At the same time, he has been invoked as a model patron of humanism and learning, a martyr for the papacy, and an example of fortune's vengeance upon those who are overly proud (or perhaps just unlucky). The process of remembering Wolsey has taken a bewildering variety of forms, and it is not yet finished. Even in the 2010s, there have appeared, in addition to Annand's sculpture, a biography, a scholarly monograph, and at least six major academic articles that take Wolsey as their topic. He has appeared prominently in studies, fictions, documentaries, and artistic works about the English Reformation that are too many to enumerate here, not least among them the international multimedia phenomenon *Wolf Hall*. The cardinal remains a subject for academic and even public interest, although perhaps more for what he has been *thought* to represent than for who he actually was.

Throughout this book, we have commented on the many factors that have shaped representations of Wolsey. While I have been careful to reject the sort of reductionism that assumes, far too simplistically, that writers of Catholic, Anglican, presbyterian, episcopalian, puritan, Marxist, or other identifiable leanings must necessarily have depicted the cardinal in terms consonant with their political and theological allegiances, it is clear that more often than not, writers and artists have approached the task of depicting Wolsey on the basis of their own presuppositions and of the circumstances within which they were working. Speaking broadly, we have encountered four sets of purposes for which Wolsey has been represented. First, and most commonly, writers, artists, and other creators have set out to explain Wolsey's role in the events leading up to the Henrician Reformation. All of the prototypes we identified in Chapter 1 and then traced through subsequent chapters seek to position Wolsey as a certain kind of actor in the drama of the king's annulment and England's subsequent break from communion with Rome. The evangelical prototype of Wolsey the papist, articulated first by Hall and Foxe but then embraced by Victorian and post-Victorian historians like Merle and Dickens, contended that Wolsey symbolized the failings of the Roman church and its clergy. The prototype constructed by Tudor Catholic writers like Vergil and especially Sander, on the other hand, figured Wolsey as a malevolent force who placed his desire for revenge above the unity of the church; for them, but importantly not for all subsequent Catholic writers, Wolsey provoked what they called the English schism on account of his personal animosity toward Katherine and Charles V rather than on account of his identity as a Catholic or a cardinal. The more sympathetic prototype that George Cavendish fashioned in his *Life* and *Metrical Visions* is that of a cardinal who sought to serve his king loyally, even when doing so meant working to achieve an outcome he had begged Henry VIII not to pursue. Here, as in the fourth, most recent pattern for characterizing the cardinal that we identified in Chapter 5, Wolsey's relationship to the Henrician reformation is not that of cause and effect but rather that of a somewhat hapless bystander, one at first left behind and then utterly destroyed by his master's determination to achieve his desires.

Cavendish's representation of Wolsey achieved only limited and mostly underground circulation for the first century after it was written. While a highly expurgated version was pressed into service in the campaigns of the 1640s, in the aftermath of the English civil wars Cavendish's representation came to inspire a series of writers who approached Wolsey with a purpose other than that of explaining the course of the Reformation. These authors, among them Fiddes, Grove, Creighton, Taunton, and most recently Gwyn, have represented Wolsey primarily in order to defend him from his critics. As in Cavendish's case, it is not surprising that many works defending the cardinal have taken the form of biographies. Those who have adopted a more critical stance, on the other hand, have tended to write longer histories either of Tudor England or the English Reformation, incorporating their condemnations of Wolsey into the broader narratives they sought to tell.

These first two categories—arguments about the cardinal's role in or responsibility for the Henrician Reformation and defenses against the critiques that have been mounted against him—comprise the vast majority of representations of Wolsey that have appeared since his death.[7] In the past two centuries, however, from roughly the first quarter of the nineteenth century through the time of this writing, Wolsey has been commemorated and represented for yet other purposes still. In Chapters 3 and 4, we investigated how Wolsey has been honored as a patron of particular institutions and localities, chief among them Hampton Court Palace, the town of Ipswich, and the foundation now known as Christ Church, Oxford. Representations of the cardinal in connection with these places have for the most part eschewed the controversies that surround the part he played in the run-up to the break between England and Rome, opting instead, as Annand's sculpture does, to pay posthumous homage to Wolsey on account of his role as a patron of architecture, art, and especially education. In addition, over the same two centuries the cardinal has appeared in a variety of works of fiction—at first, historical short stories and novels like *Freston Tower* and, later, films and television programs. Most of these fictional representations have sought to entertain at least as much as to instruct their readers and viewers. Some aimed to do the same sort of work as the biographical and historiographical narratives I described in the previous few paragraphs: The film *A Man for All Seasons*, for instance, appears to embrace Wolsey's critics' preoccupation with his wealth and worldliness, whereas *The Tudors* and *Wolf Hall* echo instead some sympathetic features of Cavendish's *Life*. Others, however, have appropriated Wolsey for purposes not related to any of our prototypes: Thus, in "Wolsey Bridge," that mid-nineteenth-century short story for youth, the cardinal appears as an emblem of the rewards of hard work and of the virtue of generosity toward one's birthplace.

I hasten to acknowledge the inherent limitations of any attempt to categorize the complex texts we have encountered throughout this volume. An author's arguments about Wolsey's role in the Reformation do not automatically preclude her or him from making biographical claims, or from reflecting upon Wolsey's relationship to particular localities, or from seeking to entertain an imagined audience. At the same time, the purpose that impels an author to represent Wolsey is only one of the factors that we have found to have informed the choice of genre or sources. Other factors are circumstantial in nature: what was happening at the time a particular representation was produced, for what audience it was produced, and with what raw materials. We have already alluded to one example: the ways in which the publication of calendars of primary sources, like the *Letters and Papers, Foreign and Domestic, of the Reign of Henry VIII*, helped prompt the reconsideration of time-honored characterizations of Wolsey. Another example comes from a few centuries earlier: In Chapter 2, we found that several representations of Wolsey cast him as a villainous predecessor to Archbishop Laud. The comparison did not long persist after Laud's execution, for it had quite literally outlived its usefulness. Instead, in the aftermath of the English civil wars, authors more sympathetic to Wolsey began to compare him with better-loved prelates, especially his Spanish contemporary Cardinal Ximenes de Cisneros.

Still other factors that have shaped the representation of Wolsey have been methodological, reflecting prevailing expectations about the rules of a particular genre or academic discipline. We have observed on a number of occasions that some long-cherished claims about Wolsey, such as descriptions of his physical appearance, emerged out of the literary conventions that shaped works like Skelton's satires. We have also noticed that debates within academic fields, such as the clash between narrative and empirical schools of historiography in the second half of the nineteenth century, have guided judgments about what kinds of evidence, and what kinds of conclusions, should carry weight. And then, on top of these factors, there are ideological ones: the ways in which an author's commitments in the spheres of theology and politics shaped her or his representations of the cardinal and other leading actors in the Henrician court. Of course, just as many of those who produced the books, articles, plays, pamphlets, films, and other sources we have been considering undertook their work for more than one reason, their representations were shaped by factors operating in tandem, including the circumstantial, methodological, and ideological impulses I have just described.

In Chapter 4, we came across Ian Hesketh's observation that the so-called scientific historians of the Victorian period were engaged in "boundary work" when they sought to bar J. A. Froude from some of the marks of full membership in the historical guild. Boundary work, Hesketh wrote, seeks to demarcate one kind of work from another. For instance, nineteenth-century scientists attempted "'to create a public image for science by contrasting it favorably to non-scientific intellectual or technical activities,'" thus constructing "a demarcation separating science from non-science in order to justify or claim scientific authority over a particular body of knowledge."[8] Nineteenth-century historians did the same thing in order to insist that their fledgling discipline was something other than literature, certainly not at all like the historical fictions becoming popular among the reading public. But if the history of the representation and commemoration of Wolsey demonstrates anything, it is that boundary work is neither exclusive to scientific enterprises nor limited to the nineteenth century. Instead, throughout this book we have encountered numerous representations of Wolsey that have functioned as forms of boundary work. At first, the boundary that writers sought to reify and police was that between England and Rome: In Chapter 1, we noted that evangelical writers like Hall represented Wolsey as a man subject to foreign influence, while representing the new Church of England as a symbol of English nationhood. Then, as the diplomatic, political, and theological chasms between England and Rome widened and no longer needed to be contested in the same way, in Chapters 2 and 3 we observed the cardinal being employed in arguments about the boundaries of the Church of England itself. Puritans like the authors of the pamphlets of 1641 figured Wolsey as an example of the dangers of high churchmanship. Later, in the debate over Catholic emancipation, in essence a debate about the compatibility of Catholic and English identities, both sides cited Wolsey. Catholics like Lingard argued that the cardinal had in fact been a loyal servant of England, whereas anti-Catholic writers like Soames regarded Wolsey as a traitor to his country. The former wished to see Catholics fully regarded as British subjects; the latter wished to keep that boundary tightly drawn. Finally, in Chapters 4 and 5 we saw different sorts of boundary work in operation. Beginning in the second half of the nineteenth century, university-trained historians sought to establish their craft as a reputable academic discipline and to defend it from the objection that it was not sufficiently rigorous. Hence, for instance, the controversy over Froude's works. In the twentieth century, as historical fictions proliferated, some historians took it upon themselves to defend multiple boundaries: correcting factual errors in fictional representations, on the one hand, while also criticizing the work of colleagues who did not enjoy the privileges of full-time academic appointments, on the other. However, it is not at all clear that these latter-day attempts at boundary maintenance have been successful: The scholars whom Shannon McSheffrey has memorably dubbed "historian-cops" appear to have been at least somewhat impotent in shaping the general public's understanding of the past, as the popularity of representations like *The Tudors* and *Wolf Hall* demonstrates.[9]

The life and career of Thomas Wolsey has proven fertile for boundary work of all these varieties and many more besides. The cardinal is a liminal figure in a number of ways—a man educated in the methods of late medieval scholasticism who came to be a patron of humanism; the last ecclesiastic to serve as lord chancellor; an Englishman whose most creative endeavors were in the field of foreign affairs; an emblem of traditional religion at a time when reform was beginning to take hold; and perhaps most of all, a commoner who rose, if not from a butcher's shop, then at least from relatively humble beginnings to become the second most influential man in England. It is not surprising that Wolsey has lent himself to so many different forms of representation or that many questions about his life will likely always go unanswered.

If it is not possible to reach definitive conclusions about Wolsey, it is my hope that *Remembering Wolsey*'s survey of representations and commemorations has validated the style of scholarship that Assmann called mnemohistory. Throughout this book, we have identified the many guises in which Wolsey has been invoked over the centuries, learning from them about the ways in which writers figured the great events of their own day—Archbishop Laud and the civil wars, the Restoration and the nonjuring movement, Catholic emancipation, World War I and twentieth-century totalitarianism. Assmann and his fellow mnemohistorical theorists have provided this book with a methodological road map, but it is a map that does not perfectly capture the contours of the early modern world. As I observed in the Introduction, the most sophisticated critiques of mnemohistorical theory have urged us to attend not only to the *producers* but also, or even more so, to the *consumers* of cultural memories. With very few exceptions, in this book we have been able to describe the circumstances within which the most influential representations of Wolsey were produced, but (with the exception of especially prominent texts like Foxe's *Actes and Monuments*) we have only rarely been able to describe their consumption, especially prior to the twentieth century. Even if the documentation was more complete, we are still continuing to learn about early modern practices of memory—ongoing research that promises to teach us better where to look for evidence of memory consumption. Of course, we may never be able fully to account for the reception of cultural memories in the early modern period, but that is no reason not to do what is possible.

At the same time, the distinction this book has offered between representations and commemorations of the cardinal may help differentiate more clearly between different vehicles of cultural memory. We have seen that a few representations—such as the Ipswich pageant of 1930 and the laudatory biographies by authors like Fiddes and Grove—have taken it as an explicit goal to recall, and usually rehabilitate, the memory of Wolsey, whereas most others have not been commemorative in quite the same way. Again, of course, the evidence has its limitations: We simply do not know and may never be able to determine to what extent any of these productions shaped the memories of their readers and audience members. Only with regard to the recent past and the present day, with the widespread popularity and international distribution of the historical fictions we surveyed in Chapter 5, is it possible to trace with greater certainty the success of any particular representation. Of course, this is not true exclusively of Wolsey: As we have seen throughout this book, the representations of other leading players in the Henrician Reformation, not least among them More, Cromwell, and the king, have all been subject to similar historiographical and commemorative shifts.

Thus much more remains to be learned not only about Thomas Wolsey, and not only about the ways in which he has been remembered and represented, but about the phenomena of collective memory that have so captivated scholars over the course of the past forty years. In the end, whatever hypotheses we may develop about the events of Wolsey's life, about the motivations and the character of a man who achieved and lost so much, and about one of the most tumultuous and dangerous periods in the history of England, it is impossible not to feel sympathy for someone whose memory has so often been deployed for ideological and propagandistic purposes. There is, indeed, no small irony here. During his lifetime Wolsey showed sensitivity to the ways in which he was being and would be represented. Reproaching Archbishop Warham for daring to refer to him as "brother," imprisoning John Roo for performing an allegory that some interpreted to be about him, commissioning an elaborate marble tomb— these and other actions are those of a man who was aware of the eyes of history. Even in the reminiscences he shared with George Cavendish during his final year on earth, Wolsey may have attempted to shape how his most faithful of servants would narrate his life after he was gone. And yet. Warham outlived Wolsey, and more than a few writers embellished the antagonism between the two men, usually to the cardinal's discredit. Roo survived, and within weeks of Wolsey's death, the far less ambiguous masque that Thomas Boleyn commissioned depicted the cardinal's soul being dragged down to hell. Wolsey's sarcophagus went unoccupied for two and a half centuries before ultimately housing the body of Horatio Nelson. And Cavendish, much as he loved his former master, drew out of Wolsey's life a lesson about the fickleness of good fortune, a lesson he did not know that a century later the puritan printer William Sheares would twist into an example of divine judgment on the wicked. Truly, as we have recently been reminded about Alexander Hamilton, another obscure man's son made good, in the end Wolsey had no control over who lived, who died, who told his story.

1. Lin-Manuel Miranda, "History Has Its Eyes on You," and "Who Lives, Who Dies, Who Tells Your Story," from *Hamilton: An American Musical* (Atlantic, 2015).

2. For reasons I will explore later in this Introduction, this book deliberately eschews the task of resolving contested questions about the historical details of Wolsey's life. Many of his biographies and biographers are discussed at length in subsequent chapters, but for an overview, see Sybil M. Jack, "Wolsey, Thomas (1470/71–1530)," *Oxford Dictionary of National Biography* (Oxford, 2004); http://www.oxforddnb.com/view/article /29854.

3. *L&P*, ii.1380. The former epithet has appeared most recently in the subtitle of the only book-length study on representations of Wolsey: Schwartz-Leeper, *Princes to Pages*. While Schwartz-Leeper has done remarkable service in delving deeply into the representation of Wolsey in select literary texts from the sixteenth and seventeenth centuries, the present book revises some of his conclusions and extends his analysis through the present day.

4. *Calendar of State Papers and Manuscripts, Relating to English Affairs, Volume 2, 1509–1519: Existing in the Archives and Collections of Venice, and in Other Libraries of Northern Italy*, ed. Rawdon Brown (Cambridge: Cambridge University Press, 1867), 560.

5. For the commemoration of Wolsey at Christ Church, see Chapter 4 in this volume.

6. The Wolsey brand, which began employing the cardinal's image in 1897, remains active to this day. Its printed advertisements featured the image of the cardinal throughout the early twentieth century. See http:// www.wolsey.com/page/history and the many advertisements preserved in the John Johnson Collection in the Bodleian Library, Oxford.

7. Clinton Rossiter, ed., *The Federalist Papers* (New York: New American Library, 1961), 41.

8. Peter Marshall, "Lollards and Protestants Revisited," in *Wycliffite Controversies*, ed. Mishtooni Bose and J. Patrick Hornbeck II (Turnhout: Brepols, 2011), 315.

9. Felicity Heal, "Appropriating History: Catholic and Protestant Polemics and the National Past," *Huntington Library Quarterly* 68, nos. 1–2 (2005): 109.

10. Among these works are Cavendish; Richard Fiddes, *The Life of Cardinal Wolsey* (London: J. Knapton, R. Knaplock, D. Midwinter, W. and J. Innys, R. Robinson, J. Osborn and T. Longman, 1726); Mandell Creighton, *Cardinal Wolsey* (London: Macmillan, 1888); and Peter Gwyn, *The King's Cardinal: The Rise and Fall of Thomas Wolsey* (London: Barrie and Jenkins, 1990); all of which, along with others, are discussed in detail in the chapters that follow.

11. For the significance and history of the plural form, recommended by revisionist historians in the 1980s and 1990s, see Chapter 5 in this volume.

12. G. A. Bergenroth, D. P. de Gayangos, et al., eds., *Calendar of Letters, Dispatches, and State Papers, Relating to the Negotiations between England and Spain* . . . , vol. 4.2 (London: Her Majesty's Stationery Office, 1882), no. 615. For discussion of this incident, see Seymour Baker House, "Literature, Drama, and Politics," in *The Reign of Henry VIII: Politics, Policy, and Piety*, ed. Diarmaid MacCulloch (New York: St. Martin's, 1995), 182.

13. As a working definition of popular culture, I will rely on that embraced by Tom Beaudoin, "Theology of Popular Music as a Theological Exercise," in *Secular Music and Sacred Theology*, ed. Tom Beaudoin (Collegeville, Minn.: Liturgical Press, 2013), xiii–xv.

14. Richard J. Bernstein, "The Culture of Memory," *History and Theory* 43, no. 4 (December 2004): 165–78; Kerwin Lee Klein, "On the Emergence of Memory in Historical Discourse," *Representations* 69 (Winter 2000): 127. It is a commonplace in recent memory studies to begin with the observation that such work has multiplied in recent years.

15. Dominick LaCapra, *History and Memory after Auschwitz* (Ithaca, NY: Cornell University Press, 1998); Ulrich Gumbrecht, "On the Decent Uses of History," *History and Theory* 40, no. 1 (February 2001): 117–27; Klein, "On the Emergence of Memory," 138–40; Susana Kaiser, *Postmemories of Terror: A New Generation Copes with the Legacy of the "Dirty War"* (New York: Palgrave, 2005); Mieke Bal, "Introduction," in *Acts of Memory: Cultural Recall in the Present*, ed. Mieke Bal et al. (Hanover, NH: University Press of New England, 1999), vii–xvii.

16. Judith Pollmann and Erika Kuijpers, "Introduction: On the Early Modernity of Modern Memory," in *Memory before Modernity: Practices of Memory in Early Modern Europe*, ed. Erika Kuijpers et al. (Leiden: Brill,

2013), 1–26; David Cressy, *Bonfires and Bells: National Memory and the Protestant Calendar in Elizabethan and Stuart England* (Berkeley, Calif.: University of California Press, 1989); and Andy Wood, *The 1549 Rebellions and the Making of Early Modern England* (Cambridge: Cambridge University Press, 2007). I am grateful to Brian Young for drawing my attention to John Guy's overview of the representation of Wolsey's successor as lord chancellor in the first chapter of his *Thomas More* (London: Arnold, 2000). Guy's book appeared in a series, Reputations, designed to "examine the reputations of some of history's most conspicuous, powerful, and influential individuals, considering a range of representations, some of striking incompatibility" (vii). William Sheils is currently undertaking a more detailed study of More's posthumous portrayal.

17. "About," *Remembering the Reformation*, http://www.rememberingthereformation.org.uk.

18. Jan Assmann, *Moses the Egyptian: The Memory of Egypt in Western Monotheism* (Cambridge, Mass.: Harvard University Press, 1997), 9.

19. Assmann, *Moses the Egyptian*, 10.

20. Assmann, *Moses the Egyptian*, 16.

21. Jan Assmann, "Collective Memory and Cultural Identity," trans. John Czaplicka, *New German Critique* 65 (Spring–Summer 1995): 125–33. See also Geoffrey Winthrop-Young, "Memories of the Nile: Egyptian Traumas and Communication Technologies in Jan Assmann's Theory of Cultural Memory," *New German Critique* 96 (Fall 2005): 119–24.

22. Particularly effusive praise for Assmann's theory can be found in the distinguished rabbinic scholar Daniel Boyarin's review of *Moses the Egyptian*, *Church History* 67 (1998): 842–44.

23. Héctor Lindo-Fuentes, Erik Ching, and Rafael A. Lara-Martínez, *Remembering a Massacre in El Salvador: The Insurrection of 1932, Roque Dalton, and the Politics of Historical Memory* (Albuquerque: University of New Mexico Press, 2007); Ronald Hendel, "The Exodus in Biblical Memory," *Journal of Biblical Literature* 120 (2001): 601–22; Ken Koltun-Fromm, "Historical Memory in Abraham Geiger's Account of Modern Jewish Identity," *Jewish Social Studies* n.s. 7, no. 1 (Autumn 2000): 109–26; John Watkins, *Representing Elizabeth in Stuart England: Literature, History, Sovereignty* (Cambridge: Cambridge University Press, 2002). I am grateful to Michael E. Lee for the first of these references.

24. Bernstein, "The Culture of Memory," 166–67; Brewster S. Chamberlin, "Remembrance Reified and Other Shoah Business," *Public Historian* 23, no. 3 (2001): 73–82; Alon Confino, "Collective Memory and Cultural History: Problems of Method," *American Historical Review* 102, no. 5 (December 1997): 1386–1403, esp. 1388.

25. Marilynne Robinson, "The Fate of Ideas: Moses," *Salmagundi* 121/122 (Winter/Spring 1999), 38–40; see also Winthrop-Young, "Memories of the Nile."

26. Wulf Kansteiner, "Finding Meaning in Memory: A Methodological Critique of Collective Memory Studies," *History and Theory* 41, no. 2 (2002): 185–86; see also Klein, "On the Emergence of Memory," 143; and Alin Coman, Adam D. Brown, Jonathan Koppel, and William Hirst, "Collective Memory from a Psychological Perspective," *International Journal of Politics, Culture, and Society* 22, no. 2 (June 2009): 125–41.

27. Winthrop-Young, "Memories of the Nile," 119; Kansteiner, "Finding Meaning in Memory"; Confino, "Collective Memory and Cultural History," 1390.

28. Susan Royal, "John Foxe's *Acts and Monuments* and the Lollard Legacy in the Long Reformation" (PhD diss., University of Durham, 2013).

29. Kansteiner, "Finding Meaning in Memory," 180.

30. On this point, see Wood, *1549 Rebellions*, 241.

31. James Fentress and Chris Wickham, *Social Memory* (Oxford: Blackwell, 1992), quoted in Wood, *1549 Rebellions*, 251.

32. In referring to public memorials and other commemorations grounded in specific places, I am indebted to Pierre Nora's influential notion of *lieux de mémoire*. See *Rethinking France: Les lieux de mémoire*, 4 vols., ed. Pierre Nora, trans. Mary Trouille (Chicago: University of Chicago Press, 2001–2010). I am grateful to Anne Fernald for drawing my attention to Nora's work.

33. Pollmann and Kuijpers, "Early Modernity of Modern Memory," 3. As these scholars observe, the obverse of early modern commemorations was what they called "acts of oblivion," or "formal agreements to forget the past" (9). Several instances of such acts will appear in this book. For other instances of early modern commemorations of turbulent events not directly related to Wolsey, see Cressy, *Bonfires and Bells*; and Wood, *1549 Rebellions*.

34. See in this volume Chapter 4 and the Conclusion for further discussion of the commemoration of Wolsey in Ipswich.

35. As Daniel Woolf is right to caution us, change does not necessarily mean improvement. He critiques what he calls the "sheer 'whiggishness'" of much work in intellectual history, which has often presumed that the craft of history has generated progressively more accurate and meaningful results over time. Daniel Woolf, *A Global History of History* (Cambridge: Cambridge University Press, 2011), 13.

36. The most recent biographies of Wolsey, Gwyn's *King's Cardinal*; Stella Fletcher's *Cardinal Wolsey: A Life in Renaissance Europe* (London: Bloomsbury, 2009), and John Matusiak's *Wolsey: The Life of King Henry VIII's*

Cardinal (Stroud: History Press, 2014), are all discussed in Chapter 5 in this volume.

37. For this ongoing debate, see the discussion in Chapter 5 in this volume.

38. Michael R. Evans, *Inventing Eleanor: The Medieval and Post-Medieval Image of Eleanor of Aquitaine* (London: Bloomsbury, 2014); Susan Bordo, *The Creation of Anne Boleyn* (Boston: Houghton Mifflin, 2013); Schwartz-Leeper, *Princes to Pages*.

39. Sybil M. Jack, "Wolsey, Thomas (1470/71–1530)"; Fletcher, *Cardinal Wolsey*, 171–94.

40. Gavin E. Schwartz-Leeper, "Turning Princes into Pages: Images of Cardinal Wolsey in the Satires of John Skelton and Shakespeare's *Henry VIII*," in *New Perspectives on Tudor Cultures*, ed. Mike Pincombe and Zsolt Almási (Newcastle: Cambridge Scholars, 2012), 78–99; as well as its more extended version in Schwartz-Leeper's monograph *From Princes to Pages*.

41. John Skelton, *Magnyfycence*, ll. 902–6, quoted in Schwartz-Leeper, *From Princes to Pages*, 35. All references to Skelton's poems are from the edition of John Scattergood, *The Complete English Poems* (New Haven, CT: Yale University Press, 1983).

42. John Skelton, *Speke, Parrot*, line 122; *Collyn Clout*, ll. 122–28, quoted in Schwartz-Leeper, *From Princes to Pages*, 40, 44–45.

43. On the *Chronicles* and their authors, see Annabel Patterson, *Reading Holinshed's Chronicles* (Chicago: University of Chicago Press, 1994); along with my discussion in Chapter 1 in this volume.

44. Holinshed (1587; STC 13569), 837, emphasis mine.

45. John Speed, *History of Great Britain* (London: Hall and Beale, 1611; STC 23045), 769.

46. William Shakespeare and John Fletcher, *King Henry VIII*, 1.1.54–57, quoted in Schwartz-Leeper, *From Princes to Pages*, 191.

47. Fletcher, *Cardinal Wolsey*, 176.

48. Two of the Gilbert paintings, *Cardinal Wolsey, Chancellor of England, on His Progress to Westminster Hall* (1887) and *Ego et rex meus* (1888), are both in London's Guildhall Art Gallery. Vivian Forbes's *Sir Thomas More Refusing to Grant Wolsey a Subsidy, 1523* (1925) is in St. Stephen's Hall, Westminster. See Fletcher, *Cardinal Wolsey*, 182–86, for further discussion.

49. For some of the exceptions, see Fletcher, *Cardinal Wolsey*, 185, 190.

50. "Fat as a Factor in Politics," *British Medical Journal* (April 20, 1901): 975–76.

51. *Calendar of State Papers . . . Venice*, 560.

52. Portrait, Bibliothèque, Arras, *Recueil d'Arras*.

53. *The Anglica Historia of Polydore Vergil*, A.D. *1485–1537*, ed. and trans. Denys Hay, Camden 3rd ser. 74 (London: Royal Historical Society, 1950), 231.

54. Oxford, Bodleian Library MS Douce 363, fols. 52r–v, 71r.

55. Greg Walker, *John Skelton and the Politics of the 1520s* (Cambridge: Cambridge University Press, 1988), 124; a later appropriation of this argument appears in Schwartz-Leeper, *From Princes to Pages*, 23–55.

1. THE BASIC INGREDIENTS (1530–C. 1600)

1. Cavendish, 184/23–24.

2. Cavendish, 185/10–13.

3. Cavendish, 186/4–5.

4. Cavendish, 187.

5. Bergenroth, de Gayangos, et al., eds., *Calendar of Letters*, vol. 4.2, no. 615.

6. In this regard, one might think of the relationship between a prototype and a specific instance of representation in terms of Ludwig Wittgenstein's notion of family resemblance. Wittgenstein argued that it is often impossible to categorize complex realities, such as biological organisms, according to a single shared common characteristic; instead, there is often a pool of characteristics that are broadly but not identically shared by all the individuals in the category. The three prototypical representations of Wolsey I identify in this chapter, therefore, might be thought about as three interrelated families of representations—not families with common historical ancestors but with sets of broadly shared traits. For further discussion of this approach, see J. Patrick Hornbeck II, *What Is a Lollard? Dissent and Belief in Late Medieval England* (Oxford: Oxford University Press, 2010).

7. Cavendish, 184/10.

8. Simon Thurley, *Hampton Court: A Social and Architectural History* (New Haven, CT: Yale University Press, 2003), 24. On the representation of Wolsey at Hampton Court Palace, see Chapter 3.

9. It is surprising that Schwartz-Leeper's monograph *Princes to Pages* does not engage these Catholic renditions of Wolsey's life in much detail.

10. Peter Lake, *Bad Queen Bess? Libels, Secret Histories, and the Politics of Publicity in the Reign of Queen Elizabeth I* (Oxford: Oxford University Press, 2016), 6.

11. J. S. Brewer, *The Reign of Henry VIII from His Accession to the Death of Wolsey*, ed. James Gairdner, 2 vols. (London: John Murray, 1884), 1:264–65.

12. Denys Hay, *Polydore Vergil: Renaissance Historian and Man of Letters* (Oxford: Clarendon, 1952), 9–14; William J. Connell, "Vergil, Polydore (c. 1470–1555)," *Oxford Dictionary of National Biography* (Oxford, 2004), http://www.oxforddnb.com/view/article/28224.

13. Vergil, *Anglica Historia*, xxix–xxx.

14. Hay, *Polydore Vergil*, 172.

15. Vergil, *Anglica Historia*, xx–xxi.

16. Hay, *Polydore Vergil*, 164–65; Vergil, *Anglica Historia*, xxxiii.

17. Thomas S. Freeman, "From Catiline to Richard III: The Influence of Classical Historians on Polydore Vergil's *Anglica Historia*," in *Reconsidering the Renaissance: Papers from the Twenty-First Annual Conference*, ed. Mario A. Di Cesare (Binghamton, NY: Medieval and Renaissance Texts and Studies, 1992), 191–214.

18. Vergil, *Anglica Historia*, 208: "Thomas Wtteley elemosinarius uir doctus ac . . . preditus ingenio, qui repente tam charus Regi effectus erat, ut pene charior fieri non posset." The ellipsis represents a word left out of the extant manuscript of Vergil's history; no corresponding gap appears in the printed edition. Here and elsewhere I base my translations on Hay's but silently differ in some small respects.

19. Compare, for instance, Vergil's treatment of Richard Empson and Edmund Dudley: *Anglica Historia*, 151.

20. Vergil, *Anglica Historia*, 225: "mirifice gloriabatur ueluti autor solus tantae felicitatis, ex eo, quod iam summa esset autoritate apud regem, sed et inuisus inde magis cum propter eam insolentiam, ac detractam simul opinionem probitatis, tum propter eius nouitatem generis."

21. Vergil, *Anglica Historia*, 295: "quia tantum abfuit, id Volsaeanum beneficium pro beneficio, ut etiam pro maleficio acceptum fuerit, quando paucos admodum, hoc est, nullos bonos impulit ad dissoluendam pristinam degendae uitae legem."

22. Vergil, *Anglica Historia*, 316: "ut Romanus pontifex gratis in Anglia male audiuerit, sed Volsaeus multo peius."

23. Vergil, *Anglica Historia*, 231: "qui tot uno ferme tempore adeptis dignitatibus, tantum superbiae animo concepit, ut sese cum regibus exaequatum existimans."

24. Vergil, *Anglica Historia*, 255–57: "se facturum breui, ut ille intelligeret se non esse ipsi parem nedum fratrem."

25. Vergil, *Anglica Historia*, 255; compare, for instance, Cavendish, 15–16.

26. Vergil, *Anglica Historia*, 325: "ei in mentem uenit mutare dominam, et unam alteram quaerere, quam aeque uita ut moribus sibi similem esse uolebat."

27. Vergil, *Anglica Historia*, 331.

28. Vergil, *Anglica Historia*, 331: "hominem tot beneficiorum immemorem in ordinem infimum redigere statuit."

29. Vergil, *Anglica Historia*, 333: "quo sic superbior fieri ac insanire desineret." For the brevity of Vergil's account of the end of Wolsey's life and of the ensuing English Reformation, see Hay, *Polydore Vergil*, 154–55.

30. Vergil, *Anglica Historia*, 333: "Volsaeus florebat dignitate et opibus, cum negotium nuptiale suscepit, quod sibi fore gaudium putauit, id extitit exitium."

31. Thomas S. Freeman, "Harpsfield, Nicholas (1519–1575)," *Oxford Dictionary of National Biography* (Oxford, 2004), http://www.oxforddnb.com /view/article/12369. For Harpsfield's later writings, see Chris Highley, "'A Persistent and Seditious Book': Nicholas Sander's *Schismatis Anglicani* and Catholic Histories of the Reformation," *Huntington Library Quarterly* 68, no. 1–2 (2005): 151.

32. Nicholas Harpsfield, *A Treatise on the Pretended Divorce between Henry VIII and Catharine of Aragon*, ed. Nicholas Pocock (London: Camden Society, 1878), 180. In contrast, Vergil alluded to the interest that Wolsey had appeared to show in gaining the papacy but concluded that this was one of the cardinal's diplomatic schemes: "Volsaeus coepit aut potius *simulauit* spem habere consequendi pontificatus." *Anglica Historia*, 292, my emphasis. For a recent discussion in agreement with Vergil's view, see D. S. Chambers, "Cardinal Wolsey and the Papal Tiara," in *Individuals and Institutions in Renaissance Italy* (Brookfield: Ashgate, 1998), item XV.

33. Harpsfield, *A Treatise on the Pretended Divorce*, 184.

34. See Highley, "'A Persistent and Seditious Book,'" 151–54, for the disproportionate lack of attention that scholars have paid to Sander's work. J. H. Pollen, "Dr. Nicholas Sander," *English Historical Review* 6 (1891): 41; see also T. F. Mayer, "Sander, Nicholas (c. 1530–1581)," *Oxford Dictionary of National Biography* (Oxford, 2014), http://www.oxforddnb.com/view/article /24621. For the publication history of the *Schismatis Anglicani*, see Lake, *Bad Queen Bess?*, 257.

35. Highley, "'A Persistent and Seditious Book,'" 157.

36. Quoted in Nic[h]olas Sander, *The Rise and Growth of the Anglican Schism*, trans. David Lewis (London: Burns and Oates, 1877), xxii–xxiii; Gilbert Burnet, *The History of the Reformation of the Church of England* (London: Chiswell, 1681), b1. See also Thomas McNevin Veech, *Dr Nicholas Sanders and the English Reformation, 1530–1581* (Louvain: Bureaux du Recueil, Bibliothèque de l'Université, 1935), esp. chap. 6. For additional discussion of Heylyn and Burnet, see Chapter 3 in this volume.

37. Sander, *De origine ac progressu schismatis anglicani* (Cologne: P. Henningium, 1585), 7v: "homo preter caeteros ambitiosus et audax." All translations from Sander are my own.

38. Highley, "'A Persistent and Seditious Book,'" 161, citing Sander, *Schismatis Anglicani*, 13v.

39. Highley, "'A Persistent and Seditious Book,'" 160.

40. Eamon Duffy, *Fires of Faith: Catholic England under Mary Tudor* (New Haven, CT: Yale University Press, 2010), 48–49.

41. Harpsfield, *A Treatise on the Pretended Divorce*, 185; for parallels in Sander, see Lake, *Bad Queen Bess?*, 260.

42. Harpsfield, *A Treatise on the Pretended Divorce*, 190.

43. Sander, *Schismatis Anglicani*, 7–7v: "Cum ea Catharinae grauitas & moderatio, eaque Henrici leuitas et libido esset, vt nihil magis repugnans et contrarium facile reperiri posset." For a discussion of Sander's characterizations of Henry and Anne Boleyn, see Highley, "'A Persistent and Seditious Book,'" 162–63.

44. Sander, *Schismatis Anglicani*, 7v: "cuius etiam opera errant regis, quam regine, operibus similiora."

45. Sander, *Schismatis Anglicani*, 15–16.

46. Sander, *Schismatis Anglicani*, 17: "Ibi tam impudice vixit, vt vulgo a Gallis appellaretur Hacnea, seu Equa anglicana. Cum autem et in regis Galliarum familiaritatem ascita esset, coepta est vocari Mula Regia."

47. Susan Bordo, in her *Creation of Anne Boleyn* (Boston: Houghton Mifflin, 2013), has commented extensively on the representation of Anne in many of the texts this chapter explores. The history of Anne's representation is as extensive and fascinating as that of Wolsey's.

48. For an extended version of this argument (pace Veech, *Dr Nicholas Sanders and the English Reformation*, 244), see Lake, *Bad Queen Bess?*, 258–61.

49. Highley, "'A Persistent and Seditious Book,'" 153.

50. Sander, *Schismatis Anglicani*, 52v: "Ob quod peccatum Henricus Volsaeum tam seuere punit, in eodem ipse pertinacissime progreditur. Propter quot inexcusabilis es o Rex."

51. Sander, *Schismatis Anglicani*, 56: "Volsaeum Cardinalem etiam Eboraci splendide agere, epulis vacare, solemnique pompa vti, ac mitram suam gemmis ornatam a rege repetere."

52. Sander, *Schismatis Anglicani*, 56v: "Sermones dissipati sunt eum sua sponte venenum sumpsisse. Illud vero constat, cum tanquam reus laesae maiestatis regiae apprehenderetur, eum dixisse, Vtinam nihilo magis laesae maiestatis divinae reus essem. Nunc autem dum nulli rei magis incubu quam vt Regi penitus inseruirem, et in Deum peccaui, et Regis gratiam non obtinui."

53. Lake, *Bad Queen Bess?*, 279, 386.

54. For Skelton, see *The Complete English Poems*, ed. V. J. Scattergood (New Haven, CT: Yale University Press, 1983); for Roy and Barlow, *Rede me and be nott wrothe for I saye no thynge but trothe* (Strasbourg: Schott, 1528; STC 1462.7); for Tyndale, especially *The Practyse of Prelates*, in *Expositions and Notes on Sundry Portions of the Holy Scriptures, Together with the Practice of Prelates*, ed. Henry Walter, Parker Society (Cambridge: Cambridge University Press, 1849), 249–344. There is an extensive scholarly literature on each of these writers, for treatment of which there is not space here.

55. Greg Walker, *John Skelton and the Politics of the 1520s* (Cambridge: Cambridge University Press, 1988), 185. See also Greg Walker, "John Skelton and the Royal Court," in *John Skelton and Early Modern Culture*, ed. David R. Carlson (Tempe, AZ: Arizona Center for Medieval and Renaissance Studies, 2008), 3–18.

56. Walker, *John Skelton*, 151.

57. Pace Schwartz-Leeper, *Princes to Pages*, 16, which inaccurately dates *Hall's Chronicle* to 1542. The first edition is STC 12721; the second, STC 12723.

58. While there is some debate about the extent of Grafton's interventions, it appears clear that Hall's own contributions run through at least the twenty-fourth year of Henry's reign (1533/34); it is therefore reasonable to attribute to Hall the chronicle's treatment of Wolsey. See Graham Pollard, "The Bibliographical History of Hall's Chronicle," *Historical Research* 10 (1932): 12–17.

59. For background on the charges presented against Wolsey and other senior clergymen, see J. A. Guy, "Henry VIII and the Praemunire Manoeuvres of 1530–1531," *Historical Journal* 97 (1982): 481–503. On the various statutes of praemunire more broadly, the classic study by W. T. Waugh, "The Great Statute of Praemunire," *English Historical Review* 37 (1922): 173–205, remains helpful.

60. Peter C. Herman, "Hall, Edward (1497–1547)," *Oxford Dictionary of National Biography* (Oxford, 2012), http://www.oxforddnb.com/view/article /11954.

61. Hall, fol. lxiii^r.

62. Hall, fols. cvi^r, lxx^r, lxxxxii^r, clxiii^v, clxvi^r, cx^v.

63. Hall, fol. lxxv^r.

64. Hall, fol. lvii^v.

65. Hall, fol. lxiiii^r.

66. Hall, fol. cxlii^r.

67. Peter C. Herman, "Henrician Historiography and the Voice of the People: The Cases of More and Hall," *Texas Studies in Literature and Language* 39, no. 3 (Fall 1997): 259–83.

68. For further discussion of this image, see Schwartz-Leeper, *Princes to Pages*, 135–37. Robert Wolsey, the future cardinal's father, was almost surely not a menial butcher but rather a substantial landowner with multiple commercial interests; nevertheless, as we will see in later chapters, this image has had a substantial afterlife. See Chapter 4 in this volume.

69. Hall, fol. clxiiii^v.

70. Hall, fols. clxv^r, clxxv^r.

71. Hall, fols. clxxiii$^{r–v}$.

72. Hall, fols. clxxxiii^{r-v}. On this book of arguments, see E. W. Ives, "The Fall of Wolsey," in *Cardinal Wolsey: Church, State, and Art*, ed. S. J. Gunn and P. G. Lindley (Cambridge: Cambridge University Press, 1991), esp. 305–8.

73. Hall, fol. clxxxx^r.

74. Hall, fol. clxxxxi^v.

75. Hall, fol. clxxxxiiii^r.

76. Hall, fols. clxxxxiii^{r-v}.

77. Hall, fol. clxxxxiiii^v.

78. Hall, fol. clxxxxiiii^v.

79. Felicity Heal, "Appropriating History: Catholic and Protestant Polemics and the National Past," *Huntington Library Quarterly* 68, nos. 1–2 (2005): 110.

80. Schwartz-Leeper, *Princes to Pages*, 118.

81. For details on the editions, see Schwartz-Leeper, *Princes to Pages*, 120–28; see also Thomas Freeman, "Texts, Lies, and Microfilm: Reading and Misreading Foxe's 'Book of Martyrs,'" *Sixteenth Century Journal* 30 (1999): 23–46.

82. There is an extensive bibliography of studies of Foxe's martyrological writings. For three classic works relevant to Foxe's historical method, see William Haller, *Foxe's Book of Martyrs and the Elect Nation* (London: Harper and Row, 1963); Richard Bauckham, *Tudor Apocalypse: Sixteenth-Century Apocalypticism, Millenarianism, and the English Reformation* (Appleford: Sutton Courtenay, 1978); and Katharine R. Firth, *The Apocalyptic Tradition in Reformation Britain, 1530–1645* (Oxford: Oxford University Press, 1979).

83. *A&M* (1563), 469.

84. *A&M* (1563), 469; for analysis, see Schwartz-Leeper, *From Princes to Pages*, 133.

85. *A&M* (1563), 470.

86. *A&M* (1563), 470.

87. *A&M* (1563), 1452. The internal page reference is to Foxe's treatment of Archbishop Arundel, a notorious persecutor of lollards, earlier in *A&M*.

88. *A&M* (1563), 1452: "Ex relatio cuiusdam qui interfuit, et morientem Cardinalem brachio sustinuit." Similar remarks appear in the three later editions: 1570, p. 1991; 1576, p. 1706; and 1583, p. 1811.

89. *A&M* (1570), 1159. This and subsequent citations are to the 1570 edition, but the text is identical in the 1576 edition (pp. 983–94) and the 1583 edition (pp. 1010–21).

90. *A&M* (1570), 1159.

91. *A&M* (1570), 1159.

92. For the identical text in these later editions, see 1576, pp. 983–94, and 1583, pp. 1010–21.

93. *A&M* (1570), 1163.
94. Schwartz-Leeper, *Princes to Pages*, 135.
95. *A&M* (1570), 1164.
96. Schwartz-Leeper, *Princes to Pages*, 141–46.
97. *A&M* (1570), 1172.
98. *A&M* (1570), 1172.
99. *A&M* (1570), 1172.
100. Among a substantial literature on discourses about martyrdom during the Reformation period, see Brad S. Gregory, *Salvation at Stake: Christian Martyrdom in Early Modern Europe* (Cambridge, Mass.: Harvard University Press, 2001).
101. *A&M* (1570), 3; for discussion of Foxe's bifurcation of the world, and indeed of his readership, into the "true" and "false," see John N. King, "Guides to Reading Foxe's *Book of Martyrs*," *Huntington Library Quarterly* 68, nos. 1–2 (2005): 140.
102. For Cavendish's biography, see the sketch by A. S. G. Edwards in the *Oxford Dictionary of National Biography* (Oxford, 2014), http://www.oxforddnb.com/view/article/4933; as well as the introduction to Sylvester's edition (xiii–xxvi); and Joseph Hunter, *Who Wrote Cavendish's Life of Wolsey?* (London: Richard and Arthur Taylor, 1814).
103. Cavendish, 3–4; for discussion, see Schwartz-Leeper, *Princes to Pages*, 77–78.
104. Sylvester, xxxi.
105. For the censorship of *Hall's Chronicle*, see Herman, "Hall, Edward."
106. For the dating of the texts, see Sylvester, xxvi–xxvii; and Schwartz-Leeper, *Princes to Pages*, 77–79.
107. A. S. G. Edwards, introduction to George Cavendish, *Metrical Visions* (Columbia: University Press of South Carolina, 1980), 4–9; see also A. S. G. Edwards, "The Author as Scribe: Cavendish's *Metrical Visions* and MS. Egerton 2402," *The Library* 5th ser. 29 (1974): 446–49; and A. S. G. Edwards, "The Text of George Cavendish's *Metrical Visions*," *Analytic and Enumerative Bibliography* 2 (1978): 3–62.
108. Derek Pearsall, *John Lydgate* (London: Routledge and Kegan Paul, 1970), 252, quoted in Edwards, introduction to George Cavendish, *Metrical Visions*, 11.
109. Edwards, introduction to George Cavendish, *Metrical Visions*, 12.
110. Cavendish, *Metrical Visions*, ln. 7.
111. On Wolsey's appearance in the *Mirror for Magistrates*, see n. 155 below.
112. See especially *Metrical Visions*, ln. 826.
113. *Metrical Visions*, ll. 85–91; see also Schwartz-Leeper, *Princes to Pages*, 84–88.

114. Cf. Edwards, *Metrical Visions*,161; Schwartz-Leeper, *Princes to Pages*, 82.

115. *Metrical Visions*, ll. 181–82.

116. *Metrical Visions*, ll. 1347–49.

117. *Metrical Visions*, ll. 218–52.

118. Dom Hilary Steuert, "Cavendish's *Life of Cardinal Wolsey*," *Downside Review* 57 (1939): 23–45; and Jonathan Crewe, "The Wolsey Paradigm?" *Criticism* 30, no. 2 (1988): 153–69. Britnell proposed that Cavendish turned to prose out of "dissatisfaction with his own conventional representation of Wolsey in the *Metrical Visions*": Richard Britnell, "Service, Loyalty, and Betrayal in Cavendish's *The Life and Death of Cardinal Wolsey*," *Moreana* 42 (March 2005): 4.

119. Sylvester's edition of 1959 identifies thirty-two manuscripts, to which Edwards has added seven more, plus a further three no longer extant. See A. S. G. Edwards, "Unrecorded Manuscripts of George Cavendish's *Life of Wolsey*," *Notes and Queries* (December 2009): 512–13. As Edwards has shown in a series of perceptive articles, and as we will see in Chapter 2, the *Life* lent itself to selective reading on the part of both Catholic and Protestant partisans. See A. S. G. Edwards, "Thomas Cromwell and Cavendish's *Life of Wolsey*: The Uses of a Tudor Biography," *Revue de l'Université d'Ottawa* 43 (1973): 292–96; A. S. G. Edwards, "A Tudor Redactor at Work," *Yearbook of English Studies* 3 (1973): 10–13.

120. Richard S. Sylvester and Davis P. Harding, eds., *Two Early Tudor Lives* (New Haven, CT: Yale University Press, 1962), x; see also Richard S. Sylvester, "Cavendish's *Life of Wolsey*: The Artistry of a Tudor Biographer," *Studies in Philology* 57 (1960): 44–71.

121. Judith Anderson, *Biographical Truth: The Representation of Historical Persons in Tudor-Stuart Writing* (New Haven, CT: Yale University Press, 1984), 36–37.

122. Warren W. Wooden, "The Art of Partisan Biography: George Cavendish's *Life of Wolsey*," *Renaissance et Réforme* n.s. 1 (1977): 24–35.

123. Schwartz-Leeper, *Princes to Pages*, 77; See *Metrical Visions*, ll. 2279–2425; Duffy, *Faith and Fire*, 188–89.

124. Wooden, "The Art of Partisan Biography," 26–27. See, e.g., Sylvester, "Cavendish's *Life of Wolsey*," 45; Edwards, "Cavendish, George."

125. Cavendish, 10/23–25.

126. The veracity of Cavendish's report, though he claims to have heard this story directly from the fallen Wolsey, has long been questioned for lack of corroborating evidence.

127. Cavendish, 12/2–3.

128. Cavendish, 28–29/36–4.

129. Cavendish, 29–34. There is an eerie (and heretofore unremarked) parallel between Anne, whom Wolsey rebuked but who finds herself in a position to procure Wolsey's fall, and Wolsey, who as chancellor punishes Sir Amias Paulet for having put the future cardinal in the stocks when he was a schoolmaster (5–6).

130. Cavendish, 34, 91–95.

131. The phrase is Schwartz-Leeper's (*Princes to Pages*, 97). See also R. H. Britnell, "Penitence and Prophecy: George Cavendish on the Last State of Cardinal Wolsey," *Journal of Ecclesiastical History* 48, no. 2 (1997): 263–81; G. F. Steiner, "A Note on Cavendish's *Life of Cardinal Wolsey*," *English* 9 (1952–53): 51–54; and Anderson, *Biographical Truth*. For extensive discussion of the parallels between the first and second halves of Cavendish's text, see Sylvester, "Cavendish's *Life of Wolsey*," 47–53.

132. Cavendish, 100/13–17.

133. Cavendish, 101–4. Cavendish himself is not nearly so reserved, asking because of Henry's "Carnall desier & voluptious affeccion of folyshe love . . . what surmysed Invencions hathe byn Invented, what lawes hathe byn enacted, what noble and auncyent monastorys ouerthrowen & defaced," and so forth (78/20–24).

134. Cavendish, 130/14–16.

135. See, e.g., Paul Wiley, "Renaissance Exploitation of Cavendish's *Life of Wolsey*," *Studies in Philology* 43 (1946): 121–46; Schwartz-Leeper, *Princes to Pages*, 109–10.

136. Cavendish, 137/11–16.

137. Cavendish, 148/6–7.

138. Cavendish, 156/27–30. A. J. Slavin, "On Henrician Politics: Games and Dramas," *Huntington Library Quarterly* 60, no. 3 (1997): 249–71, observes that this is one of many episodes in Cavendish's text that reveals the symbolic discourse of Tudor politics (255–56).

139. Cavendish, 179/13–15.

140. Cavendish, 178–79/34–1; for discussion, see Sylvester, "Cavendish's *Life of Wolsey*," 58–62; Sylvester and Harding, *Two Early Tudor Lives*, xii. As Britnell has noted, for Cavendish "loyal service" is an "absolute ideal, virtually an extension of religious obligation" ("Penitence and Prophecy," 6).

141. Cavendish, 182; on Cavendish's account of the cardinal's death, see also Wooden, "The Art of Partisan Biography," 29–33; Britnell, "Penitence and Prophecy," 267–68; Schwartz-Leeper, *Princes to Pages*, 107–8.

142. Cavendish, 188; Wiley, "Renaissance Exploitation of Cavendish's *Life of Wolsey*," 126.

143. Matthew Steggle, "Storer, Thomas (c. 1571–1604)," *Oxford Dictionary of National Biography* (Oxford, 2004), http://www.oxforddnb.com/view/article /26594.

144. On the genre of the personal elegy, see A. L. Bennett, "The Principal Rhetorical Conventions in the Renaissance Personal Elegy," *Studies in Philology* 51 (1954): 107–26.

145. Thomas Storer, *The Life and Death of Thomas Wolsey Cardinall* (London: Thomas Dawson, 1599), sig. B3.

146. Storer, *The Life and Death of Thomas Wolsey Cardinall*, sig. H3.

147. It is not surprising that Storer, a member of Christ Church, specifically elegizes Wolsey as his college's founder; for later treatments of Wolsey and Christ Church, see Chapter 4 in this volume. One of the brief works by Storer's contemporaries that introduces the 1599 edition of the poem complains that Christ Church has fallen somewhat out of favor, not least due to Wolsey's own reputation. John Sprint, a puritan Christ Church MA, mourned: "O see how widdow-like (poor soule!) she standes,/That college he began with curious frame . . . . Which though he reared, with his ambitious handes,/I dare not call him Founder of the same:/How can he be of Christchurch Founder deemde,/That of Christs church no member is esteemde?" Storer, *The Life and Death of Thomas Wolsey Cardinall*, sig. B2.

148. For these episodes, see Storer, *The Life and Death of Thomas Wolsey Cardinall*, sigs B4v, I2.

149. Storer, *The Life and Death of Thomas Wolsey Cardinall*, sig. I1.

150. Schwartz-Leeper, *Princes to Pages*, 153.

151. Schwartz-Leeper, *Princes to Pages*, 164–65.

152. Schwartz-Leeper, *Princes to Pages*, 151, quoting Patterson, *Reading Holinshed's Chronicles*, 7.

153. Schwartz-Leeper, *Princes to Pages*, 154–55.

154. Schwartz-Leeper, *Princes to Pages*, 172.

155. See Henry Summerson, "Sources: 1587," in *The Oxford Handbook of Holinshed's Chronicles*, ed. Paulina Kewes, Ian W. Archer, and Felicity Heal (Oxford: Oxford University Press, 2013), 82. It is worth noting that Stow's works appear to have been the only sources through which Fleming and his collaborators had access to Cavendish's *Life*: No part of the *Life* not quoted in Stow appears in the 1587 *Chronicles*. Others, however, like the evangelical Thomas Churchyard, who authored the section on Wolsey in the *Mirror for Magistrates*, appear also to know the *Life* directly. For instance, while Churchyard explicitly cites Stow as a source, he introduces Wolsey's father as "a playne poore honest man" (cf. Cavendish's "an honest poore mans Sonne," 4/29). Nevertheless, Churchyard's text makes it plain that he does not share Cavendish's ambivalent affection for Wolsey. Thomas Churchyard,

"How Thomas Wolsey did arise vnto great authority and government . . ." in *The Mirror for Magistrates* (London: Marsh, 1587), fols. 265–72; quotation at 265. I regret that there is not space for more extended analysis of Churchyard's representation of Wolsey.

 156. Holinshed (1587), 913; Hall, fol. clxxxxi^v.

 157. Holinshed (1587), 914.

 158. John Stow, *The Chronicles of England* (London: Newberie, 1580), 968.

 159. Cavendish, 127/13–15.

 160. Stow chooses his material from Cavendish selectively. For instance, in the section under discussion here Stow prints the logistical details of Wolsey's journey north but leaves out Cavendish's allusions to the cardinal's religious practices, such as wearing a hair shirt. Cp. Stow, 968–69, with Cavendish, 127–33.

 161. Holinshed (1587), 915.

 162. Holinshed (1587), 916–17.

 163. Cavendish, 182/3–10.

 164. Holinshed (1587), 917.

 165. Schwartz-Leeper, *Princes to Pages*, 163; Holinshed (1587), 917.

 166. Holinshed (1587), 922.

 167. Cavendish, 29/3–4.

 168. Stow, *Annales of England* (London: R. Newbury, 1592), cf. 879 and 882; see also 911, among other such instances.

2. PARCHMENT, PAMPHLETS, AND PLAYS: INTO THE EARLY STUART PERIOD (C. 1580–1641)

 1. General histories of the seventeenth century and its religious conflicts are legion; among them are D. Hirst, *England in Conflict, 1603–1660* (London: Arnold, 1999); Blair Worden, *The English Civil Wars: 1640–1660* (London: Phoenix, 2009); and Peter White, *Predestination, Policy, and Polemic: Conflict and Consensus in the English Church from the Reformation to the Civil War* (Cambridge: Cambridge University Press, 1992). Florence Higham's *Catholic and Reformed: A Study of the Anglican Church, 1559–1662* (London: S.P.C.K., 1962), remains a classic.

 2. See Chapter 1 in this volume.

 3. On the manuscripts of the *Life*, see Chapter 1 in this volume.

 4. Unfortunately, despite his excellent analysis of Cavendish's *Life* and *Metrical Visions*, Schwartz-Leeper does not examine the later history of these texts in the second chapter of *From Princes to Pages* (115–16). In this, he is not unlike many of the scholars who have studied Cavendish, with the notable exceptions of R. S. Sylvester and A. S. G. Edwards. By bringing together existing scholarship with new findings about both print and manuscript

copies of Cavendish's *Life*, this section offers the first attempt at a comprehensive account of its early modern reception.

5. Cavendish (hereafter in this chapter "Cavendish ed. Sylvester"), 272.

6. There is no evidence to indicate whether Sheares made the amendments that resulted in the edition of 1641 or whether that task was accomplished by someone else. Only for convenience's sake, therefore, I will refer to the edition as Sheares's, holding open the possibility that he printed the work of another.

7. George Cavendish, *The Negotiations of Thomas Woolsey, the Great Cardinall of England, containing His Life and Death* (London: Sheares, 1641; STC R19386) (hereafter "Cavendish ed. Sheares").

8. Eamon Duffy, *Fires of Faith: Catholic England under Mary Tudor* (New Haven, CT: Yale University Press, 2010), 188–89.

9. George Cavendish, *The Life of Cardinal Wolsey*, ed. Samuel Weller Singer (London: T. Davison, 1825).

10. Cavendish ed. Sylvester, 272.

11. Cavendish ed. Sheares, "The Table," sigs A1r–A2r; chapter numbers and headings, passim.

12. See Paul Vincent Budra, *A Mirror for Magistrates and the de Casibus Tradition* (Toronto: University of Toronto Press, 2000), esp. chap. 3.

13. Cavendish ed. Sylvester, 6/14–15; Cavendish ed. Sheares, 3.

14. Cavendish ed. Sylvester, 10/22–27; omitted from Cavendish ed. Sheares, 7.

15. Cavendish ed. Sylvester, 13/9–13; omitted from Cavendish ed. Sheares, 8.

16. Cavendish ed. Sylvester, 28/33–29/5.

17. Cavendish ed. Sheares, 23, emphasis mine. However, Sheares was deliberately cautious here: To call Anne an "Instrument" does not indicate whose instrument she was.

18. "But wee may see when Fortune doth begin to frowne, how shee can compasse a matter of displeasure, through a farre fetcht Marke." Cavendish ed. Sheares, 26.

19. Cavendish ed. Sheares, 26.

20. Schwartz-Leeper, *Princes to Pages*, 237.

21. Cavendish ed. Sylvester, 182/3–10.

22. Cavendish ed. Sheares, 115.

23. Correspondingly, and perhaps strangely for a puritan, Sheares also shortens or omits passages that praise Thomas Cromwell, Wolsey's chief agent in his exile, for his loyal management of the cardinal's affairs.

24. These omissions occur on Cavendish ed. Sheares, 80, 82, 84, 93, 95; for the corresponding passages, see Cavendish ed. Sylvester, 101–3, 110–12,

114–16, 132–49. In contrast, Sheares makes few such adjustments in the first half of the text, most notably moderating Cavendish's admiration for the cardinal's work ethic, who on one day worked from four in the morning until four in the afternoon without relieving himself. See Cavendish ed. Sylvester, 58/27–59/2; cf. Cavendish ed. Sheares, 48–49.

25. Cavendish ed. Sheares, 108.

26. Cavendish ed. Sylvester, 193.

27. Cavendish ed. Sylvester, 188/9–12.

28. This number does not include the many manuscripts, including almost all of the complete manuscripts, that omit approximately a folio of the text, a gap left blank in some manuscripts and filled up with drawings, summaries, or miscellaneous material in others. The missing text, which describes a boar hunt in France, has no discernible ideological significance, and Sylvester (226–27) has reasoned that the omission comes from a missing leaf in an early exemplar.

29. Washington, Folger Shakespeare Library V.b.111, fol. 51v. Cf. *King Richard III*, ed. James R. Siemon (London: Arden, 2009), 3.4.101–6.

30. *Henry VIII*, 3.2.459–60.

31. Philip Schwyzer, *Shakespeare and the Remains of Richard III* (Oxford: Oxford University Press, 2015), 29, quoting a December 1530 letter of Eustache Chapuys to Charles V.

32. Oxford, Bodleian Library MS Jones 14, fols. 54v–55r.

33. Oxford, Christ Church MS CLIV.

34. *A Descriptive Catalogue of the Western Manuscripts up to c. 1600 in Christ Church, Oxford*, ed. Ralph Hanna and David Rundle (Oxford: Bibliographic Society, 2017), s.v. MS CLIV, claims Tanner as the author of the annotations.

35. Oxford, Christ Church MS CLV; for such annotations, see for instance fols. 7a, 7b, 9a, 15b, 16a, 16b, and so forth.

36. Oxford, Christ Church MS CLV, fol. 11b.

37. Oxford, Bodleian Library MS Laud Misc. 591, p. 247, emphasis mine.

38. The Greek letters appear at fols. 102r, 121r, 122v, 129r, 130r, and 142r, with the omitted material at 175r–182v.

39. Rivkah Zim, "Batman, Stephan (c. 1542–1584)," *Oxford Dictionary of National Biography* (Oxford, 2011), http://www.oxforddnb.com/view/article /1704.

40. This is also true of the copy of the *Life* in London, British Library Dugdale 28, whose redaction for polemical purposes has been studied by A. S. G. Edwards in "A Tudor Redactor at Work," *Yearbook of English Studies* 3 (1973): 10–13.

41. Both annotations at Oxford, Bodleian Library MS Douce 363, fol. 48v. A similar objection appears later in the manuscript, at fol. 62v, where the annotator criticizes the cardinal for producing his own coinage: "This coyne coyned at Yorke by the Archbushop for ioyneng his Cardinals hatt at the foote of ye armes of the king & the letters of his owne name, procured no smaule suspicion to his after ouer throwe/better marked of Straungers at the firste then of Englishemen."

42. Fol. 50v.

43. Fol. 51r.

44. Fol. 65r.

45. Fol. 93v.

46. Fol. 90v.

47. For one example of an annotated early printed edition, see Oxford, Bodleian Library Gough Oxon 22, a copy of the 1667 edition that bears innumerable handwritten corrections, including sheets pasted into the book that contain passages omitted from Sheares's text. The annotator, likely the Mary Coney whose name, with the date 1676, appears on the inside front cover, labored at some length to restore the original text of Cavendish's *Life*.

48. *The Accusation and Impeachment of William Laud* (London: n.p., 1641; STC R235853). The exact number and content of the charges legally preferred against Laud remain unclear and may have differed in English and Scottish contexts. See Joong-Lak Kim, "The Character of the Scottish Prayer Book of 1637," in *The Experience of Revolution in Stuart Britain and Ireland*, ed. Michael J. Braddick and David L. Smith (Cambridge: Cambridge University Press, 2011), 24.

49. London: n.p., 1641; STC R173378.

50. *A Transcript of the Registers of the Worshipful Company of Stationers: From 1640–1708 A.D.*, *3 vols.* (London: n.p., 1913), 1:11.

51. *Canterburies Dreame*, A2r. On Overton, see Don M. Wolfe, "Unsigned Pamphlets of Richard Overton, 1641–1649," *Huntingdon Library Quarterly* 21, no. 2 (1968): 180–81.

52. *Canterburies Dreame*, A3v.

53. *Canterburies Dreame*, A4r.

54. *Canterburies Dreame*, A4r.

55. *Canterburies Dreame*, A4r, A3v.

56. *Canterburies Dreame*, A2v.

57. *Canterburies Dreame*, A2v.

58. *Canterburies Dreame*, A3r.

59. *Canterburies Dreame*, A3r.

60. The image on the cover of *Canterburies Dreame*, as Helen Pierce has shown, "is general rather than physiognomically specific, and is likely to

have been a standard woodcut used to illustrate other 'apparition' stories." In a contribution to what she calls "a cultural history of politics" and what we might dub an exercise in the history of political memory, Pierce has helpfully traced the representation of Laud in a series of antiepiscopal pamphlets of the 1640s. Helen Pierce, "Anti-Episcopacy and Graphic Satire in England, 1640–1645," *The Historical Journal* 47, no. 4 (2004): 826.

61. Thomas Kranidas, "Milton's *Of Reformation*: The Politics of Vision," *ELH* 49, no. 2 (1982): 503.

62. London: n.p., 1641; STC R23148; for the date of publication, see Kranidas, 512n4.

63. *A True Description*, A2r.

64. *A True Description*, A2r–v.

65. *A True Description*, A3v.

66. *A True Description*, A3v–A4r.

67. *Conference with Fisher*, in *The Works of the Most Reverend Father in God, William Laud* (Oxford: Parker, 1899), 2:189–90.

68. *A True Description*, A4v. The latter reference is almost certainly to Laud's 1636 trial of John Williams, Bishop of Lincoln, in Star Chamber.

69. *A True Description*, A4v.

70. See, among many others, Harry Rusche, "Prophecies and Propaganda, 1641 to 1651," *English Historical Review* 84 (1969): 752; Andrew Crome, "Constructing the Political Prophet in 1640s England," *The Seventeenth Century* 26, no. 2 (2011): 279–80. The early-twentieth-century scholar Madeleine Hope Dodds notes that political prophecies were common during the latter years of the reign of Henry VIII. See her "Political Prophecies in the Reign of Henry VIII," *Modern Language Review* 11, no. 3 (1916): 276–84.

71. Crome, "Constructing the Political Prophet in 1640s England," 281. On the collapse of censorship, see also Michael Mendle, "De Facto Freedom, De Facto Authority: Press and Parliament, 1640–1643," *The Historical Journal* 38, no. 2 (1995): 307–32.

72. Rusche, "Prophecies and Propaganda, 1641 to 1651," 754–55. For the debate on Shipton's historicity, see Laura McGrane, "Bewitching Politics and Unruly Performances: Mother Shipton Gets Her Kicks in Restoration and Eighteenth-Century Popular and Print Culture," *Forum for Modern Language Studies* 43, no. 4 (2007): 371–72. Earlier works on the subject included *The Life and Death of Mother Shipton* (London: Pearson, 1871); and William H. Harrison, *Mother Shipton Investigated* (London: Harrison, 1881).

73. *Prophesie of Mother Shipton* (London: R. Lownds, 1641; STC R12801), A2r–v.

74. See Cavendish ed. Sylvester, 127, 151. The former prophecy is that "when the cow does ride the bull, then priest beware thy skull" (127). As McGrane notes, a late-seventeenth-century play of Shipton's life includes the prophecy about the cow and the bull, here taken out of its original context and instead ascribed to "a local abbot" ("Bewitching Politics and Unruly Performances," 375).

75. This argument builds on a suggestion by McGrane, "Bewitching Politics and Unruly Performances," 373.

76. Rainer Pineas, *Tudor and Early Stuart Anti-Catholic Drama* (Nieuwkoop: de Graaf, 1972), 47.

77. Marsha S. Robinson, *Writing the Reformation: Actes and Monuments and the Jacobean History Play* (Aldershot: Ashgate, 2002), xiv.

78. In addition to those discussed in this section, we have tantalizing references to two missing contemporary plays about Wolsey: "Chettle's *The Life of Cardinal Wolsey* (1601) and *The Rising of Cardinal Wolsey* (1601) by Chettle, Drayton, Munday, and Smith." See Paul Dean, "Dramatic Mode and Historical Vision in *Henry VIII*," *Shakespeare Quarterly* 37 (1986): 176.

79. STC S10456; on the chronology of its composition and production, see Pineas, *Tudor and Early Stuart Anti-Catholic Drama*, 11.

80. Pineas, *Tudor and Early Stuart Anti-Catholic Drama*, 11.

81. Robinson, *Writing the Reformation*, 46; emphasis mine.

82. S. P. Cerasano, "Rowley, Samuel (d. 1624)," *Oxford Dictionary of National Biography* (Oxford, 2010), http://www.oxforddnb.com/view/article /24226.

83. *A Transcript of the Registers of the Company of Stationers of London, 1554–1640 A.D.*, ed. Edward Arber, 5 vols. (London: n.p., 1875–77), 3:120.

84. Robinson, *Writing the Reformation*, 14.

85. Samuel Rowley, *When You See Me, You Know Me*, ed. K. Elze (Dessau: n.p., 1874), 5–6.

86. Rowley, *When You See Me, You Know Me*, 16, 39. Historically, Thomas Cranmer was not tutor to the future Edward VI, although he advised the young king on theological matters. See Diarmaid MacCulloch, *Tudor Church Militant* (London: Penguin, 1999).

87. On Summers's role as wise fool, see Pineas, *Tudor and Early Stuart Anti-Catholic Drama*, 11; and Robinson, *Writing the Reformation*, 90–91. See also L. L. Welborn, *Paul, the Fool of Christ* (London: T & T Clark, 2005).

88. Rowley, *When You See Me, You Know Me*, 39, 25.

89. Rowley, *When You See Me, You Know Me*, 72. Summers discovers Wolsey's wealth, which the cardinal has hidden away in empty wine casks, when he goes to the cellar in search of drink. The same story appears in the later pamphlet *A Pleasant History of the Life and Death of Will Summers*

(London: Okes, 1637; STC 22917.5), which recapitulates verbatim the rhyming contest that Rowley stages between Summers, Wolsey, Bishop Bonner, and Wolsey's fool Patch. Cp. Rowley, *When You See Me, You Know Me*, 72 and 39, with *Pleasant History*, B4v–C1r and B2v.

90. Rowley, *When You See Me, You Know Me*, 76.

91. Cp. Rowley, *When You See Me, You Know Me*, 72–76, and *Hall's Chronicle*, fols. clxxxix^v–clxxxx^r.

92. Rowley, *When You See Me, You Know Me*, 76.

93. It should go without saying that a complete discussion of a play as multivalent as *King Henry VIII* is impossible in the space available here. Among the many themes I am unable to treat are the play's depiction of factionalism at Henry's court, its interventions in contemporary debates about royal authority and the rule of law, and its topical allusions to happenings at the court of James I. On these points, see especially Stuart M. Kurland, "*Henry VIII* and James I: Shakespeare and Jacobean Politics," *Shakespeare Studies* 19 (1987): 203–17; and Stuart M. Kurland, "'A beggar's book Outworths a noble's blood': The Politics of Faction in *Henry VIII*," *Comparative Drama* 26 (1992): 237–53.

94. The identity of the play's author(s) continues to evade certainty. Among other studies, see William Shakespeare and John Fletcher, *King Henry VIII*, ed. Gordon McMullan (London: Arden, 2000), 180–199; R. A. Law, "Holinshed and *Henry the Eighth*," *Texas Studies in English* 36 (1957): 3–11; and Marjorie H. Nicolson, "The Authorship of Henry the Eighth," *PMLA* 37 (1922): 484–502. Following McMullan, I presume joint authorship by Shakespeare and Fletcher.

95. Schwartz-Leeper, *Princes to Pages*, 185–91; quotes at 185 and 191. For the former suggestion, see Nicolson, "The Authorship of Henry the Eighth," 500–2. I address the performance history of *King Henry VIII* in scattered comments in the following three chapters; see also Schwartz-Leeper, *Princes to Pages*, 187–89; Stella Fletcher, *Cardinal Wolsey: A Life in Renaissance Europe* (London: Bloomsbury, 2009), chap. 7; and Arthur Colby Sprague, *Shakespeare and the Actors: The Stage Business in His Plays (1660–1905)* (Cambridge, Mass.: Harvard University Press, 1948), 76–83.

96. Larry S. Champion, "Shakespeare's *Henry VIII*: A Celebration of History," *South Atlantic Bulletin* 44, no. 1 (1979): 6. For "Foxean history," see Robinson, *Writing the Reformation*.

97. Robinson, *Writing the Reformation*, 22, 24.

98. Ivo Kamps, "Possible Pasts: Historiography and Legitimation in *Henry VIII*," *College English* 58 (1996): 210; see also Dean, "Dramatic Mode," 179.

99. Schwartz-Leeper, *Princes to Pages*, 240.

100. Martin Wiggins, "The King's Men and After," in *Shakespeare: An Illustrated Stage History,* ed. Jonathan Bate and Russell Jackson (Oxford, 1996), 35; see also John D. Cox, "Henry VIII and the Masque," *ELH* 45 (1978): 390.

101. See Peter L. Rudnytsky, "*Henry VIII* and the Deconstruction of History," *Shakespeare Survey* 43 (1991), 43–58, 55; Nicolson, "The Authorship of Henry the Eighth," 489–90; Champion, "Shakespeare's *Henry VIII*: A Celebration of History," 1.

102. *King Henry VIII,* Prol.13–17; see among others Dean, "Dramatic Mode," 176. To the contrary, others have argued that Shakespeare depended upon Rowley as "a springboard for his imagination as he sought for a fitting veracity and regal solemnity." Joseph Candido, "Fashioning Henry VIII: What Shakespeare Saw in *When You See Me, You Know Me,*" *Cahiers élisabéthains* 23 (1983), 47, quoting Bullough, *Narrative and Dramatic Sources of Shakespeare* (London, 1962), 4:442.

103. Thomas Cogswell and Peter Lake, "Buckingham Does the Globe: *Henry VIII* and the Politics of Popularity in the 1620s," *Shakespeare Quarterly* 60 (2009): 253–78, esp. 256–58. As Wiggins has noted, Villiers's contemporary critics "seized their opportunity: 'Some say he should rather have seen the fall of Cardinal Wolsey, who was a more lively type of himself'" (40).

104. Schwartz-Leeper, *Princes to Pages,* 196–99, 202. On the playwrights' use of animal imagery, which Schwartz-Leeper traces back to the poems of Skelton, see 193–95.

105. Kurland, "*Henry VIII* and James I," 207.

106. *King Henry VIII,* 231; Kurland, "*Henry VIII* and James I," 205.

107. Schwartz-Leeper, *Princes to Pages,* 196.

108. *King Henry VIII,* 2.2.72–74; on these lines, see Schwartz-Leeper, *Princes to Pages,* 204.

109. *King Henry VIII,* 2.4.140–206; see Schwartz-Leeper, *Princes to Pages,* 217.

110. See, among others, T. McBride, "*Henry VIII* as Machiavellian Romance," *Journal of English and Germanic Philology* 76, no. 1 (January 1977): 30; G. S. Brown, *Shakespeare's Prince: The Interpretation of* The Famous History of the Life of King Henry the Eighth (Macon, Ga.: Mercer University Press, 2013), 138; Champion, "Shakespeare's *Henry VIII,*" 11.

111. *King Henry VIII,* 339n124.

112. *King Henry VIII,* 3.2.212, 223–25.

113. Champion, "Shakespeare's *Henry VIII,*" 12–13; see also Kurland, "Beggar's Book," 246–47.

114. On *King Henry VIII*'s use of Cavendish as a source, see R. H. Britnell, "Penitence and Prophecy: George Cavendish on the Last State of Cardinal Wolsey," *Journal of Ecclesiastical History* 48, no. 2 (1997): 268–69.

115. *King Henry VIII*, 3.2.361–64.

116. *King Henry VIII*, 3.2.371–72; see p. 356n371.

117. *King Henry VIII*, 3.2.408–9.

118. An alternative view is that of F. Kiefer, "Churchyard's 'Cardinal Wolsey' and Its Influence on *Henry VIII*," *Essays in Literature* 6 (1979): 3–10, who argues that Shakespeare and Fletcher viewed Wolsey's fall as an instance of bad luck rather than moral reckoning.

119. *King Henry VIII*, 3.2.439–44.

120. *King Henry VIII*, 3.2.447–48.

121. Robinson, *Writing the Reformation*, 47.

122. See Rudnytsky, "*Henry VIII* and the Deconstruction of History," 48, 52; Dean, "Dramatic Mode," 182; Schwartz-Leeper, *Princes to Pages*, 236.

123. *King Henry VIII*, 4.2.33–34.

124. *King Henry VIII*, 4.2.34–35.

125. *King Henry VIII*, 4.2.64–68.

126. Rosemary O'Day, *The Debate on the English Reformation* (London: Methuen, 1986), chap. 2.

127. D. R. Woolf, "Godwin, Francis (1562–1633)," *Oxford Dictionary of National Biography* (Oxford, 2004), http://www.oxforddnb.com/view/article/10890.

128. Francis Godwin, *Annales of England Containing the reignes of Henry the Eighth, Edward the Sixt, Queene Mary. Written in Latin by the Right Honorable and Right Reverend Father in God, Francis Lord Bishop of Hereford. Thus Englished, corrected and inlarged with the author's consent, by Morgan Godwyn* (London: Islip and Stansby, 1630), A2.

129. Godwin, *Annales of England*, 67.

130. Godwin, *Annales of England*, 30, 46–47.

131. Godwin, *Annales of England*, 18, 60, 97.

132. Godwin, *Annales of England*, 97–98.

133. Godwin, *Annales of England*, 107.

134. Godwin, *Annales of England*, 112; cp. Cavendish ed. Sylvester, 178/34–179/4.

135. Godwin, *Annales of England*, 112.

136. The book was not, however, published until a decade later: Edward, Lord Herbert of Cherbury, *The Life and Raigne of King Henry the Eighth* (London: Whitaker, 1649).

137. David A. Pailin, "Herbert, Edward, first Baron Herbert of Cherbury and first Baron Herbert of Castle Island (1582?–1648)," *Oxford Dictionary of*

National Biography (Oxford, 2009), http://www.oxforddnb.com/view/article /13020.

138. Herbert, *The Life and Raigne of King Henry the Eighth*, 1–2, original emphasis.

139. Herbert, *The Life and Raigne of King Henry the Eighth*, 90. Unlike in Hall (fols. clxxiii^{r-v}), in Herbert this misfortune occurs to Wolsey on two occasions, first in 1528 and then again in 1529, where Herbert interprets the document that Cavendish describes Henry showing to the cardinal while at Grafton House to be a second piece of miscarried correspondence (121). It may not be coincidental that Herbert employs this device, writing at a time when, as we have seen, Shakespeare and Fletcher's *All Is True* was in performance.

140. Herbert, *The Life and Raigne of King Henry the Eighth*, 149, 99, 102; original emphasis.

141. Herbert, *The Life and Raigne of King Henry the Eighth*, 122–23.

3. FROM RESTORATION TO CATHOLIC EMANCIPATION: TEXTS AND PLACES (1641–C. 1860)

1. Stella Fletcher, *Cardinal Wolsey: A Life in Renaissance Europe* (London: Bloomsbury, 2009), 181. The play's popularity was not confined to London, as a collection of Yorkshire playbills from the mid-eighteenth to the early nineteenth centuries demonstrates: York, York Minister Archives and Library, SC Playbills, 1766 through 1812.

2. W. B. Patterson, "Fuller, Thomas (1607/8–1661)," *Oxford Dictionary of National Biography* (Oxford, 2008), http://www.oxforddnb.com/view/article /10236.

3. Patterson, "Fuller, Thomas."

4. Rosemary O'Day, *The Debate on the English Reformation* (London: Methuen, 1986), 38; Joseph H. Preston, "English Ecclesiastical Historians and the Problem of Bias, 1559–1742," *Journal of the History of Ideas* 32, no. 2 (April–June 1971): 205–6.

5. S. J. Barnett, "Where Was Your Church before Luther? Claims for the Antiquity of Protestantism Examined," *Church History* 68, no. 1 (1999): 19. See also Graham Nicholson, "The Nature and Function of Historical Argument in the Henrician Reformation" (PhD thesis, Cambridge University, 1990).

6. Thomas Fuller, *The Church-History of Britain: from the Birth of Jesus Christ, untill the Year M.DC.XLVIII* (London: Williams, 1655), 169.

7. Fuller, *The Church-History of Britain*, 171; see also 176. On Godwin, see Chapter 2 in this volume.

8. Fuller, *The Church-History of Britain*, 169.

9. Fuller, *The Church-History of Britain*, 178.

10. Fuller, *The Church-History of Britain*, 178.

11. Jeffrey R. Collins, "The Restoration Bishops and the Royal Supremacy," *Church History* 68, no. 3 (1999): 549–80.

12. Collins, "The Restoration Bishops and the Royal Supremacy," 571.

13. As Robert J. Mayhew has shown, Heylyn's scientific works advance a Laudian agenda just as much as his historical and theological ones: "'Geography Is Twinned with Divinity': The Laudian Geography of Peter Heylyn," *Geographical Review* 90, no. 1 (2000): 18–34.

14. Preston, "English Ecclesiastical Historians," 207–8; John Spurr, "'A special kindness for dead bishops': The Church, History, and Testimony in Seventeenth-Century Protestantism," *Huntington Library Quarterly* 68, no. 1–2 (2005): 313–34; Anthony Milton, "Heylyn, Peter (1599–1662)," *Oxford Dictionary of National Biography* (Oxford, 2015), http://www.oxforddnb.com/view/article/13171.

15. Peter Heylyn, *Ecclesia Restaurata, or, The History of the Reformation of the Church of England*, 2 vols. (London: Twyford, et al., 1660–61), 1:ix.

16. *A&M* (1570), 984; O'Day, *The Debate on the English Reformation*, 37.

17. Heylyn, *Ecclesia Restaurata*, 2:53–54; see also 2:236.

18. Heylyn, *Ecclesia Restaurata*, 2:236–39.

19. On Sander, whom Burnet calls "Sanders," see Gilbert Burnet, *History of the Reformation of the Church of England* (London: Chiswell, 1679), 1:b1, 41, *passim*; see also Chapter 1 in this volume. Burnet engaged in ongoing polemic against the supporters of Sander's history: Consider, for instance, his pamphlet "A Letter to Monsieur Thevenot, being a full Refutation of Mr. Le Grand's History of Henry VIII's Divorcing Katharine of Arragon. With a plain vindication of the same by Dr. G.B." (London: n.p., 1690).

20. Spurr, "'A special kindness for dead bishops,'" 326.

21. Mayhew, "'Geography Is Twinned with Divinity,'" 29.

22. Burnet, *History of the Reformation of the Church of England*, 1:xi–xii; discussion in Preston, "English Ecclesiastical Historians," 213.

23. Burnet, *History of the Reformation of the Church of England*, 1:8; see also 1:44–45, 82.

24. See, for instance, Burnet, *History of the Reformation of the Church of England*, 1:7, 44–45, 81.

25. Burnet, *History of the Reformation of the Church of England*, 1:8. The one exception to Burnet's negative evaluation of Wolsey's churchmanship is in connection with his attempts to reform the clergy. "He seemed to have designed the Reformation of the Inferiour Clergy by all the means he could think of, except the giving them a good Example" (1:20).

26. Burnet, *History of the Reformation of the Church of England*, 1:8.

27. Burnet, *History of the Reformation of the Church of England*, 1:c1–c2.

28. Burnet, *History of the Reformation of the Church of England*, 1:c2.

29. On John Aubrey, see Andrew Clark, "John Aubrey's Biographical Collections," *English Historical Review* 11 (April 1896): 328–35; and the introductions to the editions of the *Brief Lives* by Clark (Oxford, 1898), Oliver Lawson Dick (Ann Arbor: University of Michigan Press, 1957), and Richard Barber (London: Folio Society, 1975).

30. Adam Fox, "Aubrey, John (1626–1697)," *Oxford Dictionary of National Biography* (Oxford, 2008), http://www.oxforddnb.com/view/article/886.

31. Anthony Wood, *Athenae Oxonienses*, 2 vols. (London: Bennet, 1691–92), 1:col. 667.

32. Wood, *Athenae Oxonienses*, 1:col. 668.

33. Aubrey, *Brief Lives*, ed. Lawson Dick, 322–23.

34. Aubrey, *Brief Lives*, ed. Lawson Dick, 324; for the full poem, see Octavius Gilchrist, ed., *The Poems of Richard Corbet, Late Bishop of Oxford and of Norwich* (London: Longman et al., 1807), 171–204. Space does not permit treatment of later elegies about the cardinal, including most famously a section of Samuel Johnson's *The Vanity of Human Wishes* (London: Dodsley, 1749).

35. See Chapter 2 in this volume.

36. Vernulaeus's fascinating play falls outside the scope of the present study, both by virtue of its continental origins and its Latin language. It is worth noting that it relies primarily on Sander's *Schismatis Anglicani* and that it casts Wolsey as the prime mover of Henry's divorce. See Louis A. Schuster's excellent introduction and edition, *Henry VIII: A Neo-Latin Drama by Nicolaus Vernulaeus* (Austin: University of Texas Press, 1964).

37. See George W. Whiting, "Political Satire in London Stage Plays, 1680–83," *Modern Philology* 28 (1930): 29–43.

38. For different views on the textual history of *Vertue Betray'd*, see Edith N. Backus, "The MS. Play, 'Anna Bullen,'" *PMLA* 47 (1932): 741–52; J. M. Bastian, "James Ralph's Second Adaptation from John Banks," *Huntingdon Library Quarterly* 25, no. 3 (1962): 18–88.

39. H. Spencer, "Improving Shakespeare: Some Bibliographical Notes on the Restoration Adaptations," *PMLA* 41 (1926): 735–36; Diane Dreher, introduction to John Banks, *Vertue Betray'd: Or, Anne Bullen* (Los Angeles: William Andrews Clark Memorial Library, University of California, 1981), vii.

40. Dreher, introduction to John Banks, *Vertue Betray'd*, vi.

41. Banks, *Vertue Betray'd*, 1, original emphasis.

42. Banks, *Vertue Betray'd*, 3; see also 30, 62.

43. Banks, *Vertue Betray'd*, 31.

44. Banks, *Vertue Betray'd*, 68; see also 57.

45. J. Hopes, "Politics and Morality in the Writings of Jeremy Collier," *Literature and History* 8 (1978): 159–74, notes that Collier's decision to reject the outcome of the 1688 revolution was a defining moment in his life. See also Eric Salmon, "Collier, Jeremy (1650–1726)," *Oxford Dictionary of National Biography* (Oxford, 2004), http://www.oxforddnb.com/view/article /5917.

46. Hopes, "Politics and Morality in the Writings of Jeremy Collier," 170–71; Salmon, "Collier, Jeremy"; see also O'Day, *The Debate on the English Reformation*, 55; Andrew Starkie, "Contested Histories of the English Church: Gilbert Burnet and Jeremy Collier," *Huntington Library Quarterly* 68, no. 1–2 (2005): 335–51.

47. Jeremy Collier, *Ecclesiastical History of Great Britain*, 2 vols. (London: Keble, 1708, 1714), 2:.2.

48. Collier, *Ecclesiastical History of Great Britain*, 2:3.

49. Collier, *Ecclesiastical History of Great Britain*, 2:44. Interestingly, with regard to the cause of Wolsey's death Collier offers a novel hypothesis: Rather than committing suicide or dying from his shock and disappointment, Wolsey may have been poisoned. "If there was any foul Play, 'tis most likely 'twas received from those who had him Custody. For once at dinner, he complain'd of being taken with an extraordinary Coldness at his Stomach: Upon which, he fell into that Sickness, which carry'd him off" (2:44).

50. Collier, *Ecclesiastical History of Great Britain*, 2:22–23.

51. Collier, *Ecclesiastical History of Great Britain*, 2:37.

52. Collier, *Ecclesiastical History of Great Britain*, 2:3, 44.

53. Collier, *Ecclesiastical History of Great Britain*, 2:19–20, original emphasis.

54. Collier, *Ecclesiastical History of Great Britain*, 2:44. For Collier's treatment of the articles against Wolsey, see 2:38–43.

55. Collier, *Ecclesiastical History of Great Britain*, 2:19–20, 44.

56. Richard Sharp, "Fiddes, Richard (1671–1725)," *Oxford Dictionary of National Biography* (Oxford, 2004), http://www.oxforddnb.com/view/article /9380.

57. Fiddes, *The Life of Cardinal Wolsey* (London: Knapton et al., 1724), ii.

58. Sharp, "Fiddes, Richard."

59. Fiddes, *The Life of Cardinal Wolsey*, iii.

60. Fiddes, *The Life of Cardinal Wolsey*, iv.

61. Fiddes, *The Life of Cardinal Wolsey*, iv.

62. See, e.g., Fiddes, *The Life of Cardinal Wolsey*, x.

63. Fiddes, *The Life of Cardinal Wolsey*, xxiii.

64. Fiddes, *The Life of Cardinal Wolsey*, 157, emphasis mine. Later, Fiddes frames his presupposition more simply: "we ought to put the best Construction on the Acts of men which they will reasonably admit" (258; see also 101).

65. Fiddes, *The Life of Cardinal Wolsey*, 8, 260, among many others.

66. Fiddes, *The Life of Cardinal Wolsey*, 98, 164–65; quote at 164.

67. Fiddes, *The Life of Cardinal Wolsey*, 196–97.

68. Fiddes, *The Life of Cardinal Wolsey*, 102–112.

69. Fiddes, *The Life of Cardinal Wolsey*, 502.

70. Fiddes, *The Life of Cardinal Wolsey*, 237.

71. Fiddes, *The Life of Cardinal Wolsey*, 122.

72. Fiddes, *The Life of Cardinal Wolsey*, 20.

73. See, e.g., Fiddes, *The Life of Cardinal Wolsey*, 467–68.

74. Fiddes, *The Life of Cardinal Wolsey*, 499–50; for Collier, 44.

75. Fiddes, *The Life of Cardinal Wolsey*, 501.

76. Fiddes, *The Life of Cardinal Wolsey*, 506.

77. Sharp, "Fiddes, Richard."

78. Joseph Grove, *History of the Life and Times of Cardinal Wolsey, Prime Minister to King Henry VIII*, 4 vols. (London: Purser, 1742), 1:vi–vii.

79. For Grove's explanation, see *History of the Life and Times of Cardinal Wolsey*, 1:v.

80. See, e.g., Grove, *History of the Life and Times of Cardinal Wolsey*, 4:283–89, for Grove's narration of the fallen Wolsey joyfully receiving a token of royal favor from the hand of Henry Norris. It is unclear whether Grove had access to a manuscript of Cavendish or was instead familiar with these episodes through an intermediary like Stow.

81. See Grove, *History of the Life and Times of Cardinal Wolsey*, 2:313–14; and Joseph Grove, *Two Dialogues in the Elysian Fields, between Cardinal Wolsey, and Cardinal Ximenes, the First Prime Minister of England, and the Other of Spain* (London: Leach, 1761). While Fiddes and Grove compared Wolsey and Ximenes favorably, a contemporary political writer deployed a comparison with Wolsey against the prime minister of the day, Sir Robert Walpole: *Authentick Memoirs of the Life and Infamous Actions of Cardinal Wolsey* (London: Smith, 1732).

82. Grove, *History of the Life and Times of Cardinal Wolsey*, 1:iii–iv.

83. See, among many others, Grove, *History of the Life and Times of Cardinal Wolsey*, 2:284, 292, 4:189–91.

84. Grove, *History of the Life and Times of Cardinal Wolsey*, 3:74.

85. Grove, *History of the Life and Times of Cardinal Wolsey*, 3:161.

86. See Grove, *History of the Life and Times of Cardinal Wolsey*, 2:317; 4:189–91.

87. O'Day, *The Debate on the English Reformation*, 54.

88. O'Day, *The Debate on the English Reformation*, 54.

89. On Reformation historiography and the Catholic emancipation debate, see John E. Drabble, "Mary's Protestant Martyrs and Elizabeth's Catholic Traitors in the Age of Catholic Emancipation," *Church History* 51 (1982): 172–85.

90. John Galt, *The Life and Administration of Cardinal Wolsey* (London: Cadell and Davies, 1812). For discussion of Scott's influence on anglophone historical fiction, see Chapter 4, note 13, in this volume.

91. Galt, *The Life and Administration of Cardinal Wolsey*, 105, 266.

92. Galt, *The Life and Administration of Cardinal Wolsey*, 2.

93. Galt, *The Life and Administration of Cardinal Wolsey*, 37.

94. Galt, *The Life and Administration of Cardinal Wolsey*, 38, 14.

95. Galt, *The Life and Administration of Cardinal Wolsey*, 256.

96. Galt, *The Life and Administration of Cardinal Wolsey*, 135, 126, 53, 56.

97. Galt, *The Life and Administration of Cardinal Wolsey*, 87–89; quote at 89.

98. Galt, *The Life and Administration of Cardinal Wolsey*, 73.

99. Galt, *The Life and Administration of Cardinal Wolsey*, 187; see earlier discussion, 73–79.

100. John Vidmar, "John Lingard's *History of the English Reformation*: History or Apologetics?" *Catholic Historical Review* 85, no. 3 (1999): 383. As Drabble has demonstrated, Lingard depended for many of his arguments upon the work of Charles Butler and John Milner; they in turn had relied on moderate protestant writers such as Heylyn. Drabble, "Mary's Protestant Martyrs," 176.

101. Vidmar, "John Lingard's *History of the English Reformation*," 386–95.

102. Vidmar, "John Lingard's *History of the English Reformation*," 395.

103. John Lingard, *History of England*, 13 vols. (London: Dolman, 1844), 6:164.

104. O'Day, *The Debate on the English Reformation*, 67; Vidmar, "John Lingard's *History of the English Reformation*," 415–16.

105. Lingard, *History of England*, 6:33.

106. Lingard, *History of England*, 6:53.

107. Lingard, *History of England*, 6:113–14.

108. Lingard, *History of England*, 6:158.

109. Henry Soames, *History of the Reformation of the Church of England, Abridged from His Larger Work* (London: C. and J. Rivington, 1828), v. The full *History of the Reformation of the Church of England*, 3 vols. (London: Rivington, 1826), is barely more moderate in its presentation of the papacy. For an explicitly polemical work, see also Henry Soames, *Reasons for*

Opposing the Romish Claims (London: C. and F. Rivington, 1829). For further discussion, see Drabble, "Mary's Protestant Martyrs," 174–75.

110. Soames, *History of the Reformation of the Church of England*, 20.

111. Soames, *History of the Reformation of the Church of England*, 39, 43.

112. Adrian Tinniswood, *The Polite Tourist: A History of Country House Visiting* (London: National Trust, 1998), 139.

113. Peter Mandler, "'The Wand of Fancy': The Historical Imagination of the Victorian Tourist," in *Material Memories*, ed. Marius Kwint, Christopher Breward, and Jeremy Aynsley (Oxford and New York, 1999), 127; for data on recent visits, see Association of Leading Visitor Attractions, "Latest Visitor Figures," http://www.alva.org.uk/details.cfm?p=423.

114. Pierre Nora, *Les lieux de mémoire*, 7 vols. (Paris, 1984–1992); for discussion, see David P. Jordan, "Introduction," in *Rethinking France: Les lieux de mémoire*, trans. Mary Trouille (Chicago: University of Chicago Press, 2001), 1:xxiii–xxxiv.

115. Marius Kwint, "Introduction," in Kwint et al., eds., *Material Memories*, 2.

116. Kwint, "Introduction," 4.

117. The discovery in 2012 of the remains of King Richard III, the other historical figure entombed in the so-called Tyrants' Sepulcher in Leicester Abbey, prompted calls for renewed archaeological work to identify Wolsey's final resting place. See Hayley Dixon, "Hunt for Richard III: Now Leicester Wants to Find Cardinal Wolsey," *Guardian*, February 13, 2013.

118. In contrast with Hampton Court, the representation and commemoration of Wolsey at Christ Church has been significantly more consistent. Cp. the section "Remembering Wolsey in Public," in Chapter 5 in this volume, and Peter Curnow, "The East Window of the Chapel at Hampton Court Palace," *Architectural History* 27 (1984): 7.

119. On the significance of these last terms and on the emergence of a British "heritage industry," see Robert Hewison, *The Heritage Industry: Britain in a Climate of Decline* (London: Methuen, 1987); and Julia Parker, "Reinvention and Continuity in the Making of an Historic Visitor Attraction: Control, Access and Display at Hampton Court Palace, 1838–1938" (PhD thesis, Kingston University, 2009).

120. Edward Jesse, *A Summer's Day at Hampton Court* (London: Murray, 1840), 12.

121. Ernest Law, *History of Hampton Court Palace*, vol. 1: *In Tudor Times* (London: Bell and Sons, 1890), 115. About Law, see Simon Thurley, *Hampton Court: A Social and Architectural History* (New Haven, CT: Yale University Press, 2003), 339.

122. Schwartz-Leeper, *Princes to Pages*, 32–33.

123. As with the method of this book at large, the following section does not seek to resolve any of the outstanding archaeological and architectural controversies. For a selection of recent scholarship on the palace, see Simon Thurley, "The Sixteenth-Century Kitchens at Hampton Court," *Journal of the British Archaeological Association* 143 (1990): 1–28; Jonathan Foyle, "A Reconstruction of Thomas Wolsey's Great Hall at Hampton Court Palace," *Architectural History* 45 (2002): 128–58; and Simon Thurley, "The Cloister and the Hearth: Wolsey, Henry VIII, and the Early Tudor Palace Plan," *Journal of the British Archaeological Association* 162 (2009): 179–95.

124. R. J. Minney, *Hampton Court* (London: Cassell, 1972), 1, 4.

125. Thurley, *Hampton Court*, 30.

126. Olwen Hedley, *Hampton Court* (London: Pilkin, 1971), 3.

127. Minney, *Hampton Court*, 29–30.

128. Lucy Worsley and David Souden, *Hampton Court Palace: The Official Illustrated History* (London: Merrell, 2005), 21–23, 111–12.

129. Law, *History of Hampton Court*, 1:51.

130. Law, *History of Hampton Court*, 1:179n; June Osborne, *Hampton Court Palace* (Kingswood: Her Majesty's Stationery Office, 1984), 63.

131. G. H. Chettle, *Hampton Court Palace* (London: Her Majesty's Stationery Office, 1975), 14; Minney, *Hampton Court*, 188; Hedley, *Hampton Court*, 7.

132. Ernest Law, *History of Hampton Court Palace*, vol. 3: *In Orange and Guelph Times* (London: Bell and Sons, 1890), 324–25.

133. Mandler, "'The Wand of Fancy,'" 126.

134. Tinniswood, *The Polite Tourist*, 139–42.

135. Mandler, "'The Wand of Fancy,'" 129–39.

136. George Bickham, *Deliciae Brittanicae: Or, the Curiosities of Kensington, Hampton Court, and Windsor Castle, Delineated* (London: n.p., n.d. = 1742), 56.

137. F. Streeter, *Hampton Court: A Descriptive Poem* (Rochester: Fisher, 1778), 3–4.

138. W. H. Pyne, *The History of the Royal Residences*, 3 vols. (London: Dry, 1819), 2:1, 9.

139. Mandler, "'The Wand of Fancy,'" 139. The first official guidebook to the palace did not appear until 1930; all of those under discussion here were privately researched, published, and sold. See Parker, "Reinvention and Continuity," 26.

140. Jesse, *Summer's Day at Hampton Court*, 23, 25.

141. Felix Summerly, *A Handbook for the Architecture, Tapestries, Paintings, Gardens, and Grounds of Hampton Court* (London: Bell, 1843).

142. Law, "Wolsey at Hampton Court," 11. Twentieth-century guidebooks and histories of the palace remained divided about Wolsey. Authors such as

Osborne, *Hampton Court*; and Roy Nash, *Hampton Court: The Palace and the People* (London: MacDonald, 1983), have criticized him for corruption and greed, while others like Worsley and Souden have represented him more sympathetically.

143. Henry G. Clark, *The Royal Gallery, Hampton Court Palace: Its Pictures and Their Painters: A Hand-Book Guide for Visitors* (London, 1843), 32, quoted in Parker, "Reinvention and Continuity," 39; see also Worsley and Souden, *Hampton Court Palace*, 105.

144. Parker, "Reinvention and Continuity," 42.

145. Parker, "Reinvention and Continuity," 54.

146. Parker, "Reinvention and Continuity," 54–68; quote at 68.

147. Quoted in Parker, "Reinvention and Continuity," 57.

148. Parker, "Reinvention and Continuity," 16; Hewison, *The Heritage Industry*, 20–21.

149. Brett Dolman, personal interview, July 6, 2016.

150. Young Henry Exhibit, Hampton Court Palace, May 28, 2016.

151. Historic Royal Palaces, "Young Henry VIII: Information Folder for State Apartment Warders" (July 2007), 5. I am grateful to Brett Dolman for sharing this document with me. By "the Cause" the guide means Historic Royal Palaces' overall mission, namely "to help everyone explore the story of how monarchs and people have shaped society." See Parker, "Reinvention and Continuity," 16.

152. Historic Royal Palaces, "Young Henry VIII," 5.

153. Dolman, personal interview.

154. See the statistics compiled by the Association of Leading Visitor Attractions for the years 2007 through 2010, http://www.alva.org.uk/details .cfm?p=423; see also Tracy McVeigh, "Open Season for Tudor Tourism as Wolf Hall Effect Takes Hold," *Guardian*, January 24, 2015.

4. HISTORICAL FICTION, ACADEMIC HISTORY,
AND CIVIC PAGEANTRY (C. 1850–C. 1960)

1. Beverley Southgate, *History Meets Fiction* (Harlow: Longman, 2009), 6, original emphases.

2. Hayden White, "Introduction: Historical Fiction, Fictional History, and Historical Reality," *Rethinking History* 9, no. 2–3 (2005): 150, 149. White's massive oeuvre defies full explication here but has been seminal with regard to postmodern approaches to historiography. For helpful analysis, however, see Paul A. Roth, "Hayden White and the Aesthetics of Historiography," *History of the Human Sciences* 5, no. 1 (1992): 17–35.

3. Hilary Mantel, "Booker Winner Hilary Mantel on Dealing with History in Fiction," *Guardian*, October 16, 2009. Jerome De Groot, *Remaking*

History: Historians and Heritage in Contemporary Popular Culture (Abingdon: Routledge, 2016), 30, cites a passage from Mantel's essay, but the whole repays careful reading.

4. Shannon McSheffrey, "William Webbe's Wench: Henry VIII, History, and Popular Culture," in *The Middle Ages on Television: Critical Essays*, ed. Meriem Pagès and Karolyn Kinane (Jefferson, NC: McFarland, 2015), 56.

5. De Groot, *Remaking History*, 2.

6. Georg Lukács, *The Historical Novel*, trans. Hannah and Stanley Mitchell (Lincoln: University of Nebraska Press, 1983), 151.

7. For philosophical analysis of these features of historical fictions, see Allan Hazlett and Christy Mag Uidhir, "Unrealistic Fictions," *American Philosophical Quarterly* 48, no. 1 (2011): 33–46.

8. De Groot, *Remaking History*, 18.

9. On this point, Richard Slotkin is especially poignant in "Fiction for the Purposes of History," *Rethinking History* 9, no. 2–3 (2005): 221–36. The playful qualities of historical fictions evoke a kind of Derridean *jouissance*: Jerome De Groot, *The Historical Novel* (Abingdon: Routledge, 2010), 110.

10. Robinson Murphy, "Elizabeth Barton's Claim: Feminist Defiance in *Wolf Hall*," *Frontiers* 36, no. 2 (2015): 152–68.

11. De Groot, *Remaking History*, 7.

12. One quantitative assessment that can be made is that of Hsu-Ming Teo, who has observed that in a recent year, more than a third of the books nominated for the Booker Prize were historical in nature. Hsu-Ming Teo, "Historical Fiction and Fictions of History," *Rethinking History* 15, no. 2 (2011): 297.

13. Lukács famously characterized the first half of the nineteenth century as that of the birth of the historical novel, under the inspiration of Sir Walter Scott. While he observed that fictions set in the past could be found in earlier periods as well, he claimed that they "are historical only as regards their purely external choice of theme and costume. Not only the psychology of the characters, but the manners depicted are entirely those of the writer's own day." Lukács, *The Historical Novel*, 18. There is not space here to consider whether Lukács was right or whether we should instead accept De Groot's argument that Lukács's modernist, Eurocentric view both led him to downplay earlier works like *Don Quixote de la Mancha* and pass over in silence Asian historical fictions written as early as the sixteenth century. De Groot, *The Historical Novel*, 12–20.

14. McSheffrey, "William Webbe's Wench," 53.

15. J. F. Smith, *Wolsey! Or, the Secret Witness: An Original Drama in Three Acts* (London: Duncombe, 1845).

16. Freston Tower is now a property of the Landmark Trust, and its history is chronicled by Ed Broom at http://www.freston.net. For Wolsey Bridge, see the Suffolk County Council's heritage website: https://heritage .suffolk.gov.uk/hbsmr-web/record.aspx?UID=MSF15147-Wolsey-Bridge.

17. Both stories were still current in 1938, when Edmund Tyrrell-Green mentioned them in a survey of Wolsey's relationship to his native Suffolk: "The Constructive Genius of Cardinal Wolsey," *Essex Review* 47 (1938): 139–44.

18. The 1875 critic, the anonymous author of "Public Men of Ipswich and East Suffolk," is quoted in Ed Broom, "Cobbold Book, Author Biography," http://www.freston.net/tower/novel-bio.html. The papers were by Samuel Tymms, published in *Proceedings of the Suffolk Institute of Archaeology* 2 (1854–1859): 270–71; and C. R. Durrant, *Proceedings of the Suffolk Institute of Archaeology* 13 (1907–1909): 382–88.

19. Nicholas Orme, "Latimer, William (c. 1467–1545)," *Oxford Dictionary of National Biography* (Oxford, 2008), http://www.oxforddnb.com/view/article /16104.

20. Richard Cobbold, *Freston Tower*, 3 vols. (London: Colburn, 1850), 2:95.

21. Cobbold, *Freston Tower*, 2:188.

22. Cobbold, *Freston Tower*, 1:i–ii.

23. Cobbold, *Freston Tower*, 3:124.

24. Cobbold, *Freston Tower*, 2:138.

25. Cobbold, *Freston Tower*, 3:261–71.

26. *The Youth's Historical Cabinet: A Series of Narratives, Derived from Different Times and Countries* (Philadelphia: Hogan and Thompson, 1849), reprinted as *Romantic Stories from History* (Philadelphia: Davis, Porter, and Co., 1866), and the other collections cited in this paragraph.

27. Uncle Merry, ed., *Merry's Book of Tales and Stories* (New York: Dayton, 1860), ix.

28. Agnes Strickland, ed., *Tales from English History: For Children* (Philadelphia: Porter and Coates, 1868), 5–6, 260–64.

29. Strickland, *Tales from English History*, 167.

30. Strickland, *Tales from English History*, 167.

31. Strickland, *Tales from English History*, 173; emphases original.

32. Strickland, *Tales from English History*, 199.

33. Strickland, *Tales from English History*, 200.

34. Ranke's famous dictum, "*wie es eigentlich gewesen,*" occurs in his 1824 *History of the Latin and Teutonic Nations from 1494 to 1514*, trans. Philip A. Ashwokth (London: Bell, 1887). As Woolf has demonstrated, Ranke may not have meant this claim to be quite as sweeping as his interpreters have taken

it: Daniel Woolf, *A Global History of History* (Cambridge: Cambridge University Press, 2011), 372–73. For an overview of historiographical developments in Europe during the century covered by this chapter, see Woolf, *A Global History of History*, 345–97.

35. *Latin and Teutonic Nations*, quoted in Woolf, *A Global History of History*, 372.

36. John Dalberg-Acton, "Inaugural Lecture on the Study of History," in *Lectures on Modern History*, ed. John Neville Figgis and Reginald Vere Laurence (London: Macmillan, 1906): 7.

37. Acton, "Inaugural Lecture," 15.

38. *State Papers of Henry VIII*, 11 vols. (London: Eyre and Strahan, 1830–1852); *L&P*.

39. Brewer, *The Reign of Henry VIII*.

40. Acton, review of *Letters and Papers*, vol. 4, *London Quarterly Review* 285 (January 1877): 1.

41. Acton, review of *Letters and Papers*, 26.

42. On Merle and his family, see John B. Roney, *The Inside of History: Jean Henri Merle d'Aubigné and Romantic Historiography* (Westport, CT: Greenwood, 1996); and Blanche Biéler, *Une famille du Refuge: Jean-Henri Merle d'Aubigné, ses origines, ses parents, ses frères* (Genève: Editions Labor, 1930).

43. S. M. Houghton, introduction to J. H. Merle d'Aubigné, *The Reformation in England*, trans. H. White, 2 vols. (London: Banner of Truth Trust, 1962), 2:9, 6.

44. J. H. M. Salmon, review of Roney, *The Inside of History*, *Sixteenth-Century Journal* 27, no. 4 (Winter, 1996): 1145. On Merle's training and the sources of his historiographical method, see John Thomas McNeill, "The Interpretation of Protestantism during the Past Quarter-Century," *Journal of Religion* 6, no. 5 (September 1926): 508–9.

45. Merle, *The Reformation in England*, 1:120.

46. Merle, *The Reformation in England*, 1:124.

47. Merle, *The Reformation in England*, 1:128.

48. Merle, *The Reformation in England*, 1:130–31.

49. Merle, *The Reformation in England*, 1:143; see also 1:243–44.

50. Merle, *The Reformation in England*, 1:144–45; quote at 1:144; see also 1:456.

51. Merle, *The Reformation in England*, 1:211.

52. Merle, *The Reformation in England*, 1:278.

53. Merle, *The Reformation in England*, 1:279.

54. Merle, *The Reformation in England*, 1:330–31; cf. Hall, fol. clxxiii^{r-v}.

55. Merle, *The Reformation in England*, 1:474.

56. Samuel Martin, "Cardinal Wolsey: A Lecture" (London: Jones, 1949), 367.

57. J. A. Wylie, *The History of Protestantism*, 3 vols. (London: Cassell, 1878), 3:361, 389.

58. Lindley Murray, *The Power of Religion on the Mind in Retirement, Affliction, and at the Approach of Death* (New York: Wood, 1875), 56–57.

59. Scholarship on the Oxford movement is extensive and ongoing. Among other recent works, see C. Brad Fraught, *The Oxford Movement* (University Park, PA: Penn State University Press, 2003); S. A. Skinner, *Tractarians and the "Condition of England": The Social and Political Thought of the Oxford Movement* (Oxford: Oxford University Press, 2004); see also Rosemary O'Day, *The Debate on the English Reformation* (London: Methuen, 1986), 86–88.

60. Howard R. Murphy, "The Ethical Revolt against Christian Orthodoxy in Early Victorian England," *American Historical Review* 60 (1955): 800–17.

61. Llewleyn Williams, introduction to J. A. Froude, *Henry the Eighth*, 3 vols. (London: Dent, 1908), 1:ix. Williams's volume is an abridgement of Froude's longer *History of England*.

62. On the notion of Henry VIII as Froude's hero, see Ian Hesketh, "Diagnosing Froude's Disease: Boundary Work and the Discipline of History in Late-Victorian Britain," *History and Theory* 47 (2008): 378; see also McNeill, "The Interpretation of Protestantism," 509; O'Day, *The Debate on the English Reformation*, 91–94. Froude's willingness to believe the best about the king extended so far as to denying Henry's liaison with Mary Boleyn, on which point see J. J. Scarisbrick, *Henry VIII* (Berkeley: University of California Press, 1968), 148.

63. Paul Revere Frothingham, "Froude: Or the Historian as Preacher," *Harvard Theological Review* 2, no. 4 (October 1909): 481–99; Andrew Fish, "The Reputation of James Anthony Froude," *Pacific Historical Review* 1, no. 2 (June 1932): 179–92.

64. Hesketh, "Diagnosing Froude's Disease," 373–75, 381–82.

65. Froude, *History of England*, 1:99.

66. Froude, *History of England*, 1:106.

67. Froude, *History of England*, 1:132.

68. Froude, *History of England*, 1:129.

69. Charles Martin, *Cardinal Wolsey* (Oxford: Shrimpton, 1862), 8.

70. Martin, *Cardinal Wolsey*, 14–15; cf. Froude, *History of England*, 1:130.

71. John Henry Blunt, *The Reformation of the Church of England: Its History, Principles, and Results, Part I, AD 1514–1547*, 4th ed. (London: Rivingtons, 1878), 9, 48.

72. Blunt, *The Reformation of the Church of England*, 49.

73. Blunt, *The Reformation of the Church of England*, 50.

74. Blunt, *The Reformation of the Church of England*, 42.

75. Blunt, *The Reformation of the Church of England*, 45–47; Martin, *Cardinal Wolsey*, 8–9.

76. Martin, *Cardinal Wolsey*, 9.

77. Brewer, *Reign of Henry VIII*, 2:450.

78. Brewer, *Reign of Henry VIII*, 2:457. Among the few exceptions that Brewer mentions is Shakespeare and Fletcher's *King Henry VIII*.

79. Brewer, *Reign of Henry VIII*, 1:266; see also 1:381.

80. Brewer, *Reign of Henry VIII*, 2:49, 375.

81. Brewer, *Reign of Henry VIII*, 1:280.

82. Brewer, *Reign of Henry VIII*, 1:381–82.

83. Brewer, *Reign of Henry VIII*, 1:472–73.

84. Brewer, *Reign of Henry VIII*, 2:156.

85. Folkestone Williams concludes his entries on Wolsey in his *Lives of the English Cardinals*, 2 vols. (London: n.p., 1868), with the observation that Brewer's assessment of Wolsey is among the most laudatory of all those published to date. See 2:529.

86. Brewer, *Reign of Henry VIII*, 2:136; see also 2:449.

87. Brewer, *Reign of Henry VIII*, 2:136.

88. Brewer, *Reign of Henry VIII*, 1:580; Froude, *History of England*, 1:129; Blunt, *The Reformation of the Church of England*, 50.

89. Brewer, *Reign of Henry VIII*, 2:185.

90. Brewer, *Reign of Henry VIII*, 2:205, 222, 358.

91. Brewer, *Reign of Henry VIII*, 2:225–31; see also 2:375.

92. Brewer, *Reign of Henry VIII*, 2:446.

93. Brewer, *Reign of Henry VIII*, 1:59, 262.

94. Brewer *Reign of Henry VIII*, 2:379, 287.

95. Brewer, *Reign of Henry VIII*, 2:379.

96. Acton, review of Brewer, 26–27; quote at 27.

97. Mandell Creighton, *Cardinal Wolsey* (London: Macmillan, 1888), 2; see also 212. For comments on Creighton's dependence on Brewer, see G. J., review of *Cardinal Wolsey*, *Revue Historique* 44 (1890): 176–77.

98. Creighton, *Cardinal Wolsey*, 105–15.

99. Creighton, *Cardinal Wolsey*, 185.

100. Creighton, *Cardinal Wolsey*, 209–10.

101. Ethelred Taunton, *Thomas Wolsey: Legate and Reformer* (London: John Lane, 1901), vii, 4–6.

102. Taunton, *Thomas Wolsey*, 141.

103. Taunton, *Thomas Wolsey*, 57.

104. Taunton, *Thomas Wolsey*, 66 and *passim*; cf. Blunt, *The Reformation of the Church of England*, 49–50.

105. For the journal's current self-description, see "About the Journal," http://www.oxfordjournals.org/our_journals/enghis/about.html. On its early espousal of scientific historiography and opposition to the style of history practiced by Froude, see Hesketh, "Diagnosing Froude's Disease," 390–91.

106. T. W. Cameron, "The Early Life of Thomas Wolsey," *English Historical Review* 3 (1888): 458–77; H. E. Malden, "Wolsey's Ordination as Priest," *English Historical Review* 9 (1894): 708–9; John T. Page, "Wolsey: Ipswich Boy and Cardinal," in *Bygone Suffolk*, ed. Cuming Walters (London: Brown, 1900), 93–104; and V. B. Redstone, "Wulcy of Suffolk," *Suffolk Institute of Archaeology and Natural History* 16 (1918): 71–89.

107. James Gairdner, "The Fall of Cardinal Wolsey," *Transactions of the Royal Historical Society* 2nd ser., 13 (1899): 75–102; Herbert Thurston, "The Canon Law of the Divorce," *English Historical Review* 19 (1904): 632–45; F. J. Zwierlein, "The Delay in the Divorce Trial of Henry VIII and Katherine of Aragon: Cardinal Wolsey's Management of the Case," *Ecclesiastical Review* 53 (1915): 521–34.

108. Henry L. Thompson, *Christ Church* (London: Robinson, 1900); "The Restoration of the So Called Cardinal Wolsey's Palace in Fleet Street," *Illustrated London News* 122, no. 3465 (1905): 388; C. Caine, "Cardinal Wolsey's College, Ipswich," *Journal of the British Archaeological Association* n.s. 20 (1914): 240–41. These were followed by a number of similar investigations in the 1930s and 1940s.

109. Ernest Law, *England's First Great War Minister* (London: Bell and Sons, 1916). He was quickly followed by Charles Whibley, who published an essay entitled "Thomas Wolsey: Minister of War," in his collection *Political Portraits* (London: Macmillan, 1917), 1–19.

110. Quoted in Oliver Welch, "Wolsey's Place in History," *Downside Review* 49 (1931): 125; see also Timothy Corcoran, "Thomas, Cardinal Wolsey, Educator," *Studies* 20 (1931): 24–38. I am indebted to Welch's analysis for some of the comments that follow.

111. Patrick Collinson, "Pollard, Albert Frederick (1869–1948)," *Oxford Dictionary of National Biography* (Oxford, 2008), http://www.oxforddnb.com /view/article/35556.

112. O'Day, *The Debate on the English Reformation*, 106, 109; see A. F. Pollard, *Wolsey* (London: Longmans, Green, 1929), 26–31.

113. O'Day, 106. For Pollard's comments on title "prime minister," see *Wolsey*, 99–101.

114. Collinson, "Pollard."

115. O'Day, *The Debate on the English Reformation*, 104–5.

116. Pollard, *Wolsey*, 302.

117. Pollard, *Wolsey*, 169.

118. Pollard, *Wolsey*, 54–55, 217; see also A. F. Pollard, "The Balance of Power," *Journal of the British Institute of International Affairs* 2, no. 2 (March 1923): 51–64.

119. Pollard, *Wolsey*, 58, 312.

120. Pollard, *Wolsey*, 314–328; quotes at 314, 328.

121. Pollard, *Wolsey*, 279, 284–86.

122. Welch, "Wolsey's Place in History," 128–29.

123. Bernard Bergonzi, "Belloc, (Joseph) Hilaire Pierre René (1870–1953)," *Oxford Dictionary of National Biography* (Oxford, 2008), http://www.oxforddnb.com/view/article/30699.

124. Hilaire Belloc, *Wolsey* (London: Cassell and Co., 1930), vii.

125. Belloc, *Wolsey*, 5–6.

126. Belloc, *Wolsey*, 49, 293.

127. Belloc, *Wolsey*, 262–63.

128. On the capacity of local memories to persist quite strongly, see Andy Wood, *The 1549 Rebellions and the Making of Early Modern England* (Cambridge: Cambridge University Press, 2007), 216–17.

129. Mark Freeman, "'Splendid Display; Pompous Spectacle': Historical Pageants in Twentieth-Century Britain," *Social History* 38, no. 4 (2013): 424.

130. "Cardinal Wolsey's Town," display in Ipswich Museum, Ipswich, UK, viewed October 4, 2016. For the history of the Ipswich Charter Hangings, see http://www.ipswich-arts.org.uk/charter-hangings.

131. On Christchurch Mansion, see http://www.ipswich-lettering.co.uk/christchurch.html. For Cobbold's book, see the section "Early Historical Fictions" in this chapter.

132. *Wolsey Pageant June 23rd–28th 1930, Souvenir Programme*, foreword by A. L. Clouting and J. F. C. Hossack (Ipswich: East Anglian Daily Times, 1930), iii.

133. *Wolsey Pageant Souvenir Programme*, iv.

134. *Wolsey Pageant, Souvenir Programme*, 47; cf. *King Henry VIII*, I.2.415–16.

135. *Wolsey Pageant, Souvenir Programme*, 3.

136. *Wolsey Pageant, Souvenir Programme*, 10.

137. *Wolsey Pageant, Souvenir Programme*, 66.

138. *Wolsey Pageant, Souvenir Programme*, 68.

139. *Wolsey Pageant, Souvenir Programme*, 68; cf. *King Henry VIII*, IV.2.48–68.

140. Deborah Sugg Ryan, "'Pageantitis': Frank Lascelles' 1907 Oxford Historical Pageant, Visual Spectacle, and Popular Memory," *Visual Culture*

in Britain 8, no. 2 (2007): 63–82. See also Robert Barr, "The Pageant Epidemic," *The Idler* 31 (1907): 437–46, quoted in Freeman, "'Splendid Display; Pompous Spectacle,'" 424.

141. Sugg Ryan, "'Pageantitis,'" 72, 77.

142. H. C. Maxwell-Lyte, *History of the University of Oxford from the Earliest Times to the Year 1530* (Oxford: Macmillan, 1886), 422. Maxwell-Lyte's assessment of Wolsey's overall role in the university's history is glowing (419–29, 438–44, 478–81).

143. *The Oxford Historical Pageant June 27–July 3, 1907, Book of Words* (Oxford: Oxford University Press for the Pageant Committee, 1907), 73; for sales figures, see Freeman, "'Splendid Display; Pompous Spectacle,'" 429.

144. *Book of Words*, 73.

145. Judith Curthoys, *The Cardinal's College: Christ Church, Chapter and Verse* (London: Profile, 2012), 15–21, 40–42; quote at 42.

146. *Calendar of State Papers, Spain*, IV, part 1, ed. Pascual de Gayangos (London: Longman, 1879), 326.

147. Statutes of Cardinal College, in *Statutes of the Colleges of Oxford*, 3 vols. (London: Her Majesty's Stationery Office, 1853), ii, 53–57, 63–68; see also Wolsey's revised statutes of 1527, in *Statutes*, 164, 170–75: "Thomam Cardinalem, de Latere Legatum, Fundatorem nostrum."

148. Judith Curthoys, personal communication, August 5, 2016.

149. W. G. Hiscock, *Christ Church Miscellany* (Oxford: Oxford University Press, 1946), 104; for further material on the hat the college treats as Wolsey's, see documents in CCA, LR 45/18.

150. There are two further copies of the Strong portrait of Wolsey at Magdalen College, Oxford. See R. L. Poole, *Catalogue of Portraits in the Possession of the University, Colleges, City, and County of Oxford*, 2 vols. (Oxford: Clarendon, 1912), II, Magdalen College, nos. 12 and 14. For a full list of the representations of Wolsey in Christ Church, see *Catalogue*, II, Christ Church, nos. 7–15; for discussion of some of these images, see Roy Strong, ed., *National Portrait Gallery: Tudor and Stuart Portraits*, 2 vols. (London: Her Majesty's Stationery Office, 1969), 1:334–36.

151. The present inscription appears to have been added in 1876 or 1877. CCA xlix.a.1, minutes of Quadrangle Committee, December 16, 1876.

152. For further details, see *Catalogue*, II, Christ Church, nos. 16–17. For the Wolsey Tower, CCA xlix.a.1, *passim*; see also E. G. W. Bill, "The Belfry at Christ Church," ed. Michael Hall, *Oxoniensia* 78 (2013): 157–74.

153. "Christ Church Centenary," *Guardian*, November 11, 1846, preserved in CCA, MS Estates 125.

154. On the role of the dean and chapter prior to the reorganization of the 1880s, see Curthoys, *The Cardinal's College*.

155. Quoted in "Christ Church Centenary."

156. "Christ Church Centenary."

157. "Christ Church, 1525–1925," in CCA, 1925 Commemorations.

158. CCA, 1925 Commemorations, Founder's Prayers service leaflet, June 24, 1925.

159. CCA, 1925 Commemorations, untitled, undated newspaper article.

160. Christopher Hussey, "Christ Church, Oxford: The Fourth Centenary of Its Foundation," *Country Life*, June 20, 1925, preserved in CCA, 1925 Commemorations.

161. *The Times*, November 4, 1946, preserved in CCA, 1946 Commemorations.

162. *Times Literary Supplement*, "Makers of Christ Church," November 2, 1946, preserved in CCA, 1946 Commemorations.

163. Hugh Trevor-Roper, *Official Guidebook to Christ Church, Oxford* (Oxford: Christ Church, 1950).

5. FROM *A MAN FOR ALL SEASONS* TO *WOLF HALL* (C. 1960–PRESENT)

1. F. M. Powicke, *The Reformation in England* (Oxford: Oxford University Press, 1941), 1.

2. Sue Parrill and William B. Robison, *The Tudors on Film and Television* (Jefferson, NC: McFarland, 2013), 97–98, 36–37.

3. Parrill and Robison, *The Tudors on Film and Television*, 17; see also Susan Bordo, *The Creation of Anne Boleyn* (Boston: Houghton Mifflin, 2013), 181 and chap. 10.

4. John Guy, *Thomas More* (London: Arnold, 2000), 15.

5. Guy, *Thomas More*, 15–18.

6. See, for instance, http://www.usccb.org/issues-and-action/religious -liberty/fortnight-for-freedom/. In July 2016, relics of More and Fisher were displayed for veneration as part of the campaign. See https://cruxnow.com /church-in-the-usa/2016/07/05/relics-english-martyrs-draw-crowds-part -religious-freedom-push/.

7. Mark Freeman, "Texts, Lies, and Microfilm: Reading and Misreading Foxe's 'Book of Martyrs,'" *Sixteenth Century Journal* 30 (1999): 35.

8. Anthony Kenny, *Thomas More* (Oxford: Oxford University Press, 1983), cited in Peter Marshall, "Saints and Cinemas: *A Man for All Seasons*," in *Tudors and Stuarts on Film: Historical Perspectives*, ed. Susan Doran and Thomas S. Freeman (Basingstoke: Palgrave Macmillan, 2009), 55; see further 57–59.

9. Robert Bolt, *A Man for All Seasons* (New York: French, 1990), xiii.

10. Bolt, *A Man for All Seasons*, xiv.

11. Marshall, "Saints and Cinemas," 57.

12. See, among other works on the reception of the play, Christopher Smith, "A Drama for All Times? *A Man for All Seasons* Revived and Reviewed," *Moreana* 25, nos. 98–99 (December 1988): 51–58; Gladys Veidemanis, "A Play for All Seasons," *English Journal* 55, no. 8 (November 1966): 1006–14.

13. Gielgud, whose "lean appearance meant that he did not conform to popular notions of the cardinal," also played Wolsey in an Old Vic Theatre production of *King Henry VIII*. Stella Fletcher, *Cardinal Wolsey: A Life in Renaissance Europe* (London: Bloomsbury, 2009), 190–91.

14. Bolt, *A Man for All Seasons*, xxiv. On the use of animal metaphors for Wolsey, see the section "Wolsey the Papist," in Chapter 1 of this volume, and Schwartz-Leeper, *Princes to Pages*, 193–95.

15. Fletcher, *Cardinal Wolsey*, 191.

16. Bolt, *A Man for All Seasons*, 19.

17. Bolt, *A Man for All Seasons*, 19.

18. Bolt, *A Man for All Seasons*, 20, 22; emphasis original.

19. Bolt, *A Man for All Seasons*, 22.

20. Bolt, *A Man for All Seasons*, 23.

21. Bolt, *A Man for All Seasons*, 23–24.

22. *A Man for All Seasons* (1988), 18:12.

23. Bolt, *A Man for All Seasons*, 34; *A Man for All Seasons* (1966), 18:27; *A Man for All Seasons* (1988), 25:50; emphasis mine.

24. On Anderson's legacy as a playwright, see Esther M. Jackson, "Maxwell Anderson: Poetry and Morality in the American Drama," *Educational Theatre Journal* 25, no. 1 (March 1973): 15–33.

25. Brian Bell, review in *Fortnight* 1 (September 25, 1970): 21. For discussion of these critical reviews, see Bordo, *Creation of Anne Boleyn*, 192–93.

26. Glenn Richardson, *"Anne of the Thousand Days,"* in *Tudors and Stuarts on Film: Historical Perspectives*, ed. Susan Doran and Thomas S. Freeman (Basingstoke: Palgrave Macmillan, 2009), 63. In some ways, the difference between Bell's and Richardson's assessments of the film parallels Rosenstone's distinction between a "costume drama" and a "historical film." See Robert A. Rosenstone, *History on Film/Film on History* (London: Pearson, 2006).

27. *Anne of the Thousand Days*, 31:16.

28. *Anne of the Thousand Days*, 1:08:37ff.; 1:18:48ff.; cp. Judith Anderson, *Biographical Truth: The Representation of Historical Persons in Tudor-Stuart Writing* (New Haven, Conn.: Yale University Press, 1984), 66–67.

29. *Anne of the Thousand Days*, cp. 1:18:48 and 1:21:07.

30. Among many others, consider the film *God's Outlaw* (1986) and the novels *King's Fool* (Margaret Campbell Barnes, 1959), *Sow the Tempest* (Jane

Lane, 1962), *The King's Secret Matter* (Jean Plaidy, 1962), *The King's Pleasure* (Norah Lofts, 1969), and *The Autobiography of Henry VIII* (Margaret George, 1986). Plaidy's *The Lady in the Tower* (1986) is one of the few historical novels from this period sympathetic to the cardinal.

31. O'Day, *The Debate on the English Reformation* (London: Methuen, 1986), 102.

32. O'Day, *The Debate on the English Reformation*, 113.

33. See, e.g., Christopher Hill, *Economic Problems of the Church* (Oxford: Clarendon, 1963); Herbert Butterfield, *The Whig Interpretation of History* (London: Bell, 1931).

34. O'Day, *The Debate on the English Reformation*, 115.

35. O'Day, *The Debate on the English Reformation*, 117, summarizing Geoffrey Elton, *Henry VIII: An Essay in Revision* (London: Historical Association, 1962).

36. O'Day, *The Debate on the English Reformation*, 119–20; see, for instance, Geoffrey Elton, *The Tudor Revolution in Government* (Cambridge: Cambridge University Press, 1953), 415–27.

37. Among other works, see Geoffrey Elton's *Tudor Revolution in Government*, *England under the Tudors* (London: Methuen, 1955), and *The Tudor Constitution: Documents and Commentary* (Cambridge: Cambridge University Press, 1960).

38. Felicity Heal, "Dickens, Arthur Geoffrey (1910–2001)," *Oxford Dictionary of National Biography* (Oxford, 2009), http://www.oxforddnb.com /view/article/76115.

39. A. G. Dickens, *The English Reformation* (London: Schocken, 1964), 22–37.

40. Dickens, *The English Reformation*, 107.

41. Dickens, *The English Reformation*, 38.

42. Christopher Haigh, "Anticlericalism and the English Reformation," repr. in *The English Reformation Revised* (Cambridge: Cambridge University Press, 1987), 56–74; R. N. Swanson, "Problems of the Priesthood in Pre-Reformation England," *English Historical Review* 105 (1990): 846–69. A. G. Dickens responded to these critiques in "The Shape of Anticlericalism and the English Reformation," repr. in *Late Monasticism and the Reformation* (London: Hambledon, 1994), 151–75.

43. Dickens, *The English Reformation*, 40.

44. The historiography of the relationship between lollardy and the Henrician Reformation is at least as complex as that of the representation of Wolsey. It is likely that Dickens's interest in lollardy stemmed at least in part from his work under the supervision of the medieval historian K. B. McFarlane, who published several books on Wyclif and his followers. Heal,

"Dickens, Arthur Geoffrey (1910–2001)." For two surveys, see Peter Marshall, "Lollards and Protestants Revisited," in *Wycliffite Controversies*, ed. Mishtooni Bose and J. Patrick Hornbeck II (Turnhout: Brepols, 2011), 295–318; and J. Patrick Hornbeck II, *A Companion to Lollardy* (Leiden: Brill, 2016), esp. chap. 8.

45. Dickens, *The English Reformation*, 58.

46. Dickens, *The English Reformation*, 59–82.

47. Studies of the reception of the Reformation in individual counties proliferated in the 1970s and 1980s: O'Day, *The Debate on the English Reformation*, 150–52. Among the most influential was Christopher Haigh, *Reformation and Resistance in Tudor Lancashire* (Cambridge: Cambridge University Press, 1975).

48. For this usage, see especially Christopher Haigh, *English Reformations: Religion, Politics, and Society under the Tudors* (Oxford: Clarendon, 1993).

49. Heal, "Dickens, Arthur Geoffrey (1910–2001)"; A. G. Dickens, *The English Reformation*, 2nd ed. (London: Batsford, 1989).

50. J. J. Scarisbrick, *The Reformation and the English People* (Oxford: Blackwell, 1984).

51. J. J. Scarisbrick, *Henry VIII* (Berkeley: University of California Press, 1968), 240.

52. Scarisbrick, *Henry VIII*, 44.

53. Scarisbrick, *Henry VIII*, 42–46.

54. Scarisbrick, *Henry VIII*, 47.

55. See Scarisbrick, *Henry VIII*, 107.

56. Scarisbrick, *Henry VIII*, 154.

57. Scarisbrick, *Henry VIII*, 195.

58. Scarisbrick, *Henry VIII*, 234–35.

59. Haigh, "Anticlericalism and the English Reformation," 58–59.

60. Nancy Lenz Harvey, *Thomas Cardinal Wolsey* (New York: Macmillan, 1980). Among Harvey's errors of fact are the name of Wolsey's patron as Archbishop of Canterbury (8), the chronology of his positions before arriving at court (11), the names under which Henry VI had founded a Cambridge college (144) and under which Wolsey's Oxford college was refounded (203), the claim that he had been "stripped of his priestly power and authority" at the time of his dismissal as chancellor (185), and the identification of St. Alban's as a bishopric rather than an abbey (199); all these are in addition to numerous instances where Harvey's claims are overstated or unnecessarily sensationalistic.

61. Charles W. Ferguson, *Naked to Mine Enemies: The Life of Cardinal Wolsey* (Boston: Little, Brown, 1958), 119.

62. Ferguson, *Naked to Mine Enemies*, 435.

63. Ferguson, *Naked to Mine Enemies*, 436; see also 469.

64. Neville J. Williams, *The Cardinal and the Secretary* (New York: Macmillan, 1976), 1.

65. Williams, *The Cardinal and the Secretary*, 151.

66. Williams, *The Cardinal and the Secretary*, 150–51.

67. Guy, *Thomas More*, 14.

68. Jasper Ridley, *The Statesman and the Fanatic: Thomas Wolsey and Thomas More* (London: Constable, 1982), 1.

69. Ridley, *The Statesman and the Fanatic*, xi, 285.

70. Ridley, *The Statesman and the Fanatic*, 164; see also 94, 292.

71. Ridley, *The Statesman and the Fanatic*, 243.

72. Ridley, *The Statesman and the Fanatic*, 274.

73. Ridley, *The Statesman and the Fanatic*, 279.

74. Peter Gwyn, *The King's Cardinal: The Rise and Fall of Thomas Wolsey* (London: Barrie and Jenkins, 1990), 639.

75. Richard Rex, "Cardinal Wolsey: Review Article," *Catholic Historical Review* 78, no. 4 (1992): 607.

76. Gwyn, *The King's Cardinal*, xviii.

77. Gwyn, *The King's Cardinal*, 500.

78. Walter Roy Mathews, "The Image of Thomas Wolsey: A Study of the Depiction of the Cardinal in Historical Accounts and Biographies, 1530–1630" (MA thesis, University of Tennessee, 1966); Charles Frederick Lasher, "The Historiography of Thomas Wolsey" (PhD diss., Catholic University of America, 1973); Frank Cespedes, "Perspectives on Henry VIII and Cardinal Wolsey in the English Renaissance" (PhD diss., Cornell University, 1977); Thomas John Wyly, "Cardinal Wolsey in Tudor and Stuart Literature: Relationships between Renaissance Views of the Meaning of History and the Character of Literary Texts" (PhD diss., University of Pennsylvania, 1992).

79. Schwartz-Leeper, *Princes to Pages*.

80. Studies in each of these categories are too numerous to identify individually. For some of the most innovative work, see (on Skelton) William O. Harris, "Wolsey and Skelton's 'Magnyfycence': A Re-Evaluation," *Studies in Philology* 57 (1960): 99–122; F. W. Brownlow, "'Speke, Parrot': Skelton's Allegorical Denunciation of Cardinal Wolsey," *Studies in Philology* 65 (1968): 124–39; A. S. G. Edwards, *John Skelton: The Critical Heritage* (New York: Routledge and Kegan Paul, 1981); Arthur Kinney, *John Skelton, Priest as Poet* (Chapel Hill: University of North Carolina Press, 1987); and Greg Walker, *John Skelton and the Politics of the 1520s* (Cambridge: Cambridge University Press, 1988). On Cavendish, see the many sources

cited in Chapter 1 in this volume, and on *King Henry VIII*, likewise see the sources cited in Chapter 2 in this volume.

81. Guy's oeuvre is massive, including especially *The Cardinal's Court: The Impact of Thomas Wolsey in Star Chamber* (Totowa, NJ: Harvester, 1977).

82. R. L. Woods Jr., "Politics and Precedent: Wolsey's Parliament of 1523," *Huntington Library Quarterly* 40 (1977): 297–312.

83. See, among others, David Starkey, "Privy Secrets: Henry VIII and the Lords of the Council," *History Today* 37, no. 8 (1987): 23–31; Neil Samman, "The Henrician Court during Cardinal Wolsey's Ascendancy, c. 1514–1529," (PhD thesis, University of Wales, 1988); Greg Walker, "The 'Expulsion of the Minions' Reconsidered," *Historical Journal* 32, no. 1 (1989): 1–16; Steven J. Gunn, "The Chief Minister and the Nobles: The Dukes of Norfolk and Suffolk 1514–1526," in *Rivals in Power*, ed. David Starkey (Basingstoke: Macmillan, 1990), 50–65.

84. E.g., J. A. Guy, "Thomas Wolsey, Thomas Cromwell, and the Reform of Henrician Government," in *The Reign of Henry VIII: Politics, Policy, and Piety*, ed. Diarmaid MacCulloch (Basingstoke: Macmillan, 1995), 35–57.

85. See, among others, E. Mullaly, "Wolsey's Proposed Reform of the Oxford University Statutes: A Recently Discovered Text," *Bodleian Library Record* 10 (1978): 22–27; Claire Cross, "Oxford and the Tudor State from the Accession of Henry VIII to the Death of Mary," in *The History of the University of Oxford*, vol. 3: *The Collegiate University*, ed. J. H. McConica (Oxford: Oxford University Press, 1986), 117–49; and Susan Wabuda, "Cardinal Wolsey and Cambridge," *British Catholic History* 32, no. 3 (2015): 280–92.

86. See especially the essays by Roger Bowers, P. G. Lindley, Hilary Wayment, and Philippa Glanville in S. J. Gunn and P. G. Lindley, eds., *Cardinal Wolsey: Church, State, and Art* (Cambridge: Cambridge University Press, 1991).

87. Simon Thurley, "The Cloister and the Hearth: Wolsey, Henry VIII, and the Early Tudor Palace Plan," *Journal of the British Archaeological Association* 162 (2009): 179–95.

88. E. A. Hammond, "Doctor Augustine, Physician to Cardinal Wolsey and King Henry VIII," *Medical History* 19 (1975): 215–49.

89. L. R. Gardiner, "Further News of Cardinal Wolsey's End, November–December 1530," *Bulletin of the Institute of Historical Research* 57 (1984): 107.

90. E. W. Ives, "The Fall of Wolsey," in *Cardinal Wolsey: Church, State, and Art*, ed. S. J. Gunn and P. G. Lindley (Cambridge: Cambridge University Press, 1991), 286–315, esp. 302–3. For a longer version of Ives's argument about faction, see also his *Anne Boleyn* (Oxford, 1986), esp. 123–24.

91. Ives, "The Fall of Wolsey," 311.

92. Ives, "The Fall of Wolsey," 288, 303.

93. G. W. Bernard, "The Fall of Wolsey Reconsidered," *Journal of British Studies* 35, no. 3 (1996): 277–310; for a similar perspective, see Derek Wilson, *In the Lion's Court: Power, Ambition, and Sudden Death in the Reign of Henry VIII* (New York: St. Martin's, 2001), 135–37, 240–43, who offers the caveat that it is possible to speak of faction only after Wolsey's dismissal (294).

94. Bernard, "The Fall of Wolsey Reconsidered," 299. In his 2005 monograph *The King's Reformation* (New Haven, CT: Yale University Press, 2005), Bernard argues that Henry was always the driving force behind English policy. The king "not only found highly able servants to carry out his wishes—Wolsey, Cromwell, Cranmer, Norfolk—but also managed to get them to take the responsibility and the blame for what was done" (595). On Bernard's account, Wolsey and Henry alike saw the cardinal "above all as the king's servant," and Wolsey's dismissal advanced one of the king's diplomatic objectives: to symbolize the king's displeasure with the papacy (29, 36).

95. Keith Brown, "Wolsey and Ecclesiastical Order: The Case of the Franciscan Observants," in *Cardinal Wolsey: Church, State, and Art,* ed. S. J. Gunn and P. G. Lindley (Cambridge: Cambridge University Press, 1991), 219–38; Tim Thornton, "Cardinal Wolsey and the Abbot of Chester," *History Today* 45, no. 8 (1995): 12–17; J. J. Goring, "The Riot at Bayham Abbey, June 1525," *Sussex Archaeological Collections* 116 (1978): 1–10; Deirdre O'Sullivan, "The 'Little Dissolution' of the 1520s," *Post-Medieval Archaeology* 40, no. 2 (2006): 227–58.

96. Jonathan Arnold, "Colet, Wolsey, and the Politics of Reform: St Paul's Cathedral in 1518," *English Historical Review* 121, no. 493 (2006): 979–1001.

97. Peter D. Clarke, "Canterbury as the New Rome: Dispensations and Henry VIII's Reformation," *Journal of Ecclesiastical History* 64, no. 1 (2013): 20–44.

98. Fletcher, *Cardinal Wolsey,* 63.

99. Fletcher, *Cardinal Wolsey,* 71, 105.

100. John Matusiak, *Wolsey: The Life of King Henry VIII's Cardinal* (Stroud: The History Press, 2014), 136, 140.

101. Matusiak, *Wolsey,* 303; see also 297.

102. Lacey Baldwin Smith, "The 'Taste for Tudors' since 1940," *Studies in the Renaissance* 7 (1960): 167–83.

103. Jerome De Groot, *Consuming History: Historians and Heritage in Contemporary Popular Culture* (Abingdon: Routledge, 2009), 12–13.

104. De Groot, *Consuming History,* 213.

105. Of course, this section is not able to do justice to the many historical fictions about the reign of Henry produced in the early twenty-first century. I have chosen to focus on *The Tudors* and *Wolf Hall* because they have had the greatest impact in anglophone culture, but also important are Gregory's novels and the recent play *Anne Boleyn* by Howard Brenton (London: Bloomsbury, 2010), which foregrounds Anne's evangelical faith in ways that other fictions do not.

106. Parrill and Robison, *The Tudors on Film and Television*, 248.

107. On *The Tudors* and historical accuracy, see especially Shannon McSheffrey, "William Webbe's Wench: Henry VIII, History, and Popular Culture," in *The Middle Ages on Television: Critical Essays*, ed. Meriem Pagès and Karolyn Kinane (Jefferson, NC: McFarland, 2015). Her finding that some scenes in the series were inspired by the bowdlerized versions of historical events found in popular nonfiction works (64–66) illustrates how multiple "memory producers," in Kansteiner's terms, can collectively undergird new representations of the past.

108. Quoted in "David Starkey's Blast for the Past," *Daily Mail*, October 16, 2008.

109. Quoted in Anita Gates, "The Royal Life (Some Facts Altered)," *New York Times*, March 23, 2008. De Groot has observed that one of the most undertheorized questions about historical fictions is why people appear to enjoy and derive pleasure from them to the extent that they do. See Jerome De Groot, *Remaking History: Historians and Heritage in Contemporary Popular Culture* (Abingdon: Routledge, 2016), 151.

110. Lina Das, "Lie Back and Think of Olde England! Is This TV's Sexiest Historical Romp?" *Mail Online*, September 7, 2007; quoted in McSheffrey, "William Webbe's Wench," 58, emphasis mine.

111. *Pace* McSheffrey, "William Webbe's Wench," 56–69, see Ramona Wray, "Henry's Desperate Housewives: *The Tudors*, the Politics of Historiography, and the Beautiful Body of Jonathan Rhys-Meyers," in *The English Renaissance in Popular Culture: An Age for All Time*, ed. Gregory M. Colón Semenza (Basingstoke: Palgrave Macmillan, 2010), 28; and Jerome De Groot, "Slashing History: *The Tudors*," in *Tudorism*, ed. Tatiana C. String and Marcus Bull (Oxford: Oxford University Press, 2012), 243–60. The remainder of this paragraph is based on their arguments.

112. Thomas S. Freeman, "A Tyrant for All Seasons," in *Tudors and Stuarts on Film: Historical Perspectives*, ed. Susan Doran and Thomas S. Freeman (Basingstoke: Palgrave Macmillan, 2009), 45; on the appeal of the series to the possibility of other outcomes than the one in the historical record, see also Wray, "Henry's Desperate Housewives," 28–29, 37–39.

113. Parrill and Robison, *The Tudors on Film and Television*, 248.

114. Cavendish, 23/28.

115. Cavendish, 23/14–16.

116. Michael Hirst (writer) and Showtime (producer), *The Tudors* (2007–2010), episode 1, 28:02; episode 4, 34:16; episode 5, 50:37. Ramona Wray discusses the intertextuality of the series in her "The Network King: Re-Creating Henry VIII for a Global Television Audience," in *Filming and Performing Renaissance History*, ed. Mark Thornton Burnett and Adrian Street (Basingstoke: Palgrave Macmillan, 2011), 16–32.

117. *The Tudors*, episode 2, 50:35.

118. *The Tudors*, episode 5, 22:06.

119. *The Tudors*, episode 6, 49:15–50:13.

120. *The Tudors*, episode 2, 46:00.

121. *The Tudors*, episode 10, 42:07.

122. Wray, "Henry's Desperate Housewives," 38–39.

123. De Groot, in *Consuming History*, 11–13, uses the copula "historiocopia/historioglossia" to refer to historical fictions that are disseminated simultaneously in multiple media.

124. On Mantel, see Dominic Green, "Wolves Hall," *New Criterion* (May 2015): 25–32.

125. Hilary Mantel, *Wolf Hall* (London: Holt, 2009), 61.

126. De Groot, *Remaking History*, 23.

127. Cited in Jerome De Groot, *The Historical Novel* (Abingdon: Routledge, 2010), 42; on Mantel as theorist of historical fiction, see also Robinson Murphy, "Elizabeth Barton's Claim: Feminist Defiance in *Wolf Hall*," *Frontiers* 36, no. 2 (2015): 157–58.

128. On these effects in historical fiction more generally, see the discussion above, as well as the specific observations in De Groot, *The Historical Novel*, 3–4.

129. De Groot, *Remaking History*, 20–22.

130. Mantel, *Wolf Hall*, 144; see also 72; *Wolf Hall* (British Broadcasting Corporation, 2015), episode 1: "Three Card Trick," 56:02; episode 2: "Entirely Beloved Cromwell," 12:34.

131. *Wolf Hall*, 240; the same technique is used in the second episode of the BBC series (50:59). Cavendish's *Life* is the only sixteenth-century text that Mantel cites in her "Author's Note" at the end of the volume, where she calls it "a very touching, immediate and readable account of Wolsey's career and Thomas Cromwell's part in it" (605). Burrow, in his review of *Wolf Hall* for the *London Review of Books*, takes Mantel to task for treating Cavendish as something of a nitpicking servant: Colin Burrow, "How to Twist a Knife," *London Review of Books* 31, no. 8 (April 30, 2009): 3–5. On the genre of the author's note, see De Groot, *The Historical Novel*, 6–7.

132. Wulf Kansteiner, "Finding Meaning in Memory: A Methodological Critique of Collective Memory Studies," *History and Theory* 41, no. 2 (2002): 180. In connection with the miniseries, see Sebastian Shakespeare, "How Alastair Campbell Inspired Jonathan Wolf Hall Puppetmaster," *Daily Mail*, January 5, 2015, http://www.dailymail.co.uk/news/article-2898178 /SEBASTIAN-SHAKESPEARE-Alastair-Campbell-inspired-Jonathan -Wolf-Hall-puppetmaster.html.

133. Mantel, *Wolf Hall*, 20.

134. Mantel, *Wolf Hall*, 26; emphasis mine.

135. Mantel, *Wolf Hall*, 28; emphasis mine.

136. Mantel, *Wolf Hall*, 117; "Three Card Trick," 1:02:30.

137. De Groot, *Remaking History*, 24; Maurice Timothy Reidy, "A Man in Full," *America* (April 13–20, 2015): 31–32.

138. Ridley, *Statesman and the Fanatic*. Two English Catholic bishops criticized the miniseries on precisely these grounds: see Steve Doughty, "Inaccurate and Anti-Catholic," *Daily Mail*, February 1, 2015, http://www .dailymail.co.uk/news/article-2935693/Inaccurate-anti-Catholic-Bishops -tear-Wolf-Hall-claiming-paints-twisted-picture-English-saint-Thomas -More.html.

139. This point is well made by the unnamed editors of medievalists.net, "Review of Wolf Hall, Episode 1: Three Card Trick," April 5, 2015, http:// www.medievalists.net/2015/04/05/review-of-wolf-hall-episode-1-three-card -trick/.

140. Mantel, *Wolf Hall*, 201.

141. An early allusion to Cromwell's capacity for vengeance, overlaid again with the language of recollection, appears in the scene when he returns for the first time to York Place. Cromwell meets Mark Smeaton, formerly one of the cardinal's musicians and now one of Anne's. When Smeaton avers that he does not think of the cardinal anymore, Cromwell reflects: "To himself he says, as he moves away, you may never think of us, Mark, but we think of you. Or at least I do, I think of you calling me a felon and predicting my death" (184). In Hilary Mantel, *Bring Up the Bodies* (London: Holt, 2012), Smeaton is one of those out of whom Cromwell later extorts a confession of adultery with Anne.

142. Mantel, *Wolf Hall*, 241.

143. This unusual word, which means "Smeared, anointed, saturated, or rendered waterproof, with wax," is a homophone for *seared*. OED, s.v. cered, http://www.oed.com/view/Entry/29895. What is clear is that the image of Wolsey is indelibly imprinted on Cromwell's memory.

144. Mantel, *Wolf Hall*, 245.

145. Mantel, *Wolf Hall*, 18.

146. This point is well made by Jane Winters, reviewing the Stratford production in *History Today*, March 2014.

147. James Poniewozik, "Games of Thrones," *Time*, April 13, 2015. Not every critic has been as kind: See, for instance, Alfred Thomas, "Cromwell the Humanitarian," *Commonweal*, October 5, 2015, https://www.commonwealmagazine.org/cromwell-humanitarian.

148. De Groot, *Remaking History*, 151.

149. Peter Marshall, "(Re)defining the English Reformation," *Journal of British Studies* 48 (2009): 564–86.

150. I am careful not to label this fourth representation a "prototype," since unlike the three prototypes that we have been tracing throughout this book it is of quite recent origin and has not yet inspired the sorts of imitations and elaborations that the earlier accounts of Wolsey spawned in such great numbers.

CONCLUSION

1. "David Annand's Ipswich Statue to Honor Cardinal Wolsey," *BBC News*, April 8, 2010, http://news.bbc.co.uk/local/suffolk/hi/people_and_places/arts_and_culture/newsid_8299000/8299492.stm; on Blatchly, see "John Blatchly Obituary," *Guardian*, November 5, 2015, https://www.theguardian.com/education/2015/nov/05/john-blatchly-obituary.

2. "Cardinal Thomas Wolsey Statue Unveiled in Ipswich," *BBC News*, June 29, 2011, http://www.bbc.com/news/uk-england-suffolk-13905245.

3. For one critical review, see "Cardinal Thomas Wolsey," Recording Archive for Public Sculpture in Norfolk and Suffolk, http://racns.co.uk/sculptures.asp?action=getsurvey&id=1111.

4. "Wolsey Statue," Ipswich Historic Lettering, http://www.ipswich-lettering.co.uk/wolseystatue.html.

5. Thomas Wolsey, preface to William Lily, *Rudimenta grammatices* (Antwerp: M. de Kayser, 1535), sig. A3v.

6. "David Annand's Ipswich Statue to Honor Cardinal Wolsey."

7. It is perhaps inevitable that a book written by a church historian has dwelled primarily on controversies that are religious in nature or that have religious overtones or implications. It would be remiss of me not to note other strands of representation—those having to do with his conduct of foreign policy and, in particular, his management of the so-called balance of power among England, France, the Holy Roman Empire, and the papacy. The works that have sought to intervene in this debate, however, are dwarfed by those interested in Wolsey's role in the events that led up to the Henrician reformation.

8. Ian Hesketh, "Diagnosing Froude's Disease: Boundary Work and the Discipline of History in Late-Victorian Britain," *History and Theory* 47

(2008): 376, quoting Thomas Gieryn, "Boundary-Work and the Demarcation of Science from Non-Science: Strains and Interests in Professional Ideologies of Science," *American Sociological Review* 48 (December 1983): 781.
    9. I am grateful to Terrence W. Tilley for this observation; for the epithet "historian-cops," see Shannon McSheffrey, "William Webbe's Wench: Henry VIII, History, and Popular Culture," in *The Middle Ages on Television: Critical Essays*, ed. Meriem Pagès and Karolyn Kinane (Jefferson, NC: McFarland, 2015), 56.

BIBLIOGRAPHY

MANUSCRIPTS AND ARCHIVES

London, British Library Dugdale 28
Oxford, Bodleian Library Gough Oxon 22
Oxford, Bodleian Library MS Douce 363
Oxford, Bodleian Library MS Douce 363
Oxford, Bodleian Library MS Jones 14
Oxford, Bodleian Library MS Laud Misc. 591
Oxford, Christ Church Archives, xlix.a.1
Oxford, Christ Church Archives, 1925 Commemorations
Oxford, Christ Church Archives, 1946 Commemorations
Oxford, Christ Church Archives, LR 45/18
Oxford, Christ Church Archives, MS Estates 125
Oxford, Christ Church MS CLIV
Oxford, Christ Church MS CLV
Washington, Folger Shakespeare Library V.b.111
York, York Minister Archives and Library, SC Playbills, 1766 through 1812

PRINTED PRIMARY SOURCES

The Accusation and Impeachment of William Laud. London: n.p., 1641; STC R235853.

Arber, Edward, ed., *A Transcript of the Registers of the Company of Stationers of London, 1554–1640 A.D.* 5 vols. London: n.p., 1875–1877.

Authentick Memoirs of the Life and Infamous Actions of Cardinal Wolsey. London: Smith, 1732.

Banks, John. *Vertue Betray'd: Or, Anne Bullen.* Ed. Diane Dreher. Los Angeles: William Andrews Clark Memorial Library, University of California, 1981.

Bergenroth, G. A., D. P. de Gayangos, et al., eds. *Calendar of Letters, Dispatches, and State Papers, Relating to the Negotiations between England and Spain . . .* , vol. 4.2. London: Her Majesty's Stationery Office, 1882.

Bickham, George. *Deliciae Brittanicae: Or, the Curiosities of Kensington, Hampton Court, and Windsor Castle, Delineated.* London: n.p., n.d. = 1742.

Bolt, Robert. *A Man for All Seasons*. New York: French, 1990.

Brenton, Howard. *Anne Boleyn*. London: Bloomsbury, 2010.

Brown, Rawdon, ed. *Calendar of State Papers and Manuscripts, Relating to English Affairs, Volume 2, 1509–1519: Existing in the Archives and Collections of Venice, and in Other Libraries of Northern Italy*. Cambridge: Cambridge University Press, 1867.

Canterburies Dreame: in which the Apparition of Cardinall Wolsey did present himself unto him on the fourtenth of May last past: it being the third night after my Lord of Strafford had taken his fare-well to the World. London: n.p., 1641.

Cavendish, George. *The Life and Death of Cardinal Wolsey*. Ed. R. S. Sylvester. EETS o.s. 243, Oxford: Oxford University Press, 1959.

———. *The Life of Cardinal Wolsey*. Ed. Samuel Weller Singer. London: T. Davison, 1825.

———. *Metrical Visions*. Ed. A. S. G. Edwards. Columbia: University Press of South Carolina, 1980.

———. *The Negotiations of Thomas Woolsey, the Great Cardinall of England, containing His Life and Death*. London: Sheares, 1641; STC R19386.

Churchyard, Thomas. "How Thomas Wolsey did arise vnto great authority and government . . ." In *The Mirror for Magistrates* (London: Marsh, 1587), fols. 265–72.

Cobbold, Richard. *Freston Tower*. 3 vols. London: Colburn, 1850.

Foxe, John. *The . . . Ecclesiasticall History Contaynyng the Actes and Monuments*. London: J. Day, 1570.

Grove, Joseph. *Two Dialogues in the Elysian Fields, between Cardinal Wolsey, and Cardinal Ximenes, the First Prime Minister of England, and the Other of Spain*. London: Leach, 1761.

Harpsfield, Nicholas. *A Treatise on the Pretended Divorce between Henry VIII. and Catharine of Aragon*. Ed. Nicholas Pocock. London: Camden Society, 1878.

Johnson, Samuel. *The Vanity of Human Wishes*. London: Dodsley, 1749.

Laud, William. *Conference with Fisher*, in *The Works of the Most Reverend Father in God, William Laud*, vol. 2. Oxford: Parker, 1899.

Letters and Papers, Foreign and Domestic, of the Reign of Henry VIII. 21 vols. London: Longman, Green, Longman, & Roberts, 1862–1932.

The Life and Death of Mother Shipton. London: Pearson, 1871.

Mantel, Hilary. *Bring Up the Bodies*. London: Holt, 2012.

———. *Wolf Hall*. London: Holt, 2009.

Miranda, Lin-Manuel. "History Has Its Eyes on You," and "Who Lives, Who Dies, Who Tells Your Story." In *Hamilton: An American Musical*. Atlantic, 2015.

A Pleasant History of the Life and Death of Will Summers. London: Okes, 1637;
STC 22917.5.

The Oxford Historical Pageant June 27–July 3, 1907, Book of Words. Oxford:
Oxford University Press for the Pageant Committee, 1907.

Prophesie of Mother Shipton. London: R. Lownds, 1641; STC R12801.

Rossiter, Clinton, ed. *The Federalist Papers.* New York: New American
Library, 1961.

Rowley, Samuel. *When You See Me, You Know Me.* Ed. K. Elze. Dessau: n.p.,
1874.

Roy, William, and Jerome Barlow. *Rede me and be nott wrothe for I saye no
thynge but trothe.* Strasbourg: Schott, 1528; STC 1462.7.

Sander, Nic[h]olas. *De origine ac progressu schismatis anglicani.* Cologne: P.
Henningium, 1585.

———. *The Rise and Growth of the Anglican Schism.* Trans. David Lewis.
London: Burns and Oates, 1877.

Shakespeare, William. *King Richard III.* Ed. James R. Siemon. London:
Arden, 2009.

Shakespeare, William, and John Fletcher. *King Henry VIII.* Ed. Gordon
McMullan. London: Arden, 2000.

Smith, J. F. *Wolsey! Or, the Secret Witness: An Original Drama in Three Acts.*
London: Duncombe, 1845.

State Papers of Henry VIII. 11 vols. London: Eyre and Strahan, 1830–1852.

Statutes of Cardinal College. In *Statutes of the Colleges of Oxford,* 3 vols.
London: Her Majesty's Stationery Office, 1853.

Storer, Thomas. *The Life and Death of Thomas Wolsey Cardinall.* London:
Thomas Dawson, 1599.

Strickland, Agnes, ed. *Tales from English History: For Children.* Philadelphia:
Porter and Coates, 1868.

Sylvester, Richard S., and Davis P. Harding, eds. *Two Early Tudor Lives.* New
Haven, CT: Yale University Press, 1962.

*A Transcript of the Registers of the Worshipful Company of Stationers: From
1640–1708 A.D.* 3 vols. London: n.p., 1913.

*A True Description, or rather a Parallel between Cardinall Wolsey, Arch-Bishop
of York, and William Laud, Arch-Bishop of Canterbury.* London: n.p.,
1641.

Tyndale, William. *The Practyse of Prelates,* in *Expositions and Notes on Sundry
Portions of the Holy Scriptures, Together with the Practice of Prelates,* ed.
Henry Walter, Parker Society, 249–344. Cambridge: Cambridge Univer-
sity Press, 1849.

"Uncle Merry," ed. *Merry's Book of Tales and Stories.* New York: Dayton,
1860.

Vergil, Polydore. *The Anglica Historia of Polydore Vergil, A.D. 1485–1537.* Ed.
and trans. Denys Hay. Camden 3rd ser. 74. London: Royal Historical
Society, 1950.

Vernulaeus, Nicholas. *Henry VIII: A Neo-Latin Drama by Nicolaus Vernulaeus.*
Ed. Louis A. Schuster. Austin: University of Texas Press, 1964.

Wolsey Pageant June 23rd–28th 1930, Souvenir Programme. Ipswich: East
Anglian Daily Times, 1930.

Wolsey, Thomas. Preface to William Lily, *Rudimenta grammatices.* Antwerp:
M. de Kayser, 1535.

*The Youth's Historical Cabinet: A Series of Narratives, Derived from Different
Times and Countries.* Philadelphia: Hogan and Thompson, 1849. Reprinted
as *Romantic Stories from History.* Philadelphia: Davis, Porter, and Co., 1866.

SECONDARY SOURCES

Anderson, Judith. *Biographical Truth: The Representation of Historical Persons
in Tudor-Stuart Writing.* New Haven, CT: Yale University Press, 1984.

Arnold, Jonathan. "Colet, Wolsey and the Politics of Reform: St Paul's
Cathedral in 1518." *English Historical Review* 121, no. 493 (2006): 979–1001.

Assmann, Jan. "Collective Memory and Cultural Identity." Trans. John
Czaplicka. *New German Critique* 65 (Spring–Summer 1995): 125–33.

———. *Moses the Egyptian: The Memory of Egypt in Western Monotheism.*
Cambridge, MA: Harvard University Press, 1997.

Aubrey, John. *Brief Lives.* Ed. Andrew Clark, Oxford, 1898. Ed. Oliver
Lawson Dick, Ann Arbor: University of Michigan Press, 1957. Ed.
Richard Barber, London: Folio Society, 1975.

Backus, Edith N. "The MS. Play, 'Anna Bullen.'" *PMLA* 47 (1932): 741–52.

Bal, Mieke. "Introduction." In *Acts of Memory: Cultural Recall in the Present,*
ed. Mieke Bal et al., vii–xvii. Hanover, NH: University Press of New
England, 1999.

Barnett, S. J. "Where Was Your Church before Luther? Claims for the
Antiquity of Protestantism Examined." *Church History* 68, no. 1 (1999):
14–41.

Barr, Robert. "The Pageant Epidemic." *The Idler* 31 (1907): 437–46.

Bastian, J. M. "James Ralph's Second Adaptation from John Banks."
Huntingdon Library Quarterly 25, no. 3 (1962): 18–88.

Bauckham, Richard. *Tudor Apocalypse: Sixteenth-Century Apocalypticism,
Millenarianism, and the English Reformation.* Appleford: Sutton Courtenay,
1978.

Beaudoin, Tom. "Theology of Popular Music as a Theological Exercise." In
Secular Music and Sacred Theology, ed. Tom Beaudoin, ix–xxiv. Collegeville, MN: Liturgical Press, 2013.

Bell, Brian. Review of *Anne of the Thousand Days*. *Fortnight* 1 (September 25, 1970): 21.

Belloc, Hilaire. *Wolsey*. London: Cassell and Co., 1930.

Bennett, A. L. "The Principal Rhetorical Conventions in the Renaissance Personal Elegy." *Studies in Philology* 51 (1954): 107–26.

Bergonzi, Bernard. "Belloc, (Joseph) Hilaire Pierre René (1870–1953)." *Oxford Dictionary of National Biography*. Oxford, 2008.

Bernard, G. W. "The Fall of Wolsey Reconsidered." *Journal of British Studies* 35, no. 3 (1996): 277–310.

———. *The King's Reformation*. New Haven, CT: Yale University Press, 2005.

Bernstein, Richard J. "The Culture of Memory." *History and Theory* 43, no. 4 (December 2004): 165–78.

Biéler, Blanche. *Une famille du Refuge: Jean-Henri Merle d'Aubigné, ses origines, ses parents, ses frères*. Genève: Editions Labor, 1930.

Bill, E. G. W. "The Belfry at Christ Church." Ed. Michael Hall. *Oxoniensia* 78 (2013): 157–74.

Blunt, John Henry. *The Reformation of the Church of England: Its History, Principles, and Results, Part I, AD 1514–1547*. 4th ed. London: Rivingtons, 1878.

Bordo, Susan. *The Creation of Anne Boleyn*. Boston: Houghton Mifflin, 2013.

Boyarin, Daniel. Review of *Moses the Egyptian*. *Church History* 67 (1998): 842–44.

Brewer, J. S. *The Reign of Henry VIII from His Accession to the Death of Wolsey*. Ed. James Gairdner. 2 vols. London: John Murray, 1884.

British Medical Journal. "Fat as a Factor in Politics." April 20, 1901.

Britnell, R. H. "Penitence and Prophecy: George Cavendish on the Last State of Cardinal Wolsey." *Journal of Ecclesiastical History* 48, no. 2 (1997): 263–81.

———. "Service, Loyalty, and Betrayal in Cavendish's *The Life and Death of Cardinal Wolsey*." *Moreana* 42 (March 2005): 3–30.

Brown, G. S. *Shakespeare's Prince: The Interpretation of* The Famous History of the Life of King Henry the Eighth. Macon, GA: Mercer University Press, 2013.

Brown, Keith. "Wolsey and Ecclesiastical Order: The Case of the Franciscan Observants." In *Cardinal Wolsey: Church, State, and Art*, ed. S. J. Gunn and P. G. Lindley, 219–38. Cambridge: Cambridge University Press, 1991.

Brownlow, F. W. "'Speke, Parrot': Skelton's Allegorical Denunciation of Cardinal Wolsey." *Studies in Philology* 65 (1968): 124–39.

Budra, Paul Vincent. *A Mirror for Magistrates and the de Casibus Tradition*. Toronto: University of Toronto Press, 2000.

Bullough, Vern. *Narrative and Dramatic Sources of Shakespeare.* Vol. 4. London, 1962.

Burnet, Gilbert. *The History of the Reformation of the Church of England.* London: Chiswell, 1681.

———. "A Letter to Monsieur Thevenot, being a full Refutation of Mr. Le Grand's History of Henry VIII's Divorcing Katharine of Arragon. With a plain vindication of the same by Dr. G.B." London: n.p., 1690.

Burrow, Colin. "How to Twist a Knife." *London Review of Books* 31, no. 8 (April 30, 2009): 3–5.

Butterfield, Herbert. *The Whig Interpretation of History.* London: Bell, 1931.

Caine, C. "Cardinal Wolsey's College, Ipswich." *Journal of the British Archaeological Association* n.s. 20 (1914): 240–41.

Cameron, T. W. "The Early Life of Thomas Wolsey." *English Historical Review* 3 (1888): 458–77.

Candido, Joseph. "Fashioning Henry VIII: What Shakespeare Saw in *When You See Me, You Know Me.*" *Cahiers élisabéthains* 23 (1983): 47–59.

Cerasano, S. P. "Rowley, Samuel (d. 1624)." *Oxford Dictionary of National Biography.* Oxford, 2010.

Chamberlin, Brewster S. "Remembrance Reified and Other Shoah Business." *Public Historian* 23, no. 3 (2001): 73–82.

Chambers, D. S. "Cardinal Wolsey and the Papal Tiara." In *Individuals and Institutions in Renaissance Italy*, item XV. Brookfield: Ashgate, 1998.

Champion, Larry S. "Shakespeare's *Henry VIII*: A Celebration of History." *South Atlantic Bulletin* 44, no. 1 (1979): 1–18.

Chettle, G. H. *Hampton Court Palace.* London: Her Majesty's Stationery Office, 1975.

Clark, Andrew. "John Aubrey's Biographical Collections." *English Historical Review* 11 (April 1896): 328–335.

Clark, Henry G. *The Royal Gallery, Hampton Court Palace: Its Pictures and Their Painters: A Hand-Book Guide for Visitors.* London, 1843.

Clarke, Peter D. "Canterbury as the New Rome: Dispensations and Henry VIII's Reformation." *Journal of Ecclesiastical History* 64, no. 1 (2013): 20–44.

Cogswell, Thomas, and Peter Lake. "Buckingham Does the Globe: *Henry VIII* and the Politics of Popularity in the 1620s." *Shakespeare Quarterly* 60 (2009): 253–78.

Collier, Jeremy. *Ecclesiastical History of Great Britain.* 2 vols. London: Keble, 1708, 1714.

Collins, Jeffrey R. "The Restoration Bishops and the Royal Supremacy." *Church History* 68, no. 3 (1999): 549–80.

Collinson, Patrick. "Pollard, Albert Frederick (1869–1948)." *Oxford Dictionary of National Biography*. Oxford, 2008.

Coman, Alin, Adam D. Brown, Jonathan Koppel, and William Hirst. "Collective Memory from a Psychological Perspective." *International Journal of Politics, Culture, and Society* 22, no. 2 (June 2009): 125–41.

Confino, Alon. "Collective Memory and Cultural History: Problems of Method." *American Historical Review* 102, no. 5 (December 1997): 1386–1403.

Connell, William J. "Vergil, Polydore (c. 1470–1555)." *Oxford Dictionary of National Biography*. Oxford, 2004.

Corcoran, Timothy. "Thomas, Cardinal Wolsey, Educator." *Studies* 20 (1931): 24–38.

Cox, John D. "Henry VIII and the Masque." *ELH* 45 (1978): 390–409.

Creighton, Mandell. *Cardinal Wolsey*. London: Macmillan, 1888.

Cressy, David. *Bonfires and Bells: National Memory and the Protestant Calendar in Elizabethan and Stuart England*. Berkeley: University of California Press, 1989.

Crewe, Jonathan. "The Wolsey Paradigm?" *Criticism* 30, no. 2 (1988): 153–69.

Crome, Andrew. "Constructing the Political Prophet in 1640s England." *The Seventeenth Century* 26, no. 2 (2011): 279–98.

Cross, Claire. "Oxford and the Tudor State from the Accession of Henry VIII to the Death of Mary." In *The History of the University of Oxford*, vol. 3: *The Collegiate University*, ed. J. H. McConica, 117–49. Oxford: Oxford University Press, 1986.

Curnow, Peter. "The East Window of the Chapel at Hampton Court Palace." *Architectural History* 27 (1984): 1–14.

Curthoys, Judith. *The Cardinal's College: Christ Church, Chapter and Verse*. London: Profile, 2012.

Dalberg-Acton, John. "Inaugural Lecture on the Study of History." In *Lectures on Modern History*, ed. John Neville Figgis and Reginald Vere Laurence, 1–30. London: Macmillan, 1906.

———. Review of *Letters and Papers*, vol. 4. *London Quarterly Review* 285 (January 1877): 1–2.

De Groot, Jerome. *Consuming History: Historians and Heritage in Contemporary Popular Culture*. Abingdon: Routledge, 2009.

———. *The Historical Novel*. Abingdon: Routledge, 2010.

———. *Remaking History: Historians and Heritage in Contemporary Popular Culture*. Abingdon: Routledge, 2016.

———. "Slashing History: *The Tudors*." In *Tudorism*, ed. Tatiana C. String and Marcus Bull, 243–60. Oxford: Oxford University Press, 2012.

Dean, Paul. "Dramatic Mode and Historical Vision in *Henry VIII*." *Shakespeare Quarterly* 37 (1986): 175–89.

Dickens, A. G. *The English Reformation*. London: Schocken, 1964.

———. *The English Reformation*. 2nd ed. London: Batsford, 1989.

———. "The Shape of Anticlericalism and the English Reformation." Reprinted in *Late Monasticism and the Reformation*, 151–75. London: Hambledon, 1994.

Dodds, Madeleine Hope. "Political Prophecies in the Reign of Henry VIII." *Modern Language Review* 11, no. 3 (1916): 276–84.

Drabble, John E. "Mary's Protestant Martyrs and Elizabeth's Catholic Traitors in the Age of Catholic Emancipation." *Church History* 51 (1982): 172–85.

Duffy, Eamon. *Fires of Faith: Catholic England under Mary Tudor*. New Haven, CT: Yale University Press, 2010.

Durrant, C. R. *Proceedings of the Suffolk Institute of Archaeology* 13 (1907–1909): 382–88.

Edwards, A. S. G. "The Author as Scribe: Cavendish's *Metrical Visions* and MS. Egerton 2402." *The Library* 5th ser. 29 (1974): 446–49.

———. "Cavendish, George." *Oxford Dictionary of National Biography*. Oxford, 2014.

———. *John Skelton: The Critical Heritage*. New York: Routledge and Kegan Paul, 1981.

———. "The Text of George Cavendish's *Metrical Visions*." *Analytic and Enumerative Bibliography* 2 (1978): 3–62.

———. "Thomas Cromwell and Cavendish's *Life of Wolsey*: The Uses of a Tudor Biography." *Revue de l'Université d'Ottawa* 43 (1973): 292–96.

———. "A Tudor Redactor at Work." *Yearbook of English Studies* 3 (1973): 10–13.

———. "Unrecorded Manuscripts of George Cavendish's *Life of Wolsey*." *Notes and Queries* (December 2009): 512–13.

Elton, G. R. *England under the Tudors*. London: Methuen, 1955.

———. *Henry VIII: An Essay in Revision*. London: Historical Association, 1962.

———. *The Tudor Constitution: Documents and Commentary*. Cambridge: Cambridge University Press, 1960.

———. *The Tudor Revolution in Government*. Cambridge: Cambridge University Press, 1953.

Evans, Michael R. *Inventing Eleanor: The Medieval and Post-Medieval Image of Eleanor of Aquitaine*. London: Bloomsbury, 2014.

Fentress, James, and Chris Wickham. *Social Memory*. Oxford: Blackwell, 1992.

Ferguson, Charles W. *Naked to Mine Enemies: The Life of Cardinal Wolsey.*
Boston: Little, Brown, 1958.

Fiddes, Richard. *The Life of Cardinal Wolsey.* London: J. Knapton, R. Knaplock,
D. Midwinter, W. and J. Innys, R. Robinson, J. Osborn and T. Longman,
1726.

Firth, Katharine R. *The Apocalyptic Tradition in Reformation Britain, 1530–
1645.* Oxford: Oxford University Press, 1979.

Fish, Andrew. "The Reputation of James Anthony Froude." *Pacific Historical
Review* 1, no. 2 (June 1932): 179–92.

Fletcher, Stella. *Cardinal Wolsey: A Life in Renaissance Europe.* London:
Bloomsbury, 2009.

Fox, Adam. "Aubrey, John (1626–1697)." *Oxford Dictionary of National
Biography.* Oxford, 2008.

Foyle, Jonathan. "A Reconstruction of Thomas Wolsey's Great Hall at
Hampton Court Palace." *Architectural History* 45 (2002): 128–58.

Fraught, C. Brad. *The Oxford Movement.* University Park: Penn State
University Press, 2003.

Freeman, Mark. "'Splendid Display; Pompous Spectacle': Historical Pageants
in Twentieth-Century Britain." *Social History* 38, no. 4 (2013): 423–55.

Freeman, Thomas S. "From Catiline to Richard III: The Influence of
Classical Historians on Polydore Vergil's *Anglica historia*." In *Reconsidering
the Renaissance: Papers from the Twenty-First Annual Conference,* ed.
Mario A. Di Cesare, 191–214. Binghamton, NY: Medieval and Renaissance
Texts and Studies, 1992.

———. "Harpsfield, Nicholas (1519–1575)." *Oxford Dictionary of National
Biography.* Oxford, 2004.

———. "Texts, Lies, and Microfilm: Reading and Misreading Foxe's 'Book
of Martyrs.'" *Sixteenth Century Journal* 30 (1999): 23–46.

———. "A Tyrant for All Seasons." In *Tudors and Stuarts on Film: Historical
Perspectives,* ed. Susan Doran and Thomas S. Freeman, 30–45. Basingstoke:
Palgrave Macmillan, 2009.

Frothingham, Paul Revere. "Froude: Or the Historian as Preacher." *Harvard
Theological Review* 2, no. 4 (October 1909): 481–99.

Froude, J. A. *Henry the Eighth.* 3 vols. London: Dent, 1908.

Fuller, Thomas. *The Church-History of Britain: from the Birth of Jesus Christ,
untill the Year M.DC.XLVIII.* London: Williams, 1655.

G. J. Review of *Cardinal Wolsey.* *Revue Historique* 44 (1890): 176–77.

Gairdner, James. "The Fall of Cardinal Wolsey." *Transactions of the Royal
Historical Society* 2nd ser., 13 (1899): 75–102.

Galt, John. *The Life and Administration of Cardinal Wolsey.* London: Cadell
and Davies, 1812.

Gardiner, L. R. "Further News of Cardinal Wolsey's End, November–December 1530." *Bulletin of the Institute of Historical Research* 57 (1984): 99–107.

Gieryn, Thomas. "Boundary-Work and the Demarcation of Science from Non-Science: Strains and Interests in Professional Ideologies of Science." *American Sociological Review* 48 (December 1983): 781–95.

Gilchrist, Octavius, ed. *The Poems of Richard Corbet, Late Bishop of Oxford and of Norwich.* London: Longman et al., 1807.

Godwin, Francis. *Annales of England Containing the reignes of Henry the Eighth, Edward the Sixt, Queene Mary. Written in Latin by the Right Honorable and Right Reverend Father in God, Francis Lord Bishop of Hereford. Thus Englished, corrected and inlarged with the author's consent, by Morgan Godwyn.* London: Islip and Stansby, 1630.

Goring, J. J. "The Riot at Bayham Abbey, June 1525." *Sussex Archaeological Collections* 116 (1978): 1–10.

Green, Dominic. "Wolves Hall." *New Criterion* (May 2015): 25–32.

Gregory, Brad S. *Salvation at Stake: Christian Martyrdom in Early Modern Europe.* Cambridge, MA: Harvard University Press, 2001.

Grove, Joseph. *History of the Life and Times of Cardinal Wolsey, Prime Minister to King Henry VIII.* 4 vols. London: Purser, 1742.

Gumbrecht, Ulrich. "On the Decent Uses of History." *History and Theory* 40, no. 1 (February 2001): 117–27.

Gunn, Steven J. "The Chief Minister and the Nobles: The Dukes of Norfolk and Suffolk 1514–1526." In *Rivals in Power*, ed. David Starkey, 50–65. Basingstoke: Macmillan, 1990.

Gunn, S. J., and P. G. Lindley, eds. *Cardinal Wolsey: Church, State, and Art.* Cambridge: Cambridge University Press, 1991.

Guy, J. A. *The Cardinal's Court: The Impact of Thomas Wolsey in Star Chamber.* Totowa, NJ: Harvester, 1977.

———. "Henry VIII and the Praemunire Manoeuvres of 1530–1531." *Historical Journal* 97 (1982): 481–503.

———. *Thomas More.* London: Arnold, 2000.

———. "Thomas Wolsey, Thomas Cromwell and the Reform of Henrician Government." In *The Reign of Henry VIII: Politics, Policy, and Piety*, ed. Diarmaid MacCulloch, 35–57. Basingstoke: Macmillan, 1995.

Gwyn, Peter. *The King's Cardinal: The Rise and Fall of Thomas Wolsey.* London: Barrie and Jenkins, 1990.

Haigh, Christopher. "Anticlericalism and the English Reformation." Reprinted in *The English Reformation Revised*, 56–74. Cambridge: Cambridge University Press, 1987.

————. *English Reformations: Religion, Politics, and Society under the Tudors.* Oxford: Clarendon, 1993.

————. *Reformation and Resistance in Tudor Lancashire.* Cambridge: Cambridge University Press, 1975.

Haller, William. *Foxe's Book of Martyrs and the Elect Nation.* London: Harper and Row, 1963.

Hammond, E. A. "Doctor Augustine, Physician to Cardinal Wolsey and King Henry VIII." *Medical History* 19 (1975): 215–49.

Hanna, Ralph, and David Rundle, eds. *A Descriptive Catalogue of the Western Manuscripts up to c. 1600 in Christ Church, Oxford.* Oxford: Bibliographic Society, 2017.

Harris, William O. "Wolsey and Skelton's 'Magnyfycence': A Re-Evaluation." *Studies in Philology* 57 (1960): 99–122.

Harrison, William H. *Mother Shipton Investigated.* London: Harrison, 1881.

Harvey, Nancy Lenz. *Thomas Cardinal Wolsey.* New York: Macmillan, 1980.

Hay, Denys. *Polydore Vergil: Renaissance Historian and Man of Letters.* Oxford: Clarendon, 1952.

Hazlett, Allan, and Christy Mag Uidhir. "Unrealistic Fictions." *American Philosophical Quarterly* 48, no. 1 (2011): 33–46.

Heal, Felicity. "Appropriating History: Catholic and Protestant Polemics and the National Past." *Huntington Library Quarterly* 68, no. 1–2 (2005): 109–33.

————. "Dickens, Arthur Geoffrey (1910–2001)." *Oxford Dictionary of National Biography.* Oxford, 2009.

Hedley, Olwen. *Hampton Court.* London: Pilkin, 1971.

Hendel, Ronald. "The Exodus in Biblical Memory." *Journal of Biblical Literature* 120 (2001): 601–22.

Herbert, Edward, Lord of Cherbury. *The Life and Raigne of King Henry the Eighth.* London: Whitaker, 1649.

Herman, Peter C. "Hall, Edward (1497–1547)." *Oxford Dictionary of National Biography.* Oxford, 2012.

————. "Henrician Historiography and the Voice of the People: The Cases of More and Hall." *Texas Studies in Literature and Language* 39, no. 3 (Fall 1997): 259–83.

Hesketh, Ian. "Diagnosing Froude's Disease: Boundary Work and the Discipline of History in Late-Victorian Britain." *History and Theory* 47 (2008): 373–95.

Hewison, Robert. *The Heritage Industry: Britain in a Climate of Decline.* London: Methuen, 1987.

Heylyn, Peter. *Ecclesia Restaurata, or, The History of the Reformation of the Church of England.* 2 vols. London: Twyford et al., 1660–1661.

266

Bibliography

Higham, Florence. *Catholic and Reformed: A Study of the Anglican Church, 1559–1662*. London: S.P.C.K., 1962.

Highley, Chris. "'A Persistent and Seditious Book': Nicholas Sander's *Schismatis Anglicani* and Catholic Histories of the Reformation." *Huntington Library Quarterly* 68, no. 1–2 (2005): 151–71.

Hill, Christopher. *Economic Problems of the Church*. Oxford: Clarendon, 1963.

Hirst, D. *England in Conflict, 1603–1660*. London: Arnold, 1999.

Hiscock, W. G. *Christ Church Miscellany*. Oxford: Oxford University Press, 1946.

Holinshed, Raphael, et al. *The First and Second Volume of Chronicles . . .* London: J. Hunne, 1577 and 1587; STC 13569.

Hopes, J. "Politics and Morality in the Writings of Jeremy Collier." *Literature and History* 8 (1978): 159–74.

Hornbeck, J. Patrick, II. *A Companion to Lollardy*. Leiden: Brill, 2016.

———. *What Is a Lollard? Dissent and Belief in Late Medieval England*. Oxford: Oxford University Press, 2010.

House, Seymour Baker. "Literature, Drama, and Politics." In *The Reign of Henry VIII: Politics, Policy, and Piety*, ed. Diarmaid MacCulloch, 181–201. New York: St. Martin's, 1995.

Hunter, Joseph. *Who Wrote Cavendish's Life of Wolsey?* London: Richard and Arthur Taylor, 1814.

Hussey, Christopher. "Christ Church, Oxford: The Fourth Centenary of Its Foundation." *Country Life*, June 20, 1925.

Ipswich Historic Lettering. "Wolsey Statue." http://www.ipswichhistoriclettering.com.

Ives, E. W. *Anne Boleyn*. Oxford, 1986.

———. "The Fall of Wolsey." In *Cardinal Wolsey: Church, State, and Art*, ed. S. J. Gunn and P. G. Lindley, 286–315. Cambridge: Cambridge University Press, 1991.

Jack, Sybil M. "Wolsey, Thomas (1470/71–1530)." *Oxford Dictionary of National Biography*. Oxford, 2004.

Jackson, Esther M. "Maxwell Anderson: Poetry and Morality in the American Drama." *Educational Theatre Journal* 25, no. 1 (March 1973): 15–33.

Jesse, Edward. *A Summer's Day at Hampton Court*. London: Murray, 1840.

Jordan, David P. "Introduction." In *Rethinking France: Les lieux de mémoire*, vol. 1, trans. Mary Trouille. Chicago: University of Chicago Press, 2001.

Kaiser, Susana. *Postmemories of Terror: A New Generation Copes with the Legacy of the "Dirty War."* New York: Palgrave, 2005.

Kamps, Ivo. "Possible Pasts: Historiography and Legitimation in *Henry VIII*." *College English* 58 (1996): 192–215.

Kansteiner, Wulf. "Finding Meaning in Memory: A Methodological Critique of Collective Memory Studies." *History and Theory* 41, no. 2 (2002): 179–97.

Kenny, Anthony. *Thomas More*. Oxford: Oxford University Press, 1983.

Kiefer, F. "Churchyard's 'Cardinal Wolsey' and Its Influence on *Henry VIII*." *Essays in Literature* 6 (1979): 3–10.

Kim, Joong-Lak. "The Character of the Scottish Prayer Book of 1637." In *The Experience of Revolution in Stuart Britain and Ireland*, ed. Michael J. Braddick and David L. Smith, 14–32. Cambridge: Cambridge University Press, 2011.

King, John N. "Guides to Reading Foxe's *Book of Martyrs*." *Huntington Library Quarterly* 68, no. 1–2 (2005): 133–50.

Kinney, Arthur. *John Skelton, Priest as Poet*. Chapel Hill: University of North Carolina Press, 1987.

Klein, Kerwin Lee. "On the Emergence of Memory in Historical Discourse." *Representations* 69 (Winter 2000): 127–50.

Koltun-Fromm, Ken. "Historical Memory in Abraham Geiger's Account of Modern Jewish Identity." *Jewish Social Studies* new ser. 7, no. 1 (Autumn 2000): 109–26.

Kranidas, Thomas. "Milton's *Of Reformation*: The Politics of Vision." *ELH* 49, no. 2 (1982): 497–513.

Kurland, Stuart M. "'A beggar's book Outworths a noble's blood': The Politics of Faction in *Henry VIII*." *Comparative Drama* 26 (1992): 237–53.

———. "*Henry VIII* and James I: Shakespeare and Jacobean Politics." *Shakespeare Studies* 19 (1987): 203–17.

LaCapra, Dominick. *History and Memory after Auschwitz*. Ithaca, NY: Cornell University Press, 1998.

Lake, Peter. *Bad Queen Bess? Libels, Secret Histories, and the Politics of Publicity in the Reign of Queen Elizabeth I*. Oxford: Oxford University Press, 2016.

Law, Ernest. *England's First Great War Minister*. London: Bell and Sons, 1916.

———. *History of Hampton Court Palace*. Vol. 1: *In Tudor Times*. London: Bell and Sons, 1890.

Law, R. A. "Holinshed and *Henry the Eighth*." *Texas Studies in English* 36 (1957): 3–11.

Lindo-Fuentes, Héctor, Erik Ching, and Rafael A. Lara-Martínez. *Remembering a Massacre in El Salvador: The Insurrection of 1932, Roque Dalton, and the Politics of Historical Memory*. Albuquerque: University of New Mexico Press, 2007.

Lingard, John. *History of England*. 13 vols. London: Dolman, 1844.

Lukács, Georg. *The Historical Novel.* Trans. Hannah Mitchell and Stanley Mitchell. Lincoln: University of Nebraska Press, 1983.

MacCulloch, Diarmaid. *Tudor Church Militant.* London: Penguin, 1999.

Malden, H. E. "Wolsey's Ordination as Priest." *English Historical Review* 9 (1894): 708–9.

Mandler, Peter. "'The Wand of Fancy': The Historical Imagination of the Victorian Tourist." In *Material Memories,* ed. Marius Kwint, Christopher Breward, and Jeremy Aynsley, 125–42. Oxford and New York, 1999.

Marshall, Peter. "Lollards and Protestants Revisited." In *Wycliffite Controversies,* ed. Mishtooni Bose and J. Patrick Hornbeck II, 295–318. Turnhout: Brepols, 2011.

———. "(Re)defining the English Reformation." *Journal of British Studies* 48 (2009): 564–86.

———. "Saints and Cinemas: *A Man for All Seasons.*" In *Tudors and Stuarts on Film: Historical Perspectives,* ed. Susan Doran and Thomas S. Freeman, 46–59. Basingstoke: Palgrave Macmillan, 2009.

Martin, Charles. *Cardinal Wolsey.* Oxford: Shrimpton, 1862.

Martin, Samuel. "Cardinal Wolsey: A Lecture." London: Jones, 1949.

Matusiak, John. *Wolsey: The Life of King Henry VIII's Cardinal.* Stroud: History Press, 2014.

Maxwell-Lyte, H. C. *History of the University of Oxford from the Earliest Times to the Year 1530.* Oxford: Macmillan, 1886.

Mayer, T. F. "Sander, Nicholas (c. 1530–1581)." *Oxford Dictionary of National Biography.* Oxford, 2014.

Mayhew, Robert J. "'Geography Is Twinned with Divinity': The Laudian Geography of Peter Heylyn." *Geographical Review* 90, no. 1 (2000): 18–34.

McBride, T. "*Henry VIII* as Machiavellian Romance." *Journal of English and Germanic Philology* 76, no. 1 (January 1977): 26–39.

McGrane, Laura. "Bewitching Politics and Unruly Performances: Mother Shipton Gets Her Kicks in Restoration and Eighteenth-Century Popular and Print Culture." *Forum for Modern Language Studies* 43, no. 4 (2007): 370–84.

McNeill, John Thomas. "The Interpretation of Protestantism during the Past Quarter-Century." *Journal of Religion* 6, no. 5 (September 1926): 504–25.

McSheffrey, Shannon. "William Webbe's Wench: Henry VIII, History, and Popular Culture." In *The Middle Ages on Television: Critical Essays,* ed. Meriem Pagès and Karolyn Kinane, 53–77. Jefferson, NC: McFarland, 2015.

Mendle, Michael. "De Facto Freedom, De Facto Authority: Press and Parliament, 1640–1643." *The Historical Journal* 38, no. 2 (1995): 307–32.

Merle d'Aubigné, J. H. *The Reformation in England.* 2 vols. Trans. H. White. London: Banner of Truth Trust, 1962.

Milton, Anthony. "Heylyn, Peter (1599–1662)." *Oxford Dictionary of National Biography.* Oxford, 2015.

Minney, R. J. *Hampton Court.* London: Cassell, 1972.

Mullaly, E. "Wolsey's Proposed Reform of the Oxford University Statutes: A Recently Discovered Text." *Bodleian Library Record* 10 (1978): 22–27.

Murphy, Howard R. "The Ethical Revolt against Christian Orthodoxy in Early Victorian England." *American Historical Review* 60 (1955): 800–17.

Murphy, Robinson. "Elizabeth Barton's Claim: Feminist Defiance in *Wolf Hall.*" *Frontiers* 36, no. 2 (2015): 152–68.

Murray, Lindley. *The Power of Religion on the Mind in Retirement, Affliction, and at the Approach of Death.* New York: Wood, 1875.

Nash, Roy. *Hampton Court: The Palace and the People.* London: MacDonald, 1983.

Nicolson, Marjorie H. "The Authorship of Henry the Eighth." *PMLA* 37 (1922): 484–502.

Nora, Pierre, ed. *Rethinking France: Les lieux de mémoire.* 4 vols. Trans. Mary Trouille. Chicago: University of Chicago Press, 2001–2010.

O'Day, Rosemary. *The Debate on the English Reformation.* London: Methuen, 1986.

O'Sullivan, Deirdre. "The 'Little Dissolution' of the 1520s." *Post-Medieval Archaeology* 40, no. 2 (2006): 227–58.

Orme, Nicholas. "Latimer, William (*c.* 1467–1545)." *Oxford Dictionary of National Biography.* Oxford, 2008.

Osborne, June. *Hampton Court Palace.* Kingswood: Her Majesty's Stationery Office, 1984.

Page, John T. "Wolsey: Ipswich Boy and Cardinal." In *Bygone Suffolk*, ed. Cuming Walters, 93–104. London: Brown, 1900.

Pailin, David A. "Herbert, Edward, first Baron Herbert of Cherbury and first Baron Herbert of Castle Island (1582?–1648)." *Oxford Dictionary of National Biography.* Oxford, 2009.

Parrill, Sue, and William B. Robison. *The Tudors on Film and Television.* Jefferson, NC: McFarland, 2013.

Patterson, Annabel. *Reading Holinshed's Chronicles.* Chicago: University of Chicago Press, 1994.

Patterson, W. B. "Fuller, Thomas (1607/8–1661)." *Oxford Dictionary of National Biography.* Oxford, 2008.

Pearsall, Derek. *John Lydgate.* London: Routledge and Kegan Paul, 1970.

Pierce, Helen. "Anti-Episcopacy and Graphic Satire in England, 1640–1645." *The Historical Journal* 47, no. 4 (2004): 809–48.

Pineas, Rainer. *Tudor and Early Stuart Anti-Catholic Drama*. Nieuwkoop: de Graaf, 1972.

Pollard, A. F. "The Balance of Power." *Journal of the British Institute of International Affairs* 2, no. 2 (March 1923): 51–64.

———. *Wolsey*. London: Longmans, Green, 1929.

Pollard, Graham. "The Bibliographical History of Hall's Chronicle." *Historical Research* 10 (1932): 12–17.

Pollen, J. H. "Dr. Nicholas Sander." *English Historical Review* 6 (1891): 36–47.

Pollmann, Judith, and Erika Kuijpers. "Introduction: On the Early Modernity of Modern Memory." In *Memory before Modernity: Practices of Memory in Early Modern Europe*, ed. Judith Pollmann and Erika Kuijpers, 1–26. Leiden: Brill, 2013.

Poole, R. L. *Catalogue of Portraits in the Possession of the University, Colleges, City, and County of Oxford*. 2 vols. Oxford: Clarendon, 1912.

Powicke, F. M. *The Reformation in England*. Oxford: Oxford University Press, 1941.

Preston, Joseph H. "English Ecclesiastical Historians and the Problem of Bias, 1559–1742." *Journal of the History of Ideas* 32, no. 2. (April–June 1971): 203–20.

Pyne, W. H. *The History of the Royal Residences*. 3 vols. London: Dry, 1819.

Ranke, Leopold von. *History of the Latin and Teutonic Nations from 1494 to 1514*. Trans. Philip A. Ashwokth. London: Bell, 1887.

Redstone, V. B. "Wulcy of Suffolk." *Suffolk Institute of Archaeology and Natural History* 16 (1918): 71–89.

Rex, Richard. "Cardinal Wolsey: Review Article." *Catholic Historical Review* 78, no. 4 (1992): 607–14.

Richardson, Glenn. "*Anne of the Thousand Days*." In *Tudors and Stuarts on Film: Historical Perspectives*, ed. Susan Doran and Thomas S. Freeman, 60–75. Basingstoke: Palgrave Macmillan, 2009.

Ridley, Jasper. *The Statesman and the Fanatic: Thomas Wolsey and Thomas More*. London: Constable, 1982.

Robinson, Marilynne. "The Fate of Ideas: Moses." *Salmagundi* 121/122 (Winter/Spring 1999): 23–46.

Robinson, Marsha S. *Writing the Reformation: Actes and Monuments and the Jacobean History Play*. Aldershot: Ashgate, 2002.

Roney, John B. *The Inside of History: Jean Henri Merle d'Aubigné and Romantic Historiography*. Westport, CT: Greenwood, 1996.

Rosenstone, Robert A. *History on Film/Film on History*. London: Pearson, 2006.

Roth, Paul A. "Hayden White and the Aesthetics of Historiography." *History of the Human Sciences* 5, no. 1 (1992): 17–35.

Rudnytsky, Peter L. "*Henry VIII* and the Deconstruction of History." *Shakespeare Survey* 43 (1991): 43–58.

Rusche, Harry. "Prophecies and Propaganda, 1641 to 1651." *English Historical Review* 84 (1969): 752–70.

Salmon, Eric. "Collier, Jeremy (1650–1726)." *Oxford Dictionary of National Biography* (Oxford 2004).

Scarisbrick, J. J. *Henry VIII*. Berkeley: University of California Press, 1968.

————. *The Reformation and the English People*. Oxford: Blackwell, 1984.

Schwartz-Leeper, Gavin. *From Princes to Pages: The Literary Lives of Cardinal Wolsey, Tudor England's "Other King."* Leiden: Brill, 2016.

————. "Turning Princes into Pages: Images of Cardinal Wolsey in the Satires of John Skelton and Shakespeare's *Henry VIII*." In *New Perspectives on Tudor Cultures*, ed. Mike Pincombe and Zsolt Almási, 78–99. Newcastle: Cambridge Scholars, 2012.

Schwyzer, Philip. *Shakespeare and the Remains of Richard III*. Oxford: Oxford University Press, 2015.

Sharp, Richard. "Fiddes, Richard (1671–1725)." *Oxford Dictionary of National Biography*. Oxford, 2004.

Skelton, John. *The Complete English Poems*. Ed. John Scattergood. New Haven, CT: Yale University Press, 1983.

Skinner, S. A. *Tractarians and the "Condition of England": The Social and Political Thought of the Oxford Movement*. Oxford: Oxford University Press, 2004.

Slavin, A. J. "On Henrician Politics: Games and Dramas." *Huntington Library Quarterly* 60, no. 3 (1997): 249–71.

Slotkin, Richard. "Fiction for the Purposes of History." *Rethinking History* 9, no. 2–3 (2005): 221–36.

Smith, Christopher. "A Drama for All Times? *A Man for All Seasons* Revived and Reviewed." *Moreana* 25 (December 1988): 51–58.

Smith, Lacey Baldwin. "The 'Taste for Tudors' Since 1940." *Studies in the Renaissance* 7 (1960): 167–83.

Soames, Henry. *History of the Reformation of the Church of England*. 3 vols. London: Rivington, 1826.

————. *History of the Reformation of the Church of England, Abridged from His Larger Work*. London: C. and J. Rivington, 1828.

————. *Reasons for Opposing the Romish Claims*. London: C. and F. Rivington, 1829.

Southgate, Beverley. *History Meets Fiction*. Harlow: Longman, 2009.

Speed, John. *History of Great Britain*. London: Hall and Beale, 1611; STC 23045.

Spencer, H. "Improving Shakespeare: Some Bibliographical Notes on the Restoration Adaptations." *PMLA* 41 (1926): 727–46.

Sprague, Arthur Colby. *Shakespeare and the Actors: The Stage Business in His Plays (1660–1905).* Cambridge, Mass.: Harvard University Press, 1948.

Spurr, John. "'A special kindness for dead bishops': The Church, History, and Testimony in Seventeenth-Century Protestantism." *Huntington Library Quarterly* 68, no. 1–2 (2005): 313–34.

Starkey, David. "Privy Secrets: Henry VIII and the Lords of the Council." *History Today* 37, no. 8 (1987): 23–31.

Starkie, Andrew. "Contested Histories of the English Church: Gilbert Burnet and Jeremy Collier." *Huntington Library Quarterly* 68, no. 1–2 (2005): 335–51.

Steggle, Matthew. "Storer, Thomas (*c.* 1571–1604)." *Oxford Dictionary of National Biography.* Oxford, 2004.

Steiner, G. F. "A Note on Cavendish's *Life of Cardinal Wolsey.*" *English* 9 (1952–1953): 51–54.

Steuert, Dom Hilary. "Cavendish's *Life of Cardinal Wolsey.*" *Downside Review* 57 (1939): 23–45.

Stow, John. *Annales of England.* London: R. Newbury, 1592.

———. *The Chronicles of England.* London: Newberie, 1580.

Streeter, F. *Hampton Court: A Descriptive Poem.* Rochester: Fisher, 1778.

Sugg Ryan, Deborah. "'Pageantitis': Frank Lascelles' 1907 Oxford Historical Pageant, Visual Spectacle, and Popular Memory." *Visual Culture in Britain* 8, no. 2 (2007): 63–82.

Summerly, Felix. *A Handbook for the Architecture, Tapestries, Paintings, Gardens, and Grounds of Hampton Court.* London: Bell, 1843.

Summerson, Henry. "Sources: 1587." In *The Oxford Handbook of Holinshed's Chronicles,* ed. Paulina Kewes et al., 77–92. Oxford: Oxford University Press, 2013.

Swanson, R. N. "Problems of the Priesthood in Pre-Reformation England." *English Historical Review* 105 (1990): 846–69.

Sylvester, Richard. "Cavendish's *Life of Wolsey*: The Artistry of a Tudor Biographer." *Studies in Philology* 57 (1960): 44–71.

Taunton, Ethelred. *Thomas Wolsey: Legate and Reformer.* London: John Lane, 1901.

Teo, Hsu-Ming. "Historical Fiction and Fictions of History." *Rethinking History* 15, no. 2 (2011): 297–313.

Thomas, Alfred. "Cromwell the Humanitarian." *Commonweal,* October 5, 2015.

Thompson, Henry L. *Christ Church.* London: Robinson, 1900.

———. "The Restoration of the So Called Cardinal Wolsey's Palace in Fleet Street." *Illustrated London News* 122, no. 3465 (1905): 388.

Thornton, Tim. "Cardinal Wolsey and the Abbot of Chester." *History Today* 45, no. 8 (1995): 12–17.

Thurley, Simon. "The Cloister and the Hearth: Wolsey, Henry VIII and the Early Tudor Palace Plan." *Journal of the British Archaeological Association* 162 (2009): 179–95.

———. *Hampton Court: A Social and Architectural History.* New Haven, CT: Yale University Press, 2003.

———. "The Sixteenth-Century Kitchens at Hampton Court." *Journal of the British Archaeological Association* 143 (1990): 1–28.

Thurston, Herbert. "The Canon Law of the Divorce." *English Historical Review* 19 (1904): 632–45.

Tinniswood, Adrian. *The Polite Tourist: A History of Country House Visiting.* London: National Trust, 1998.

Trevor-Roper, Hugh. *Official Guidebook to Christ Church, Oxford.* Oxford: Christ Church, 1950.

Tymms, Samuel. *Proceedings of the Suffolk Institute of Archaeology* 2 (1854–1859): 270–71.

Tyrrell-Green, Edmund. "The Constructive Genius of Cardinal Wolsey." *Essex Review* 47 (1938): 139–44.

Veech, Thomas McNevin. *Dr Nicholas Sanders and the English Reformation, 1530–1581.* Louvain: Bureaux du Recueil, Bibliothèque de l'Université, 1935.

Veidemanis, Gladys. "A Play for All Seasons." *English Journal* 55, no. 8 (November 1966): 1006–1014.

Vidmar, John. "John Lingard's *History of the English Reformation*: History or Apologetics?" *Catholic Historical Review* 85, no. 3 (1999): 383–419.

Wabuda, Susan. "Cardinal Wolsey and Cambridge." *British Catholic History* 32, no. 3 (2015): 280–92.

Walker, Greg. "The 'Expulsion of the Minions' Reconsidered." *Historical Journal* 32, no. 1 (1989): 1–16.

———. *John Skelton and the Politics of the 1520s.* Cambridge: Cambridge University Press, 1988.

———. "John Skelton and the Royal Court." In *John Skelton and Early Modern Culture*, ed. David R. Carlson, 3–18. Tempe: Arizona Center for Medieval and Renaissance Studies, 2008.

Watkins, John. *Representing Elizabeth in Stuart England: Literature, History, Sovereignty.* Cambridge: Cambridge University Press, 2002.

Waugh, W. T. "The Great Statute of Praemunire." *English Historical Review* 37 (1922): 173–205.

Welborn, L. L. *Paul, the Fool of Christ*. London: T & T Clark, 2005.

Welch, Oliver. "Wolsey's Place in History." *Downside Review* 49 (1931): 124–32.

Whibley, Charles. "Thomas Wolsey: Minister of War." In *Political Portraits*, 1–19. London: Macmillan, 1917.

White, Hayden. "Introduction: Historical Fiction, Fictional History, and Historical Reality." *Rethinking History* 9, no. 2–3 (2005): 147–57.

White, Peter. *Predestination, Policy, and Polemic: Conflict and Consensus in the English Church from the Reformation to the Civil War*. Cambridge: Cambridge University Press, 1992.

Whiting, George W. "Political Satire in London Stage Plays, 1680–83." *Modern Philology* 28 (1930): 29–43.

Wiggins, Martin. "The King's Men and After." In *Shakespeare: An Illustrated Stage History*, ed. Jonathan Bate and Russell Jackson, 23–44. Oxford, 1996.

Wiley, Paul. "Renaissance Exploitation of Cavendish's *Life of Wolsey*." *Studies in Philology* 43 (1946): 121–46.

Williams, Folkestone. *Lives of the English Cardinals*. 2 vols. London: n.p., 1868.

Williams, Neville J. *The Cardinal and the Secretary*. New York: Macmillan, 1976.

Wilson, Derek. *In the Lion's Court: Power, Ambition, and Sudden Death in the Reign of Henry VIII*. New York: St. Martin's, 2001.

Winters, Jane. Review of *Wolf Hall* (stage production). *History Today*, March 2014.

Winthrop-Young, Geoffrey. "Memories of the Nile: Egyptian Traumas and Communication Technologies in Jan Assmann's Theory of Cultural Memory." *New German Critique* 96 (Fall 2005): 103–33.

Wolfe, Don M. "Unsigned Pamphlets of Richard Overton, 1641–1649." *Huntingdon Library Quarterly* 21, no. 2 (1968): 167–201.

Wood, Andy. *The 1549 Rebellions and the Making of Early Modern England*. Cambridge: Cambridge University Press, 2007.

Wood, Anthony. *Athenae Oxonienses*. 2 vols. London: Bennet, 1691–1692.

Wooden, Warren W. "The Art of Partisan Biography: George Cavendish's *Life of Wolsey*." *Renaissance et Réforme* n.s. 1 (1977): 24–35.

Woods, R. L., Jr. "Politics and Precedent: Wolsey's Parliament of 1523." *Huntington Library Quarterly* 40 (1977): 297–312.

Woolf, D. R. "Godwin, Francis (1562–1633)." *Oxford Dictionary of National Biography* (Oxford 2004).

Woolf, Daniel. *A Global History of History*. Cambridge: Cambridge University Press, 2011.

Worden, Blair. *The English Civil Wars: 1640–1660.* London: Phoenix, 2009.

Worsley, Lucy, and David Souden. *Hampton Court Palace: The Official Illustrated History.* London: Merrell, 2005.

Wray, Ramona. "Henry's Desperate Housewives: *The Tudors,* the Politics of Historiography, and the Beautiful Body of Jonathan Rhys-Meyers." In *The English Renaissance in Popular Culture: An Age for All Time,* ed. Gregory M. Colón Semenza, 25–42. Basingstoke: Palgrave Macmillan, 2010.

———. "The Network King: Re-Creating Henry VIII for a Global Television Audience." In *Filming and Performing Renaissance History,* ed. Mark Thornton Burnett and Adrian Street, 16–32. Basingstoke: Palgrave Macmillan, 2011.

Wylie, J. A. *The History of Protestantism.* 3 vols. London: Cassell, 1878.

Zim, Rivkah. "Batman, Stephan (*c.* 1542–1584)." *Oxford Dictionary of National Biography.* Oxford, 2011.

Zwierlein, F. J. "The Delay in the Divorce Trial of Henry VIII and Katherine of Aragon: Cardinal Wolsey's Management of the Case." *Ecclesiastical Review* 53 (1915): 521–34.

FILMS AND TELEVISION PROGRAMS

Anne of the Thousand Days.

Hirst, Michael (writer), and Showtime (producer), *The Tudors* (2007–2010).

A Man for All Seasons (1966).

A Man for All Seasons (1988).

Wolf Hall (British Broadcasting Corporation, 2015).

ARTWORKS AND MUSEUM EXHIBITS

"Cardinal Wolsey's Town," display in Ipswich Museum, Ipswich, UK.

Forbes, Vivian. *Sir Thomas More Refusing to Grant Wolsey a Subsidy, 1523.* 1925. St. Stephen's Hall, Westminster.

Gilbert, John. *Cardinal Wolsey, Chancellor of England, on His Progress to Westminster Hall.* 1887. London, Guildhall Art Gallery.

———. *Ego et rex meus.* 1888. London, Guildhall Art Gallery.

Historic Royal Palaces. "Young Henry VIII: Information Folder for State Apartment Warders." July 2007.

Portrait of Thomas Wolsey, Bibliothèque, Arras, *Recueil d'Arras.*

Recording Archive for Public Sculpture in Norfolk and Suffolk. "Cardinal Thomas Wolsey."

Strong, Roy, ed. *National Portrait Gallery: Tudor and Stuart Portraits.* 2 vols. London: Her Majesty's Stationery Office, 1969.

NEWS REPORTS

BBC News. "Cardinal Thomas Wolsey Statute Unveiled in Ipswich."
June 29, 2011.

———. "David Annand's Ipswich Statue to Honor Cardinal Wolsey."
April 8, 2010.

Daily Mail. "David Starkey's Blast for the Past." October 16, 2008.

Das, Lina. "Lie Back and Think of Olde England! Is This TV's Sexiest
Historical Romp?" *Mail Online,* September 7, 2007.

Dixon, Hayley. "Hunt for Richard III: Now Leicester Wants To Find
Cardinal Wolsey." *Guardian,* February 13, 2013.

Doughty, Steve. "Inaccurate and Anti-Catholic." *Daily Mail,* February 1,
2015.

Gates, Anita. "The Royal Life (Some Facts Altered)." *New York Times,*
March 23, 2008.

Guardian. "Christ Church Centenary." November 11, 1846.

———. "John Blatchly Obituary." November 5, 2015.

Times Literary Supplement. "Makers of Christ Church." November 2, 1946.

Mantel, Hilary. "Booker Winner Hilary Mantel on Dealing with History in
Fiction." *Guardian,* October 16, 2009.

McVeigh, Tracy. "Open Season for Tudor Tourism as Wolf Hall Effect
Takes Hold." *Guardian,* January 24, 2015.

Poniewozik, James. "Games of Thrones." *Time,* April 13, 2015.

Reidy, Maurice Timothy. "A Man in Full." *America,* April 13–20, 2015.

Shakespeare, Sebastian. "How Alastair Campbell Inspired Jonathan Wolf
Hall Puppetmaster." *Daily Mail,* January 5, 2015.

UNPUBLISHED PAPERS, THESES, AND DISSERTATIONS

Cespedes, Frank. "Perspectives on Henry VIII and Cardinal Wolsey in the
English Renaissance." PhD diss., Cornell University, 1977.

Lasher, Charles Frederick. "The Historiography of Thomas Wolsey." PhD
diss., Catholic University of America, 1973.

Mathews, Walter Roy. "The Image of Thomas Wolsey: A Study of the
Depiction of the Cardinal in Historical Accounts and Biographies,
1530–1630." MA thesis, University of Tennessee, 1966.

Nicholson, Graham. "The Nature and Function of Historical Argument in
the Henrician Reformation." PhD thesis, Cambridge University, 1990.

Parker, Julia. "Reinvention and Continuity in the Making of an Historic
Visitor Attraction: Control, Access and Display at Hampton Court
Palace, 1838–1938." PhD thesis, Kingston University, 2009.

Royal, Susan. "John Foxe's *Acts and Monuments* and the Lollard Legacy in
the Long Reformation." PhD diss., University of Durham, 2013.

Samman, Neil. "The Henrician Court during Cardinal Wolsey's Ascendancy, c. 1514–1529." PhD thesis, University of Wales, 1988.

Wyly, Thomas John. "Cardinal Wolsey in Tudor and Stuart Literature: Relationships between Renaissance Views of the Meaning of History and the Character of Literary Texts." PhD diss., University of Pennsylvania, 1992.

PERSONAL INTERVIEWS AND COMMUNICATIONS

Judith Curthoys, personal communication, August 5, 2016.

Brett Dolman, personal interview, July 6, 2016.